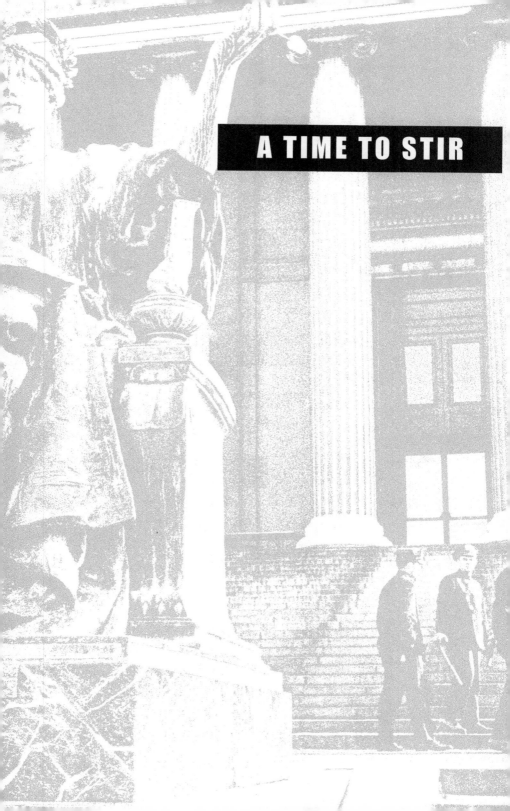

A TIME TO STIR

PAUL CRONIN, EDITOR

A TIME TO STIR

COLUMBIA '68

Columbia University Press   New York

Columbia University Press
Publishers Since 1893
New York Chichester, West Sussex
cup.columbia.edu

Copyright © 2018 Columbia University Press

Library of Congress Cataloging-in-Publication Data
Names: Cronin, Paul, editor.
Title: A time to stir : Columbia '68 / edited by Paul Cronin.
Description: New York : Columbia University Press, 2017. | Includes
   bibliographical references.
Identifiers: LCCN 2017024004 (print) | LCCN 2017040035 (ebook) |
   ISBN 9780231544337 | ISBN 9780231182744 (alk. paper)
Subjects: LCSH: Columbia University—Student strike, 1968. | Students for
   a Democratic Society (U.S.). Columbia University Chapter. | Columbia University.
   Students' Afro-American Society. | Student movements—New York (State)—
   New York—History—20th century. | African American student movements—
   New York (State)—New York—History—20th century. | Student protesters—
   New York (State)—New York—Biography.
Classification: LCC LD1250 (ebook) | LCC LD1250 .T56 2017 (print) |
   DDC 378.747/1—dc23
LC record available at https://lccn.loc.gov/2017024004

Columbia University Press books are printed on permanent
and durable acid-free paper.
Printed in the United States of America

Cover design: Lisa Hamm
Cover image: Archive Photos/Getty Images

In memoriam
Peter Haidu
and
Harold Wechsler

When the country, into which I had just set my foot, was set on fire about my ears, it was time to stir. It was time for every man to stir.

—THOMAS PAINE

Columbia's problem is the problem of America in miniature.

—TOM HAYDEN

CONTENTS

FOREWORD

by Paul Berman

In the spring of 1968, I was a wide-eyed freshman at Columbia College and a militant agitator for the left-wing cause, and the student uprising that broke out at my university seemed to me to be one of history's hugest events, on a par with the Peloponnesian War or the Russian Revolution. Half a century later, I have tempered my evaluation—and yet, I have to confess, not in every regard. The Columbia University student uprising was, in fact, authentically large. And it was mysteriously dynamic, which made it larger still. Perhaps the dynamism was not obvious to everyone at the time. The professors who watched in astonishment failed to see it sometimes, and so, too, did the journalists. But we students saw it. We felt it in the flesh. We trembled.

My own organization in those days was an august left-wing youth movement with an ancient history, founded in 1905 as the Intercollegiate Socialist Society, under the leadership of none other than Jack London. The Intercollegiate Socialist Society was a noble movement, and it evolved after a while into a practical movement, too. It became a youth auxiliary of the social-democratic trade unions under a more modern-sounding name, the Student League for Industrial Democracy, or SLID. And it took on a mighty responsibility, which was to train young people in the grandest traditions of the American Liberal Left—the traditions that are prolabor, pro–civil rights, egalitarian, and democratic. Maybe SLID was not a good acronym. At the start of the sixties, the members wisely changed the name yet again to Students for a Democratic Society, or SDS. Only, a war between the generations was by then beginning to break out, and the student leaders of the renamed organization could no longer get along with their adult sponsors. The sponsors were hardboiled social democrats in the Old Left style, and they demanded conformity to social-democratic dogma. The students demurred. The elders changed the locks. SDS, like a young reprobate who has been thrown out of the family home, wandered off on its own, bereft of adult guidance but free, at least, to follow the dictates of youthful whim. And somehow the mysterious dynamism began to stir.

By the spring of 1968, the SDS chapter at Columbia had blossomed into a vigorous campus organization, commanding the allegiance of perhaps two or three hundred students, with a few dozen people as the activist core and an "Action Faction" of red hots in the leadership. Every last person among those hundreds of SDSers was upset in the extreme about America's participation in the Vietnam War—upset that, in the early days of 1968, a thousand American soldiers a week were getting killed in Vietnam, and many more Vietnamese. Everyone was upset about civil rights—perhaps not as intensely for the moment, but upset, in any case. Then came April, and Martin Luther King, Jr. was assassinated, and a new moment arrived. Riots broke out in a variety of cities. Riots seemed to be a hair away from breaking out in Harlem, down the hill from the Columbia campus. And, in that atmosphere—sulfuric, enraging, disorienting—the SDS chapter struck up an alliance or coalition with one other student group.

The students in SDS's Columbia chapter were white, except for a few. The coalition partner, however, was the Students' Afro-American Society, or SAS, whose own membership consisted of the first sizeable contingent of black students ever to enroll at Columbia—not everybody within that contingent, but a large enough portion to be able to make claims for the black students as a whole. The alliance between those two groups, SDS and SAS, was entirely logical but not especially easy. The students of SAS, in their sundry currents of opinion, had by no means broken with their own elders, and their connections to the broader black community conferred on them (or so I thought at the time, and still think) a more sophisticated appreciation of American reality than could sometimes be found among SDSers. Still, the two organizations held a joint rally. And, by joining together, the two groups touched off an explosion

FOREWORD XXIII

of unexpected emotion, and a chain of further explosions, something really extraordinary—an explosion of political anger among a few hundred students, and then a few thousand, and more thousands, together with some of the younger and radical professors and friends and families: an anger that could no longer be expressed by oratory or pamphlets or chants and slogans, but only by physical action. The explosion of anger produced the sequence of events that you will read about in the pages of this book—a minor scuffle with the police, which led to the seizure of a classroom building, which led to the seizure of still more buildings, which led the university president to call in a large number of police, which led to a couple of nights of fighting and a great many injuries (most of them superficial, some of them grave and lasting, with a policeman the most gravely injured of all), and many hundreds of arrests, which led to still larger crowds, sometimes from outside the university, marching through the uptown streets amid clouds of rage, bitterness, alienation, and confusion: a genuine insurrection, mostly nonviolent (apart from those two terrible nights), unplanned, mass, emitting fumes of utopian exhilaration. Such was America in the spring of 1968.

Then came the summer, and the Columbia uprising gave way to the police-versus-demonstrator rioting outside the Democratic National Convention in Chicago; and the fall, when any number of additional student revolts broke out around the country; and the spring of 1969, likewise; and the fall; until, in the spring of 1970, a national antiwar student strike succeeded in mobilizing millions of the students, which amounted to one of the largest protests ever to take place in the United States. Nor did Columbia manage to calm down during those next years, as I well remember. The uprising of 1968 receded into the past, and, even so, the embers went on smoldering, and some of us students were always demonstrating, or plotting to demonstrate, or marching here and there, always with the expectation that, at any moment, the original insurrection might break out anew.

The mysterious dynamism at Columbia in 1968, then—what was the source of that dynamism, finally? The book that Paul Cronin has put together, *A Time to Stir*, contains more than sixty essays or statements by people who participated on one side or the other in the Columbia events, and the contributions make clear that, on a first level, nothing about it was really mysterious. Anger is a combustible, and it combusted. Still, there were other levels. Everyone who thinks back on those times will recall that a variety of thoughts and feelings, some of them fairly vague, without immediate connection to any particular outrage or campus issue, entered into the insurrectionary mood. Among a good many students, not just the radicals, there was a suspicion that American society as a whole had taken a wrong turn—a worried suspicion that impersonal institutions had lost contact with ordinary humanity and with moral behavior, and the whole of society had begun to lose its human quality. Maybe there was another suspicion, which was shared by a lively vanguard. It was a suspicion that traditional ways of organizing the relations of men and women and of sexuality in general had ceased to make sense, or perhaps had never made sense—a suspicion that every last social custom and habit needed to be reexamined and reinvented, not just in the political world but in the realms of private behavior and domestic life. That was a shapeless idea for the moment. And yet, the shapeless idea kept intruding into student actions, and uprisings broke out within the student uprising, with young women rebelling, or muttering under their teeth in preparation to rebel, against their uncomprehending comrades, the young men—a rebellion within the rebellion that would turn out to be massively influential in years to come.

Or maybe the dynamism at Columbia drew on still another source, deeper and broader than everything else, and yet oddly invisible—an impulse to rebel whose existence can be inferred from a mass of evidence, but, like some unknown particle in physics, cannot otherwise be detected or described. The mass of evidence in this case was worldwide. The uprising at Columbia was spectacular, but it was not unique. In several parts of the world, similar uprisings, sometimes nearly identical in style, broke out during those same weeks and months. The largest and most spectacular uprising of all, roughly simultaneous to the one at Columbia, got started in a small way in the last week of March 1968 at a university in the Paris suburbs. The uprising spread to the Sorbonne in Paris itself, then produced something that is accurately denominated the "Night of the Barricades," then spread to further schools elsewhere in France, and ultimately made the leap into the zones of organized labor, where it generated perhaps the largest general strike the world has ever seen, quite as if France as a whole were teetering on the brink of revolution. The French student uprising spread to Italy and West Germany and, in varying degrees, to everywhere else in Western Europe. Even Spain, which was a Fascist dictatorship in those days, underwent a few tremors. People in North Africa felt the vibrations. An enormous student uprising took place in Mexico City (and elsewhere in Mexico), only to be suppressed with a massacre by the police at Tlatelolco Plaza in October 1968, which produced dozens of deaths, or perhaps hundreds—no one has known for sure. And the Mexican student uprising spread elsewhere in Latin America. The student movement in Japan was significant, and likewise in South Korea.

Student protests broke out in the Soviet Bloc countries of Central and Eastern Europe and even, ever so slightly, in Moscow. The protests in Warsaw, in February and March, were among the earliest of the student rebellions of 1968, although hardly anyone knew about them in the rest of the world, given the Polish censorship. The young people's fervor in what was then Czechoslovakia became, by contrast, exceptionally visible, if only because a reform wing of the Communist Party rose to power in Prague and, in the months before the Soviet Union sent in the tanks, tolerantly indulged the ebullience of the younger generation. Among the many young people's protests and uprisings around the world in 1968, the ones in Poland and Czechoslovakia and other East Bloc countries eventually proved to be, all in all, the most consequential, judged from a conventional political standpoint. Every one of those Eastern Bloc protests was suppressed. The leaders sometimes ended up in jail, sometimes for several years. And yet, from those protests emerged a series of tiny dissident movements, which germinated underground, until, in 1989, the tiny movements blossomed into mass insurrections and democratic revolutions, typically under the leadership of the by-then grizzled veterans of 1968. There was the example of Václav Havel, a leading personality among the young dissidents of Prague in 1968. In the spring of that year, an opportunity came Havel's way to visit New York. And, because the Columbia uprising was under way, he made a point of going uptown to take a look, which meant that among the sympathetic faces in the enormous crowds at Columbia was his own face. Many a young hero in the Columbia rebellion of 1968 dreamed of one day leading a revolution, and here was a man who actually did it—the Velvet Revolution of 1989, than which no revolution in modern times has been more beautiful or more successful.

Only, what can account for the worldwide impulse to rebel—the impulse in 1968? It could not have been a reaction to any particular set of concrete issues or controversies. America's political movements for civil rights and withdrawal from Vietnam mattered greatly to people in many countries, and yet, in each country, the rebelling students and young people had reason to emphasize priorities of their own, which were not necessarily America's or Vietnam's. Was the causal factor something abstract, a political belief perhaps, which, having arisen in one place or another, proved to be irresistibly attractive? A political belief that spread contagiously around the world? That may well be the explanation. I do think so, even if the explanation begs the question of what causes political contagions. No one can deny that, in university neighborhoods all over the world in 1968, on both sides of the Cold War, students and young people did seem to share an ideal. They considered themselves to be idealists of the Left, in some fashion or other. Only, what did it mean to be on the Left in those days and settings? On this matter, a worldwide consensus did not exist.

There was not much agreement even within the few small blocks of the Columbia campus. The largest single sentiment among the rebelling students there, and among their faculty friends, was an exasperated and radicalized liberalism in the American vein, an angry left-liberalism perhaps, even if the word "liberal" had come to sound darkly criminal. Naturally, the Columbia left-liberalism came in many stripes. There were Christian radicals of different sorts, beginning with the religious-minded admirers of Martin Luther King. Dwight Macdonald showed up on campus on a couple of occasions to orate on behalf of his version of anarchism, which likewise had its liberal side; and he, too, had admirers, in a small way. Then again, there were sophisticated champions of a post-Trotskyist anti-Stalinism, who might have regarded "liberal" as an insult; philosophical disciples of the Frankfurt School Marxists; radical pacifists; admirers of Malcolm X (who renamed the university after him in the course of the uprising); an occasional Communist Party recruiter from the 1930s, skulking about; and whole crowds of countercultural "freaks," who sneered at "politicos" and participated in the uprising only when some demonstration promised to be historic (which was all the time, for a few weeks), or when musicians were performing.

The ideological variations and divagations and contradictions within SDS were especially complex. Once the uprising was under way, the members of the SAS and their friends and allies elected to pursue an autonomous course, which strengthened the rebellion ten times over by attracting a warm and fervent support from the larger black community—but also left SDS free for a few weeks to dominate the rest of the uprising. And SDS's political philosophy turned out to be several things at once. The particular strand of American social democracy that had given birth to SDS was liberal, socialist, and aggressively democratic, which meant anti-Communist in the trade-union style—and, at Columbia in 1968, the social-democratic legacy still clung to life, in spite of everything. The SDS literature table on the steps of Low Library distributed a pamphlet about Che Guevara, but it also distributed the old SDS manifesto, the Port Huron Statement, from 1962, before SDS and the old-time social democrats had severed relations. The Port Huron Statement offered many sharp and well-phrased social criticisms, not just of American society. It said, "As democrats we are in basic opposition to the communist system"—which the social democrats of the older generation would have applauded (but Che would have condemned). I do not know how many students at Columbia actually read the Port Huron Statement, but I am guessing that most of the people who did so must have felt the way that I felt. I loved it. I was proud to belong to a student organization that possessed such a lofty manifesto. I suspect that, without its historic connection to socialist tradition and the ideas to be found in the Port Huron Statement—without phrases like "participatory democracy"—the SDS chapter at Columbia would not have attracted as big a following as it did.

On the other hand, within the chapter itself, people were by then reading pamphlets from *The Little Lenin Library*, which the old social democrats would never have allowed. Stalin's *On the National Question* was passed from hand to hand. Some of the SDS leaders—some of the very people who found themselves thrust for a while into leadership of the mainstream of the insurrection—were beginning to define themselves, at least in private, as "revolutionary Communists." That was a fateful phrase, and it hinted all too strongly at the gods of destruction and self-destruction that already were beginning to seduce one SDSer after another, my own circle of friends, under the Guevarist name of guerrilla Marxism: a miserable tragedy in the months to come. It did not help that, within SDS, the main opposition to the ultras in the leadership came from a pro-Chinese splinter of the American Communist Party called the Progressive Labor Party, whose cadre at Columbia exuded an exhaust-pipe fume of fanaticism and Maoist dogma, which everybody else had to inhale. Still another faction consisted of the brainy disciples of a cracked and incoherent cult leader from a Trotskyist background known as Lyn Marcus, or Lyndon LaRouche, who promoted apocalyptic conspiracy theories. Here, then, was a tumult of ideological confusion. The tumult spilled outward from SDS meetings into the public events. The oratory at student rallies was pretty wild, sometimes. The sundial must have blinked in astonishment. Solid doctrines and mad theories went marching arm in arm through the quads. It was the revolution of 1848 as described by a horrified Flaubert. The best of people were sane today and out of their minds tomorrow. And this was true of student uprisings across the world.

In Mexico City, the students ardently yearned for democracy, and just as ardently venerated the megalomaniacal dictator of Cuba, without appearing to notice the contradiction. In France, where the level of left-wing political education was exceptionally high, the most prominent leader of the uprising was Danny the Red, or Daniel Cohn-Bendit, who, on anarchist grounds, regarded himself as a "visceral anti-Communist"— and, even so, a great mass of the rebelling students aligned themselves with a sprinkling of Trotskyist sects, and a still greater mass identified with a sprinkling of Maoist proto-guerrilla sects. In the Eastern Bloc countries the student rebels were politically more consistent, at least on the topic of Communism, about which no one had any illusions. And, even so, the Eastern Bloc '68ers admired their Western counterparts in Paris and Frankfort and New York and California and everywhere else, and yearned for the freedom to resemble them.

What did it add up to, then, the worldwide student uprising? You could easily conclude that it did not add up. Somehow it did, though. Young people around the world certainly felt that it did. This was obvious at the time, and, in any case, I know it to be true because, over the years, my labors as writer and citizen have brought me into conversations on comparative insurrectionary themes with the radical student leaders of 1968 from maybe a dozen countries. Each and every one of those conversations has reminded me of how vividly felt was the spirit of solidarity from one country or continent to another, and how warmly the veterans of those rebellions have tended to recall the spirit in later years—even if, in one country after another, the old veterans have also shuddered in recollection of the spirit of destruction. Those people felt a solidarity back in the day because they pictured themselves as a generational cohort that had been thrown into conflict with their elders—not in every instance, but often enough. They felt a solidarity because they shared—they knew they shared—a disdain for the conventional symbols and hierarchies of success and power, another worldwide phenomenon. They shared an impulse for cultural impudence. They shared a sense of themselves as people engaged in a revolutionary project to make a better world—even if there was not the slightest consensus on how to picture the better world, or on how to get there, or on how to avoid falling into the nihilist chasm. They shared—they knew they shared—a notion that, whatever might be the proper philosophy for a young people's movement, the reasons to rebel were undeniable, even if some of those reasons were inscrutable, and young people *ought* to rebel, and they ought to do so right now: a belief so urgent it felt explosive.

And so, they rebelled.

Paul Berman *('71CC) is the author of, among other books, two volumes on the Generation of 1968 around the world,* A Tale of Two Utopias *and* Power and the Idealists, *which have been translated into many languages. He has contributed to the* New York Times Book Review *since 1979 and has been a columnist or on staff at the* New Republic, *the* New Yorker, *the* Village Voice, Slate, Tablet, *and other magazines. He has taught at several universities and has received fellowships from the National Endowment for the Humanities and the MacArthur and Guggenheim foundations. He is a member of the editorial board of* Dissent *magazine.*

INTRODUCTION

April 1968. Hundreds of emboldened Columbia University students, many allied to two groups—Students for a Democratic Society (SDS) and Students' Afro-American Society (SAS)—take direct action against what they regard as their university's racist and militaristic policies by barricading themselves inside five buildings on campus. All of them together, behind locked doors, with a unified vision, issuing demands: Columbia must end construction of a gymnasium in nearby Morningside Park (public parkland situated within a primarily black neighborhood—"Gym Crow Must Go!") and disaffiliate with the Institute for Defense Analyses (IDA), which is conducting weapons research for the Department of Defense and so connects Columbia to war in Vietnam.

Immediately are unleashed, and made crystal clear, the schisms that have long existed on campus. As Columbia's unresponsive administration—controlled by businessmen-trustees and overseen by a dithering president—attempts to defuse the situation, as faculty meet and discuss the issues, as undergraduates opposed to the occupiers mobilize a raging reaction to their classmates' rebellion, hundreds of New York City Police officers are assembling. After six days, with neither side leaning toward compromise, with no hope of reconciliation, law enforcement remove the protesters—more than seven hundred, of whom nearly two hundred are not Columbia students—from their makeshift, self-governing communes, one of which is held exclusively by black students. The "bust" has a clarifying effect on many who otherwise would have paid little attention to the world of politics around them. Students who had sidestepped the protests, who never would have thought of involving themselves in disruption of any kind, are galvanized, and a fresh wave of turmoil surges across Columbia, helping to set in motion similar actions at colleges and universities—public, private, rural, and urban—across the United States.

The social and political issues that had energized the campus and the student protest movement for years reflected a formidable and transformative populist uprising that was engulfing whole swathes of the nation, even the globe—a rejoinder to the perceived inadequacies of mainstream institutions and politics. By 1968, in the shadow of a war that was pulling in hundreds of thousands of young American men, and only three weeks after the assassination of Martin Luther King, Jr., Columbia University—so close to the center of the world's media industries and even closer to the African American community of West Harlem—became one place where the academy's plight during the Vietnam quagmire, and the culture wars of the era, were conspicuously played out.

A Time to Stir presents several dozen firsthand testimonies from a cross section of participants in those events of 1968, many of whom never before have written about their experiences of this dramatic moment, all bringing with them insights gleaned from the past half-century. The group includes members of the Columbia chapter of SDS; women from Barnard College; two students of architecture and urban planning; a student lawyer-in-training; members of each of the four white-held buildings, including some resistant to SDS militancy; six representatives of the black-only-occupied Hamilton Hall; a long-time resident of the Columbia neighborhood; one student involved in community organizing in Harlem and another in campus draft counseling; the president of Columbia University's Student Council; a journalist from the underground press; two "outside agitators"; several members of the Columbia faculty; a prosecutor from the district attorney's office; an aide to New York City Mayor John Lindsay; Columbia undergraduates who objected to the building occupations; students who worked at Columbia's WKCR radio station and *Spectator* newspaper; two police officers who helped clear the occupied buildings; and members of the moderate groups Students for a Restructured University and Alumni for a New Columbia. Two of the shrewdest political commentators working in the United States today—Paul

Berman and Juan Gonzalez, both intimately involved in the events of 1968 at Columbia—have offered up, respectively, a foreword and afterword. The book opens with a chronology of events (drawn from reports in the *Columbia Daily Spectator* student newspaper and subsequent book, written by *Spectator's* dogged journalists, entitled *Up Against the Ivy Wall*) that details incidents from the 1966–1967 and 1967–1968 academic years.

By presenting such an array of perspectives, *A Time to Stir* tells the compelling story of the unprecedented protests that paralyzed an Ivy League institution. The book documents this watershed event and the debates that animated it by pulling at myriad threads, but at its core must inevitably be the students behind the inciting incident, to whom everyone else responded. In their stories, we learn about the disillusionment of male undergraduates at Columbia College, the pent-up frustrations, the persistent and earnest activism, and the spontaneous occupation of five buildings by what student leader Mark Rudd described as a "motley mob."[1] Here was a ragtag collection of disaffected constituencies, a crowd—passionate, polemical, and reliant on instinct—with diverse political commitments but commonality of purpose, brought together by circumstance and a series of improvisational encounters, with a more or less group-centered leadership.

Each occupied building quickly developed its own personality, drawing in a particular kind of activist. Low, Avery, Mathematics, and Fayerweather became dynamic enclaves packed with hundreds of undergraduates and graduate students, holed up side-by-side with a host of sympathetic outsiders who suspected that Columbia would prove fertile recruiting ground for action on the streets beyond campus. Of vital importance, too often forgotten today, or more likely simply unknown, was the fact that Hamilton Hall was held by a group of contemplative, disciplined black Columbia students who proved to be the strategic and moral centrifuge of the protests. For these men and women, pledged to the ideal of self-determination, some enthralled by the rise of Black Power, the act of closing ranks was made easier by the fact that most already knew each other. Initially suspect of the level of commitment of white students,

---

1. "Symbols of the Revolution" in *Up Against the Ivy Wall: A History of the Columbia Crisis*, eds. Jerry Avorn et al. (New York: Atheneum, 1969), 291.

and with practical support offered by Harlem locals, these black students were, from the start, on a different trajectory than the other protesters.

Every individual on the Columbia campus in 1968—no matter whose company they sought or kept, which organization or ideology they aligned themselves with, how committed they were to allegiances, or how fiercely they vowed to remain unaffiliated—was motivated by different reasons. With the enduring absence of a monolithic student bloc, with pulses beating ever faster and a stunning lack of stability to the situation, with rival factions proliferating by the day, consensus and conciliation would never be easy to reach. There wasn't a groupuscule that was not, at one time or other, at odds with every other groupuscule. This was a contest of ideas, a confluence of mismatched concerns making for an extraordinarily stimulating learning curve that no one had ever before experienced. Whether aware of it or not, everyone active in the protests was showing one another, once the textbooks were put away and the classroom doors were sealed, how living through a historical moment could be an educational windfall, a potent form of vivification.

As several of those who have contributed their memories to this book make clear, the tumult had been brewing for years. Study the *Spectator* from 1965 onward and read about a centralized administration offering paper-thin promises and desperate to prevent dissent from upsetting its fund-raising efforts, alongside a marked acceleration of student protest and voice-raising, a drive toward transgression and extreme measures, the jettisoning of complacency, and the censuring of conformity: an expanding number of single-issue political groups operating on campus; provocative antiwar gatherings around New York involving Columbia students; the steady, sometimes reluctant abandonment of conventional, moderate tactics as seen through increasingly contentious campus rallies, including protests against the Reserve Officer Training Corps and recruitment by the Central Intelligence Agency and the Marines Corps; students involving themselves in community outreach in Harlem; civil rights activism and furor over the draft, and the prospect of conscription and the brutality of the Vietnam body count; demonstrations at the site of Columbia's proposed gymnasium; heated student and faculty responses to the university's heavy-handed purchasing of neighborhood buildings and subsequent evictions; and picketing at Columbia dining halls in support of better conditions for its workers. Each of these actions fueled the next.

Worried about your grades? About being thrown out of Columbia? Consequences, be damned!

By 1968, it was clear that students were becoming a vital and effective political force and that inflexible university administrators across the nation would be unwise to ignore calls for change. Demands from students to become part of the decision-making processes were thunderous, with "relevance" a new watchword when it came to curriculum reform. But change could come only if workable channels of communications and possibilities for meaningful dialogue existed, and many vocal students felt that those who ruled Columbia had constructed a paternalistic, archaic culture of opaqueness (see Dan Pellegrom's essay, with its mention of the Student Life Report). In October 1965, David Truman, then dean of Columbia College, spoke to an interviewer about student civil disobedience, declaring that "the circumstances under which such protest would be acceptable are extremely rare."[2] As with Berkeley in 1964, the battleground became one of free speech. On the first day of the fall 1967 semester, in an attempt to stave off disruption, a ban on protest inside campus buildings was instituted.

Columbia students were part of a cohort of headstrong youngsters immersed in a set of subcultures that by 1968 had permeated deeply and were helping to cultivate in millions of people a sense of personal responsibility for institutional behavior. Many of them, for the first time in their lives, saw the necessity for direct action. This may have been a coterie of ludic, hedonistic hipsters who gravitated to subterranean downtown festivities, smoked dope and hung out in cafés, or just lingered in dorm rooms sprinkled with psychedelia and burning incense. But there was a counterpoint: this was also a nucleus of sincere, bookish students who just as often could be found at the uptown end of the 1 train, standing on the sundial at the center of the Columbia campus, drawing in fellow students with precocious analyses of world affairs and leftist politics, fastidiously recounting frank historical narratives largely unavailable in the mainstream press, deflecting criticisms and fielding questions. Some of them, like their Berkeley '64 compatriots, had gone South to assist civil rights organizations with voter registration and educational programs.

---

2. "Truman Terms Disobedience Unacceptable," *Columbia Daily Spectator*, October 14, 1965.

Others—too young for that—had been taken by parents to the nation's capital in August 1963 to hear Martin Luther King, Jr. enthrall the nation. Some were classic red (or pink) diaper babies, or children of devoted New Deal Democrats. A few had parents who had suffered under McCarthy or were survivors of the European Holocaust, still so fresh in mind. Some had cousins who had fought in Spain, who had copies of Paul Goodman, David Riesman, and C. Wright Mills about the place, who subscribed to the *National Guardian* or the muckraking *I. F. Stone's Weekly*, that warehouse of subversion. This was, all in all, by 1968, a hyperpoliticized group, indelibly influenced and schooled by television imagery of Operation Rolling Thunder's jungle war and Bull Connor's dogs, plus the duck-and-cover absurdity of mutually assured destruction. These rapturous, sloganeering students were swept up into the whirlwind, inflamed by a feverish, idealistic conviction that the hour for action had arrived.

Behind the brick walls of the campus, inside the occupied buildings, some kind of conversion experience was occurring, with great leaps of faith being taken, with boundaries being dissolved, the negation of alienation finally, if temporarily, achievable. The challenges came from all directions, including a battalion of Columbia students who declared that the occupiers' tactics were an affront to the intellectual spirit of the university. Anxious to show the world that another face of Columbia existed, counterprotesters were determined to neutralize the infectious, invasive demonstrations by retaliating against the mobocracy and marching feet around them. These short-haired, suit-and-tied athletes (the "jocks") weren't necessarily opposed to the final aims and long-range goals of the protesters (the "pukes"), who had immobilized the campus and shut down classes, but would have preferred, at the very least, that some form of rational persuasion be practiced instead. "There shall be no use of coercion, disruption, or blackmail to influence the future of this great academic institution," read a flyer produced by a coalition of groups worried about escalating violence on campus and—staggered by the Columbia administration's inaction—progressively ready to take matters into their own hands. "Numbers and reason—not force and emotionalism—shall decide."

The largest mass of students, those cautious tenderfoots, stood on the sidelines, struggling to understand precisely what was going on, but knowing enough that they couldn't let this historic moment pass them by.

Through the maelstrom stumbled an incredulous, outdated, and painfully vulnerable university administration, ill equipped for the problem-solving tasks with which it suddenly was faced, accused of having its reputation tarnished by incestuous connections with the New York power elite and, more broadly, the nation's establishment matrix. Foot soldiers from the mainstream media and the underground press congregated on campus, cameras rolling and typewriters at the ready, transforming a few square blocks of Morningside Heights into a fishbowl for the entire world to stare into. They installed themselves wherever the New York City Police Department (NYPD) and clutches of concerned parents—bearing chicken soup and bail money—weren't taking up space.

It might be said that the efforts of most everyone at Columbia during those days were both legitimate and inappropriate, that everyone conducted themselves both honorably and improperly. To be sure, everyone made mistakes. The faculty, for example—only a small number of whom would have considered themselves radical—advanced itself as an honest broker but immediately lost its footing, revealing just how powerless it really was, and for the most part refused to take a genuine political stance. Almost overnight, liberal professors—convinced that the campus was a sanctuary to be protected at all costs—became, in the mind of radical students, a lost cause. Some, who had long been identified as progressive, were overtaken by events and, like their hardline colleagues, found themselves dubbed reactionary dinosaurs. As Columbia professor of French Richard Greeman explained in a 1968 essay, faculty sympathetic to the aims of the student dissidents but who considered their tactics "coercive" were hypocrites and cowards. These people, wrote Greeman, "would never have dared to consider taking a position on the gym, of which they all disapproved, had it not been for the mass student pressure from below expressed through direct action."[3]

That pressure came most vehemently from adaptive, swaggering twenty-year-old rebels who were learning as they went along—a bull-headed sliver of whom were drawn to the Bolshevik notion of the vanguard and the heroic guerrilla Che's *foco* theory, to the cadre's leadership of an armed insurrection. ("That's out of date," aspiring Columbia SDSers

---

3. Richard Greeman, "The Center Falls Out: The Role of the Faculty in the Columbia Strike," SDS Radical Education Project, 1968.

were being told by 1968 of the Port Huron Statement, the organization's relatively placid and reformist Jeffersonian founding document, issued six years earlier. "We're reading Lenin's *The State and Revolution* and Che's speeches by now.") The activities of these agitators—who had little regard for the potentially damaging consequences of their strategy—ran counter to the antihierarchical participatory democracy that blossomed amid the often joyous, sensual atmosphere of the occupied buildings. The restructuring of the university, for example—which in the months that followed became a focus of graduate student groups—was deemed by them a hopeless and co-optive act. Some firebrands were intent on turning the campus into little more than the staging ground for their revolutionary aims, and it is no surprise that a direct line can be drawn from Columbia '68 to the infamy of Weatherman. Years later, novelist and Mathematics occupier Paul Auster wrote that 1968 was the year he went "crazy."[4] *A Time to Stir* suggests that the real story isn't what the tribe did once they reached that frenzied state, but how they *became* crazy.

However one feels about what happened at Columbia University in 1968, the events, and the contents of this book, serve as a rich case study, an opportunity to investigate broad themes, all not only relevant to campus events but also emblematic issues of the late sixties.

THE ROLE AND RESPONSIBILITY OF DEMOCRATIC CITIZENSHIP

Throughout American history, citizens have used a variety of means— political organizations, voluntary associations, journals of opinion, public rallies, and protests—to exercise their democratic rights and make political and policy preferences known to elected officials. Few periods of American history were as fecund (and chaotic) with such revitalizing expressions of citizen activism as the sixties, especially in terms of the creation and use of grassroots democratic tools, most prominently in the form of social change movements—often led by those feeling marginalized by mainstream politics. In 1960, Columbia professor Daniel Bell noted in his *The End of Ideology* that "one can have causes and passions only when one knows against whom to fight," before asking: "Today, intellectually

---

4. Paul Auster, "The Accidental Rebel," *New York Times*, April 23, 2008.

and emotionally, who is the enemy that one can fight?"[5] By the end of the decade, for some students at Columbia University, with their heightened consciousness and lists of interlocking grievances, that question was all too easy to answer. The year 1968 tested the seams of the American quilt like no other, and the deluge of antiwar protests and student activism in the second half of the sixties is a significant chapter in the story of postwar democratic inventiveness and effectiveness. Fundamental questions were raised about the citizen's ethical responsibility to counter laws and politics considered unjust or illegal. Inequitable mandates needed to be defied. Where previously apathy was the standard, dissent thrived. Dissent became protest, from protest to resistance, resistance was overtaken by confrontation, and then confrontation jumped to militancy. The range of strategies employed by students to facilitate change on campus and beyond represented a vivid challenge to the assumption that authorities should be respected without question. Disruptive insurgency ruled the day. There would be no business as usual.

In his 2016 obituary for human rights attorney and activist Michael Ratner, one of the few Columbia Law School students who plunged into the protests of 1968, David Cole wrote: "Ratner knew that when you sue the powerful, you will often lose. But he also understood that such suits could prompt political action, and that advocacy inspired by a lawsuit was often more important in achieving justice than the litigation itself."[6] These lines replay an idea expressed as early as June 1968 in *Ramparts* magazine: "Columbia was no revolution because those who created it could never really hope to take power."[7] Students went straight to the heart of a mighty university, one backed by New York's legal, political, and media power industries. Armed with little more than slingshots, many figured it likely would be an impossible fight, even with a global spirit of rebellion behind them, even when in solidarity with compadres on other continents. But at Columbia in April and May 1968, a prototype operation was presented to the world. Within days of the events, newspapers reported copycat happenings across the country.

---

5. Daniel Bell, *The End of Ideology: On the Exhaustion of Political Ideas in the Fifties* (New York: Collier, 1962), 301.
6. David Cole, "Michael Ratner, 1943–2016," *The Nation*, May 11, 2016.
7. "The Siege of Columbia," *Ramparts*, June 15, 1968.

Given that plans for the gymnasium needed to be abandoned and Columbia's disaffiliation from the IDA was a non-negotiable issue, students felt that they were committing a justified act of nonviolent civil disobedience. Needless to say, some saw it differently, urging that the occupations upset the rightful order of institutional procedure and jeopardized the university's special status as a much-needed enclave set apart from politics, war-making, and the like. What happened to the campus as a bastion for the steady maintenance of basic notions and practices of academic freedom? What good could ever come from shutting down a university and inflicting upon it a potentially mortal wound? Richard Nixon, declaiming against anarchy and stumping for law and order, trumpeted Columbia '68 as the first volley in attempts by a lunatic fringe to seize control of the nation's campuses, while J. Edgar Hoover's Federal Bureau of Investigation used the events as a pretext to go after New Left organizations with added fervor.

Michael Neumann, in his contribution to this book, writes that what the campus protests might have achieved beyond the boundaries of Morningside Heights is scarcely worth thinking about. His trenchant case against Columbia '68 begins with accusations that the insular, self-satisfied protesters, relishing the carnivalesque atmosphere, were more involved with "therapeutic" self-expression than any kind of meaningful political activity. Todd Gitlin famously noted that "[w]hile the Right was occupying the heights of the political system, the assemblage of groups identified with the Left were marching on the English department."[8] The gym and the IDA were, of course, to a certain extent only pretexts, a spur to action. Yet the symbolic value of the protests—"bringing the war home"—was pivotal. As Eleanor Stein writes in her essay, symbolism "is an enormously important, motivating, inspiring and engaging aspect of human existence and life." Such debate frames one of the central issues of A Time to Stir: what is it that constitutes legitimate and effective political action—especially when it emerges from the ground up, from those with limited power?

THE ROLE OF THE UNIVERSITY IN AMERICAN SOCIETY

In the final years of the sixties, Columbia University displayed in crisp focus the crisis of the liberal academy amid the cultural, racial, and

---

8. Todd Gitlin, *Twilight of Common Dreams* (New York: Metropolitan, 1995), 148.

political dramas of the time. Of protesting students, renowned historian and Columbia history professor Richard Hofstadter noted in 1968
that "to imagine that the best way to change a social order is to start by
assaulting its most accessible centers of thought and study and criticism
is not only to show a complete disregard for the intrinsic character of
the university but also to develop a curiously self-destructive strategy
for social change."[9]

But for Columbia students, what better place to vent their anger? The
doctrine of academic freedom prevented the university administration
from openly opposing the pointless war being waged in Vietnam, even
while many of its faculty and students—as well as President Grayson Kirk
and Vice President David Truman—did so with mounting conviction.
More troubling was that several faculty members were consultants for
the IDA, on the board of which Columbia's president served, thus giving the university an appearance of connivance with the war. Students
saw this as a sign of hypocrisy, the worst marker of academic complicity
in the military chain of command. At the same time, Columbia's practical
need for space and expanded facilities resulted in a land grab from a public park in West Harlem, an eerie echo to the kinds of thefts of property
and persons familiar in previous centuries. What better indication than a
vast gymnasium with a symbolically segregationist back door did anyone
need to understand that Columbia—expected to have an evolved, even
enlightened approach to racial politics and the interaction between town
and gown—was so shamefully out of step with the era? The gym proved
to be just one element of the university's nefarious, exclusionary dealings
in Morningside Heights, with its sanitization of the neighborhood and
removal of undesirables from newly purchased residential buildings.

More generally, after the Free Speech protests at Berkeley in 1964,
students' realization of themselves as cogs in a faceless bureaucratic
system, as personnel to be molded, became increasingly ubiquitous.
This stoked the anomie and resistance of its young charges, sullying
the notion of Columbia as a virtuous community of scholars. For many
students, Columbia—though smaller than public universities, such as
Berkeley, the size of which encouraged protest on a larger scale—did
not provide the cohesive, collegiate experience that its status in the Ivy
League seemed to promise. As the *Report of the President's Commission*

---

9. Richard Hofstadter, Commencement Day Speech, Columbia campus, June 4, 1968.

on *Campus Unrest* stated in 1970, too many faculty appeared to the average freshman "more like corporation executives than cloistered scholars," more committed to academic training that prepared students to fit the requirements of Cold War militarism than anything else.[10] Disenchanted, with an unhappy understanding of the coercive university as an embodiment of the outside world, these youngsters had been steadily disabused of the notion that the ivory tower was a neutral entity, able to keep its hands clean of the Vietnam War and institutional racism. As Columbia student radical David Gilbert wrote in 1968, the structures of American higher education were "dedicated to the social functions required by modern capitalism."[11]

These issues were exacerbated for students of color, with the university's handful of black students resentful of a distant, unresponsive, and overwhelmingly white institution. Columbia's Core Curriculum—requiring undergraduates to study classics in Western civilization's literary and philosophical heritage—was for some an oppressive celebration of imperialist values. Recent acknowledgments by antebellum universities of their participation in the slave trade have generated a new and robust reckoning with how intimately and interwoven the academy was with systemic oppression.

RACIAL JUSTICE IN SIXTIES AMERICA

Three weeks before Columbia students occupied the campus, Dr. Martin Luther King, Jr. was assassinated in Memphis, setting in motion a furious, grief-stricken response throughout the nation's urban communities that lead to many deaths. King's murder contributed to a decisive shift within the civil rights movement—from nonviolence and peaceful self-defense to Black Power, a militant demand for black freedom. These changes manifested themselves at Columbia in early 1968 with a change in SAS leadership, and then, after the joint SDS–SAS rally and sit-in at Hamilton Hall—that poignant, if brief, flash of interracial solidarity—with SAS telling white Columbia students they had to depart Hamilton and hold their own building. This segregationist move recapitulated the wider struggle

---

10. *Report of the President's Commission on Campus Unrest* (Washington, DC: US Government Printing Office, 1970), 75.
11. David Gilbert, "Just a Few Express Stops from Wall Street," *Ripsaw*, December 1968.

and mimicked larger structures, as articulated by the Student Nonviolent Coordinating Committee (SNCC). In a 1966 statement, SNCC explained that "white people who desire change in this country should go where that problem (of racism) is most manifest."[12] Reflecting the call for white activists to leave the South and head home to the urban North, before dawn on April 24 protesting white Columbia students—accused of indecision, feeling rejected and down-hearted—departed Hamilton, as requested by their black comrades. The doors barricaded behind them, this small group moved across campus and smashed their way into the president's office in Low Memorial Library, the university's main administrative building. The "community of common commitment" was still there, but a new chapter in the fragile alliance between blacks and whites at Columbia was beginning.

Hamilton Hall remained "black only" for the rest of the weeklong occupation, under the leadership of SAS, which asserted that above all it represented the interests of Harlem's working-class community. The entrance into Hamilton of Stokely Carmichael (former SNCC chairman) and H. Rap Brown (current SNCC chairman) on April 26 linked Columbia to a wider spectrum of societal concerns. Whether or not white SDSers were aware of it at the time, SAS's control of Hamilton provided the basis for the sustained occupation of not just that building, but the four others too, primarily because the NYPD were fearful of how Harlem might respond if they moved in to clear the campus. As such, the importance of Hamilton (renamed by students "Malcolm X Hall") cannot be overstated. By closing ranks the way they did—efficiently, peaceably—its inhabitants demonstrated that Black Power ideology wasn't necessarily the incendiary polar opposite of the civil rights movement. Instead, when put into practice, its approach represented a carefully structured and restrained operation, displaying tactical skill and moral fortitude. The black students' actions were made all the more compelling when one considers the risks they were taking in invading private property of the rich and powerful. For white students, there were likely to be few serious negative repercussions and especially no threat to life and limb. For African Americans, who could not expect such a soft landing and for whom the recent killings in February 1968 of three black students at

---

12. Student Nonviolent Coordinating Committee, "The Position of SNCC on Its Black Power Philosophy," *New York Times*, September 10, 1966.

Orangeburg, South Carolina, reverberated far more strongly, the situation was different. Unlike some white students, they saw no nobility in being arrested and beaten up—or worse. Juan Gonzalez, author of this book's afterword, recalls in interviews that within hours of the occupation of Hamilton Hall, he saw guns inside the building, brought in by Harlemites determined to prevent any overreaction by the authorities.

PARTICIPATORY DEMOCRACY

Even as the United States has been a dynamic society whose promise of equality, liberty, and freedom of expression has offered the American people great opportunity, those same values have also produced intense social tension. Time and again, citizens have wrestled with the need for change. In the sixties, the conflict between those who advocated rapid, even radical, adjustment and those committed to traditional ideas of political and social order was made manifest across the country—from small-town politics to national debate, from inner cities to remote academic enclaves.

Columbia University was a focal point for that contest, one of the sites where a new radical activism was emerging. The self-rule that developed within the optimism of the occupied buildings, filled with people who envisioned a society in which citizens would fully share in the decisions shaping their lives, was a memorable reflection of Thoreau's call: "Cast your whole vote, not a strip of paper merely, but your whole influence."[13] It was truly a mass movement—enmeshed in situations of unusual turmoil, fluidity, and, occasionally, histrionics—that shook Columbia's foundations, even if the media threw up Mark Rudd as antihero of the hour, and even if a number of protesters clearly moved beyond tactics that were perceived by most as strategically acceptable.

By 1968 at Columbia, influence had flowed into the hands of a small group of voluble and well-read (Mao, Debray, Gramsci, Fanon) SDSers whose approach differed markedly from traditional nonviolent New Left ideology. With long-range goals, and feeling betrayed by spineless liberalism, they had been, by 1968, engaged in years of political activity and "base-building"—via strategizing, dorm canvassing, teach-ins, meetings and rallies, and the writing and distribution of petitions and broadsides.

13. Henry David Thoreau, *Walden and Civil Disobedience* (Boston, MA: Houghton Mifflin, 2000), 26.

Once the five buildings were taken and everyone knew the NYPD would soon be arriving, with the media spectacle swelling (day after day the protesters were demonized on the front page of the *New York Times*), these advocates were somehow in the pilot's seat, at least to the extent that they were able to set a context and wield influence for three or four days. This small faction believed it could be the single force—the spark—capable of igniting a powerful revolutionary spirit, and that, in response, the power of the state, through a violent police action, would reveal itself, thus pulling off the fence all those previously unresponsive to SDS appeals.

The authoritarianism that marked this tiny minority of protesters meant they clashed with many inside the buildings and were accused of practicing "manipulatory democracy." Note the essay by Joshua Rubenstein who, while inside Fayerweather, confronted—and resisted—what he felt were SDS strong-arm tactics. Contributions from Nancy Biberman and Carolyn Rusti Eisenberg are revealing in different ways, as they touch on SDS's macho, unegalitarian tendencies, with its treatment of women, in the years—months, even—before the full power of the women's movement took hold. According to a common line from female interviewees on their experiences of the occupation, "the men told us they had important work to do and that we should go make sandwiches." The emancipation of female Barnard college students did not begin inside Fayerweather Hall, yet looking back, both women and men of the movement acknowledge that the seeds of consciousness were starting to take root.

In his book about Berkeley Free Speech Movement activist Mario Savio, Robert Cohen writes of the historicizing of the New Left, the suggestion of some scholars and activists that the movement's "approach to grassroots organizing" during its early years was "democratic, nonviolent, undogmatic, and innovative." This phase is followed by an implosive, irrevocable period of "alienation, cynicism, and revolutionary fantasies." Other (mostly younger) historians, adds Cohen, see the historical progression differently, proposing that alongside the sectarianism that split apart SDS came mass protests that "surged on the campuses."[14] Within the context of what is today known as the "good sixties–bad sixties" interpretation, Columbia '68 can be looked on as a temporal hinge, the moment

---

14. Robert Cohen, *Freedom's Orator: Mario Savio and the Radical Legacy of the 1960s* (New York: Oxford, 2009), 8.

when the tone darkened and, for some, revolutionary fantasies became more harmful than anything else. At the same time, while the hothead Morningside Heights revolutionaries always shouted the loudest, they were only ever a small proportion of the protest movement, one that grew in pragmatic strength, both on and off campus, following the bombing of Cambodia and the killings at Kent State.

What of the protesters today? What came next? Although for some participants there was certainly a performative, apolitical aspect to time inside the buildings (see Gene Slater's essay), for many, the rebellion signaled a shift of priorities that sent them down a path of social engagement they have been walking ever since. As Thomas Paine wrote of "panics": they might last only a short time, but "the mind soon grows through them, and acquires a firmer habit than before." [15]

The late Allan Silver, a Columbia sociology professor who fumed against the protesters, insisting that they had "violated basic rules," also described his best students of those years (including Ted Gold, killed in 1970 when a bomb he and colleagues were making in a Greenwich Village townhouse accidentally exploded) as among "the most incandescently brilliant" he had ever taught. Look at student publications from the period, as well as the many flyers and handouts produced, and note the sophistication of written material produced by twenty-year-olds. Beyond their obviously fierce intelligence, this is a group that has long estranged itself from apathy and inertia. To this day, many of the campus protesters remain politically ambitious, committed to social change, and have, in their own ways, continued to practice Marcuse's liberating Great Refusal. One hears all too often about the sixties radical-turned-company man (the "Jerry Rubin syndrome"). But take a cross section of the most active Columbia protesters and today find a group of committed retirees, still suffused by the consciousness-raising energy of the sixties. Unlike so many youthful protesters in 1968, today's activists have a generation (or two) of knowledgeable, contrarian grandparents (often networked together, still challenging the status quo) to call on for guidance and counsel when it comes to facing any number of travails—political and otherwise. Given the exigencies of raising children and paying the mortgage, to say nothing of the predicaments of old age, a certain level of engagement has inevitably slipped away.

15. Thomas Paine, "December 23, 1776," in *The American Crisis* (London: R. Carlile, 1819), 12.

But as we come face to face with new threats and embark on our own epochal battles, these folks can school us in how to confront the long odds and hard knocks, to help us understand our shared experiences. They are available to tutor us out of quiescence, to show us how to build up the spirit, and to stave off discouragement, as one obstacle morphs into the next.

Among the veterans of the Avery commune (the School of Architecture) who I interviewed, for example, are no billionaire property developers, instead only socially conscious designers, urban planners, and community developers. In his *Gates of Eden: American Culture in the Sixties*, Morris Dickstein (an assistant professor of English at Columbia in 1968) wrote of the twentieth-anniversary celebrations of 1968, a campus meeting of strike veterans. For Dickstein, "it was remarkable how many had somehow remained true to their ideas . . . Few, it seems, had just gone for the money, despite the Gilded Age ethics of the Reagan years. It was clear that some sense of community responsibility would continue to shape the remainder of their lives."[16] And indeed it has, something I can attest to, having caught up with many hundreds of Columbia's protest veterans—public servants, doctors, teachers, academics, writers—some thirty years after Dickstein. Mark Rudd, these days working as intensely and urgently as he was five decades ago, has, over the years, been an especially important presence for me. An energetic, compassionate rabble-rouser, currently training young leadership in strategic organizing and how to build structures and create definitive outcomes that will carry the movement forward in New Mexico (where he has lived for forty years), generations into the future, Mark is today anxious to let it be known what mistakes were made. "Out of Columbia came the belief that militancy will do everything," he explained in a 2007 interview with me. "We happened to be lucky at that moment. There had been base-building and politicization of the campus, years of education, confrontation and agitation, and years of talking with people. It was real organizing that went on. But coming out of Columbia it was our militancy that we seized on. We thought that militancy could become a strategy, when really it's only a tactic which sometimes, occasionally, if you're lucky, works." The young leadership of Columbia SDS was hoping not just to understand the world, but to change it—by any means necessary. Base-building and long-term organizational strategies were seen as of secondary importance.

16. Morris Dickstein, *Gates of Eden: American Culture in the Sixties* (New York: Penguin, 1989), x.

As the scope of the essays that follow shows, the uprising at Columbia University can be understood through many perspectives and stories. There is no one narrative, but many. All can be considered, however, in one common and vital way: as a microcosm of the nation's wider concerns. There remain, of course, at least as many avenues open for exploration, including those that tackle post-1968 Columbia. The university was changed forever, most immediately with the imperious, prideful President Grayson Kirk—who in April 1968 described the young people of America as having "taken refuge in a turbulent and inchoate nihilism"[17]—and Vice President David Truman both dethroned; the Columbia Senate ("a policy-making and legislative body with full jurisdiction and power to deal with all matters of University-wide concern"[18]) established the following year; the revision of disciplinary procedures implemented (including the dissolution of the more patronizing elements of *in loco parentis*); and the hiring of more black faculty, including Charles Hamilton in the government department.

By documenting the story of a generation of politically committed citizens who came of age in a world painfully out of equilibrium and who sought to reshape that world, *A Time to Stir* has the potential to deepen our understanding not just of the widespread social unrest that pervaded the final years of the sixties in the United States and beyond, but also the theory and practice of contemporary protest and debate. The year 1968 was the high point of an era when the fight between those who advocated rapid adjustment of norms and values and those who were committed to maintaining traditional ideas of political and social order erupted in every direction. To delve into the campus events of that year means to explore an array of ideas, ideologies, histories, disputes, groups, and individuals, and so let loose a range of themes that are unmistakably as germane and worthy of investigation today as they were all those years ago. Every significant beat of this story finds a contemporary analog at least as pertinent today as it was five decades ago. We ignore these resilient problems, these present-day struggles, these issues and fundamental questions of culture, politics, and society, at our peril. Motivated by an intention to put forth a description of historic events, to fuse the skirmishes of 1968 to the present day, adventuresome readers are challenged to ask themselves: what would I have done fifty years ago?

---

17. Quoted George Keller, "Six Weeks That Shook Morningside," *Columbia* magazine, Spring 1968, 13.
18. "The University Senate," *Columbia Daily Spectator*, February 18, 1969.

In his final book *Hell No: The Forgotten Power of the Vietnam Peace Movement,* Tom Hayden, who continues to hover—inspiringly—over my nearly two-decades-long 1968 projects (Chicago and Columbia), wrote of the campaign that must be fought against loss of memory. Our digital culture is exponentially amnesiac, which makes even more important the task of soliciting stories from a generation that activated itself into one of the most powerful antiwar and social justice movements in American history. Those more arcane and iconoclastic retellings of events that we might think have been exhausted are, in fact, indispensable. And so here, for today's readers and tomorrow's scholars, is a collection written by participants and witnesses, men and women whose tales need to be remembered by history. On that note, the creation of a book composed of new testimonials about student protest written fifty years after the fact brings with it the issue of range and scope. Men and women who were twenty years old in 1968 are more likely to be available today for the task of remembrance than those who were, as part of Columbia's administration and faculty, middle age or older. As such, *A Time to Stir* might be said to lack balance. There are offerings from those who, five decades ago, were on Columbia's faculty, but voices from the university's administration do not appear.

Everyone who contributed to this book also gave an interview for an accompanying panoramic, multichapter documentary, which complements, expands on, and illustrates the contents of this book, making use of several hundred newly recorded conversations and an archive of many thousands of newly discovered photographs. My thanks to them, as well as to all my interviewees over the years. Appreciation also to Neal Hurwitz for his expansive remembrances of 1968; Stacey Knecht for her thoughtful comments on the manuscript; Jocelyn Wilk at Columbia's archive in Butler Library, which houses the wondrous Protest and Activism Collection; and Philip Leventhal at Columbia University Press.

When deciding what to write about, each contributor made his and her own decisions, although in some instances I suggested certain starting points and directions in which the essays might move. While I cannot agree with everything contained in what follows and might consider some of the descriptive language unfair and the interpretations misguided, there is nothing of import presented here that I know to be egregiously in error.

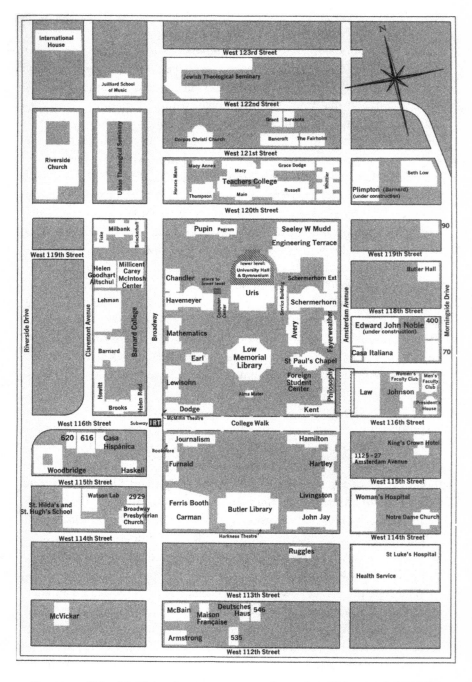

Figure 0.1 Columbia University campus, c. 1968. *Image from University Archives, Rare Book and Manuscript Library, Columbia University in the City of New York.*

CHRONOLOGY OF EVENTS

A ll quotes are from *Spectator*, Columbia's student-run newspaper, unless otherwise specified. http://spectatorarchive.library.columbia .edu/. Some details that follow are from *Up Against the Ivy Wall*, edited by Jerry Avorn et al. (New York: Atheneum, 1969).

SEPTEMBER 1966

"After a delay of nearly seven years, the new Columbia Community Gymnasium in Morningside Park is due to become a reality. Ground-breaking ceremonies for the $9 million edifice will be held early next month." Two weeks later it is reported that there is a delay "until early 1967."

OCTOBER 1966

Tenants in a Columbia-owned residence organize "to protest living conditions in the building." One resident "charged yesterday that there had been no hot water and no steam 'for some weeks.' She said, too, that Columbia had offered tenants $50 to $75 to relocate."

A new student magazine—"a forum for the war on Vietnam"—is published. The first issue of *Gadfly*, edited by Paul Rockwell, "will concentrate on the convictions of three servicemen who refused to go to Vietnam."

The Columbia chapter of Students for a Democratic Society (SDS) organizes a series of workshops "to analyze and change the social injustices which it feels exist in American society," while the Independent Committee on Vietnam, another student group, votes "to expand and intensify its dissent against the war in Vietnam." A collection of Columbia faculty, led by Professor Immanuel Wallerstein, form the Faculty Civil Rights Group "to study the prospects for the advancement of civil rights in the nation in the coming years."

NOVEMBER 1966

Columbia Chaplain John Cannon and fifteen undergraduates, including Ted Kaptchuk, embark upon a three-day fast in protest against the war in Vietnam.

"More than two hundred students marched from a noon rally at the sundial into Dodge Hall yesterday to 'ask a few questions' of a recruiting agent of the Central Intelligence Agency. . . . The march was organized and conducted by the Columbia chapter of Students for a Democratic Society." The following day "A group of about 150 students marched on President Grayson Kirk's office in Low Memorial Library yesterday to present a letter to him protesting the University's involvement with the Central Intelligence Agency [CIA]." Five days later more than five hundred students confront President Kirk with demands that he not allow the CIA to recruit on campus. When asked why students are not being consulted on certain decisions made by the university, President Kirk responds: "Many decisions cannot appropriately be made by those moving on in three or four years."

A group of black students petition to establish a chapter of Omega Psi Phi, which would become the first black fraternity on campus. In April of the following year, there are an initial eleven pledges.

Professor Seymour Melman accuses Columbia of compromising its integrity because of the "secret research" it is conducting for the federal government. "There is secret work going on in the electrical engineering research labs at the Hudson Labs, and there is a history of research in nerve gas and the like at the College of Physicians and Surgeons." Nearly 50 percent of Columbia's budget, says Melman, comes from the Department of Defense, the Atomic Energy Commission, and NASA.

DECEMBER 1966

"Maurice T. Moore, chairman of the Board of Trustees, said this week that there is virtually no likelihood that students could be included in the activities of the Trustees. 'I don't think it would be practical,' Mr. Moore said, 'to bring students into what you might call the actual decision-making.' However, the chairman said, 'We're always interested in responsible expressions of opinion from students.'"

FEBRUARY 1967

A group of students stage a sit-in outside a room in Dodge Hall, protesting the presence on campus of a CIA recruiter. They refuse to disperse "despite a warning that their actions might lead to expulsion from the University." The two CIA recruiters are trapped in an office for five hours. The following day, President Kirk appoints a "six-man tripartite committee" (administration, faculty, students) to hear the students' cases. "In a break with a tradition of secrecy on disciplinary cases, the hearings will be open to the press. The accused students will be allowed to call witnesses." A poll of College seniors shows that 80 percent are in favor of allowing the CIA to recruit on campus.

City Councilman J. Raymond Jones asks New York City Mayor John Lindsay "to re-negotiate the terms of the lease between Columbia and the city for the two acres of parkland to be used for the planned University gymnasium." He writes in his letter: "Columbia, having received an unusual and rich plum, shall not retain the lion's share of the fruit while doling out to the community no more than the pit."

Arthur Ochs Sulzberger, president and publisher of the *New York Times*, is elected to Columbia's Board of Trustees.

MARCH 1967

Students from the "ROTC-off-the-Campus" group, refusing to recognize naval officers as members of the faculty, attend two Naval Reserve Officer Training Corps classes on campus without authorization. Michael Neumann, a leader of the group, says that "no disruptive tactics" are planned, but as sit-ins continue "clashes with the NROTC instructors will probably occur." By the end of the month, it is announced that ROTC at Columbia will be phased out over the next five years. "Columbia thus becomes the first college or university to actually break its contract with the Department of the Navy."

An unnamed, "high-ranking member of the Advisory Committee of the Faculties" advocates that the body become "an academic senate with the power to make decisions binding on the University administration." He explains that "the present system of government of Columbia is similar to that of Tsar Nicholas II. It is up to the faculty to assert its need and desire to change this system."

Bob Feldman, an undergraduate SDS researcher, discovers that "Columbia is institutionally affiliated with the Institute for Defense Analyses [IDA], an organization which deals exclusively in military research for the government. In addition, several members of the Columbia faculty are or have been engaged in classified defense work for the Institute on an individual basis." Feldman explains that IDA's function is one of "converting technical advances into new elements of military power—for guiding technology in the creation of new and more effective foundations of strategy." Ralph Halford, dean of graduate faculties, previously denied that Columbia was connected with IDA, stating, "These things are not in the purview of faculty or students . . . This is a matter for the Trustees of the University to decide."

APRIL 1967

The Committee of Graduate Students to End the War in Vietnam is formed, having amassed seven hundred signatures of students who are "deeply concerned about the war in Vietnam and its continuing intensification."

"The Social Action Committee of the Students' Afro-American Society [SAS] last week issued proposals calling for the improvement of food services employees' working conditions and for salary raises." SAS demands include that "full-time workers should receive a 10-cent-an-hour raise, and student employees two annual raises beginning next year." Meanwhile, after several months of campaigning, Columbia's Progressive Labor organization abandons attempts to unionize university library employees.

Later in the month, several students picket John Jay cafeteria "to protest current working conditions and food quality."

Fifty students, many "identified as athletes or members of the Naval Reserve Officers Training Corps," confront three hundred SDS supporters in the lobby of John Jay Hall dormitory, leading to an hour-long clash over the issue of Marine recruitment. "The fist fights broke out as the two factions jockeyed for position in the tightly-packed lobby. Many verbal arguments ended in physical violence." The following day, as Marines recruit in the lobby of a nearby dormitory, more than eight hundred SDS supporters calmly march for an hour and a half around the Van Am Quadrangle while "five hundred bystanders and hecklers glared and jeered from behind a hedge several feet away." Soon thereafter, for the second consecutive year, President Kirk cancels the annual ROTC review.

Herbert Deane, vice dean of Graduate Faculties, defends Columbia's membership in the IDA and insists that "student or faculty opinion should not in itself have any influence on the formation of administrative policy." He gives what becomes known as "The Strawberry Statement": "A university is definitely not a democratic institution . . . When decisions begin to be made democratically around here, I will not be here any longer . . . Whether students vote 'yes' or 'no' on an issue is like telling me they like strawberries."

MAY 1967

"Secret defense research violates the aims and integrity of science," says Professor Morton Fried, one of eight faculty members of the Anthropology Department who have declared they will not conduct classified research for the federal government.

JUNE 1967

Copies of *Jester*, the College humor magazine, are seized by African American students from the *Jester* offices and destroyed. They claim that an article published in the magazine "on the recently established all-Negro Columbia chapter of Omega Psi Phi was 'offensive' to the Negro race. 'It goes beyond the bounds of satire,' one Negro student said."

David Truman is appointed to the combined position of vice president and provost of Columbia University.

AUGUST 1967

The tripartite Advisory Committee on Student Life—established in 1965 to study and define the "proper boundaries of civil disobedience" at Columbia and examine "matters concerned with student-faculty and student-administration relationships as they relate to student rights and responsibilities"—issues its report to President Grayson Kirk.

SEPTEMBER 1967

President Kirk begins the academic year by initiating a ban on indoor picketing and demonstrating. Infractions of the ban "will be followed by appropriate disciplinary action, including the possibility of suspension or dismissal." This policy "was made in anticipation of possible student protests this year." Several days later, in his convocation speech, Vice President Truman offers "a firm warning . . . that the administration will not tolerate efforts to make the University an instrument of opposition to the established orders of society." The rights of students, he declares, cannot be extended so far that Columbia is permitted "to become an agent of revolt against the government of the United States."

OCTOBER 1967

Controversy over the planned construction of Columbia's new gymnasium facility, a few blocks from campus, continues. "Members of the West Harlem Tenants Association may well throw themselves in front of the bulldozers that will break ground for the $9-million structure if the University refuses to cancel plans to build, Robert McKay, a member of the group, predicted." Under an agreement with the City of New York, construction must begin by November 30. The university asks for an extension until January 1968.

In light of impending recruitment sessions on campus by groups such as Dow Chemical (manufacturer of napalm), IDA and the Marine Corps,

Professor Allan Silver is named chairman of a five-man committee that will "examine the entire matter of recruiting of Columbia College students on campus by all outside agencies." Later in the month a referendum of students is held, with the result that 67 percent vote "in favor of open campus recruiting for all organizations."

Paul Rockwell discovers that Columbia has been secretly receiving $125,000 a year from the CIA for research being done at the School of International Affairs, immediately confirmed by the university. The disclosure precipitates an outdoor demonstration and calls for a "permanent committee on free inquiry to investigate secret projects and dealings involving the University." Students hand-deliver a letter to President Kirk "demanding that the University sever its connections with the military establishment." Ted Kaptchuk, chairman of Columbia SDS, stresses that "the University will face 'widespread resistance' if the administration does not meet SDS demands."

University Chaplain John Cannon announces the establishment of an "extensive program of draft counseling" at Columbia, "the first on a major university campus." Cannon explains that "by the end of last year he was spending two to three hours a day personally counseling students, and found it an inefficient system."

NOVEMBER 1967

A new directive from the Selective Service System is announced: students who obstruct military recruiting may lose their draft deferment. The faculty of Columbia College "vote overwhelmingly to request that President Kirk suspend all military recruiting on campus."

SAS invites H. Rap Brown, chairman of the Student Nonviolent Coordinating Committee (SNCC), to campus. "White students have a role in the black man's struggle in America," he explains, "but not within the black community. They must organize among whites and awaken those who don't know what is happening. We don't need missionaries, we need revolutionaries."

Eight Columbia students—including Mark Rudd and Ted Gold of SDS—are arrested at a demonstration outside the Hilton Hotel in midtown Manhattan, protesting an appearance by Secretary of State Dean Rusk.

DECEMBER 1967

Stop the Draft Week. Hundreds of students attend an eight-hour conference on campus as "scholars, journalists and government officials discuss—and often debate—the causes and effects of the war in Vietnam."
Several Columbia students are arrested later at a protest at the army
induction center on Whitehall Street, downtown Manhattan.

A groundbreaking ceremony for the gymnasium in Morningside Park
is called off because various local community organizers insist they will
protest any such event. H. Rap Brown speaks at a community meeting in
Harlem, telling the assembled crowd: "If they build the first story, blow it
up. If they sneak back at night and build three stories, burn it down. And
if they get nine stories built, it's yours. Take it over, and maybe we'll let
them in on the weekends."

JANUARY 1968

The Faculty Civil Rights Group submits a letter to the Columbia administration "requesting that the University declare a temporary moratorium
on the relocation of tenants in Columbia-owned buildings until comprehensive expansion plans have been formulated in conjunction with neighborhood groups and city agencies."

The establishment of a committee to study Columbia's relationships
and contracts with "outside agencies"—including the CIA and IDA—is
announced by David Truman.

A group of some twenty-five faculty members at Columbia come
together to form an organization that will assist students refusing to be
inducted into the armed forces.

FEBRUARY 1968

A twelve-foot-high chain-link fence is constructed around the site of
the proposed gymnasium in Morningside Heights. A few days later,
twelve people, including six Columbia students, are arrested during a
demonstration at the site. "For the third time in the past two years, a
bill to stop the construction of the Columbia gymnasium may be submitted to the state Assembly next week, according to Assemblyman

Charles B. Rangel, the author of the bill." A week later, thirteen people, including twelve Columbia students, are arrested while protesting at the site.

The Selective Service System cancels deferments for most graduate students, meaning undergraduate seniors may face induction within months. A letter signed by two dozen faculty members is circulated. It reads: "We, members of the faculty of Columbia University, will support those Columbia students who decide to refuse cooperation with Selective Service because they consider our war in Vietnam unjust and immoral."

"Over eighty Columbia and Barnard students blocked the entrance to a recruiting office in Dodge Hall for almost two hours Friday, causing two recruiters from the Dow Chemical Company to cancel seven afternoon appointments."

MARCH 1968

"About one hundred students protesting Columbia's affiliation with the Institute for Defense Analyses picketed a tea held for the Trustees and faculty in the Engineering Terrace lounge yesterday. The demonstrators, organized by Students for a Democratic Society, were joined by the Pageant Players, a mime theater group, who performed an anti-IDA skit during the demonstration."

The *Spectator* editorial, March 13: "A day of relevant learning. A protest against American involvement in the war in Vietnam. A search for answers about how to react to the challenges which Vietnam forces students to confront. A review of possible alternatives to military service. Moratorium Day at Columbia." Most classes are canceled as students gather across campus to hear a variety of speakers, including Noam Chomsky, Dwight Macdonald, Joseph Heller, and Robert Lowell.

Mark Rudd, an adherent of "confrontation politics," is elected chairman of the Columbia chapter of SDS.

Seventeen Columbia students and two faculty members are arrested at a demonstration in the lobby of the Rockefeller Plaza offices of the Dow Chemical Company. The same day, the director of the New York City headquarters of the Selective Service System is hit in the face with a lemon meringue pie during a talk on campus. "According to several

observers, the pie was thrown at Col. Paul Akst when several demonstrators staged an apparent diversionary melee at the rear of the
auditorium."

Following a rally and speeches at the sundial, a group of students, led
by SDS, enters Low Memorial Library to deliver to President Kirk a petition requesting that Columbia's ties with IDA be severed. In violation of
the ban on indoor protest, "The students chanted slogans, carried placards and used a bull horn inside the building." The administration lets it
be known that it plans to discipline six students, all from the SDS steering committee.

APRIL 1968

The Columbia University Student Council asks that President Grayson
Kirk release the Student Life Report, which he received in August 1967 but
has yet to make public. A few days later, Kirk does so, alongside a minority opinion written by four of the five student members of the Advisory
Committee on Student Life, which "severely criticized the majority report
on the subject of the extent of the student's role in the University decision-
making process."

The university administration announces that it plans to "terminate
formal institutional sponsorship" of IDA, but President Kirk will remain
on the IDA board. Mark Rudd describes this move as "a sham . . . Nothing
has changed except the words 'institutional affiliation.'"

Just before Vice President and Provost Truman delivers his address
at the university's official memorial service for Dr. Martin Luther King,
Jr., Mark Rudd interrupts events by walking up to the speaker's platform,
describing the service as an "obscenity," and calling on the administration to end its racist policies in the neighborhood. Rudd then leads several dozen SDS supporters out of St. Paul's Chapel.

The "IDA 6"—those students identified after the recent Low Memorial Library protest—are placed on disciplinary probation because they
refuse to meet with a dean to discuss their participation in the event.
The students "demand an open hearing" instead. SDS and SAS plan a
joint rally on April 23 to protest. "We will go into Low Memorial Library.
We will ask to see President Kirk and present him with a petition," says
Mark Rudd.

TUESDAY, APRIL 23

Noon   Five hundred demonstrators gather at the sundial, at the center of campus. Members of SDS and SAS give speeches to the crowd. Faculty members are present to prevent clashes between demonstrators and the fifty counterdemonstrators who have gathered on the steps of Low Memorial Library. Members of SDS lead the crowd to the security door of Low but fail to gain entrance. A section of the crowd, numbering more than three hundred, moves off campus, crossing Amsterdam Avenue, and then walks down to the gymnasium construction site in Morningside and tears down the fence. New York City Police arrive and one student is arrested.

1 P.M.   Demonstrators return to the sundial where SDS and SAS leaders speak to the crowd. A sit-in begins in the lobby of Hamilton Hall. Dean Henry Coleman, held "hostage" in his office inside Hamilton with two others, confers with university officials on the telephone. A steering committee, composed of members of SDS, SAS and others, is established.

2:30 P.M.   Six demands are formulated and read to the crowd (see p. lxxi). Demonstrators decide not to leave Hamilton until these demands are met.

4:30 P.M.   Dean Coleman emerges from his office and announces that Vice President and Provost Truman has informed him by phone that he will meet with demonstrators in Wollman Auditorium to discuss their grievances. The demonstrators reject the offer. Coleman returns to his office as the crowd grows inside Hamilton. President Kirk, who is off campus, is informed of the protests and immediately suggests that police be brought in to clear Hamilton Hall. Several members of the faculty arrive and speak to the crowd in Hamilton. A student band plays a concert in the lobby. Community activists and Harlem residents begin arriving, and students drift upstairs to find places to spend the night. Professor Eugene Galanter gathers the twenty signatures necessary to call a special faculty meeting, and later in the day the entire faculty of Columbia College is notified.

10 P.M.   David Truman appears outside Hamilton before meeting students in the lobby of Hartley Hall. "We will discuss anything," he tells the audience, "but we will not act under coercion. There will, and

necessarily must be, punishments, or we will be torn apart by a willful minority that will have its way no matter what" (*Up Against*, p. 59).

WEDNESDAY, APRIL 24

2 A.M.   The Hamilton steering committee splits into two separate groups: SDS and SAS. SAS wants to barricade the building, whereas SDS would rather seal off the dean's office and let students come in and out of the building. Mark Rudd prefers "to radicalize students to build a mass movement rather than alienate them from the start by barricading them out of their morning classes" (*Up Against*, p. 61). Moreover, "The slow, wavering nature of SDS's participatory democracy irritated the blacks who preferred more centralized decision-making and felt that SDS would not have the discipline or resolve to 'go all the way'" (*Up Against*, p. 61). Rumors circulate that there are guns in the building.

5:30 A.M.   White students are evicted from Hamilton by black students. Dean Coleman and the two other individuals locked inside his office barricade themselves inside by pushing two desks against the locked door.

6:15 A.M.   Students break into Low Memorial Library and seize President Grayson Kirk's office. Some rummage through files and copy documents, extracts of which are later published in underground New York newspapers.

7 A.M.   The occupants of Low are told that if they surrender their identification cards and remove themselves from the building, they will face only university discipline and no criminal trespass charges. The proposal is rejected.

7:45 A.M.   After police enter Kirk's offices, some students, including Mark Rudd, escape from the office by jumping out the windows. The police remove a $450,000 Rembrandt from the wall but make no arrests.

10 A.M.   Faculty begin to meet informally inside Philosophy Hall. State Sen. Basil Paterson heads to campus and meets with black students inside Hamilton, while Deputy New York Major Robert Sweet telephones the Columbia administration to ask if they want the mayor's Urban

Task Force troubleshooters to intervene. Several of the mayor's aides are eventually sent to campus, where they spend several days. The black students make it clear that there are two preconditions for negotiations: no criminal prosecutions and no university discipline for any student involved in the protests.

3 P.M.   The faculty of Columbia College meet and condemn the holding of Dean Coleman before recommending suspending construction of the gym and proposing the creation of a tripartite body that will advise on any disciplinary action arising from the protests.

3:30 P.M.   After twenty-six hours inside his office, Dean Henry Coleman and two others leave Hamilton Hall.

4 P.M.   Crowds of demonstrators and counterdemonstrators gather outside Hamilton. The administration cancels all evening classes.

5 P.M.   President Kirk and Vice President/Provost Truman meet with Basil Paterson, Borough President Percy Sutton, and State Assemblyman Charles Rangel.

8 P.M.   The administration attempts to negotiate separately with the black students inside Hamilton. A promise is made that if demonstrators leave the building they will not be suspended, although they will be placed on disciplinary probation. The Hamilton Hall occupiers reject the offer. A line of faculty, each wearing a white armband, stands outside Hamilton "to discourage outbreaks of violence between students" (*Up Against*, p. 87).

10 P.M.   Architecture students working inside Avery refuse to leave the building when asked to by security guards.

THURSDAY, APRIL 25

2 A.M.   Fayerweather Hall is occupied by various groups and the building is barricaded.

11 A.M.   President Kirk calls on Professors Lionel Trilling, Eugene Galanter, and Carl Hovde to recommend "the structure, the personnel, and the appropriate procedures for the tripartite commission" (*Up Against*, p. 89).

1:30 P.M.   Counterdemonstrators ("conservatives") meet in the Columbia gymnasium to organize their response and form themselves into the Majority Coalition. Shortly thereafter, Kirk and Truman give a press conference. "We cannot give in on amnesty," Truman says, referring to one of the protesters' demands. "This goes far beyond this university" (*Up Against*, p. 90). Truman then speaks to the faculty assembled in Philosophy Hall, explaining that Columbia cannot indefinitely halt construction of the gymnasium "because it would cost six million dollars to break the contracts" (*Up Against*, p. 91).

4 P.M.   Some faculty begins to coalesce into what becomes known as the Ad Hoc Faculty Group, which remains in continuous session until April 30. A four-point proposal is passed by the group requesting (1) cessation of excavation at the gym site, (2) the university administration delegates all disciplinary powers to the tripartite committee, (3) students leave the buildings immediately, and (4) faculty stand in front of the occupied buildings in the event of police being called in.

7 P.M.   The proposals are taken into the four occupied buildings by various faculty members. In each case, strikers explain that they will vacate the buildings only "when the University grants our six demands as stated" (*Up Against*, p. 95).

8 P.M.   Harlem activists address a rally at the Columbia gates.

9:30 P.M. Counterdemonstrators attempt to invade Fayerweather Hall before sending a representative to speak to the faculty in Philosophy Hall and then at a meeting at Wollman Auditorium, where a discussion between students and faculty takes place. The Ad Hoc Faculty Group is "condemned as illegitimate, Kirk and Truman excoriated for their inaction" (*Up Against*, p. 103).

FRIDAY, APRIL 26

1 A.M.   David Truman arrives in Philosophy Hall and announces an imminent police action. "The room exploded. There were cries of 'Shame! Shame!' as faculty members booed the vice president loudly" (*Up Against*, p. 108). Professor Alan Westin and a small group of faculty meet with Mark Rudd and others, but these negotiations prove fruitless. Faculty put on white armbands and take up position

outside the buildings, which they informally patrol all day, to prevent violence among students. "A roaring chant of 'KIRK MUST
GO!' rose from the crowd into the cold spring air" (*Up Against*,
p. 114). Plainclothes policemen clash with the faculty line around
Low Memorial Library.

1:15 A.M.   Mathematics Hall is occupied. Around this time, WKCR, Columbia's student-run radio station, announces that broadcasts have
been suspended after David Truman's suggestion "that WKCR is
contributing to an unhealthy atmosphere" (*Up Against*, p. 114). This
is followed shortly afterward by another announcement: WKCR
will be allowed to continue broadcasting after all.

3:30 A.M.   Truman announces the cancellation of the police action, that construction on the gymnasium has been suspended, and that the university will be closed until Monday.

11 A.M.   "Two hundred black high school students marched to Columbia and
held a rally at 116th Street and Amsterdam Avenue in support of the
black students in Hamilton Hall. At 11:15 they streamed onto campus,
sprinting toward the Sundial" (*Up Against*, p. 133).

1:15 P.M.   H. Rap Brown (SNCC national chairman) and Stokely Carmichael
(former SNCC national chairman) enter campus, breaking through
the police line on Amsterdam Avenue. They are surrounded by a
group of black high school students who escort them to Hamilton Hall, where the two spend approximately forty minutes before
appearing on the steps of the building. "Brown calmly read the text
of a press statement that had been issued the previous evening by the
students in Hamilton. When he finished, he added a few words of his
own. Shaking his fist, he shouted, 'If the University doesn't deal with
the brothers in there, they're going to have to deal with the brothers
out on the streets'" (*Up Against*, p. 134).

4 P.M.   The Trilling-Galanter-Hovde Committee submits proposals for the
tripartite commission on discipline: five Columbia College students,
five faculty, and two administrators to handle punishment of demonstrating students, with specific penalties for specific acts.

5 P.M.   Led by Professor Lowell Harriss, approximately two hundred students opposed to the building occupations, who earlier in the day
issued a statement ("Amnesty is out of the question"), march to

Philosophy Hall. Professor Harriss warns his fellow faculty that "Unless the insurrection is ended soon, by the police, if necessary, there will be widespread student violence" (*Up Against*, p. 137).

7:30 P.M.   At a Strike Coordinating Committee press conference, Mark Rudd insists that the key issue is whether the administration will grant the demonstrators amnesty. He urges the faculty "to cease mediating and to take sides with the students" (*Up Against*, p. 138).

9 P.M.   Professor Alan Westin and his team meet with the Strike Coordinating Committee.

SATURDAY, APRIL 27

1 A.M.   Mark Rudd addresses the Ad Hoc Faculty Group and declares his recent conversations with Alan Westin as "exploratory, more in the line of bullshit" (*Up Against*, p. 140). He reiterates that the only way to resolve the crisis is by granting students amnesty.

10:30 A.M.   A statement from Columbia's Board of Trustees is released: "In common with the administration and those great majorities, the Trustees deplore the complete disruption of normal University operations and the illegal seizure and occupation of University buildings, perpetrated by a small minority of students, aided and abetted by outsiders who have injected themselves into the situation." The statement notes that there will be no amnesty for the protesters, that construction of the gymnasium has been temporarily halted, and that President Grayson Kirk "shall maintain the ultimate disciplinary power," thus negating the Trilling-Galanter-Hovde Committee proposals and further polarizing the campus (*Up Against*, p. 143).

11:30 A.M.   A faculty cordon is established around Low Memorial Library. No students will be allowed access "except those officially designated as mediators" (*Up Against*, p. 146).

6 P.M.   Five hundred antiwar demonstrators who have come from a rally in Central Park mass at 116th Street and Amsterdam Avenue. Ted Kaptchuk, Mark Rudd, and Tom Hayden address the crowd.

11 P.M.   The Ad Hoc Faculty Group recognizes that both sides are "entrenched in intransigence" and that the situation is now at a deadlock. The

students "do not intend to settle" and the administration is determined to "hold the line" (*Up Against*, p. 154–7).

SUNDAY, APRIL 28

8 A.M.   The Ad Hoc Faculty issues a final set of proposals (the "bitter pill") to end the crisis, announcing that if these are not acceptable to both sides, all negotiating efforts will be ended. The four elements of this proposal: (1) establishment of a tripartite commission to have ultimate judicial review on all matters concerning university discipline; (2) the establishment of a tripartite committee of community, trustees, and faculty to find an alternative to the gym; (3) students to vacate the buildings and submit themselves to due process once the administration has accepted the proposals; and (4) if President Kirk rejects the proposals, the faculty will try to prevent the use of force, but if students reject them, faculty will no longer interpose themselves between administration and students. The proposals are accepted by a vote of 200 to 3.

10 A.M.   A meeting of the Morningside Faculties is held in the Law School, with more than five hundred members attending. Professor Peter Kenen's motion (condemnation of building occupations, commendation of gym suspension and consultation with local community, and endorsement of tripartite commission for discipline) is passed 466 to 40.

Noon   At a press conference, the Strike Coordinating Committee rejects the Ad Hoc Faculty Group proposals and reaffirms their six demands before asking the faculty to stop mediating, "take a political position," and come out in support of the six demands (*Up Against*, p. 161).

5:15 P.M.   After the results of a campus survey are released (of 5,500 people surveyed, most are not in favor of amnesty or the tactics of the protesters, but most want to end construction of the gym and to sever ties to IDA), the Majority Coalition establishes a blockade around Low Memorial Library to prevent people and supplies from entering. By midnight there are 250 students (all wearing coat and tie) in the cordon.

11:30 P.M.   Richard Eagan and Andrea Boroff are married inside Fayerweather Hall.

MONDAY, APRIL 29

3:30 P.M.   President Kirk issues a statement in response to the "bitter pill." He calls for (1) a tripartite commission proposed by Galanter, Hovde, and Trilling, (2) disciplinary measures to be reexamined in light of the tripartite committee's recommendations, (3) the matter of uniform penalties to be referred to the tripartite commission, and (4) discussions relating to the gym construction. The Ad Hoc Faculty leaders declare that the statement falls far short of their proposals. Outside at Low Memorial Library, there is a five-minute skirmish as supporters try to crash through the Majority Coalition line, then proceed to throw food over the line through the windows of Low.

6:30 P.M.   The Strike Coordinating Committee reaffirms the six demands and rejects the "bitter pill."

TUESDAY, APRIL 30

2 A.M.   Telephone and water lines into the five occupied buildings are cut. The police enter Hamilton Hall and the building's occupants are peacefully removed and loaded into police vans. "As knowledge of the bust spread across campus, faculty and students began to assemble at the security entrance to Low, resolved to use all means within their power to prevent a solution of the crisis by force" (*Up Against*, p. 186). People also congregate at the entrances to the three other occupied buildings.

2:30 A.M.   Armed with "blackjacks and flashlights" (*Up Against*, p 189), the police charge through the lines of faculty and students outside each of the buildings and enter Low Memorial Library, Avery, Fayerweather, and Mathematics. Some 80 percent of the 712 arrestees are Columbia or Barnard students. "Makeshift medical centers were set up by volunteers in Earl Hall, the building which normally houses the chaplain and his staff, and in the lounge of Philosophy Hall where the Ad Hoc Faculty Group had debated three hours before" (*Up Against*, p. 191). Crowds of observers on campus, including counterdemonstrators, are rushed by a line of police. "The students who ran slowest in the stampede were struck with clubs, tripped or kicked." Students forced off campus onto Broadway are confronted with mounted policemen who "charged into them" (*Up Against*, p. 195). The Civilian Complaint Review Board later receives 120 charges of police brutality, "the largest number of complaints ever received in New York City for a single police action" (*Up Against*, p. 196).

10 A.M. Hundreds of students join with the Strike Coordinating Committee, which has called for a campus-wide strike.

4 P.M. A Joint Faculties meeting takes place in St. Paul's Chapel, where the Executive Committee of the Faculty is established, which is designed to have the power "to call the faculty together and to take other needed steps to return the University to its educational task at the earliest possible moment" (*Up Against*, p. 213). Later, the Executive Committee meets with a group of student leaders to discuss "the question of restructuring the University" (*Up Against*, p. 218).

WEDNESDAY, MAY 1

Students clash with the police as 750 people attend a Strike Steering Committee rally at Amsterdam Avenue and 116th Street.

At a meeting in Wollman Auditorium, a new Strike Coordinating Committee is created. Any group pledged to support the strike can send one delegate to the SCC for every seventy constituents. By the following day, "the credentials of thirty-seven delegates had been approved" (*Up Against*, p. 225). The SCC eventually grows to represent four thousand students.

THURSDAY, MAY 2

The College Committee on Instruction meets and decides that for each class taken, a student can opt for either "a letter grade, a grade of 'P' indicating only that he had passed the course, or an 'incomplete' which would mean that he would have a year to make up any work necessary to receive a grade" (*Up Against*, p. 225).

FRIDAY, MAY 3

The SCC rejects "the efforts of the Executive Committee, comparing it to the disregarded Committee on Student Life and to President Lyndon

Johnson's commissions on civil disorders and the draft. 'The committee has neither the proper democratic structure to represent the interests of those studied, nor the power to effect meaningful change,' SCC charged" (*Up Against*, p. 232).

SATURDAY, MAY 4

At a meeting "over three hundred students passed by acclamation an SCC motion to picket academic buildings on Monday. To prevent the strike from losing the momentum it had acquired from the bust, the group decided to hold a rally every day at noon for the next week" (*Up Against*, p. 226). The Strike Education Committee announces the creation of the Liberation School. "Counter-classes," some of which take place outside on lawns in front of campus buildings, will help students "exercise their *freedom* to experiment with and create new and different forms and content, according to a continuing *democratic procedure*" (*Up Against*, p. 226).

SUNDAY, MAY 5

Columbia College faculty meet and endorse the Executive Committee of the Faculty's call "for structural reforms to give faculty members a larger share of decision-making power in the College" (*Up Against*, p. 229). The Executive Committee announces the membership of a five-member fact-finding panel, led by former US Solicitor General Archibald Cox, "to establish the chronology of events leading up to the recent disturbances on the Columbia campus" and to inquire into their "underlying causes" (*Up Against*, p. 235). Black students representing Hamilton Hall occupiers make it clear that they will not testify before the Cox Commission, while the SCC contends that the commission does not represent the interests of the faculty or the students, and is merely diverting attention from the issues of the strike.

THURSDAY, MAY 16

The university reopens, but students continue their participation in a boycott of classes and picketing outside buildings. John Thoms leads twenty

Figure o.2 A flyer distributed on campus, Thursday, April 25. In the early hours of the following day, Mathematics Hall is occupied, taking the total number of buildings held by protesters to five. *Image from University Archives, Rare Book and Manuscript Library, Columbia University in the City of New York.*

delegates in a walk-out from the SCC and forms the moderate group Students for a Restructured University.

FRIDAY, MAY 17

Community activists seize a Columbia-owned apartment building on 114th Street, which is scheduled for demolition, planning "to transform it into a neighborhood action center for Morningside Heights" (*Up Against*, p. 241). In support, a thousand Columbia students congregate outside the building; 117 people are arrested, 56 of whom are Columbia students.

TUESDAY, MAY 21

Approximately two hundred students reoccupy Hamilton Hall in protest against the disciplining of four SDS leaders, who have been threatened with suspension because of their involvement with previous demonstrations. At around 2:30 A.M., police enter Hamilton and empty the building, arresting approximately one hundred students and thirty outsiders. Shortly afterward, demonstrators throw bricks through the windows of Low Memorial Library and other buildings, and fires are reported to have been started in Hamilton and Fayerweather. The New York City Fire Department is called and the police clear the campus.

TUESDAY, JUNE 4

Columbia holds its 214th Commencement Exercise at the Cathedral of Saint John the Divine. At the start of Professor Richard Hofstadter's address, several hundred graduating students walk out of ceremonies and hold a countercommencement, organized by Students for a Restructured University, in front of Low Memorial Library.

AUGUST 1968

Grayson Kirk announces his early retirement as president of Columbia University. Andrew Cordier, dean of Columbia's School of International Affairs, is appointed acting president.

JANUARY 1969

David Truman resigns and is appointed president of Mount Holyoake College in Massachusetts.

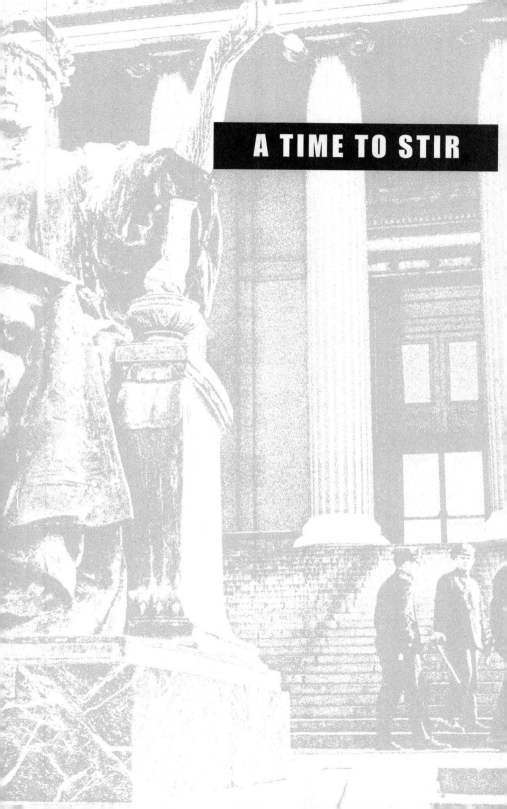

A TIME TO STIR

Barnard undergraduate/Strike Coordinating Committee

CHILDREN OF THE NEW AGE

We were an optimistic and righteous generation, many of us raised by parents who had survived World War II. My dad was an Army combat vet who fought in the South Pacific and trained GIs on the use of top-secret proximity fuse weaponry. My four refugee grandparents fled persecution in Russian shtetls, arrived in America penniless, and spoke Yiddish and Russian at home. They were hopeful yet wary, with "one foot in the suitcase" in case they had to go back. Despite their caution, I blossomed into a high school liberal activist in the sheltered suburbs of Philadelphia.

From my father and television I learned about the world. My dad, an engineer, built an early version of a TV; we were the first in the neighborhood to get one. From that box in the corner of our tiny living room I found out about civil rights and the intimidation and murder of Southern blacks for attempting to register to vote. I saw Sheriff Bull Connor unleash his dogs and fire hoses on young blacks, many no older than me. By the time I was a high school senior the Vietnam War, this nation's first televised war, filled my home with images of napalmed children and burning villages, as people ran from American cluster bombs, their bodies charred black by my country's lethal chemical warfare. I watched generals on TV talking about "the enemy" in words that made no sense.

I decided I wanted to go to college at Barnard mainly because it was located in New York City, teeming with the diversity I craved as a Philly teenager. By the time I arrived on campus, my new friends and I all knew of high school classmates who had returned from Vietnam in body bags. Learning about and organizing against the war was what I did with my time outside of classes. The early months of 1968 unfolded: the Tet Offensive, the assassination of Dr. Martin Luther King, Jr. followed by black rebellion in cities across the country. Students and faculty at Columbia and elsewhere were talking about the war and civil rights. Students for a Democratic Society (SDS) had a strong presence on college campuses, and, in today's parlance, became the thought-leader of the antiwar movement, holding rallies and teach-ins. At Columbia, the SDS chapter published critiques of the university for its affiliation with US Defense Department contractors. SDS also paid attention to how the university related to its largely African American neighborhood. When it became known that Columbia was planning to build a private gym for its students in a public park that separated the university from Harlem, the antiwar and civil rights movements converged.

On April 23, 1968, hundreds of students, including me, stormed into and "occupied" a university building. Within a matter of days, four more buildings were occupied and barricaded by hundreds of students. I was eventually charged with criminal trespass, spent a night in jail, and was released the following morning. (Columbia later dropped all charges against its students, and my graduation ceremony a year later took place at virtually the same spot where I had been arrested.)

Life inside Columbia's occupied buildings was intense, intoxicating, and profoundly pre-feminist. We believed we were making history by shutting down the university, but even at the time I and many other women felt that our views were not being heard and that we were somehow being excluded from real decision-making meetings—from leadership.

Columbia strike alums have come together on most decade anniversaries of the student rebellion to reflect on what happened, and what it meant. On the anniversary of the first decade, my recollections were laced with anger, and I decided not to go. Ten years after that, in 1988, I was asked to speak on a panel of "strike leaders." I was taken aback at the notion I had been any kind of a leader, but agreed to participate. In preparation for the panel I reread *Up Against the Ivy Wall*, published in 1969 by a group of student journalists who had reported daily on strike activities for the university newspaper. Rereading the book as history was a revelation. It makes no mention that of the more than seven hundred students arrested, almost two hundred—graduate students and under- grads from Barnard—were women. Only once in three hundred pages is a woman mentioned by name, and she is the mother of one of the male strikers. Barnard students are called only "girls" or "coeds," never simply "students." The book's appendix is a cast of characters listed by name, which includes seventeen students, seven administrators, twenty-five fac- ulty, and ten community leaders and city officials. Not one is a woman.

When describing the events of one of the mass arrests, *Up Against the Ivy Wall* records "one girl, speaking from the floor" who "gave a tearful, angry appeal for staying."[1] It is the only use of the word "tearful" in the entire book. In a description of the communal cohesion inside the build- ings, the authors write that students "formed and joined task forces to serve the needs of the other occupants; some stood guard at points of contact with the outside, some kept up communications via phone and walkie-talkie with friendly buildings, and others—mostly girls—managed food and housekeeping details."[2] As the campus flooded with police in full riot gear, there is this observation: "'It's beautiful,' one girl sighed as she watched students perched high on the barricade screaming obsceni- ties at the cops."[3]

Being expunged from the pages of our own history reflects our deval- uation by our brothers and lovers in this movement for social change. We pre-feminists felt demeaned and angry that our contributions to the Columbia strike were marginalized. We doubted ourselves, and too many people apparently doubted that women could be reliable witnesses to our own lives. In the years since, I and other women I know from those times have, in one way or another, fought for the right to have ideas, to be in possession of facts, to be acknowledged.

In hindsight, I better understand how unsettled we felt. After all, we grew up in egalitarian families that took our intellects as seriously as those of our brothers. I certainly believed that my engagement with the New Left was no different from any guy I knew. We all believed in the

1. Jerry L. Avorn, with Andrew Crane [and others] of the staff of the *Columbia Daily Spectator*, *Up Against the Ivy Wall* (New York: Atheneum Press, 1969), 118.
2. Avorn et al., *Up Against*, 254.
3. Avorn et al., *Up Against*, 263.

inseparability of ends and means, of participatory democracy, of integrating politics into our personal lives. Yet, as I look back on 1968, the sense of euphoria that was emblematic of the Columbia strike is tempered by uneasy feelings. As Todd Gitlin put it in his book *The Sixties*, movement men sought women out, recruited us, took us seriously, and honored our intelligence, yet demoted us to girlfriends, wives, note-takers, and coffee-makers. We cherished our personal relationships with guys, at least in part because without them we could not have participated in the endless, informal, high-level meetings taking place. Yet quietly we resented being there on male sufferance, or if our consciousness had not yet clarified those amorphous feelings into resentment, we were at the very least confused.

The occupied buildings became our homes, and we lived with each other, cooked, ate, cleaned up (women were in the forefront of that effort) and talked politics into the wee hours. One couple inside occupied Fayerweather got married in a candlelit ceremony with hundreds of witnesses, as officiated by Columbia's Episcopalian Chaplain, who to the delight of everyone declared them "Children of the New Age."

There were a few women who had the guts and vision to speak up back then, including the newlywed bride. I will never forget a sign, hung over a typewriter inside occupied Fayerweather Hall, that read: "To all women: You are in a liberated area. You are urged to reject the traditional role of housekeeper unless, of course, you feel this is the role that allows for creative expression. Speak up. Use your brains." I wrote in an article at the time about "male ego-trips," and that I, like many others, were trying to create a new form of leadership, "one that recognized us as women, yet also as political people with thoughts and actions which must be communicated."

People speak of Columbia as a transforming event, a unique time when we bonded intensely with each other, some of us total strangers. We placed our lives and futures in each other's hands. We ate, slept, breathed, and loved our political activism. "Everybody tries to find too much emotional motivation in our protests," I was quoted in 1968 by the *New York Times* as saying, trying to explain how seriously we took our political beliefs. "We're not just alienated."

Nearly fifty years after the Columbia strike, my husband and I flew from New York to Saigon, now Ho Chi Minh City. Spending time in this tiny country that shaped me as a young adult, consumed me from high

school through law school, and nourished my morality as parent and professional, was gut-wrenching. The war, it took me five decades to learn,
was vastly more destructive—in the number of bombs dropped and in
the use of chemical and biological warfare—than I, aged eighteen, knew
at the time. We traveled the country for a month from the Mekong Delta
to the Central Highlands, north to Hanoi and mountain villages less than
ten miles from the China border. We swam in the Gulf of Tonkin and saw
monuments at Quang Tri and the ancient imperial city of Hue, which was
leveled in 1968. We climbed through the Vinh Moc tunnels, which housed
an entire rural community during the war—hundreds of families escaping the bombing—thirty meters below ground. Babies were born in the
tunnels as doctors made use of an operating table fabricated from metal
salvaged from a downed American plane. The day I spent at the Vietnamese Women's Museum in Hanoi was when I flashed back to being a young
woman at Columbia. The museum portrays women's lives throughout
Vietnamese history as a tapestry of vital roles: mother, soldier, student,
all with strong and feminine qualities, all whole and essential. Vietnamese
women seemed to be guilelessly self-determined agents of their own des-
tinies, never victims.

    While at the women's museum, I finally began to grieve for what our
country had done to these women and their families. Later, emerging from
the claustrophobic Củ Chi tunnels near Ho Chi Minh City, in which North
Vietnamese soldiers lived and which they used as a base of operations,
I started sobbing. Our guide embraced me and told me not to cry, saying
that it was all in the past and the Vietnamese had "moved on." Perhaps
Buddhism—its loving kindness, compassion, sympathy, equanimity—
encourages this thinking. Again and again I repeated his words to myself
as we visited tombs, battlefields, and museums that recalled vivid details
of the war. By the time we returned from Saigon to New York, President
Obama had set out for Vietnam and Laos. While in Laos he acknowledged
that 270 million American bombs had been dropped in what was then a
top-secret operation aimed at destroying "supply routes" along the Ho Chi
Minh Trail. About a third of the bombs to hit Laos never exploded, and to
this day, unexploded ordnance dropped by American bombers kills and
maims hundreds of people every year.

    Most of my professional life has been based in the South Bronx, long
a poster child for warlike destruction masquerading as urban renewal.

In 1988, I began work to redevelop twenty-three abandoned, burned-out buildings, once home to more than seven hundred families. Across the façade of one building were the words "Persistence of Memory." That idea has animated my life and work. After all, things that are destroyed and buried can be forever forgotten. History and memory are fragile and easily manipulated, or erased.

My father never ceased talking about his wartime combat experiences—he hated the enemy he fought—even as his memory succumbed to Alzheimer's. He fought the just war, yet supported me as I fought against an unjust one. In the hazy weeks after he died in 2015, I visited Washington, D.C., and walked through the memorials—to the World War II veterans, to FDR, to the American soldiers killed in Vietnam. Standing at the Martin Luther King, Jr. Memorial, I recalled a trip my husband and I had taken with two of our children, then nine and fourteen, to see the death camps at Auschwitz and later the beaches of Normandy. We wanted them

Figure 1.1 Graffiti on a blackboard inside occupied Fayerweather Hall. *Photograph by Gerald Adler.*

to learn to recognize evil in the world and to begin their own lifelong dialogues with themselves about how a moral person acts in the face of immorality. Etched on the Martin Luther King, Jr. Memorial are these words, from 1967: "I oppose the war in Vietnam because I love America. I speak out against it not in anger but with anxiety and sorrow in my heart, and above all with a passionate desire to see our beloved country stand as a moral example of the world."

We knew that as students we could not stop the Vietnam War, nor could we end racism. But we could do our part, which at Columbia in 1968 was to broadcast as loudly as we could that students were willing to put their lives and futures at risk to end this awful war. What we learned during those six days of the building occupation was the transformative power of individuals working together in pursuit of justice. Ho Chi Minh once said that his people were never anti-American, only against the American government, and that the war would end when the American people stopped their government from pursuing it. Perhaps we Columbia protesters can take some credit for catalyzing the student movement in the United States against the war, which in turn helped catalyze the rest of the nation. Perhaps we saved some lives. We did the best we could. In hindsight, we should have done more. But we were, like all who were fighting, so young.

Nancy Biberman ('69BC) is president of WHEDco, a community development organization in the South Bronx she founded in 1992. She pioneered a process of community-driven contextual development grounded in the preservation, memory and history of the South Bronx by renovating old buildings or constructing new structures on vacant land to anchor and preserve neighborhoods. She began her career as a legal services lawyer representing tenants, immigrants and women in abusive relationships. She is married and the mother of three grown children.

J. PLUNKY BRANCH

*Columbia College undergraduate/Students' Afro-American Society/
Hamilton Hall occupier*

INSIDE ALIENATION, OUTSIDE AGITATOR

I arrived on campus in September 1965 as one of only sixteen black freshmen included in the approximately eight hundred students in the class of 1969, effectively doubling the number of black students at Columbia College. We were a mixed group: prep school graduates, gifted athletes, recruits from down South, New Yorkers, and others. Doubtless we were intended to add to campus diversity while preparing ourselves to be leaders, but in many ways, we were outsiders who, by our very presence, became agents for change at Columbia.

I was born and raised in the segregated city of Richmond, Virginia, once the capital of the Confederate States of America. At Columbia, I was pleasantly surprised at how easily I adjusted to interactions with the multiracial student body. In dorm rooms, lobbies, and other social settings I witnessed and participated in intense and enlightening debates with my fellow undergrad students on any number of subjects. Yet there was one important residue from my upbringing. I had had few occasions to meet white people in Richmond, and as black kids—and especially black males—we were taught not to look white people in the eye. My Columbia friends would say to me, "I saw you on Broadway yesterday and waved, but you didn't wave back." The fact is that I wouldn't even have noticed them. I would walk into the crowded Lion's Den, the campus grill, but my eyes would see only black people. My avoidance of looking certain people in the eye, learned as a child in Richmond, meant that when I arrived in New York, I had to teach myself to see white people.

I came to Columbia planning to become a chemist and then return home to Richmond to work at the DuPont plant ("Better Things for Better Living Through Chemistry" was the company slogan). I had fallen in love with chemistry at age nine, when I found my father's college textbook and believed it to be a noble profession, as I would surely, eventually, invent some new synthetic and help make people's lives better. But that career path would be altered by the arguments of my more politically astute and radical fellow students.

While in Richmond, I had little or no experience in questioning the validity and value of the war in Vietnam, but at Columbia, I encountered an active cadre of antiwar activist students and faculty who challenged my thinking and my apathy. In conversations and debates about the origins and prosecution of the war, I became convinced that to become a chemist would mean I likely would end up making napalm and other weapons that would contribute to the military-industrial complex. Rather than taking a role in the killing of innocent people in Southeast Asia and elsewhere, I decided I would pursue a career in the liberal arts.

The mid-sixties was the time of the maturing of the civil rights movement, and the range of possibilities being explored in the black community, as well as being discussed and debated by black students at Columbia, was vast. Dr. Martin Luther King and his Southern Christian Leadership Conference (SCLC) had gained national prominence, while groups such as the Student Nonviolent Coordinating Committee (SNCC); Congress for Racial Equality; the ever-present National Association for the Advancement of Colored People; and several local, state, and regional groups were all organizing protests and political actions, as well as devising strategies, which added to the movement's widespread impact. SCLC was intent on maintaining a national movement, whereas SNCC and other groups focused on more locally directed, student-led activities. Some organizations emphasized voter registration in the South, others tackled specific issues like employment, desegregation, and unfairness of the draft in sending black men to war. The Nation of Islam, led by Elijah Muhammad and Malcolm X, and later the Black Panthers, advocated more aggressive, confrontational strategies as alternatives to nonviolent protests. Black nationalists, pan-Africanists, and cultural nationalists put forth different views and alternative pathways to achieve local, national, and international goals for black people. We students were foot soldiers, a source of energy and political will that fueled the movement, and an important part of the debates and strategies being waged and executed. We also likely were to become some of the primary future beneficiaries of the push for voting rights and equal opportunity under the law.

My early years at Columbia were in some ways typical of undergrad student life, with their share of study; sex, drugs, and rock 'n' roll; and political activism, as well as meeting new people and exploring boundaries without local parental oversight. But some layers of concerns and activities were specific to being black at Columbia. Some of my black classmates were totally committed to excelling in their academic endeavors. Some were establishing chapters of national fraternities. Some were enduring discrimination on football and basketball teams. Some were politically active, both on and off campus. Most were trying to find themselves and lay the groundwork for their careers. But all of us were part of a generation that had been repeatedly told: "You have to do your absolute best at all times. You have to be *better* than everyone else, and not just for personal gain. When you step out in public, you are representing not just yourself but the entire race." We were conspicuous examples of the "talented tenth," whose role it was to be public intellectuals and black leaders.

Influenced by a range of new philosophies that destabilized some of the assumptions of my upbringing, I had my own personal issues with alienation and the disorientation of having shifted my projected career from chemistry to who knew what. My own personal proclivity to push boundaries in social areas also complicated my relationship with fellow students, administrators, and campus politics. I was a social bad boy and a ladies' man. And I started a dance band on campus, the Soul Syndicate, fourteen pieces of driving soul, doing James Brown and Motown songs for college mixers and disco club audiences. Leading the band—my own infusion of Southern soul culture at the college—gave me some modicum of celebrity on campus. In January 1968, at the end of the first semester of my junior year, I dropped out of Columbia. Few people knew it at the time because I remained on campus and kept up most of my activities, still socializing, debating political philosophies, and leading the band.

The war and civil rights were the twin overriding issues of the time. Students for a Democratic Society (SDS) was the main, largely white, antiwar organization on campus, whereas the Students' Afro-American Society (SAS) was the leading black advocacy group. In the spring of 1968, the political topics were the presidential election, ending the Vietnam War, and stopping Columbia's expansion into West Harlem. In April, Dr. Martin Luther King, Jr. was assassinated. Our reaction on campus to the death of Dr. King was not as visceral, maybe not as physical as the people who rioted in the streets. But it charged us with the idea that we were going to have to come up with the intellectual justification for the coming revolution. If dark forces could kill Dr. King, a messenger of peace, then certainly other options to nonviolence had to be seriously considered.

Nearly three weeks after King's assassination, a demonstration was planned to protest Columbia's building of a gymnasium in Morningside Park and the university's involvement with the war. The night before, Paul, my band's trombonist, arranged a meeting between Cicero, our drummer, who was also a leader of SAS, and Mark, the chairman of Columbia's SDS chapter, to coordinate plans for their groups' activities the next day. I wasn't at the gym site on April 23 and don't remember how I got the information that SDS and SAS were staging a sit-in at Hamilton Hall. I just recall being crowded inside the lobby of Hamilton, with Dean Coleman, my advisor, trapped in his office, and along with many others realizing that we would have to formulate coherent plans as to what to do next. How long would we stay? What were our demands? What would be the response of campus security and later the police? What might the consequences be to individual students? Would there be violence and what would be our response to it?

Stopping the gym and supporting Harlem was, for us in SAS, the primary issue, stoked in no small part by the death of Dr. King. SDS and other groups, meanwhile, had come out in support of progressive action and to press for the university to suspend all support for the war. We were all in it together: Columbia men, Barnard women, blacks, whites, and others. But inside Hamilton Hall, it quickly became clear that each group had a different emphasis. For SAS, civil rights dominated, whereas for SDS, it was the war. There were two different agendas: rallying support for black struggles and creating a searing antiwar event. Maybe two different methodologies: one nonviolent and the other not necessarily so.

I was not a part of the leadership in the discussions between SAS and SDS, so I don't know the details, but it was decided that all white protesters would depart and take over another building, leaving Hamilton Hall to SAS and the blacks. Once we had Hamilton to ourselves, the atmosphere was upbeat but serious. We were happy to be in control of our own agenda, imagery, and messaging, and from behind the building's barricaded doors we issued our demands: Columbia must abandon its plans to build a gym. By doing so, we were pledging solidarity with black causes across the nation, even the world.

In those first hours, we set about the various tasks of securing the doors and windows, designating separate areas for women and men, and assigning other responsibilities. Operating one of the old-style phone systems had been my freshman work-study job, so I assumed control of the main campus telephone switchboard located in the building. I manned the switchboard for fifty straight hours, fielding innumerable incoming calls to the college from the press, administrators, and parents, all of whom wanted to know what was going on, who was in control, when was the occupation going to end, and how? It was April, and acceptance letters had just gone out to the incoming freshman class, so parents were calling to find out what would happen for the next semester (Hamilton Hall was, and still is, the classroom building of the undergraduate population at Columbia). I told some of them, "There might not be a university here next year!" When university administrators and news media phoned, I was the one who connected them to SAS leadership. We were constantly in touch with SDS at the Strike Coordinating Committee, and discussions were ongoing about objectives and tactics.

Nearly a hundred people encamped and sleeping in a building that was not designed as a residence can be a massive challenge. But in some ways this was an adventure, with us sometimes hanging out on the second-floor balcony, waving and shouting to a throng of students and others crowded around below. Black students on the outside, as well as Harlem mothers, community church groups, and civil rights leaders were all supportive, bringing food, sleeping bags, and messages of encouragement. We regarded this as a powerful validation of our actions, despite the fact that the public relations spin of the Columbia administration made a clear demarcation between students and "outside agitators." They wanted it to appear as if the protesters were being sustained by dangerous, dark external forces, people with a bigger agenda—like the destruction of the university. It was a convenient way of handling things, but of course had nothing to do with the truth. Those "outside agitators" were our brothers and sisters. This was yet another example of Columbia's inability to understand precisely what the protests were about, and more specifically how aggrieved we black students were with the operations of the university.

Like the white students in the other four buildings, we were given ultimatums to leave Hamilton Hall. Deadlines were set and passed. It was clear the standoff would come to an end very soon. The administration and the police made it clear that students would not be coddled or granted amnesty unless they left peaceably, and that outsiders and nonstudents would be deemed trespassers and thus handled differently from Columbia students. Because I was no longer registered at the college, I would not have been afforded the same leniency as a student, so I decided I would not stay until the confrontational conclusion. On the night before the end of the siege, under the cover of darkness, I slipped out of Hamilton Hall and left the campus, which—packed with police—was looking increasingly dangerous.

The occupations came to a riotous end, although the expulsion of the blacks from Hamilton Hall was peaceful. Not even our SAS leaders were roughed up, even though we had understood that this was likely. Whatever came down—whether the cops came in by force or whether we negotiated—the people who would be most likely to face retribution would be the student leaders. This is why, during the debates inside Hamilton Hall in which we openly discussed the issues as a group, all final decisions ultimately were taken by the leadership. This was a democratic process, but as a group, we were happy to defer to those three or four men who stepped out in front and became our public face. In a broader context, black leaders always have been targeted. From the time of slavery through the twenty-first century, Nat Turner, Gabriel Prosser, Harriet Tubman, Frederick Douglass, Marcus Garvey, Paul Robeson, Malcolm X, Medgar Evers, Stokely Carmichael, H. Rap Brown, Fred Hampton, Jessie Jackson, Al Sharpton, Nelson Mandela, Martin Luther King, and many others have paid dearly, some with their lives. We in the black community have always been supportive of our leaders, those who sometimes have placed themselves at grave risk to serve the greater good.

Memory is a faulty tool for recall, especially for details. But there are things I won't forget. The lessons learned constituted a turning point in my life. Our protest changed the lives of many as well as influenced other campus demonstrations and occupations across the country that followed. As college students we took a stand, and some of us never lost the sense of ourselves as the activists we became because of that experience. After Hamilton Hall in 1968, many of us, having witnessed and taken physical and political action, would be better equipped to be leaders—and agitators.

***

J. Plunky Branch *is a jazz and soul saxophonist, producer, songwriter, documentary filmmaker, educator, and political activist living in Richmond, Virginia. In 2015, he was recognized by the Library of Virginia as one of the Strong Men and Women in Virginia History. His book* Plunky: Juju Jazz Funk & Oneness— A Musical Memoir *was published in 2016.*

RAYMOND M. BROWN

*Columbia College undergraduate/Students' Afro-American Society/
Hamilton Hall occupier*

RACE AND THE SPECTER OF STRATEGIC BLINDNESS

T he Black Students of Hamilton Hall knew that the Columbia protests
of April 1968 were not the "revolution," even though Chairman Mao
did send us a congratulatory telegram. (We were amused.) For us,
those events occurred because we valued our relationships with the larger
black community and to each other. These events also demonstrated that
our fervent desire to obtain degrees from Columbia did not outweigh our
opposition to the university's attempt to grasp resources belonging to the
West Harlem community.

As the events of that spring played out, the Grey Lady covered our
activities every day up to and including our arrests. Nonetheless, the *New
York Times* and the rest of the fourth estate never seemed to understand
that the black students' occupation of Hamilton Hall was the pivotal act
of the Columbia protest, not an ancillary coda to a New Left uprising.
Our presence confronted university and government decision-makers
with the possibility that careless use of force could lead to violence in
Harlem—a deep concern that arose just weeks after the assassination of
Dr. Martin Luther King, Jr. That this strategic reality escaped the notice
of many observers then and now is a perverse tribute to the ability of
implicit racism to blind our world to critical truths. In the summer of '68,
I attributed this press blindness to "collusion" with the administration.[1]

---

1.   Stephen Donadio, "Columbia: Seven Interviews," *Partisan Review* 35, no. 3 (Summer 1968): 354–92.

I am no longer convinced that the administration was facile enough to conspire in this way.

Although most of the press missed this point, the steady stream of visitors to Hamilton Hall who sought to buttress our position appreciated our strategic position. They came from the West Harlem Tenants Association and other community groups with whom some of us had toiled in opposition to the university's appropriation of Morningside Park for its gym. They offered food, love, and the specter of alliances. Stokely Carmichael, H. Rap Brown, Borough President Percy Sutton, State Senator Basil Paterson, and others of the black political elite stopped by to offer advice. (*Be strategic, don't throw away your futures and believe your own bluff. No telling how the people of Harlem will respond to what happens up on Morningside Heights.*) We thus faced a three-dimensional challenge constructed from our commitment to stopping a powerful institution, our comprehension of the reluctance of the authorities to use force, and the knowledge that the community's support might prove to be chimerical.

Of course, the stress created by our strategic posture was exacerbated by anxious parents who called constantly on the phone in the dean's office inside Hamilton Hall, offering encouragement, threats, admonitions, and endless forms of parental advice. I later learned that some of our parents (including my dad) had been lurking outside the building in case things got funky. Yet the fact that we governed ourselves in a highly disciplined manner under these stressors will remain a treasured memory. Of equal satisfaction is the fact that the gym was never constructed in Morningside Park and that no black student was injured during the arrests or prevented from matriculating. Finally, I derive pleasure from the fact that Columbia ended its relationship with the Institute for Defense Analyses (IDA), a demand adopted by the black students and shared with others.

THE CLASS OF '68 ARRIVES—FOLLOWED BY THREE MORE: IRONIES ABOUND

Science tells us that memory is not a tape recorder, that the "acquisition," "retention," and "retrieval" of memory are affected by many external variables. In fact, some of the "memories" of 1968 were forged in advance.

Many black students were the children of men who had served in World War II and returned home to form the backbone of the postwar phase of the "movement."

Of course, it was not just outsiders to the university who helped form memories in advance of that spring. The handful of us who arrived in the fall of 1964 comprised the largest group of African Americans to enter Columbia College. We did not form a monolith, but whether from north or south, from professional families or the first to attend college, we were greeted by an institution unprepared for our arrival. The school's leadership never understood that we weren't just white students with black masks. More to the point, our continuous efforts at dialogue were generally ineffective and characterized by lip service highlighted in my mind by the indelible image of the famous provost Jacques Barzun shooting his elegant cuffs and ignoring our proposed discourse.

For those who came from homes or communities directly involved in the "movement," our connection to the larger black world was manifest. (My father was the greatest civil rights leader I ever knew, and my first picket line was Woolworth's in Jersey City, in support of student sit-ins in North Carolina.) All of us were progeny of *Brown v. Board of Education*, which did more to undermine the legitimacy of the doctrine of white supremacy than to desegregate primary education. *Brown* helps frame the irony of the university's obliviousness to the special circumstances created by our presence on campus. As I recall it, virtually every black student in my class had been actively recruited to attend Columbia in light of the dawning consciousness about racial equality. Few of us would have been on Morningside Heights had that outreach not occurred. In my case, Henry Coleman, the dean who was "stuck" in his office when we occupied Hamilton Hall, had sought me out in 1963, urged me to apply, and ensured my admission.

My own political consciousness was formed in a segregated housing project in Jersey City (named for Booker T. Washington) and in marches with the National Association for the Advancement of Colored People (NAACP) outside Woolworth's and an indifferent City Hall. My father and his colleagues actively fought the local corrupt Democratic machine, and he was extremely knowledgeable about African American history. It wasn't possible to grow up in that world and not become an intensely political being, acutely aware of being black.

Shortly after our arrival at Columbia, James Baldwin was invited to speak on campus by the Students' Afro-American Society (SAS), the black student organization founded in 1964 by Hilton Clark, son of famed psychologist Kenneth Clark. The campus newspaper reported that Baldwin commented on the spokesmen of the civil rights movement, telling us, "I disagree with the present leadership, so I look to you for the future of the movement."[2] My recollection is of Baldwin sitting with us until 2 A.M., surprised to find young black men and women at Columbia and Barnard interested in his thoughts about our relationship to the larger struggle. He explained that our presence as students at an Ivy League university was more important than we ourselves realized, and that our complaints about our treatment were minor issues compared with the fact of our presence and our search for connections to the larger struggle.

CONTOURS OF OUR CONNECTIONS TO OTHER BLACKS

As a group, we came to think of ourselves as more connected to the Harlem community than to Columbia. This stemmed largely from the fact that we attended school at an intense time in the larger movement. We were constantly interacting with Student Nonviolent Coordinating Committee activists like Courtland Cox and Cleveland Sellers, and Southern Christian Leadership Conference stalwarts like Reverend James Bevel. We were also in continuous contact with pan-Africanist and Nationalist leaders in New York like John Henrik Clarke, Queen Mother Moore, and Charles 37X Kenyatta.

Additionally, however, we were confronted by a persistent insensitivity on the part of the administration. It was not uncommon, for example, for a group of students—black and white—to be entering the campus with security guards stopping only the black students, asking for ID cards. The sense we got was that we had been invited into an environment in which we weren't really welcome. This led to frequent, though slightly hyperbolic, comparisons between our day-to-day life on campus and the

---

2. Mark Minton, "Baldwin Criticizes Dr. King, Calls for New, Tough Leaders," *Columbia Daily Spectator* (New York), November 24, 1964.

realities of South Africa's pass system. Our daily reality—compounded by the fact that there was only one tenured black faculty member on the Morningside campus, no visible blacks in the university administration, and little sensitivity to the changes we sought to make in the curriculum— created a profound sense of alienation for many of us.

Among our critiques of the curriculum was the absence of black studies courses and the failure to acknowledge in any systemic way the contribution of black people to American history. Additionally, some of the faculty members with whom we attempted to dialog on the subject were astoundingly oblivious to our history and culture, or the contemporary relevance of figures like W. E. B. DuBois, Langston Hughes, and even James Baldwin. Our anger was further fueled by the administration's unwillingness to seriously discuss what we felt were deep biases in Columbia's Core Curriculum, which emphasized Western civilization and the humanities as they evolved from Greek and European enlightenment history, but contained virtually nothing on Asian and African culture. Ironically, this nondebate was taking place at a moment when it seemed as if the entire world was engaged in seething ferment about the effects of colonialism and neocolonialism. In the face of consistent efforts to seriously engage on these subjects, the administration remained adamantly close-minded.

RACE AND HAMILTON HALL

It is important for me to pause here for an additional word about race. This is, after all, a narrative about ninety or so black students who took and held a building for a week in the face of the imminent threat of the use of force amid a swirling vortex of political power in the hands of the city and university administration. The Black Students of Hamilton Hall had attended Columbia carrying our own and our families' hopes of matriculation in the university and society at large. The common bond we forged was a belief that we should not be forced to sacrifice our racial identity, culture, or beliefs to achieve those goals.

That bond had evolved as we had continued to build Hilton Clark's SAS into a forum in which we could flesh out some of the issues raised by being black in a white institution. This involved vigorous discussion among ourselves and with an indifferent administration. Along the way, some underclassmen had established a chapter of the national black fraternity, Omega Psi Phi, led by Cicero Wilson. Its founding and rituals had been greeted with racist ridicule by the campus humor magazine, *Jester*, in its May 1967 issue. In response, a group of students identified as "Negroes" by the *Spectator* broke into the office of the *Jester* and destroyed all copies of the offending issues. The article in question quoted an imaginary "Overseer of Admissions," saying, "It only means we take a few less kikes. Colored folks are good for our community. Ask the man who owns one." The Omega Phi Psi chapter was referred to as a "colony" of Pamphratria, and an imaginary student was quoted as saying, "I don't care what they call themselves; they're just a bunch of big ants in purple beanies." This episode promoted outrage among black students and a series of publicized but ineffectual meetings with the dean's office. There was no feeling that white students on campus felt the same way.

The athletic department had recruited some talented football players, among then Zachary Husser, Larry Frazier, and Al Dempsey, but the coaches proceeded to "stack" all these athletes at the same position so that no more than one would ever appear on the field at the same time. Across Broadway, at Barnard, black women were not only supportive of our struggles at Columbia but also brought to the table a set of challenging engagements. The list of offenses against our dignity are too numerous to list and too painful to remember. But they added up.

A group like ours was so diverse in its religious, regional, political, ideological, and class composition that virtually every issue discussed among us produced profound differences. Organizing around race is complex. A four-year history of sharp internal differences over many issues surrounding "double consciousness," however, created a bond of which we were not fully aware until the spring of '68. Of course, the bond wasn't entirely subconscious. There was virtual unanimity in our opposition to the Vietnam War and to the determination of the university to build a gymnasium in Morningside Park. What struck us about the dynamics surrounding the gym had been the university's refusal to bargain in good faith with community groups, many of which were supported by SAS. We regarded this posture as infused with racism, and it rankled.

Much of the discourse about race and the events of '68 has focused appropriately on the administration and faculty. A much more emotional component, however, concerns the student body. Ironically, my focus here is on the Left, which, at least from my point of view, was more inclined to address issues of race than the balance of the student body, but it also drew critical attention from black students. Although I haven't consulted him on this characterization, I would say that William Sales and I were on the "progressive" end of the political spectrum among black students. Neither of us ever joined Students for a Democratic Society or Columbia's Congress of Racial Equality (CORE) chapter, or any of the New Left or old-line Marxist organizations on campus. We were, however, more likely than other black students to attend their fora and debate them, formally or informally, on issues ranging from Herbert Marcuse and Frantz Fanon to the gym or the plight of cafeteria workers employed by Columbia.

APRIL 1968

The supreme irony is that the night before the demonstrations, Mark Rudd or Juan Gonzalez (I cannot remember which) asked Sales and myself to attend a meeting to discuss whether there would be any further demonstrations about the gym before the graduation of the class of '68. (Some folks remember Cicero Wilson being present at the meeting, which is quite likely as he had just been elected to the presidency of SAS. Perhaps, he has disappeared from my memory because I cannot imagine Cicero being wrong, like the rest of us, in assessing how students felt.) In delightful testimony to the tendency of "leadership elements" to overestimate their grasp of the *zeitgeist* of their own communities, we unanimously agreed that the student body was tired, apathetic, and unlikely to engage further on the issue. There was agreement, however, that we should hold one final joint rally next morning at the sundial.

The history of that morning has been told a thousand times. For my purpose, what matters is that during one of our speeches to a hundred or so students, an unknown voice shouted, "Let's take Low Library!" In the minute that it took that swelling group of students to move toward Low, the administration building was locked down. When it became clear that no entry would be granted to the building, another voice (or was it the same one?) said, "Let's go to the gym site!" The leaderless but growing group of students ran to the site, only to quickly realize that a hole in the ground provides a poor prop for a demonstration. After an inconclusive skirmish with the New York City Police Department (NYPD), the ever-expanding group of students returned to campus, where it was perhaps that same anonymous—and maybe now chastened—provocateur, who suggested a "teach-in" at Hamilton Hall.

At Hamilton Hall, a racially mixed steering committee consisting of the folks who had concluded the night before that student apathy would prevent any meaningful demonstrations that spring was hastily elected, with the addition of a black graduate student, Drew Newton, whom no one seemed to know. As the day wore on, the numerous ideological groupings represented in that building began to manifest. All manner of demands and potential meetings with the administration were proposed around issues ranging from stopping the war to stopping the gym to starting the revolution.

Immediately, the black students began to meet separately upstairs. Cicero Wilson joined Sales, myself, and Newton as the steering committee of the Black Students of Hamilton Hall. With surprising clarity and speed, we decided to embrace a simple subset of the numerous demands that had been bruited about during the day: ceasing construction on the gym and ending the university's ties to IDA. We also decided to barricade the building and ask the still-disorganized white students to leave. Barricading the building proved a successful tactic. Our victories on the gym and IDA have long been manifest. The request for white students to leave and "seize other buildings on your own" hung pregnantly in the air for forty years.

Ten years ago, at the end of the forty-year commemoration of the student strike, after days of panels on strategy, reminiscences, and the status of Columbia's then-current relationship to the community, a large gathering was held in the Law School auditorium. It was a racially mixed enclave consisting of several of the most active participants from '68. The open forum started slowly but came alive when a number of white students expressed their chagrin and continuing anger in asking, "Why had they been asked to leave Hamilton Hall during the first day of occupation?" I was astounded that their sense of hurt and rejection had lasted so long. I thought our reasons had been obvious and that our tactics had been proven correct by the result. This was an assumption evidently not shared by many white students.

What struck me overall about the evening was its tone. Although there was deep emotion underpinning the white students' question, it was not offensively accusatory. Interestingly, the black student response, while direct, was not defensive. Precise explanations were offered about the social, athletic, and personal offenses faced daily by black students in those years and about the fact that white students had remained oblivious to issues like "stacking," the *Jester* incident, and the constant checking of ID cards. It became clear that these differences had been exacerbated by the differences in political culture and were not overcome by the coincidence of opposition to the war and the gym.

Finally, someone explained the process by which the black students had built a bond that seemed to transcend the events of that week, and which had manifested itself in our being more disciplined in our demands, approach to security, and maintenance (we took pride in leaving the building cleaner than we found it). This discourse about our posture, discipline, and cleanliness lasted long into the night. In some ways, it presaged the discussion currently surrounding the Black Lives Matter movement about "respectability politics." Randall Kennedy and Ta-Nehisi Coates have been among the publicly opposing voices in this debate. This discourse is centred on the extent to which black protest movements in the sixties focused on the acceptable characteristics of iconic protesters like Rosa Parks, in contrast with the need for contemporary movements to embrace their human subjects as they find them, particularly when young black men, sometimes with criminal records, are victims of police brutality.

Why raise the question of police violence in a piece of twenty-first-century writing about a black student demonstration in the sixties? Because consciousness about violence bedevils every black confrontation with society. The Black Students of Hamilton Hall received some unfriendly criticism after the arrests that ended the demonstration. Why were there no casualties among black students as there were among whites? What kind of unprincipled compromises had we made to bring about this result?

From the moment we barricaded Hamilton Hall, we understood the advantages and risks. This entire essay has been about the strategic advantages. The risks, however, were clear to us from the beginning. As soon as the white students left Hamilton Hall, we began drilling for what we believed were likely arrests. We worked on assembling peaceably and protecting ourselves against the use of gas. Our experiences in life and in past demonstrations told us that under normal conditions we were at greater risk than our white counterparts.

We made contact with William Booth of the City Human Rights Commission and arranged for the NAACP Legal Office to assign us Robert F. Van Lierop and a team to be present at our arrests and arraignments. Through these and other contacts, we communicated to the NYPD that we did not intend to resist or offer violence. In return, the NYPD indicated that it would send a black-led unit to arrest us (they did) and give us adequate notice of the moment of arrest (they did not).

DO YOU KNOW MARK RUDD?

This aide-mémoire for the future wasn't easy for me to write. I generally like writing, but this subject has a special resonance for me and this essay has been difficult to finish. Perhaps it's because the most important part

Figure 3.1 A meeting of the African American occupiers of Hamilton Hall. *Photograph by Clarence Davis.*

of what happened in the spring of '68 was the creation of esprit de corps with a number of black folks with whom I had shared a deeply spirited period of my life. That's almost a private moment that I am not inclined to share broadly. Perhaps it's because the spring of '68 was the capstone of a period of intense intellectual stimulation when I couldn't walk five feet on campus or in Harlem or near the West End bar without being challenged on ideas both critical and small.

Perhaps it has been difficult because ultimately the most important point mirrors the general experience of black folks in America. For one week, the media and the people of the most dynamic city on the planet focused on a demonstration taking place on Morningside Heights, but virtually none of them knew that black students were the key element of those events. Perhaps I am just tired of making this point to ears that cannot hear it.

I am reminded of this when, from time to time, someone learns of my participation in the spring events and asks, "Do you know Mark Rudd?" For years I found this inquiry irksome, until the past decade, when I bantered with Rudd about it. He has had the grace and insight to supply a proposed answer: "Ask Mark Rudd if he knew about the Black Students of Hamilton Hall."

Raymond M. Brown *('69CC) is a partner at Greenbaum Rowe Smith and Davis in New Jersey, where he heads the White Collar Crime and International Human Rights Due Diligence Practice Groups. He is a cofounder of the International Justice Project, which for ten years has been engaged in the struggle against genocide in Darfur. He represents victims in Darfur at the International Criminal Court in The Hague and has represented an accused at the Special Court for Sierra Leone.*

GEORGE CAVALLETTO

Liberation News Service

LIBERATION NEWS SERVICE AND THE COLUMBIA STUDENT REVOLT

The year 1968 was the peak of a few charismatic years when increasing numbers of people across the country—and the world—dropped what they were doing, threw self-interest to the wind, dedicated themselves to alternatives, and began expressing an energetic willingness to work in a collective situation with little remuneration. For many of these people, this was a moment when everything was up for grabs, when a strong and vivid divide existed between not only old and young people but also between progressives and conservatives in all matters of life.

In town after town, one of the things these people did was set up a newspaper, which in many cases became the organizational center of those communities. Sometimes there wasn't a local chapter of Students for a Democratic Society—there wasn't even a college campus. It was maybe just a bunch of high school students who got together at a coffee shop after realizing that if they wanted to know what was really going in the world around them, it was likely that lots of other people did too. What became known as the underground press developed into an important way of communicating to hundreds of thousands of people what was happening with the countercultural and antiwar movements. What helped sustain these publications, what at times helped give focus to them, was Liberation News Service (LNS), an organization that twice a week sent packets of material—a couple of dozen pages full of articles and sheets of photographs that could be cut out and used on offset printers—to any newspaper that wanted it. Enough publications paid for this material that LNS could cover costs.

In an atmosphere when the national press, if it even covered certain events, did so with pronounced adversarial bias, the theory was that activists on college campuses and in all these small towns needed a supply of researched and well-written stories about what was going on. Look at some of those publications from the late sixties and you will see that much of the cultural coverage, much of the international coverage, and a fair amount of national political coverage was provided by LNS writers, who made no pretense of "objectivity," preferring instead a journalism of participation and commitment. The *New York Times* was known as the newspaper of record, but its legitimacy was questioned by not only radicals but also many liberals. Although alternatives did exist—in 1963, for example, *The New York Review of Books* was born—the perception was that the mainstream, establishment media was captive to a middle-of-the-road perspective. By 1968, an environment existed in which great legitimacy was given by a large percentage of young people to the underground press. For them, these locally produced newspapers helped fill the gap and were the only place where they regularly could find out what was really happening. For a short but crucial time, LNS played an important role in helping hold these publications together, offering direction and content, and giving them a sense of national context and connection.

I became involved with alternative media in the opening months of 1968. I had been a graduate student at Columbia University since 1963, living on Claremont Avenue, just north of Teachers College. While I had been to a few demonstrations and was an avid listener to Bob Fass on WBAI (whose broadcasts were for me an enthusiastic breath of fresh air, full of the kind of information and analysis I couldn't find anywhere else), in early 1968, I was still at work on my thesis, about the young Wordsworth and his embrace of radical ideas. Around me in Columbia's English department were disillusioned left-liberals who had decided that the masses needed high culture, not political action, a point of view from which I was becoming increasingly alienated. The world, after all, was changing so quickly.

It was fortunate, then, that one day, while walking to class on Broadway, a few blocks from campus, I saw a sign in a shop window: "Anti-War News Service being established here. Meeting tonight, 8 P.M." That evening I found myself in a room with thirty people. It was explained to us by a representative of the Student Communication Network, which was run by a Protestant church group, that the idea was to set up a coordinated network of telex machines between New York, Madison, and Berkeley. From those three hotspots, news would be communicated to other centers of activity, in an attempt to coordinate the antiwar movement. People were needed to work out of the newly set-up New York office. One person would be in charge, to open up in the morning, close up at night, and generally be responsible for the place. No one else in the room volunteered, so I raised my hand. That was it for me. I dropped out of school and began working full time. I placed an ad on the back page of the *Village Voice* asking for volunteers—journalists and photographers—and was inundated with people who wanted to get involved. Within a couple of weeks, I had the office staffed by at least two people at every hour of the day, and began sending people off to report on news stories almost as soon as they showed up at the office, pointing them in different directions depending on what they were interested in writing about. The energy level was astonishing. For me it was a new lease on life. Such intoxicating freedom, such a sense of momentum!

Somewhere along the way I learned about LNS, which had been set up some months before in Washington, D.C. and was having a hard time holding itself together. Our office in New York was such a hive of activity that I contacted LNS and suggested we start sending them news. Soon more and more of what was appearing in the LNS packets was coming from us, and after discussing logistics, it was decided that the D.C. office would close and its operations be moved to New York. This happened at more or less the same time I had leased a large office space on Claremont Avenue—sixteen hundred square feet, $200 a month, which even in those days was a bargain—only a few blocks from the Columbia campus. In preparation for the LNS relocation, a group of us spent four weeks rebuilding the place. Walls were torn down, desks built, psychedelic paintings appeared around the place, and a slew of IBM Selectric typewriters were purchased (from a fence) and installed.

Left-wing activism was new to me, so I sought out and took advice from anyone who had been involved with successful leftist organizations, including Mike Locker and Fred Goff at the North American Congress on Latin America. Fred suggested that LNS be run as a cooperative, explaining that this was the most efficient way of doing things. I became convinced that I wanted LNS to be organized as a working collective, where everything important was voted on and where those who did the work made the decisions. During the early months of 1968, this vision of LNS was only partially realized. There was real fluidity to the organization as the Washington and New York operations merged, and there was often a chaotic coterie of hangers-on in the office. By the summer, however, strict voting procedures were established and a competent staff of twelve was formed. The best moments occurred when, once a packet was sent out, we would meet around a table, decide what should be in the next packet, and hand out new assignments. Someone would propose something, angles to stories would be formulated, and two days later people would start turning in articles. Then we would have critique sessions, where everyone's material was read by everyone else. In the early months after the merger, this collective editing process, where no editor-at-large held sway, faced opposition. Marshall Bloom—who in the fall of 1967 had cofounded LNS in Washington with Ray Mungo and Allen Young, and who in New York in the early months of 1968 still imagined himself the guiding genius of the organization—occasionally would show up at the last moment, red pen in hand, and go through everything, editing and throwing out what he didn't like, and adding things he did. He would then rush out of the office as the staff undid his impositions.

In April, the building occupations at Columbia exploded across the neighborhood, the city, the country, even the world. It was an important starting point for us because although we were doing things on a shoestring—it was only later that people were paid a whopping $25 a week—we had the resources of a range of Columbia students who were happy to assist (some even dropped out of school to work with us 24/7), knowing that LNS was an important organization, or at least had the potential to become one. I went up to campus that first night, when students had just taken over President Grayson Kirk's office, and was hoisted up into Low Memorial Library, where people were going through his filing cabinets and desk drawers. (Later I was the recipient of a file of stamps from Kirk's office, which we used to mail out a packet when we were short of money.) Members of LNS were probably the only members of the press permitted inside the occupied buildings, which I visited several times. I would have stayed longer but had to be back at the office to take care of things, and I knew we had a handful of good writers on campus, including Steve Diamond, who wrote a fifteen-page account of the protests entitled "Columbia: The Revolution Is Now," and that served as the basis of a (much rewritten) *Ramparts* article. Later, once it was all over, I negotiated a book deal with a publisher, and we rented a house upstate to allow LNSers to sit and write a book about the student protests. But for one reason or another, it never happened.

One powerful memory, a riveting experience that has never left me, was a meeting inside occupied Mathematics Hall led by Tom Hayden, who employed techniques I have borrowed ever since. Although it was clear he had plenty of opinions of his own and had an idea of where he wanted the discussion to end up, Tom never pushed anything on people. But he wasn't passive, looking for a nice town hall discussion. Instead, with a strong sense of what problems we were facing, and what solutions might best be offered, he allowed everyone to come to their own conclusions. He did this by carefully and respectfully listening, by bringing people in, and then gently questioning every person who wanted to say something. Those conclusions, of course, happened to be the ones he had been nudging us toward all along. It was a powerful lesson for me, someone new to this kind of direct political action. How stunning to watch all these combinations of ideas coming into play. I learned that you can't permit rhetoric and rabble-rousing to overwhelm a crowd.

Max Weber wrote in *Economy and Society* about three types of social order, each of which was held together by belief in the legitimacy of its authority structures. The first order (Weber was referring to bureaucratic Western democracy) was characterized by "legal legitimacy," "resting on the belief in the legality of enacted rules and the right of those elevated to authority under such rules to issue commands." Second was traditional order, the legitimacy of which rested "on an established belief in the sanctity of immemorial traditions and the legitimacy of those exercising authority under them." This second order included feudalism, that great chain of command with the king or emperor at the top. The third social order rested "on devotion to the exceptional sanctity, heroism or exemplary character of an individual person, and of the normative patterns or order revealed or ordained by him." Weber dubbed this form of legitimacy "charismatic," and in his writings, he extended this notion to include concepts of "charismatic communities" and "charismatic movements."[1]

---

1. Max Weber, *Economy and Society*, ed. Guenther Roth and Claus Wittich (Berkeley: University of California Press, 1978), 215.

We can look back now and see 1968 as a time when significant portions of a generation were swept up into a broad-based countercultural movement composed of young people who otherwise might have remained relatively compliant and obedient to the strictures associated with mainstream capitalist society. The year 1968 occasioned a charismatic break from such mainstream orientations. It was a historic moment, when people suddenly were willing to give up everything and offer their lives to a nonhierarchical order, an exciting, revelatory, and novel culture. This was the type of movement that Weber characterized as "sharply opposed to . . . everyday forms of domination" and "the everyday routine world."[2] Regretfully, it was also short-lived. For a whole complex of reasons, the fervor of its ideals could not last for long, and in the most general terms, its dissolution followed the pattern that Weber foresaw of all charismatic formations: its ideals compromised, routinized, and co-opted.

George Cavalletto *('63GS, '66GSAS) continued to do left-wing presswork after 1968. In the late eighties, he returned to graduate school, earned a Ph.D. in sociology from CUNY, and taught for twenty years at Brooklyn and Hunter Colleges. After his wife, Sheila Ryan, died in 2013, he decided to pursue art photography as a full-time vocation, studying at the International Center of Photography.*

---

2. Weber, *Economy and Society*, 244.

MARK DONNELLY

Student, School of General Studies

A WORKING CLASS VETERAN'S PERSPECTIVE

I was twenty-four years old when, in the fall of 1966, I entered Columbia's School of General Studies. I had a working-class background and had gone to high school in Memphis, Tennessee, a racially segregated city. I had been in the military for six years before attending Columbia, spending several years in the 101st Airborne Division, during which time I received riot control training. Notably, in 1962, I was with federal troops when James Meredith entered Ole Miss, standing guard outside his dormitory for almost a week. I later joined the Navy, and in 1965 was on an aircraft carrier off Vietnam. I was also active in the antiwar movement and was a founding member of Vietnam Veterans Against the War.

At Columbia, opposition to the gym and the university's involvement in the Institute for Defense Analyses were issues to which I was sympathetic. I cared more about the gym because after living in a segregated society and directly experiencing racial hatred among students in Mississippi, I found a gymnasium with a separate entrance for the people of Harlem to be particularly offensive. Regardless, I was too busy studying and working to get involved with anything beyond my antiwar activities, which that year were minimal.

When the occupation of the buildings began, I was simply an observer. I witnessed events at the gym site on the first day and stood outside Hamilton Hall in the rain on the second. Over the next few days I was on the campus at all hours, and one evening even went into Fayerweather for a brief moment. I had moral qualms about occupying buildings and effectively closing down the campus. I was also not a particular fan of Students for a Democratic Society, too many members of which I thought were extremely arrogant.

As tension built, I joined a group known as the Green Arm Bands. As far as I know there was never a leader or even a founding meeting. Word just passed around between people who felt that matters should be settled by giving the occupiers amnesty and that on no account should police be brought on campus. I was ambivalent about amnesty, but knew that if the police showed up, there would be violence.

At some point in the early evening of Monday, April 29, talk began about the police arriving within hours. At about two o'clock in the morning I was sitting on the steps in front of Low Memorial Library when we heard that the police were moving into action. I got up and immediately ran with other students and faculty to the security entrance at Low. I remember thinking that the people around me had no idea what was about to happen. Most students were from upper-middle-class families, but in high school, I had friends whose fathers were policemen. I knew that the police on the Columbia campus thought of the protesters as ungrateful, spoiled little rich brats who, in the words of one officer, deserved "a good spanking." The New York City Police Department (NYPD) was determined to administer this treatment.

As I arrived, I saw several rows of students and faculty already blocking the door. The police directly in front of this group gathered outside were three or four ranks wide and eight to ten deep. I noticed through the glass in the door that there were also police inside the building.

I joined the ranks of students with some foreboding, because at that moment I was in the front row, but soon more people joined us and I found myself several rows from the front. I watched students running up. They would look at us, then at the line of police, then back at us, and then make the decision to join the lines. There was a great deal of noise and yelling from our side, but the police remained silent. At some point our group began singing "We Shall Overcome," the anthem of the civil rights movement.

We stood there for what seemed quite some time, and on at least two occasions were read a statement about our being in violation of the law. An order to disperse was given. No one moved. Then came another few minutes of waiting. Suddenly bright lights were switched on and the police charged. There was screaming and shouting. As they came at us, the lines of students in front of me were pushed back, and we were shoved to the ground. It seemed as if the police were literally walking over us as much as through us. But despite all this, many people were determined to block the door. To this day, I can hear shouts of "Hold your ground!" and "Push to the center!" The plainclothes police standing on the side made use of their blackjacks and saps. I was thrown over a hedge and as I rolled to one side falling to the ground I saw a sap pass just over my head as one of them tried to hit me. Others were not so lucky.

I spent the rest of the evening watching the police enter Avery and prepare to take Mathematics. I ended up with a small group of people caught between Mathematics and Low. The police, now determined to clear the campus, began pushing us toward Pupin Hall, north of Mathematics. What concerned everyone was that you reached Pupin by going down a metal staircase into an unlit lower area that could not be seen from the campus. Some people shouted their concerns, saying that we shouldn't go. They were afraid we would be in an isolated dark area where the police would be free to beat us up. Given the behavior of the NYPD over the past few hours, this fear didn't seem misplaced. At this point, my riot control training kicked in. A cardinal rule is never to push a crowd into a corner with no place to escape, because they will panic and fight back. I was sure the gate to the street by Pupin would be open and began yelling as such. Sure enough, I was right. When I reflect on what I saw that night and heard about the next day all I can say is this: thank God. I really had no reason to believe those gates would be open. The police pushed us down onto Broadway and closed the gates behind us. It was around four in the morning. At that point I decided it was time to go home.

The next day, on the corner of 116th Street and Broadway, I engaged some police officers in conversation. I told them I had been at Mississippi in 1962 and that the night before they had broken some basic rules of riot control. I was immediately confronted by one cop who had been an MP at Ole Miss. I reminded him that we took a lot of "crap" from the students then and had not been allowed to touch them. He replied by saying he was in the Army then and had to obey orders. Now he was a police officer and didn't need to take that "crap."

I was a veteran in an old Army field jacket, and several other cops decided that somehow I was someone they could talk to. After we spoke about events the night before, one cop suddenly asked me, "How did you get in here?" He was not questioning my intelligence, but the fact that I didn't conform to the image he had of Columbia students. I told them about General Studies and all the vets who attended the school. We talked for the next few minutes. One of the older officers rhetorically asked, "Do you think Kirk will be president of this university after what we did last night?" He answered his own question by laughingly saying that the president wouldn't last the summer. He was right. By August, Kirk was gone.

Mark Donnelly *('70GS) is a retired marketing consultant for financial institutions, living in Manhattan.*

THOMAS EHRENBERG

Columbia College undergraduate/Strike Coordinating Committee

CONSTRUCTIONS OF POWER

The civil rights movement, which had been steadily gaining ground amid great struggle and sacrifice, had focused most of its energies in the South, particularly in the areas of segregation and voter rights. Avenues including civil disobedience, court challenges, and legislative reform all bore fruit, albeit way too slowly, with lives still being lost at the hands of white dominance. Awareness was growing—particularly among northern whites—that racism and oppression of people of color was not limited to the southern states and that there was plenty of work to be done right at home. In addition, voices were starting to emerge questioning the effectiveness of nonviolence, as well as the role of whites within the movement.

The country was still in the post–World War II, Korean War, Cold War era, with the Cuban Missile Crisis only a few years behind us and rhetoric like the "Soviet Menace" and the "domino theory" a part of the normal national discourse. (Ours was a generation of schoolchildren periodically hiding under our desks in elementary school because a Russian nuclear attack was thought to be imminent.) Another way of saying this is that the struggle between the "superpower" states of the Soviet Union and the United States for spheres of influence, following the defeat of the dominant powers in Europe and Asia, was still being played out. One focal point of this struggle was the former French colony of Vietnam, the "responsibility" for which, following World War II, the French handed off to the Americans. By 1968, the Vietnam War was at full throttle, with lives from both sides being lost and ruined in obscene numbers, and increasing numbers of the American people rejecting the premises "justifying" the war. Resistance to the war was becoming a moral calling, and the institutional involvement of Columbia in the war effort was beyond unacceptable.

While (at least to my knowledge) the phrase "white male privilege" had not yet been coined, there was a growing awareness of some of its underlying concepts. Feminism in the form we came to know it in the seventies was beginning to be understood and articulated in broader and more complex terms than earlier calls for suffrage, and although the place of women in movement activity remained on the threshold of a genuinely independent voice, the oppression of women was beginning to be seen as a set of issues integrally related to racial and class oppression. In addition, ours was a generation raised by parents who had lived through the Great Depression and the New Deal, and who understood labor organizing and unions as a necessary part of the economic, social, and political landscape.

The Columbia chapter of Students for a Democratic Society (SDS) was articulate about its understanding of leftist social theory. In addition they had, among various groups on campus, one of the most often heard and clearest messages about the nature and structure of oppression and class, and those institutional systems supporting class oppression. The Students' Afro-American Society (SAS) was also active in articulating the nature of structural oppression, and the way issues of race affected college campuses were reflections, and manifestations, of the racism present in the larger society.

There is a long history, at Columbia and other schools, of support for (and sometimes challenges to) war efforts. However, Columbia's involvement in the Institute for Defense Analyses (IDA, a Pentagon think tank) and in the Reserve Officers Training Corps (the on-campus military training program) became identified as part of the Vietnam War machine. The administration's interlocking directorates and complicity with corporate interests and New York City politics, which helped facilitate the virtual stealing of public parkland for use by Columbia students, was becoming more exposed and less tolerable to the student body. The administration's arrogance in dealing with these issues, in handling student and community objections, and in exercising its entitlement and power—implicitly through the planned gymnasium and explicitly in its lack of response to students—came to be seen as exemplars of pervasive and abhorrent white privilege.

In April 1967, a year before the strike, Dr. Martin Luther King, Jr. spoke to an overflow crowd (including many from Columbia) at Riverside Church, just up the street from campus. In this, one of his most famous and pivotal speeches, Dr. King eloquently connected the dots between the war in Vietnam and segregation and racism in America. The observation that we would not have been annihilating the Vietnamese people had they been white, while perhaps a given to many now, was worldview altering for many who heard him. The additional reality that people of color were greatly overrepresented in the American military at the time, and that had the military been composed of privileged whites the war probably would have ended years earlier, underscored the message.

A year later, on April 23, 1968, a rally in the middle of campus moved down into Morningside Park. Students tore down some of the fence around the gym construction site, and then returned to campus to hold a sit-in at Hamilton Hall until there was a satisfactory response from the administration. Subsequent events unfolded organically, out of frustration and anger, fueled by the intransigence of the university's power structure. The occupation of Hamilton and other buildings, the strike and meteoric growth of support for the occupation, the support services to make it all work, and the rallies and press releases and development of a coherent set of demands and positions all came from decisions made on the spot, in the moment or the hour or the day. Planning was immediate and in response to needs, political positions and realities, and the activities of Columbia's administration and New York City's government.

Many on campus were frustrated over one or more issues around the war, civil rights, the administration's high-handedness, and so on. The tendency of the Left was to see oppression through the lens of capital and fight it through class struggle, whereas the tendency of the civil rights movement was to see oppression through the lens of racism as the bulwark of American power. But our unity was not only not undermined by those differences but also probably strengthened (notwithstanding the way things ultimately played out between the black and white students). The interrelatedness of the issues for every student involved made possible a powerful convergence. It was the perfect storm.

For many of us, our political and social understanding at the time included a reassessment of the role of leadership and similar notions within the conceptual framework of oppressive social constructs. We were grappling with the understanding that there were, in the reality of one person having the authority and power to tell others what to do, not just the seeds of oppression ("power corrupts") but structural hierarchies that typically, and historically, were based on certain factors (e.g., skin color, country of origin, gender, wealth, land holdings, beauty, an ability to speak well in public, physical size/height, strength/skill at fighting, family of origin, charisma) that form the basis for that power and subsequent privilege of one group over another. Thus, "power" deriving as just described, and "authority" as being derived from a legitimizing source, are not necessarily conceptually interchangeable. This, of course, raises questions about what might constitute legitimate grounds for authority (e.g., God and church; financial power, military power, etc.; consent or request of those being governed; suitability, i.e., "I am qualified to rule because I do a good job"; family, social rank, or bloodline). Although these might seem abstract and academic, it must be remembered that we were, after all, in the academy and were, particularly in light of the war and racial oppression, actively engaging with such questions. One of the ways this engagement manifested was in an active effort to avoid creating and enacting systems that reflected the hierarchical privilege-based structures we were battling.

I do not argue that the strike as a movement or the groups that had come together around the strike explicitly shared this distrust and challenge to authority-based structures. The civil rights movement had strong leadership and much "top-down" organization, while the power-centrism of socialism and Communism, and its preference for state organization and solutions, did not include a suspicion of power exercised on behalf of the working class. Nor would I argue that these concerns were front and center in our discourse. But they were present, and they informed our approach, choices, and responses. We were suspicious of our "leaders"— on a national and at the university level—who consistently acted without regard for truth, for what was right, or for any moral sensibility. They had lost both credibility and legitimacy, just like the hierarchical and privilege-based system that had spawned them.

The major way these implicit concerns manifested during the strike was in the absence of any hierarchical structure. The strike at Columbia was not top down: there was no top, middle, or bottom. There was, fundamentally, no leadership in any meaningful sense. This was a true mass uprising. Early and right on through, the groups involved made the decisions. What was and was not negotiable, what were the core concerns, how we should proceed, and when to stand firm were all decided by participants, sometimes in meetings that went on for hours. Even tactical decisions—what buildings to occupy, when to hold rallies, whom to get to speak, who should negotiate and for what—were all made on a group basis. This point is extremely important, because it was a convenient conceit of the press and the Columbia administration to characterize the strike as a riot led by a small cadre of (mostly SDS and so-called outside) left-wing agitators. This, of course, was a way of marginalizing the whole strike. How much less threatening to regard the entire venture as being led ("manipulated") by a bunch of misguided college students, duped by sophisticated agents of Moscow. To acknowledge it as a mass uprising—as a groundswell of civil disobedience in response to legitimate outrage over the war, the university's involvement in the military, the gym, and Columbia's participation in the racist power structure—would have required engagement and response. How much the characterization of the strike as a "riot," one "led" by professional agitators, stemmed from outright ignorance; from wishful thinking; from having no other framework for understanding dissent and the extent of the challenge; and, truth be told, from claims made by some involved in the strike, I do not know. But I do know that this was genuine participatory decision-making without the benefits— and liabilities—of centralized leadership.

Through the ensuing years, I have thought about what constitutes legitimate authority. To my mind, government derives its authority from the will of those governed, and the closer decision-making is to the people, the more integrity and legitimacy it has. I recognize that some of this view runs contrary to much of what has shaped Communist, parliamentary, and other forms of representative democracies in our republic and others around the world since the post-Enlightenment period of state-building. I also acknowledge the belief held by some that people are not fit to self-govern, that they (read "we") need leadership provided by those with experience or expertise (either by virtue of class, rank, etc.) to look after the greater good, and that leadership must, in a democracy, be a force to correct the will of the ignorant masses. Nonetheless, I retain my confidence in self-governance, and find that the "self-governance versus more expert and centralized governance" counterpoint presents regularly in my life.

I prefer to make my own decisions, and for others to do so, whether or not the decision would be deemed to be a good one by others, or even by myself, at a later time. I prefer it because the greatest hope for significant social justice is and must be rooted in the exercise of power in the hands of the people. That preference and hope is tied to many of the same anchors in my politics that fueled my participation in the 1968 strike. I remain suspicious of arbitrary authority, whether wielded for good or evil. People who wield power for evil, whether waging war in Vietnam or exercising racial oppression, do not typically believe they are being evil. On the contrary, they believe wholeheartedly in the rightness of what they do. Despite the undeniable reality (made starkly clear in the labor, civil rights, and antiwar movements) that power is not readily given up and sometimes must be confronted by power (as in April 1968), during the strike, we also tried to face some of the inherent pitfalls in the exercise of power.

My experiences in the late sixties and later have made me aware that one of the fundamental blocks to creating a more socially just society is people's subjective sense of powerlessness, of not having control over their own lives, nor having sufficient social power to make a difference. When people feel powerless, they can't or won't make a revolution. At their core, the civil rights movement and mass action against the war in Vietnam were challenges to that powerlessness, an invitation to something different. To us and many around the world, the Columbia strike was a potent example of the shift from powerlessness to the exercise of power. This is what made it so important. The strike's ability to exercise collective power was a great lesson, one of many in that decade. The earlier conventional wisdom that the state and its apparatus maintain hegemony over the exercise of power was challenged successfully.

People feel powerless for many reasons: because they are from a social group that has been denied power by those who are more powerful than they, because they are afraid of exercising power, because they have been victimized, because they feel hopeless. I fully recognize the conundrum in the reality that people frequently feel powerless because they indeed *are*, or because they are members of a social group that systematically or otherwise is denied power. Nonetheless, history is rife with examples of members of such groups claiming their due—and getting it. Nor am I so naïve that I think that if people recognize their power it automatically will make the world a better place. And I certainly am not interested in contributing to creating a world in which people *feel* powerful while they (we) fundamentally remain powerless. I simply maintain that acknowledging and being prepared to use one's power is an important prerequisite to social change. For me, the transformation from powerless to having and exercising power (personal, interpersonal, or social) is more important than the short-term goal of getting it right in a particular instance. This is my life's work. It was before 1968, it was during 1968, and it remains so.

Thomas Ehrenberg *('68CC) grew up in New York City and attended city public schools. While at Columbia, he was active in several programs in the Citizenship Council, including the Harlem Education Program. After Columbia, he worked as a cabdriver, fundraiser, and telephone switchman. He relocated to Vermont in 1971, working in construction before settling into a career in education and counseling. He has had his own psychotherapy and consultation practice since 1984.*

CAROLYN RUSTI EISENBERG

Graduate student, History/Fayerweather Hall occupier

YOU GAVE US HOPE

I t was a strange coincidence. When Mark Rudd's e-mail arrived in March 2009, I was staying at a Huế hotel, conducting research for my book on US foreign policy during the Nixon years. With the help of the US–Vietnam Friendship Society, I had been interviewing political and military actors from that time. With the exception of Huế, interviewees in varied locations from Hanoi to the Mekong Delta had been cordial and forthcoming. In this one city, the Vietnamese translator could not conceal the impatience and hostility of the participants.

To concentrate on my Vietnam travels, I had limited e-mail to my children back in the United States. But when Mark asked if I would speak at his book launch party at the old West End bar on Broadway, across the road from the Columbia campus, I readily agreed. This involved some messaging back and forth, raising a question, "Why in the world am I exchanging e-mails with Mark Rudd, when I'm communicating with nobody else?" After all, I had never liked Mark in the first place.

That "first place" was Columbia University in the spring of 1968, during which student protesters occupied five buildings. I was representing Fayerweather Hall on the hastily assembled Strike Steering Committee. This body, which met in Columbia's student center, was largely dominated by male undergraduates from Students for a Democratic Society, with Mark Rudd functioning as its leader and public spokesman.

As a graduate student, a newcomer to Columbia, and the only woman in this initial group, I was an instant misfit.

Gender was a huge problem, both before and during the Columbia strike. To say that the atmosphere was macho is akin to saying it's warm on the Equator. A group of twenty-year-old white men, many of them close friends, paralyzing an entire university in New York—the media capital of the world—was an electrifying experience. It didn't help matters that during the first night of the occupation, the young black men from Columbia's Students' Afro-American Society had thrown them out of Hamilton Hall, with the invidious comparison that "we are prepared to die here and you are not." It was a stinging reproach, which never ceased to fester, creating an additional impetus for male assertiveness on the steering committee.

Meanwhile, television and newspapers magnified the drama. With each passing day, they drew an ominous picture of the occupation at Columbia as a revolutionary event, and its long-haired perpetrators as the local equivalents of Fidel and Che. Some of this was plainly ridiculous. I remember sitting in meetings and somebody would come in and say, "Mark, it's your mother again! You'd better take it." And sure enough, the revolutionary leader would rush dutifully to the phone, while we all waited patiently until he returned and the conversation could proceed.

But the media coverage was heady stuff and fostered a certain conviction in the steering committee that here at Columbia we really were setting a revolutionary example, that we weren't simply challenging certain university policies, but rather the legitimacy of the institution and of society as a whole. Moreover, in making strategic decisions about next steps, our job was not to represent the people in our buildings, but rather to function as a cadre, prodding people to new levels of militancy. Everyone had apparently read Régis Debray, the revolutionary who had articulated this point of view with particular force and clarity.

I remember arguing against these ideas, believing they were melodramatic and destructive of the genuine sense of community emerging in the buildings. When people voted on representatives to the steering committee, they were choosing individuals to reflect their concerns, not to dictate tactics. This disagreement became especially sharp when the steering committee was notified by the New York City mayor's office that a "bust" was imminent. Was our responsibility to alert the occupants that this was happening, so they could decide for themselves whether to stay or leave? Or should we, as true revolutionaries, let the police appear without advance notice and allow the bloody confrontation to develop, as it surely would? On this latter item, tempers flared. Because I was advocating for transparency, one person identified me as "a known CIA agent." Nobody laughed.

In Huế, standing outside the Citadel, I had a flashback to how, in the weeks just before the Columbia strike, many of us had watched television coverage of US Marines blasting the walls and flattening portions of the city. Our official demand of Columbia University was that it cease doing

Figure 7.1 SDS member David Gilbert (checkered jacket) speaks to students outside occupied Hamilton Hall. *Photograph by Barney Edmonds.*

weapons research for the Department of Defense. It was an arid-sounding request. But the emotional reality it expressed was how we hated the war, how painful it was to see American troops storming a city, or Vietnamese kids screaming, or our soldiers setting fire to villages.

We were very young then. But the beards and long hair notwithstanding, we were youthful patriots, watching our country devastate another society. And in 1968, most grownups seemed quiescent or even complicit in the damage. By then, it no longer seemed adequate to go on being our regular selves, but it was hard to find a different identity that was adequate to the challenge. Faced with such carnage, some imagined themselves Third World revolutionaries, whereas others invested fresh hope in the power of a peaceful community. Yet in that year, the killing went on and nothing seemed to work.

One striking aspect of my Vietnam travels was meeting contemporaries from that nation, whose lives had been upended by the conflict. Apart from Hué, the friendliness was overwhelming. The reasons were similar: "We knew Americans were protesting! It meant so much to us to know we weren't alone! It gave us hope!"

Against this backdrop, I found myself in Vietnam writing to Mark Rudd. He had long ago morphed into a warm and thoughtful adult and the hatchet was buried. But the deeper questions were generational and not personal: How do we understand the bitter quarrels of that time? What mistakes were made? What did we accomplish? And perhaps most pertinent in today's militarized country: What should be our contribution to a more peaceful future?

Carolyn Rusti Eisenberg *('71GSAS) is a professor of US foreign policy at Hofstra University. She received her Ph.D. in American History from Columbia in 1971 and is the author of* Drawing the Line: The American Decision to Divide Germany. *A cofounder of Brooklyn for Peace in 1983, for the past ten years she has been a legislative coordinator for United for Peace and Justice.*

BOB FELDMAN

Columbia College undergraduate/Students for a Democratic Society/
Fayerweather Hall occupier

A PEOPLE'S PREHISTORY OF COLUMBIA, 1968

The white student Left at Columbia was nearly invisible during freshman week in 1965. Before one of the week's events, George Gruenthal, a Columbia undergraduate, tried to sell some kind of leftist newspaper to freshmen lined up to go inside Ferris Booth Hall. The newspaper claimed that Columbia University was controlled by Wall Street and was nothing more than an instrument of these corporations, so was not really an institution concerned about the pursuit of knowledge. From the freshmen on the line who bothered to notice George, there was much snickering and some taunting of him for being a "commie." After glancing at his newspaper's headlines and listening to his sales pitch, I thought to myself that this view of Columbia was intellectually simplistic and inaccurate and that it was ridiculous to argue that Columbia University was "just another US multiversity like Berkeley." But the more time I spent at Columbia, the more my own views about the place began to change.

The one student speaker during freshman week who impressed me was the representative of Columbia's liberal political organization, Action. The group had organized an antiwar, anti–Reserve Officers Training Corps (ROTC) demonstration in the spring of 1965, which the Columbia administration had broken up by calling in cops to arrest the less than one hundred and fifty demonstrators. The Action speaker was the only student who mentioned the need to oppose the war in Vietnam on campus. His presentation was interrupted by jeers from right-wing Columbia freshmen and by much heckling. When it came time to sign up for campus activities, I signed Action's mailing list. But early in fall 1965, Action became defunct because most hardcore Columbia and Barnard activists joined the Independent Committee on Vietnam (ICV).

Once the semester began, at lunchtime and in the early afternoon, I found myself habitually hanging around the ICV table on the plaza in front of Low Memorial Library. A Teachers College student named Mel Baron generally would set up there and sit behind his table from about 11:30 A.M. until sunset. Mel seemed to know Vietnamese history and the history of US military intervention in Vietnam better than anyone else at Columbia. He had been a Peace Corps volunteer in Algeria, and this experience had caused him to become disillusioned with the reality of American foreign policy. As the war continued to escalate, Mel's presence at the ICV table at Columbia reinforced my opposition to US government policy in Vietnam. Students would stop by the table and debate with him the morality of US policy, and I would stop by to listen to Mel whenever I saw a crowd around the table. His talk seemed more relevant and interesting than any classroom discussions going on inside Columbia's classrooms.

"We're committing genocide in Vietnam. Napalm bombings and carpet bombings are designed to kill civilians. The Geneva Accords of 1954 required an election to unify Vietnam in 1956. Even Eisenhower admitted Ho Chi Minh would have won the 1956 elections if the United States and the Diem dictatorship hadn't violated the Geneva Accords," Mel argued passionately, day after day. Sometimes he would be joined around the table by other antiwar students. Every three or four weeks, the ICV would hold an antiwar rally around Columbia's sundial during which Mel and Columbia College senior Dave Gilbert would stand up on the sundial and patiently explain to other students gathered there why US military intervention in Vietnam was an immoral crime against humanity, in violation of the Nuremberg Accords.

Supporters of the war could not justify US policy on moral grounds when confronted with Mel's knowledge of the facts, and it's fair to say that he influenced me more than any Columbia professor did that year. Mel's moral passion and detailed critique of US foreign policy convinced me that the American military's role in the Third World was antidemocratic and violated the self-determination rights of Third World nations. His personal dedication, at the expense of his career preparation and studying time, to raising consciousness about the war in Vietnam caused me to completely question the American mass media version of contemporary history.

Soon after that I attended my first off-campus antiwar rally, where, for the first time, I heard Dave Dellinger and the elderly War Resisters League head A. J. Muste speak, as well as other anti-imperialist speakers, and I immediately knew that they made more sense than the Democratic and Republican Party politicians I had seen on TV when I was growing up. When I read through all the free antiwar literature I had accumulated during the day, it made much more sense to me than what the *New York Times* was printing about Vietnam.

I became a Students for a Democratic Society (SDS) activist in November 1966, along with most other ICV activists. Along with Dave Gilbert, John Fuerst was most responsible for establishing an SDS chapter at Columbia. In 1965, John had been involved in the antiwar student disruption of the Columbia ROTC awards ceremony. As a result of this protest, which was busted up by the Columbia administration with the aid of New York City police, John had received a disciplinary warning letter from Columbia College Dean David Truman. In November 1966, John took the initiative on campus when it was learned that the Central Intelligence Agency (CIA) was coming to recruit students in Dodge Hall. Columbia SDS sponsored a sundial rally to protest the CIA's presence on campus and demanded that the Columbia administration not allow them to use university facilities to recruit. Speakers at the sundial during a lunch hour rally explained what the CIA already had done around the world before 1966: it had overthrown the democratically elected government of Iran in 1953, overthrown the democratically elected government of Guatemala in 1954, planned the Bay of Pigs invasion of Cuba in 1961, and helped set up the Diem dictatorship in Vietnam.

Fed up with US foreign policy, fed up with racism, fed up with the endless mass murder in Vietnam, and fed up with the Columbia University administration's failure to speak out against all this and its "business as usual" attitude, I was one of the students who marched into Low Memorial Library and gathered in the rotunda as Columbia President Grayson Kirk uneasily read a statement in which he argued that the university should make no value judgments and take no political positions regarding US government policy, and that therefore organizations like the CIA would continue to have the right to recruit on campus.

After Kirk left the rotunda, Dave Gilbert was the first activist to speak to the rest of us: "Those are his values. But we have different values. And if we want Columbia University policy to reflect our values, we're going to have to build a movement here that fights for student power and participatory democracy at Columbia. And that's why we have to build a Columbia SDS chapter." There was more discussion, and the antiwar students were enthusiastic about attempting to build a Columbia SDS chapter that would fight the Columbia administration on a multi-issue basis, attempt to win student power at Columbia, and work to build a mass-based radical student movement in the United States. A time for follow-up meetings was agreed upon and we broke up for the day. My feeling was that John and Dave's Columbia SDS chapter-building approach seemed more dynamic than the ICV's relatively quiet approach, and soon thereafter a Columbia SDS chapter was established as a mass-based student campus group. New Columbia SDS recruits quickly learned that we all shared a sense of political powerlessness, antiwar and antidraft rage, and a militant antiracist and anticapitalist value structure. We all wanted to build a radically new world and new social order.

A Columbia SDS steering committee began to meet publicly every Friday afternoon on campus, although when necessary informal meetings were held at Teddy Kaptchuk's apartment. Around this time, other leftist students became involved, forming "Praxis Axis," the hardcore faction of Columbia SDS. "Praxis" was a political term used by national SDS people to describe political theorizing and strategizing that related to daily radical activism. Around this same time, a regional SDS conference was held in Princeton, New Jersey, at which Dave read his Port Authority Statement (cowritten with Bob Gottlieb and Gerry Tenney), which was intended as an updated equivalent of SDS's Port Huron Statement. Its basic argument was that "the new working class" of technocrats, technicians, and middle-class professionals was going to be the agent of revolution in the United States, instead of the traditional industrial working class, which was declining in numbers and social power because of technological change. In 1967, given the general political passivity of US industrial workers in relationship to the war machine, and given the growing enthusiasm of white, middle-class, preprofessional college students for radical politics, Dave's New Working-Class Theory seemed to explain reality.

In March 1967, I discovered by accident Columbia's institutional affil-iation with the Institute for Defense Analyses (IDA), a think-tank that did weapons research for the Pentagon, which connected the university directly with the war in Vietnam. I read all the IDA annual reports, which bragged about how crucial IDA was to carrying out the Pentagon's Cold War military mission and how important a contribution university fac-ulty were making to the US war machine by being involved with IDA. I immediately felt that if the Columbia administration didn't resign its institutional membership in IDA, the Columbia Left might be able to cre-ate a Berkeley 1964 revolt-type situation, as a way of effectively protesting both the insanity and immorality of US military intervention in Vietnam and the political powerlessness and lack of generational freedom felt by students. Columbia's IDA affiliation symbolized the degree to which the university's research budget depended on Pentagon research contracts. Moreover, it turned out that both Columbia University President Gray-son Kirk and Columbia Trustee William Burden were also IDA trustees and members of IDA's executive committee, even though Columbia Dean of Graduate Faculties Ralph Halford had claimed at an early 1967 cam-pus forum that there was "no institutional connection" between Colum-bia and IDA.

In April 1967, Columbia SDS learned that the US Marines were coming to recruit on Columbia's campus. There was a two-hour meeting in Ferris Booth Hall's Hewitt Lounge where about twenty of us discussed how we would greet the recruiters. As usual, there was division over whether to peacefully picket, hold an indoor demonstration, conduct a sit-in, ask embarrassing questions, or physically throw the Marines out of the John Jay Hall dormitory lobby. The consensus was that the Marines did not have the moral and democratic right to recruit students from Columbia to participate in a war that violated the Nuremberg Accords. But it was also agreed that although most students were against military intervention in Vietnam, they were not politically radical enough to support Columbia SDS denying the Marines their freedom of speech or right to recruit on campus. Left-liberal antiwar students likely would consider Columbia SDS to be anti–civil libertarian if we stopped the Marines from recruiting.

A brief antiwar rally was held at the sundial on Thursday, April 20, 1967, attended by about three hundred antiwar students, who then marched to the John Jay lobby to peacefully and nonviolently confront the Marines, raise the issue of Columbia's complicity with war crimes, and build support for more draft resistance. Once inside, we suddenly faced not only the two Marine recruiters, but also twenty jocks from Columbia's football team. They started to individually shove and push the physically smaller Columbia SDS people and antiwar demonstrators out of the lobby. The effect of this violence against us was to politicize hundreds of other Columbia and Barnard students on campus who never previously had taken Columbia SDS seriously. At the postattack sundial rally, Mark Rudd, an active SDS member, spoke spontaneously in an easygoing, humorous, theatrical, clear, emotionally open, nonrhetorical, nonacademic, nonpedantic, charismatic way. I had not considered him an especially impressive speaker until that moment, but now Mark appeared to be the Mario Savio figure we apparently needed to repeat the Berkeley Student Revolt. His spirited and wild-eyed approach for New Left politics was now appealing to me.

For the rest of the afternoon, people were talking about radical politics in small groups. The Columbia SDS steering committee and Columbia professor of sociology Vernon Dibble, our strongest faculty supporter, retreated to the back of the West End bar on Broadway to plan what to do next. "You let them push you out of John Jay Hall today. You have to go back there again tomorrow to keep your credibility as a radical student group," Professor Dibble insisted.

Everyone agreed we had to go back to confront the Marine recruiters the next day. The major point of debate was whether we would gain more politically and win more mass support by stopping campus Marine recruitment and possibly fighting it out with other students—the right-wing protectors of the Marines—or by having a more mass-based, nonviolent antiwar demonstration directed at protesting the policies of our main enemy, the Columbia administration.

"The administration likes nothing better than to have students fighting other students," said Ted Gold, "because then it can portray itself as 'above politics' and as 'neutral.' We shouldn't fall into the administration's trap and alienate our new mass student support by leading students into a violent confrontation, which is what the administration now wants us to do."

Ted's views were pretty much supported by the rest of the Columbia SDS leadership. Our April 21, 1967, demonstration of the next day was going to be nonviolent, disciplined, and focused more on protesting the Columbia administration's policies than on the jocks. Martin Luther King's Southern Christian Leadership Council aide, James Bevel, would be invited to address the campus rally. That evening, my dorm counselor Bill Sales, a member of the Students' Afro-American Society (SAS), called me into his dorm room and bawled me out.

"How could SDS let itself get pushed out of the John Jay lobby when you outnumbered them three hundred to thirty?" Bill asked sharply, with a tone of disdain.

"We weren't ready. But we win politically by being seen as the victims of right-wing violence in the eyes of all the white liberal antiwar students," I answered half-heartedly.

Bill thought for a second and then replied,: "Well, maybe you can turn it to your advantage." Then he smiled and added, "But if SDS actually wants to fight those jocks and needs some help, the black student karate club might be willing to stand by your side."

"If they attack us again tomorrow," I said, "SDS may take you up on your offer." For the first time, Bill appeared to be now taking Columbia SDS's campus organizing efforts more seriously.

In the fall of 1967, Columbia SDS continued to spend its weekly general assembly meetings in long discussions of political strategy. Mark Rudd started to participate more actively in these debates, and at an SDS general assembly meeting argued in favor of working to build a student strike at Columbia, around university complicity with the Pentagon issues, six months later, in April 1968. He circulated mimeographed copies of a position paper, which argued in favor of Columbia SDS adopting this strategy, and because of which he became known as a leading member of the "Action Faction" (as opposed to the Praxis Axis). What was good about Mark's paper was that (unlike the dominant figures in the Praxis Axis), he recognized that unless Columbia SDS was seen by the mass of student radicals as concretely working for some kind of spring strike (and not just simply working to educate students without mobilizing them to act concretely), as the academic year progressed, campus radicals would drift away from active participation in local organizing work. What was bad about Mark's paper was that it failed to show how locking Columbia SDS into a plan to call for a student strike six months later would lead to the mass politicization and radicalization of students any faster than would the dorm canvassing, meetings, educational activities, and petition-circulating being carried out under the Praxis Axis leadership. Mark's plan appeared to overestimate the degree to which Columbia and Barnard students already had been radicalized and were ready to express their new radicalism in militant nonviolent action. The mass of Columbia SDS members voted down most of Mark's proposals because they seemed overambitious and unrealistic.

The heavy Columbia SDS theoreticians were still much glibber than Mark when it came to discussing political strategy with SDS members. Praxis Axis Marxist intellectuals dismissed him as being, at best, a "vulgar Marxist" and, at worst, "an anarchist hippie." Any Columbia SDS person who dared question the chapter's emphasis on nonalienating, pedantic leftism and consciousness-raising—instead of moralistic, militant nonviolent direct actionism—as a means of developing a mass campus base was accused by Columbia SDS's theoreticians of having "no politics." My own strategic position was that Columbia SDS should continue to do dorm canvassing and other kinds of radical education work in the context of continuing to demand an end to Columbia's membership in IDA and should not alienate the mass of antiwar left-liberal students by small, premature, left-sectarian actions that demanded an end to the Columbia-IDA connection. But when we had won enough people through this kind of educational work to stage a sit-in of five hundred people in Low Memorial Library, I felt it then would be most practical to nonviolently disrupt business as usual at Columbia until the university's IDA ties were severed. Like other Praxis Axis people on Columbia SDS's steering committee, I felt it wasn't enough for Columbia SDS to be a cute guerrilla-theater, radical-education, draft-counseling, petition-signature-gathering, purely agitational organization. But the intellectualism and intellectual certitude of others within the Praxis Axis leadership made me assume that they knew what they were doing.

By December 1967, it was clear that unless Columbia SDS activists felt their organizing was going to lead to some spring '68 confrontation or sit-in or strike, they would tend to retreat from day-to-day political activism. And unless there was some kind of spring '68 confrontation, sit-in, or strike, the mass of Columbia and Barnard students surely would remain apathetic, unpoliticized, and unradicalized. Columbia SDS had to stop verbalizing about what we ought to be doing and as soon as possible start doing what we really felt like doing: shutting down the university until it cut ties to the US war machine. Mark and I wrote a position paper entitled "How to Get SDS Moving Again and Screw the University All in One Fell Swoop," but the SDS Praxis Axis immediately challenged serious consideration of our ideas.

"We can't start working for a spring confrontation or strike now because it's too early to know whether we will have enough student support," Ted Gold said to us. Mark attempted to explain to Ted that the whole point of the paper was to ensure that by motivating chapter hardcore activists with the promise of a spring confrontation, we would gather enough student support for a spring disruption.

"We still have to just focus on developing mass radical consciousness," maintained Ted. "That's more important than whether or not we have a spring strike or confrontation."

"As long as Columbia is disrupting the lives of the Vietnamese through its IDA sponsorship, we have a right and an obligation to disrupt its campus," I argued.

"That's just thinking morally, not strategically or politically," said Ted. "It's not a question of whether we have a moral right to disrupt the campus. It's a question of being politically sophisticated enough to know when it's more important to educate the campus and not alienate people through confrontation. Otherwise we'll end up isolated."

By February 1968, it was clear to me that rank-and-file Columbia SDS people were becoming increasingly dissatisfied with the nonconfrontational, overly academic, frivolous Praxis Axis approach of Ted Gold and Columbia SDS chapter chairman Teddy Kaptchuk. The majority of students at Columbia College who had voted in a nonbinding referendum were opposed to Columbia's ties to IDA and the war, but they still felt that freedom of speech included the right of organizations like the CIA and Dow Chemical to recruit on campus. This meant that Ted and Teddy were unwilling to prevent Dow Chemical recruitment on campus on February 23, 1968, to avoid alienating the majority of liberal students on campus that SDS still was trying to organize. On other campuses around the country, however, antiwar students had held sit-ins to stop Dow Chemical recruiting on campus, regardless of what the majority opinion of students on their campus was, on the grounds that it was morally wrong. So when Ted and Teddy tried to persuade Columbia SDS's rank and file to limit—"on tactical grounds"—the anti-Dow protest to just picketing Low Memorial Library, everybody ignored them and marched up to Dodge Hall to sit in and stop Dow's recruitment process. Despite these developments, it still appeared in early March 1968 that the majority of students at Columbia was more interested in its Ivy League championship basketball team than in political activity.

In March 1968, Howard University students occupied their administration building in support of their demands, something that influenced Columbia's African American student activist leaders. I read about the Howard University occupation, but, insofar as I could envision a spring shutdown of Columbia, I still could imagine a mass sit-in only inside Low.

That same month, Columbia SDS held elections for its 1968–1969 officers and steering committee members. Mark was elected chairman and there was an expectation that he was going to push Columbia SDS in a more confrontational direction. On March 20, Col. Akst, the New York City Director of the Selective Service System, came to campus to speak about the draft options of students. At a meeting held by Columbia SDS's Draft Counseling Committee, it was suggested by the Praxis Axis that the most effective way to respond to Akst's presence was to "ask probing and embarrassing questions." Mark, however, had argued that this response was not dramatic enough and that SDS people should use guerrilla theater in the middle of Akst's speech to disrupt the speech of a war criminal. A declassified FBI "Red Squad" document of March 22, 1968, describes what happened:

Approximately 150 students had assembled in the hall at 4:00 P.M. when Col. Akst began his talk. He had spoken about one-half hour, when a group of students, identified as Students for a Democratic Society (S.D.S.) members, entered through the rear of the audience and proceeded to cause a commotion. The invading students were equipped with an American flag; some were masked, and some carried toy pistols and fake rifles. They conducted what was purported to be a mock war. While everyone's attention was drawn to the rear of the hall, one or two youths sneaked up on the stage and threw a lemon meringue pie at Col. Akst. The pie struck the Colonel on the left shoulder and left side of his face. The perpetrators escaped before they were apprehended.

The Praxis Axis SDS members were furious. They considered the incident as infantile and irresponsible, and there was talk that Mark should be ousted as Columbia SDS chairman. "You had no democratic right to go off and plan such a politically childish action on your own," said Ted. "It hurts us politically on campus because it alienates us from most of the liberals who still have hang-ups about free speech." Mark's response—an indication that he was clearly in control, and able to lead in a free-wheeling, charismatic way, with the enthusiastic support of the bulk of Columbia SDS's hard core—was powerful: "The issue isn't really a question of democratic forms or whether the pie-throwing was a good tactic. The issue is whether the old leadership is going to really surrender control of the chapter to me and stop trying to block those of us who want to use more creative tactics to build the movement."

On March 27, two hundred SDS members marched into Low Memorial Library. We felt that challenging President Kirk's ban on indoor demonstrations was the only way we could encourage the mass of apathetic antiwar students who had mobilized behind us in the April 1967 confrontation with the Marines to go into political action again. A few days later, just after Martin Luther King's assassination, the Columbia administration decided to discipline six students (who appeared to be randomly chosen, including Mark and Ted) for this demonstration inside Low. Columbia SDS protested by having the six students ignore requests that they report to the office of Assistant Dean Alexander Platt, thus refusing to acknowledge the legitimacy of his disciplining authority.

The problem the IDA 6 faced was that if they all refused to accept the right of Columbia College to discipline them for their political activism, they conceivably could be suspended. This was in an era when suspension meant losing your student deferment and being drafted. Emboldened by the support of their Columbia SDS peers, the six held firm and demanded that they be given an open hearing before any administration disciplinary action was taken against them. Not wanting to grant an open hearing, but also not wanting to throw these six students out of school because it might provoke more protest, the Columbia administration put the six on "disciplinary probation."

In response, Columbia SDS decided that on April 23, 1968, it would attempt to march into or sit in at Low Memorial Library until the IDA 6 were taken off disciplinary probation for exercising their First Amendment rights. A well-attended Columbia SDS general assembly meeting was held in Fayerweather Hall to plan our strategy for the April 23 rally. Bill Sales and Ray Brown of SAS sat near the front of the classroom where the meeting was held, listening and observing, while the hundred white SDS people debated possible tactics. Bill and Ray only attended Columbia SDS meetings when they expected that genuine white radical action might soon follow. Mark and the other New Left Action Faction people—and even the Praxis Axis people—all agreed with the proposal to march into Low and confront Kirk, but felt it was too premature to call for a student strike until we saw how many students turned out for the initial confrontation. Before the meeting ended in a state of excitement and anticipation, Mark made the following comment: "The usual life span for a leftist organization at Columbia is two years. Columbia SDS is approaching the end of its second year. And we may not survive the administration's attempt to repress us. But let's fight for our right to be free and our right to act politically on this campus as Columbia SDS, for as long as we can."

A paper had been passed around for volunteers to sit behind the Columbia SDS table on Low Plaza on April 23, 1968, and I signed up for the 12 to 1 p.m. slot. Consequently, I was the last Columbia SDS activist to be at the table before the sundial rally turned into the student revolt, and a new political situation suddenly developed on Columbia's campus. Sitting there, observing people as they gathered around the sundial, it became obvious that we had mobilized more than the four hundred leftist students required to finally hold a mass sit-in at Low.

April 23, 1968, marked the last day I sat in a Columbia College classroom as an undergraduate, after nearly three years of being a Columbia College student. It marked a personal turning point in my life, as well as a political turning point in sixties history.

Bob Feldman *('69CC) is Boston-based antiwar movement writer-activist. A former Columbia SDS steering committee member, in retirement he is a member of the Massachusetts Senior Action Council elderly rights group. A weekly columnist for alternative newspaper* Downtown *throughout the nineties, in recent years, his writing has appeared on various websites, including* Toward Freedom, The Rag Blog, *and* Bob Feldman 68. *Some of his songs are on his protestfolk YouTube channel.*

LARRY GARNER

Graduate student, Department of Public Law and Government/
Fayerweather Hall occupier

"POSSIBILISTES" VS. "MAXIMALISTES":
HOW IT WENT DOWN IN FAYERWEATHER

I was a graduate student in Columbia's Department of Public Law and Government in the spring of 1968, and my reasons for participating in the occupation of Fayerweather Hall were pretty much the same as my fellow "trespassers": the university's perceived complicity in the Vietnam War (e.g., contracts with the Institute for Defense Analyses; Reserve Officers Training Corps programs; Marine Corps and Central Intelligence Agency recruitment on university grounds; Dow Chemical— of Agent Orange fame—permitted to recruit on campus); the crisis in race relations (that same month had seen the assassination of Martin Luther King, Jr.) manifested *in nuce* by the arrogant decision of a large white institution to build a new gymnasium in a park traditionally seen as West Harlem's turf; and the structure and quality of graduate education.

This last issue was particularly important for those of us graduate students who chose to take over Fayerweather Hall. This is not to say that we were any less concerned about the other two issues, but we inside Fayerweather were distinguished from the occupants of the other buildings precisely because we raised these other matters as well. Because the issues related to the war and race are well known and self-explanatory, I will focus here on the intra-university questions.

To be a graduate student at Columbia in the sixties, and particularly in the Department of Public Law and Government, meant taking large lecture classes with enrolments of more than a hundred students, with professors who seemed distant and were thoroughly absorbed in their research. Perhaps most disenchanting, they seemed to be part and parcel (at least in the social sciences) of the ideological grid underpinning the established regime. Columbia had long since lost the professors (C. Wright Mills, Herbert Marcuse, Franz Neumann) who saw themselves as ideological adversaries of the existing system. In their place was that cohort of American social scientists who marveled at the "American genius," whether in government institutions, political culture, social norms, or economic systems. We were being told, in essence, that the United States was number one in the world in virtually every category (often despite outward appearances starkly to the contrary). Those of us who entered graduate school in the midst of the Vietnam War and the upheaval in race relations were looking for something other than the apologetic pabulum fed us by our Columbia professors.

Many of us had become convinced that a radical or Marxist perspective would find a place on the faculty only if students themselves became part of the hiring and firing process. This question, in the case of Columbia, went well beyond ideology, for Columbia had lapsed into a kind of in-house cronyism whereby many professors brought on board their favorite Columbia Ph.D.'s, some of whom were less than stellar. In any case, in our view, the revolutionary task confronting intellectuals was to begin the "long march" through the institution that was our field of activity: the university. By bringing more radical faculty to Columbia, we would be doing our part to establish the cultural hegemony of progressive thinking in America. In place of a culture that identified happiness with material wealth, individual success and the vicarious euphoria of imperial might, we would be the bearers of cultural values emphasizing solidarity, community, and social justice, at home and abroad.

This matter of opening up Columbia to new and radical voices of social scientific inquiry, and how to incorporate that demand within the ongoing negotiations between Students for a Democratic Society (SDS) leadership and the university administration, was a constant subject of debate during our occupancy of Fayerweather. Discussions on this subject, and on whether we were prepared to accept a "slap on the wrist" or settle for nothing less than unqualified student "amnesty," were heated. Our plenary discussions held in the basement adhered strictly to *Roberts' Rules of Order*, because—as we discovered early in our meetings—chaos ensued whenever we had anything short of parliamentary discipline. One of the occupants was a former University of Michigan student body president who knew the rules implicitly and was effective in presiding over "orderly" discussions of the many resolutions proposed. So here you had this bunch of shaggy, long-haired, pot-smoking, and generally disheveled radicals who were "seconding the motion" and "calling the question."

One of the most divisive questions was amnesty for students as opposed to that "slap on the wrist." The issue here was whether we were prepared to accept the latter in exchange for substantive reform in all areas of our grievances. Fayerweather consistently devised and sent out resolutions in favor of that position and passed them on to the SDS negotiating committee. These resolutions went nowhere. And now, in retrospect (and even shortly after the police "bust," I must say), it is clear that SDS leadership never had any interest in coming to terms with the university. Many in that leadership subscribed to the view that it was necessary to force the bourgeoisie to remove the "velvet glove" that masked the "mailed fist" of the bourgeois state. They thought that a confrontation with the police would have a beneficent effect: the impact of police billy clubs on the skulls of students would set off an instantaneous radicalizing of student consciousness.

A few in the SDS camp, however, were convinced that they held the trump cards and could achieve their maximalist objectives. There was, after all, the very unlikely prospect of Harlem rising up *en masse* should anything happen to the black students in Hamilton. And then there was the suggestion by JJ (John Jacobs), a Columbia undergraduate and one of the loonier characters in occupied Math, that if we all stripped and went buck naked at the time of the police raid, the police would be so grossed out that they would back off and allow the occupation to continue.

The night of the bust, I was outside Fayerweather and could see the police massing to enter Low Memorial Library. A group of us spontaneously formed a human barrier to their entrance and began singing "America the Beautiful." I remember linking arms with the persons to my right and left as the police meticulously put on white gloves and prepared themselves for their phalanx-like charge, and at the moment they advanced upon us, I tightened up on the arm of a fellow graduate student. Later I was to discover that this maneuver, together with the force of the police charge, dislocated his shoulder, and he went careening in pain off into the bushes. I escaped with nary a bruise and headed over to the steps of Low, where one of my professors said something to the effect that "after tonight, relations between colleagues will never be the same." I remember rejoining that if those relations disintegrated under the pressure of divergent *prises de position* on serious political matters, they didn't amount to much in the first place. I also recall seeing one student pushed through a plate glass window at the Lion's Den, a campus café, and numerous others clubbed on the head (whether they were instantaneously radicalized for life as a result, I have my doubts).

The next fall the Department of Public law and Government made a token attempt to hear the opinions of graduate students in matters of faculty recruitment. I can recall sitting in on the presentations of prospective candidates, critiquing their talks, and passing on our views to the faculty. I don't know whether this practice ever became institutionalized, since by the fall of 1969, I was no longer in residence. I also edited a short-lived newsletter of graduate studies from the perspective of the more radical of us. Its title was *Traumerei* and—inspired by utopian ruminations on the future of the social sciences—it bore a quote from Dante's *Inferno* on its front page: Abandon all hope ye who enter.

Larry Garner *('74GSAS) wrote his dissertation on the Marxism of Antonio Gramsci, played semipro baseball in Italy, fought the "class struggle in theory" (Althusser) at DePaul University for twenty years, and for the past two decades has been acting on the stages of Chicago theaters.*

MICHAEL GARRETT

Graduate student, Columbia Law and Business Schools

ATTEMPTING TO "HOLD THE CENTER" AT COLUMBIA, 1968

The ceremony of innocence is drowned;
The best lack all conviction, while the worst
Are full of passionate intensity.

And what rough beast, its hour come round at last,
Slouches towards Morningside to be borne?

"THE SECOND COMING" (WITH APOLOGIES TO WILLIAM BUTLER YEATS)

The buttoned-down, conservative quietude of the fifties ended in the mid-sixties with the emergence of a cornucopia of issues and causes that became the subject of discussion, demonstration, and protest on the Columbia campus. During my Columbia College years, 1962–1966, those events were characterized by sincere debate and respectful good cheer. Everyone took their cause seriously, but no one took themselves all that seriously. And no one even considered that the occupation of a building was an option that could possibly further their cause. For instance, I remember a demonstration, in 1964, in front of Ferris Booth (now Alfred Lerner) Hall in support of higher wages for cafeteria workers. The sign-carrying demonstrators were marching in a circle singing "We Shall Overcome," when the football team, walking to their prepractice lunch, formed a circle around the demonstrators, and broke out a chorus of "We Shall

i

Overeat." Everyone laughed and then quietly discussed the issues. In 1965, Columbia's humor magazine, *Jester*, sponsored, and at least five hundred people attended, the "All-Purpose Protest," at which such pressing causes such as "Help Stamp Out Flaming Ducks!" were represented on placards and in wise and witty speeches.

In the spring of 1966, Adolf Berle, the last of the Roosevelt cabinet and an adjunct professor at the Law School, offered an undergraduate seminar on his massive study *Power*. The dozen of us who were fortunate enough to be accepted into the seminar ranged from Ron Bryant, the head of the Conservative Club, on the Right, to David Gilbert, one of the founders of the Columbia chapter of Students for a Democratic Society (SDS), on the Left, and ten of us in between. Berle had world-class experts read the papers we wrote and then join us at an elegant, black-tie dinner at his Gramercy Park South townhouse. It was so exhilarating and inspiring that, at the end of the evening, about eight of us walked the seven miles back to Morningside.

On that long walk, I expressed to David Gilbert that I felt SDS was sounding far more radical and militant in recent months. There was even rhetoric that began to justify obstructive and violent action. I asked him where it was leading and whether or not he could see himself as the leader of that sort of organization. He replied that he was well aware of the trend and not at all sure if he would embrace it. He speculated, however, that the Berle dinner might well be the last time he either wore a tuxedo or spoke civilly to the establishment. (True to that insight, David took his place among the most radical students and, after leaving Morningside, joined the Weatherman and was convicted of felony murder, and sentenced to forty years to life, for the shooting death of a Brinks guard and two police officers in the course of a robbery in Westchester County.)

In early 1968, in the context of demonstrations and protests that were boisterous but still well within bounds, Columbia Vice President and Provost David Truman was proud of the past, satisfied with the present, and inspired by his nearly certain future as president of the university. His roles as scholar, author, teacher, dean, and provost had been performed with distinction, and the support for his succeeding president Grayson Kirk was widespread and enthusiastic. To prepare for that lofty office, he had assembled a loose network of his most trusted faculty, administrators, trustees, alumni, and students. The network acted as an informal focus group for his proposed procedures, policies, and programs. Also, being very aware of the arch personae that Presidents Butler, Eisenhower, and Kirk presented to Columbia, Truman engaged us in his ontological inquiry into who he should be for each of the university constituencies. I worked with Dean Truman as an undergraduate at the College and Provost Truman as graduate student at the Law and Business Schools.

A few short months later, "the future wasn't what it used to be." The time-honored, civilized processes with which the university carried out its sacred mission—the free exchange of ideas in a respectful community of learning—had been shattered, or at least "radically" altered. A few hundred of Columbia's seventeen thousand students were occupying university buildings and preventing nonoccupiers from entering. They flaunted a series of demands that they knew from the outset were either not within the university's control (the Vietnam War and the civil rights movement) or would not be acceded to just because buildings were occupied (the gymnasium in Morningside Park and on-campus military research). The black militant students, having occupied the college's principal classroom building, Hamilton Hall, and ejected all nonblack occupiers, spurred the rejected whites to prove themselves by acting even "more radical than thou." The faculty was running around in circles flapping its wings, wringing its hands in naïve collective guilt and confusion, and producing a great deal of unconstructive noise both orally and in writing. Some students agreed with the occupation, or at least were in sympathy with the issues selected by the occupiers to justify their actions. Other students, inaccurately calling themselves the Majority Coalition, were harshly and crudely demanding that the occupiers be ejected as brutally as possible from the buildings. The vast majority of students, however, were a herd of sophomoric deer blinded by the headlights of the events and failing utterly to perceive the dire severity of the crisis within the ongoing spectacle.

Faced with this complex and unprecedented scenario, the world's most enlightened university administration would be hard pressed to successfully address all the attendant issues, constituencies, and courses of action. Columbia was no exception. To add insult to injury, the president's office was being occupied and gleefully trashed and desecrated by its occupiers. To further complicate matters, President Kirk remained away from the campus most of the time, and when present, was in hiding and—as all agreed—ineffectual. Kirk and some vocal trustees wanted only to end the occupation, apparently oblivious to any other aspect of the crisis. Accordingly, they tightly constricted the range of policy options and actions that Provost Truman was authorized to take, while making it appear he was solely in charge. Truman found himself, as he expressed to me and others, faced with a staggering combination of frustration with his constraints, disappointment at the naïveté and passivity of the faculty, and bewilderment at the attitudes and actions of the intransigent students in and outside the buildings. I sensed he also felt that he might never see the implementation of the plans he made for his presidency. Yeats's poesy of fifty years earlier, *The Second Coming*, was eerily current and on point:

> Things fall apart; the centre cannot hold;
> Mere anarchy is loosed upon the world,
> The blood-dimmed tide is loosed, and everywhere
> The ceremony of innocence is drowned;
> The best lack all conviction, while the worst
> Are full of passionate intensity.[1]

I was shaken by the events and further shaken by the irresponsibility of the university constituencies and the profundity of the predicament in which Dr. Truman was entrapped. We shared the fear that the rational core of the university was exploding in slow motion around us and might never be put right. I wasn't sleeping, and during the day, it was as if I were in a nightmare in which I could see but not affect the madness that swirled around me. I had recurring thoughts—the English major in me—of the Yeats poem, particularly with the coincidence that Yeats had selected a lion and that Jerusalem and Morningside enjoyed the same scansion. I was also convinced that the "radical" students were being manipulated by the SDS national organization, particularly because I had met the purported student leader, Mark Rudd, and believed that he was neither intellectually nor constitutionally capable of conceiving or authentically leading all that was occurring. I felt I must do something—anything—beyond offering Dr. Truman any assistance that I could render

---

1.   W. B. Yeats, "The Second Coming," in *The Collected Works of W. B. Yeats*, 2nd ed. (New York: Scribner, 1997), 1: 189.

to rally the center and preserve the university. I foolishly failed to perceive the Herculean and Sisyphean nature of that task.

"Alumni for the Preservation of Columbia University" was the less-than-modest moniker I bestowed on our tiny desert island of sanity in the sea of madness that was Morningside. That island was populated by me and a few of my college classmates who shared my dread that our world was coming apart. Our only accomplishment was spending too much time composing a letter, which was published in the *New York Times* on May 2, 1968. In calling for restraint and cautious reconciliation, and to get everyone to the table, we gave far more respect and credence to all sides than we believed they deserved. To our great disappointment, our letter was met with a silent ovation, leaving us with our worst fears and our enervating powerlessness.

My overwhelming reaction to the night of the bust was a deep aching sadness. I had accompanied a Columbia administrator to one of the well-intentioned briefings concerning restraint and procedures that took place at every one of the police precincts that sent officers to the campus. While there appeared to be complete agreement with the cautionary approach prescribed by the university, the officers had not been trained for this kind of event, and looked frightened and out of their depth from the moment they arrived on Morningside. Set out in long lines, they looked for all the world like the Victorian constabulary in *Pirates of Penzance* about to sing "A Policeman's Lot Is Not a Happy One." Ultimately, their supervision was inadequate, individuals panicked, and the charge began. No better than the students' occupation of buildings, which brutalized the very soul of the university as the forum for the respectful free exchange of ideas, the police randomly brutalized the bodies of participants on all sides, and bystanders as well.

Six months after the bust, I was elected to the Committee on University Governance that was formed to address the major issues facing Columbia as it attempted to work its way back from anarchy to academy. I became cochair of the University Presidential Search Committee, which was composed (for the first time ever at Columbia) of six trustees, six faculty members, and six students. With the dark cloud of the past May hovering over us, we sought to find a president who would heal the ghastly wounds inflicted on Columbia and bridge the chasms of mistrust that separated the components of the university. I strongly advocated for David Truman, but, fairly or unfairly, he was so inextricably identified with the painful crisis that he was no longer a viable candidate, regardless of his merits.

After considering virtually all the bright lights in higher education, we chose Chancellor William McGill of the University of California at San Diego (and former Columbia psychology professor) as the best person to lead the recovery—to regain the center. His devotion to understanding people and their motivations and goals, engaging in dispute resolution, and building consensus, and his record of accomplishing those goals, was impressive. In his full Committee interview, one of the student Committee members threw out the challenge that had been carefully designed by the Committee: "Okay, McGill, I'm in your office, smoking' your cigars, and readin' and trashin' your papers—so you gonna call the cops to bust my head and drag me out?" Chancellor McGill replied, "If discussion didn't get you to leave quickly, I'd call in the police." The student responded "So you value bricks and mortar more than the lives of students?" McGill rose from his chair, confronted the student, and said "Young man, if you don't understand that the Columbia buildings are infinitely more than mere bricks and mortar, and that an attack on those structures was in fact an

Figure 10.1 Occupiers entering and leaving Low Library. *Photograph by Richard Howard.*

assault on the very concept of a university, then you don't belong here and you should leave now." McGill was the only candidate who did not give a convoluted process answer. While he faced the issue squarely, clearly, and with deep conviction—and we were all very impressed—we also recognized that it was going to be a difficult and perilous task for Dr. McGill to translate his profound observation into the successful reconstitution and reinvigoration of the university. As Yeats wrote,

> The darkness drops again; but now I know
> That twenty centuries of stony sleep
> Were vexed to nightmare by a rocking cradle,
> And what rough beast, its hour come round at last,
> Slouches towards [Morningside] to be born?[2]

While I have remained a loyal and active alumnus, many of my classmates are alienated from Columbia because they did not see 1968 coming and still feel both blind-sided and violated by what occurred. As I look back fifty years on those terrible and traumatic events, and the sweep of development since then, I know that the center has held, but I am hard pressed to identify the event and moment that has made it so. I do remember my first real surge of optimism occurred when Michael Sovern took over as president. Whether or not the center was made secure at that moment, as Yeats foretold, the lion has slouched toward Morningside and been reborn. Far beyond any rational expectation in 1968, Columbia has grown (and matured) in every dimension, while remaining true to its center.

In Lumine Tuo Videbimus Lumen. Amen.

Michael Garrett *('66CC, '69LAW, '70BUS) has served as general counsel of global financial businesses; as leader of nonprofits related to the September 11 attacks, higher education, and employment within underserved populations; and as an executive coach, all while remaining an active parent and grandparent, Columbia alumnus, photographer, pianist, and world traveler.*

---

2. Yeats, "Second Coming," 190.

Columbia College undergraduate/Students for a Democratic Society

THE MAN WHO SHOOK MY HAND

N early all of us who were involved in the Columbia strike have, at one time or another, used our magnifying glasses to examine those events. Mine is now put away. Although we strikers still carry intimate knowledge and emotions related to the core weeks of the strike, from April 23 to May 22, 1968, I have shifted my focus from fact-finding to trying to understand the experiences that have turned out to be critical elements of the prism that give me perspective on the world and on my life.

Dr. David Truman was dean of Columbia College and an influential professor in the university's Department of Public Law and Government. More important, he was part of Columbia's brain trust and heir-apparent to President Grayson Kirk. I first met Truman in September 1966. He stood inside the doorway of what is today Alfred Lerner Hall, his staff arrayed about him, half entourage and half receiving line. Eight hundred strong, the freshmen of the class of 1970 shuffled in for the opening session of a week-long orientation. Political scientist by trade but politician at heart, Truman shook us by the hand as he expertly stepped forward, at once an unconscious gesture of friendship and control. Although relaxed, his face was ashen, a grayness complemented by a dark suit and charcoal tie. His body language expertly transmitted the sense that he knew something special about each of us.

I was all of sixteen (and a half!), but the hand that Truman clasped had already worked its way up and onto a ladder of some significance in the parts from which I hailed. It had been shaken by Queens County (New York) Democratic Party bosses, congressmen, state senators, judges, and even our beloved Sen. Robert Kennedy. In my ambitious mind, those handshakes were both the instruments and objects of a single scheme: to get into a school such as Columbia, broaden my base (of important hands shaken, I suppose), and climb onto a more significant political and social ladder. Truman shook my hand and inadvertently shook up a piece of my soul. Avuncularly, he looked me in the eye, introduced himself, and asked, "How do you feel, son?" Of course, I reciprocated the introduction, but wasn't sure if he expected an enthusiastic "Great!" or a well-mannered "So excited to be here, sir." As a working-class kid, I had not yet learned that it's best not to respond with anything more than a peppy, positive answer in these types of situations with people in authority.

My newly tried-on mask of Ivy League refinement quickly crumbled. I revealed my Bronx first-kid-to-go-to-college origins with a monosyllabic and quite ungrammatical reply: "Real scared!" Did Truman think that his team had let "a bad one" slip through their admissions process? Or did he sense my potential rather than my momentary fear? Truman had no choice, really, about what to say. Still, I would like to believe he responded earnestly. He held on to both of my hands for a few extra seconds and said, "Don't be, son. I'm sure you'll be just fine."

I began my journey at Columbia an orderly, studious, and ostentatious freshman who read the *New York Times* each morning. But by the fall of 1967, I was oversleeping, skipping breakfast, and tearing across campus to arrive, barely on time, for class. I was consumed with knowing more than anyone else about *every* debate within *every* social movement across *every* continent.

By 1968, my view of Columbia was that of a Students for a Democratic Society (SDS) organizer (part of the so-called Sophomore Caucus) who would do all he could to speed up the cultural and political changes that were taking place across the nation. I just happened to be a student, and I squeezed lectures and life in between SDS gatherings and door-knocking. Although SDS is remembered by many for the factionalism and hypermilitancy that plagued it in 1969 and 1970, SDSers who worked on issue campaigns were people with a great work ethic. Right up to the eve of April 23, when the rally and building occupations that launched the strike took place, we devoted a large amount of our leisure time to structured political work. We worked in small groups but assembled at least monthly to share news, techniques, and ideas. We would leave meetings drained, but the next evening there we were, again engaged in seemingly endless canvassing in Columbia and Barnard dorms, overly energetic argumentation at the ready. We invited sympathetic faculty and regional SDS speakers to give our organization credibility, and we held outdoor rallies both to draw political discussion literally into the center of the campus and to strengthen the emotional ties we had to each other and to our movement.

While working in SDS, I joined the Citizenship Council, a campus volunteer group, and spent regular amounts of time working for the Harlem Education Program. The youths who participated after school hours or on weekends ranged in age from about seven to fourteen. They came from poor families and attended awful schools. Theirs was the African American ghetto life whose rhythms and realities made the Bronx that I had known shine like a wealthy suburb. I was the leader of an Adventure Club, taking kids out of their compressed neighborhoods and into the iconic play spaces of the city (Central Park, Bronx Zoo, Wollman Rink, Empire State Building) and helped organize a Science Club, which had its own workspace (at the edge of an abandoned lot covered in ankle-deep trash). A pair of Columbia premeds led this activity, and I marveled not only at the consistency of their work, but their likeability, shared insights about the kids, and effectiveness. A generation away from tenement life myself (my grandparents lived above a storefront in a poor part of Brooklyn, my grandfather had me make price signs for the vegetable cart motored by his rented horse), I decided that as long as I remained a student, I would spend at least one day a week out in the world that I wanted to change.

As I got on the subway each colder and colder Saturday morning to head up to Harlem, the intensification of the pro- versus antimilitary split at Columbia shadowed me. Muhammad Ali had refused military service, and in 1967, Martin Luther King, Jr. began to speak out against the Vietnam War. Walking across campus during freshman year, it did not take long to run into people who wore Navy uniforms one day a week and were enrolled in the Reserve Officers Training Corps (ROTC). I had thought about ROTC as a way to finance my enrollment at Columbia from the time I learned about it in the fall of 1965 right up to the start of school in

September 1966. The idea was quickly slapped down at my high school by newly found antiwar friends. I agreed. It would be hard to be against the war, as I firmly was from the end of 1966 on, if I was financially dependent on the military to get me through school. But I was getting a Regents Scholarship (from New York State), a federally subsidized bank loan, and a federally funded work-study job. It always gnawed at me how convenient it was to draw a line in the sand against working for and receiving ROTC funds.

On my eighteenth birthday, a letter from the Selective Service System arrived at my dorm reminding me that I had correctly registered for the draft but that my student status had not been verified. The presumptiveness of the letter's wording rang loud and clear to me: "Take this letter to your registrar or university administration office in order to ensure that you receive your deferred status." But this had not been unintentional on my part. Asking for a student deferment was just not in my bones. Unlike many of my classmates, black and white alike, who automatically accepted this right, I always refused it and was at all times ready to undergo military conscription while still at school. Consistency demanded I share at least some of the risks that others in society faced.

During this time, changes were taking place among many people in and around SDS, both at Columbia and across the nation. Those who supported the goals of SDS but remained outside of it built their politics around a fear that direct action, whether by individuals or groups, would personally or politically isolate student activists. At the same time, we in the core of the organization at Columbia cultivated a personal and organizational knack for confrontation. Outside the campus, in the antiwar demonstrations in midtown New York and San Francisco, or even larger ones in Washington, D.C., we found ourselves led into small confrontations with police or opponents of the movement itching for a fight. These became as much a part of our movement experiences as dorm-canvassing. Up through the end of 1967, we returned to Columbia after each national event with determination, to lick our wounds and intensify the mostly educational and occasionally confrontational activities that we managed to create week to week. From January 1968 on, world events and racist violence overshadowed patient, passive dormitory-organizing or even loud outdoor rallies. Those engaged in SDS activities (assisted by the maturity of the organization, with its morale-boosting

New York Regional Office), and those who joined us in believing that important things were amiss, were looking to realize our political potential and take more significant action.

April 24, 1968, wasn't simply the day after another outdoor rally. Early morning, when black students initiated the discussion about our leaving, what they really were doing was allowing us to give in to historical momentum. That momentum was brewing inside us in January, when Mark Rudd had returned from Cuba to a campus full of what many of us considered to be "overenthusiasm." It was brewing in February, when community and non–SDS student activists had been arrested at the newly broken ground of the construction site of Columbia's "Jim Crow gym." It was brewing in March, when the administration thoughtlessly upped the ante by "reminding" everyone on campus of the rules against indoor demonstrations.

It was 2 A.M. I and others disturbed the sleep of white students occupying Hamilton, marched them out of the building, and led them into the night to seize Low Memorial Library and expand the strike in coordination with the leaders of the black students. At Low, we faced helmeted, club-bearing campus security guards behind a bolted and chained glass door. As the wooden board I was carrying bounced off not only the wooden frame of the door but also the vulnerable sheet of glass at its center, our hoped-for historical moment was in danger of becoming farce. To save face, several of us used the board to pry the door partially open. The bulk of the crowd still stood back. Again with help, I grabbed a nearby bench with which we finally shattered the door glass. The distinct shattering sound filled the night air, and the raised eyebrows of Captain DeNisco, head of campus security, was enough of a "signal" to send his men fleeing in several directions, a few retreating upstairs, leading some of the less informed among us straight to the office of Grayson Kirk.

Those of us occupying Kirk's office spent the night carefully picking through his private files, which proved to be a surprising treasure trove of documents. By dawn, as our adrenaline levels normalized and our minds cleared, we knew a lot more about what David Truman and other university executive team members had been doing when they weren't teaching or writing. We finally had proof of the lies and narrow interests upon which the power, influence, and, to some extent, even the purposes of the university had been built.

If someday we recover Truman's appointment book, it may show that he and I had two or three private—and rather gentlemanly—discussions in the months and years before 1968, each concerning academic matters. Beyond these businesslike chats, our only other encounter—initiated by Truman, and a very public one—came a day after the April 30 beating and arrest of many hundreds of strikers by the New York City Police Department (NYPD). The direct action phase of our strike seemingly concluded, the real strike—changes in the grading system, courses of study more relevant to our interests, the ending of gender-separated dorms—was just beginning. The Strike Coordinating Committee (SCC) joined several faculty subgroups in seeking the resignations of Kirk and Truman, and demanded the resignation of several university trustees linked to military industries and international media.

Truman's political instincts were failing him. He believed too much in his own political theories and ignored the evidence at hand. The strategy of using mass arrests, beatings, and partial police occupation of the campus did clear out the buildings, but it failed completely to change campus sentiment and, ultimately, led to the reoccupation three weeks later of both Hamilton Hall and a building in the community slated for urban renewal. Truman, however, remained convinced that the administration could win back the loyalty of key faculty and even, he argued privately, a sizeable core of the literally wounded and angry student body. All he needed to bring picketers to heel and wean striking students from SCC-organized liberation classes was to show the flag of his touted social and political sophistication This, thought Truman, would revive the normal rhythms of academic life in those final days of the 1968 academic year.

With timing typical of historical figures with whom he shared this type of hubris, Truman chose day one of the campus-wide strike for a mid-morning walking tour of picketed buildings. Many picketers limped on the picket lines, sporting various bumps, bruises, and stitched-up wounds obtained courtesy of the NYPD's Tactical Patrol Force and accompanying plainclothes detectives. From my perch on the Fayerweather steps, where I was speaking to a crowd, I saw Truman enter the quad with a small entourage that included Captain DeNisco. In the distance, Truman appeared intent, poking his finger in the air and working his jaw as if speaking with some anger. He waded into the edge of the crowd and arrived a few yards from the stairs where I was standing. His index finger came to a stop and was pointed at me like a gun. "Shut up! Shut up!" he hollered. I asked the picketers to pass me the bullhorn and, ignoring the obviously defanged Truman, continued to speak about the liberation classes and picketing schedule. Truman increasingly (and I believe intentionally) brushed against the crowd as the students demonstrated their newfound confidence by closing around the steps to protect the doors

Figure 11.1 Ted Gold (checkered jacket and glasses), Mark Rudd (duffel coat), and others on the sundial, April 23, 1968. *Photograph by Barney Edmonds.*

against any potential breach. With the bullhorn going full blast, whatever Truman was trying to tell the crowd went unheard. He turned to the closing phalanx of strikers, looked each one in the eye, and again barked his mantra: "Shut up! Shut up!"

What had to happen next was all too obvious. The all-powerful Truman, who days before gave the final approval the for the police action, found himself mocked and powerless. The crowd of striking students encircled him and his small entourage. The crowd rhythmically chanted and pointed "No, *you* shut up! No, *you* shut up!" and parted as the now silenced Truman was hustled away to his next destination. Although I remained on campus for another full year, I never saw Dr. Truman out-and-about on the quads again.

Stuart Gedal *is a Harvard-trained executive coach and language trainer. Admitted to Columbia as a member of the Class of 1970, he left Columbia at the end of the 1969 academic year and became a blue collar worker (US Steel) and community organizer (tenants' rights and antiracism) into the eighties. As a program designer and consultant, he then worked with industry and government to link diversity, teamwork, and technology to workforce development. Today, he focuses on skill development for non-native English speakers working in US and global businesses.*

Manhattan District Attorney's Office

IN THE SPIRIT OF RECONCILIATION

The role of the prosecutor is to vindicate the rule of law. Who, if not the prosecutor, does this? The police make arrests and the judge makes the final decision, but it's the prosecutor who makes all key decisions, who decides when the law has been infringed and which legal procedures should be used to hold the offender accountable. It's the prosecutor who has to understand the awesome power that he or she has.

The events at Columbia in 1968 are a fascinating example of the way the power structure of the United States functions. When it came to prosecuting the hundreds of people arrested on the Columbia campus during the police bust that ended the building occupations of April 1968, it was obvious to me from the outset that none of the students were in need of incarceration or rehabilitation. I knew this partly because it was simple common sense that most participants in demonstrations and disturbances of the era were generally passive and peaceful, and also because the students of Columbia, and students on campuses across the country, were more interested in constructive participation with society than the destruction of the world in which they lived. These were idealistic people standing up for a cause in which they passionately believed.

Moreover, their message—about racism, about the waging of an unpopular war, about corporate America—was one I was sympathetic to. I shared many of their views and was deeply concerned with the issues about which they were so passionate. At Horace Mann prep school, I was offended by the ostentatious wealth displayed by so many students around me, and later, after my first year at NYU Law School, I went down as a volunteer to Hattiesburg, Mississippi, for Freedom Summer 1964. I worked for the Law Students Civil Rights Research Council and assisted in the voter registration program by coordinating lawyers—including William Kunstler and Arthur Kinoy—who were coming into the community for two-week stints. Not long after that, alongside many thousands of other Americans, I marched in antiwar parades in New York, even while I was working in the district attorney's (DA's) office as a prosecutor, where I started in 1967.

Deserved or not, we had a reputation as being one of the most nonpartisan, fair-minded, and effective prosecutor's office in the country. Whether working down in Mississippi or as a prosecutor in New York City, I was obligated to defend the Constitution, enforce the law, and uphold the rights of everyone, no matter who they were. I had no problem with prosecuting antiwar demonstrators, for example, so long as our office dispensed justice fairly and consistently with the rights of every defendant. I was handed the cases of hundreds of men and women, a hodgepodge of Columbia students who had been sitting in the buildings for nearly a week, each of whom had been charged with criminal trespass, a class B misdemeanor. The accused is guilty of trespass after being in a place he has no right to be and, when ordered to leave, refuses to do so. I set about speaking to the police officers who had made the arrests, and it immediately struck me how difficult it would be to prosecute these cases. The police had gone inside, grabbed the demonstrators, pulled them out, and handed them to other police officers, who in turn handed them over to someone else, who brought them downtown in buses, booked them, and then had them arraigned before a judge. The fact that the students were processed en masse, that so many people were arrested that night at Columbia, worked against us.

Weeks later, as I interviewed each police officer, I asked, "So you arrested John Doe. Can you testify that John Doe was sitting in a particular building?" The response was usually something like: "Well, I don't know. I was handed Joe Doe by a fellow officer. I couldn't tell you exactly where he came from."

"Who handed John Doe to you?"

"I don't remember."

And so on.

Without reliable witnesses, or photographs to document the events of that night, I wondered whether I could prove that the defendants had committed the crime of criminal trespass, or even been inside the buildings. These were all, at best, tenuous cases.

There was, at the time, a battle in the DA's office over whether we should be prosecuting these cases at all. Criminal trespass is really a crime against property, against someone who wants their property freed from interference. Did the trustees of the university—as owners of the buildings—really want to prosecute hundreds of its students? What message would that send? During those years, I had become a student of civil disobedience, reading anything I could find on the subject, and I thought about it as much as any philosophical subject. As far as I was concerned, the students arrested at Columbia had been conducting legitimate acts of civil disobedience. All the usual reasons for imposing punishment didn't seem to apply here. There was certainly no deterrence value, as the wave of campus protests in the months and years that followed made clear. Did representatives of Columbia's administration really want to come into court as complaining witnesses, stand before the world, and explain their side of the story?

For many of us in the DA's office, Columbia reaching for its pound of flesh looked unnecessarily petty and vindictive. It seemed obvious that any self-respecting university is in the business of education, not trying to throw its students in jail. By dropping the cases, perhaps some kind of rapprochement might be brought about. As some people recommended at the time, this should all be kept in the family. Some degree of discipline might be exercised on students, but only according to university statues and rules. Any remedy other than calling in the DA's office was preferable. Only then could the requisite "healing" take place and divisions on campus be repaired.

Eventually, after what I gather was much internal discussion, and in the spirit of reconciliation, Columbia decided to throw in the towel. It didn't want to proceed with the cases. On September 18, 1968, the *Columbia Daily Spectator* reported that the newly installed Columbia President Andrew Cordier, "to appease the moderate elements on campus," was asking the courts for "maximum leniency" in the cases of more than four hundred arrested students.[1] The powers that be, those in charge of this prominent university, an internationally respected institution that had been featured on several front pages of the *New York Times* throughout the week of the student protests, didn't want to retaliate in ways that surely would have generated much negative publicity. I was glad about this good faith move on the part of the university because, after all, there had been no real damage to the buildings. It was almost as if the only real casualty was Columbia's pride, so when it was decided to put an end to what I considered to be corrosive litigation, I figured that the paperwork stacked up on my desk could be filed away for good. What made things troublesome was that my boss, Frank Hogan, the legendary district attorney—"a minister of justice," as the *New York Times* described him in a hagiographic article from 1967,[2] and a man I revered—was a member of Columbia's Board of Trustees, so the building occupations had been for him a personal issue. He felt victimized and violated by what had happened at his beloved alma mater (his undergraduate and law degrees were from Columbia, and the place was an integral part of his existence).

Hogan insisted on prosecuting the students, despite Columbia's protestations and despite my reiteration that the cases had evidentiary weaknesses, that we had limited resources, and that it wouldn't look good to take on a thousand dubious cases when we had many much more serious crimes to deal with. (In early October 1968, a motion to disqualify Hogan from the case because of his close ties to Columbia was turned down.) I did some research and discovered that if the complainant in a criminal trespass case doesn't want to prosecute, the DA's office can still move forward if it feels that the public interest demands it. We could, in theory, continue with these cases, even though—as I explained to Hogan—it probably would be more difficult because the jury would presumably wonder why the complainant wasn't there in court.

Hogan insisted we push on. At this point, I said to him that for moral and logistical reasons I couldn't do it. "I don't think I can stand up in court and strongly argue against the motions that the defense attorneys for

---

1. Martin Mayer, " 'Hogan's Office' Is a Kind of Ministry of Justice," *New York Times* (New York), July 23, 1967.
2. "Leniency Sought in Trespass Cases," *Columbia Daily Spectator* (New York), September 18, 1968.

these individuals will make," I said. "I cannot, in good conscience, make a credible and sincere argument in opposition. These are unwinnable cases." Having recused myself, the job fell to my bureau chief, Joe Stone, who stood in a crowded courtroom, before Justice Arthur Goldberg, a handful of the best civil rights attorneys in New York (some of whom were friends of mine), and Columbia's lawyers, and proceeded to make what I can only describe as a series of half-hearted arguments. These included, notably, the suggestion that these cases were a testing ground for whether or not students across the nation would be able to escape punishment after committing what Hogan and others considered riotous behavior. It was almost as if Joe were doing it just for the record, going through the motions. This in contrast to the array of lawyers on the other side, all of whom made a series of convincing and impassioned statements. The issue ultimately became whether or not the judge would go along with Columbia's desire to dismiss the criminal trespass cases. I found it all rather comical.

After listening to everyone, Judge Goldberg said he would return in fifteen minutes with his decision, and the courtroom was adjourned. He came back and immediately, irrevocably dismissed every case. End of story. No more prosecutions. The joke was that in one day I lost more cases than my colleagues had throughout their entire careers. True! But I wasn't too upset about it.

Bennett Gershman *is one of the original faculty members at Pace Law School, where he still teaches. Between 1967 and 1972, he worked in the office of Frank S. Hogan, district attorney, New York County, and in 1969, he was a member of the Mayor's Committee for the Enforcement of Law During Civil Disorders. He is the author of many books and articles and is an expert on prosecutorial misconduct.*

IRA GOLDBERG

Columbia College undergraduate/Office of Public Information

HOW I BECOME A NATIONAL NEWS SOURCE: COLUMBIA'S OFFICE OF PUBLIC INFORMATION

I n the spring of 1968, I was a senior at Columbia College, working between ten and fifteen hours a week in the Office of Public Information, the main public affairs office of Columbia University. With the exception of the annual Pulitzer Prizes, when the office became a fairly large national facility, it was a steady and uneventful operation, with most of its output devoted to various academic awards won by members of the faculty. At times, however, the office became a hive of activity. My colleagues there would talk about Columbia professor Charles Van Doren winning thousands of dollars on the weekly television quiz show *Twenty One*, or Pat Boone signing up for classes in the School of General Studies. Little did we know, at the start of the 1967–1968 academic year, that we would experience perhaps the most frenetic moment in Columbia's history.

The first unusual event was initiated across Broadway, at Barnard, the all-female undergraduate college. In 1968, Barnard's students living in the dormitories were subject to strictly enforced curfews. First-year students were required to be back in their dormitories by 10:30 P.M. during the week and all on-campus students had to be in their rooms by 1 A.M. on weekends. Barnard required that all students under twenty-one were to either live in the dormitories or at home. An exception was made for married students, who were permitted to live with their husbands. Of course, students at the all-male Columbia College had no curfews during their four-year stint on Morningside Heights. Both Barnard and Columbia

College had strict single-sex dorms with no members of the opposite sex allowed above the first "social" floors. When Columbia first allowed women to visit men's dorm rooms, it was limited to Sunday afternoons. Female guests were required to be signed in at a security desk and doors were required to remain open the "width of a book," a definition that was quickly expanded by students to include matchbooks. Sign-in security desks lasted well into 1968.

It was obvious that student mores, especially with respect to the burgeoning "sexual revolution," were changing, and the New York Times decided to do a story on student living arrangements in New York City. During their investigations, they interviewed a Barnard student under twenty-one who admitted to living off-campus with her Columbia College boyfriend. Although not identified by name, the student said she came from New Hampshire. With so few students from that state registered, it did not take long for Barnard authorities to identify the student as Linda LeClair. The president of Barnard held a brief hearing, and it was decided to expel Ms. LeClair from Barnard for breaking campus directives. Her boyfriend, of course, faced no such disciplinary action. New York and national media picked up on the story, and soon our office was transformed into a busy pressroom for all kinds of media outlets. I was surprised at how quickly public interest in the matter waned. Barnard authorities eventually reversed their decision to expel Ms. LeClair and the story became old news. I remember chatting with my boss John Hastings and mentioning that since we were now heading toward the end of April, we could expect a quiet ending to the academic year in June.

Throughout that year, antiwar sentiment against the continuing war in Vietnam was steadily growing. Tensions were heightened in March when the Selective Service System, the government agency in charge of running the military draft, announced that all graduate school deferments were to be ended, with the exception of students studying for a medical degree. On April 4, Martin Luther King, Jr. was assassinated. The university held a memorial service on campus, in St. Paul's Chapel, during which Mark Rudd—chairman of Columbia's Students for a Democratic Society (SDS) chapter—burst onto the stage and accused Grayson Kirk, president of the university, of blatant hypocrisy. In Rudd's opinion, the policies of the university, especially with respect to the minority groups living in the surrounding Morningside Heights neighborhood, were racist. Although these actions of direct confrontation with the university were new, the story remained on campus and had little effect on the operations of the office.

On April 23, 1968, I was heading to the office for a normal after-class shift of mimeographing articles and stuffing envelopes. A rally was scheduled at the sundial that afternoon, something common enough in the spring of 1968, but when I arrived at the office, I discovered that this was not going to be a normal afternoon shift. The rally at the sundial ended with a large group of students walking over to the Morningside Park construction site of the new Columbia gymnasium. After a tussle with local police, students marched to Hamilton Hall where they confronted Dean Henry Coleman in the lobby. He had a few words with some of the students before going into his ground-floor office. Then the most extraordinary thing happened. The students decided not to leave the building.

Rumors about this possible sit-in reached our office, and I was asked to go to Hamilton and see what was happening. I was amazed to find hundreds of students either milling about in the lobby, blocking the door to Dean Coleman's office, or scattered through the various floors of the building and making themselves at home. I went back to the office and reported these events. By then we were in touch with President Grayson Kirk's office but no overt intervention was planned. A wait-and-see attitude was our policy. The festive atmosphere inside Hamilton quickly changed when early the next morning the African American students "invited" all of the white students to find their own building to occupy. They barricaded the doors to Hamilton Hall and stated that they were not planning to leave until their list of demands was met. The white students, apparently spontaneously, broke into Low Memorial Library and occupied the offices of the president. By the time I arrived at the office for my normal afternoon work-study job, the story had spread beyond the campus and the first outside reporters arrived at our door. They explained that the Public Affairs Office seemed like a logical place to find out what was going on.

Within a day or two, the story of the Columbia occupations became a national one, and the office began to assume the role of de facto headquarters for the national press. John Hastings met with all student employees and told us that we would have to be available on a twenty-four-hour basis. Cheap rollaway beds were installed in one of the suboffices and we were told that we no longer had to keep track of our hours because from now on we would be working twenty-four hours a day. As more reporters and cameramen began to rely on us for the dissemination of information, our normal operations became less important, and all the professional staff, as well as the part-time students, found themselves involved with dealing with this army of outsiders roaming the campus. There was plenty of action to be recorded. Blackboards were wheeled in from the buildings, and some classes met outside of the occupied buildings, while tension between students for and against the protests led to at least one fistfight involving dozens of people on both sides. Motorcycle couriers, looking as if they had just come from the set of the Marlon Brando classic *The Wild One*, would drive onto campus and park outside the office to take 16 mm film canisters downtown to the network headquarters, where the footage would be developed, edited, and prepared for broadcast on that evening's news.

Along with my fellow part-time students, I spent most of my time walking around campus, trying to ascertain the mood of the fast-moving events, and fielding endless telephone calls from across the country. Technology was primitive: we had nothing but bulky black phones, the only innovation of which was that each had buttons to allow for calls to be transferred to other telephones in the office. In most cases, people were attempting to find out why the university was continuing to allow the situation to linger. I recall one phone call from I. F. Stone. After identifying myself as a mere student employee, he still insisted that I give him a detailed report of the past five days and further asked me to give him a scoop as to future events. I got to know several of the reporters who had moved into our office, including Nicholas von Hoffman of the *Washington Post* and Fox Butterfield of the *New York Times*. I recall the persistent von Hoffman insisting that he be granted a one-on-one interview with Grayson Kirk. After a great deal of prodding, he was given time with the president.

Tensions continued to mount on campus. By the last days of April, it was apparent that negotiations between faculty, the university administration, and students had reached a deadlock. People on all sides were going without sleep, and in the office, we were becoming increasingly exhausted, resting whenever we could on our uncomfortable temporary beds and munching on the same monotonous sandwiches. By the evening of April 30, everyone knew that matters would be coming to a close. Although we student employees had been very much involved in disseminating information to the increasingly demanding press corps, we now found ourselves virtually shut out of the university's plans to bring the situation to an end. As evening came and John Hastings was called to Grayson Kirk's office, it was clear that something big was about to take place. John returned to the office clutching a document that was to be read to student occupiers, demanding that they immediately end their occupations or they would be removed by the New York City Police. This single sheet was mimeographed and distributed to several university personnel who then left the office—accompanied by several policemen— and delivered the message to the various occupied buildings.

There appeared to be nothing further that I could do at the immediate moment, so I left the office and wandered over to Avery Hall, home to the School of Architecture and one of the occupied buildings. I stood about seventy-five feet from the entrance as the university's demands were read to a group of some fifty students sitting at the entrance, blocking the doors, and singing, "We Shall Not Be Moved."

The narrative as to what happened that night has been told from many different perspectives. I would simply state, at a distance of fifty years, that I saw confusion, anger, violence, and fear as hundreds of police

Figure 13.1 President Grayson Kirk (left) and Vice President David Truman give a press conference, April 25, 1968 *Image from University Archives, Rare Book and Manuscript Library, Columbia University in the City of New York.*

chased hundreds of students through the campus. When I returned to the office, John Hastings asked what I had seen. I started to relate what I had seen but stopped midsentence, caught my breath, and exclaimed, "John, it was awful."

After the police action, in which more than seven hundred people were arrested, the office became surprisingly quiet. Most of the stories that were to appear in the morning newspaper editions were being edited and printed downtown, and almost every reporter had left the campus. At about 4 A.M., the office received news that the university would be formally closed that day, and we prepared a short statement reflecting this decision. About an hour later, I happened to be the person who answered a call from WKCR, Columbia's student radio station. They wanted confirmation about the closure, so I told them that a formal statement had just been released by the university. I was asked to read that statement live on the air. John Hastings was sitting about ten feet away from me at another desk as I relayed the request to him. With a great deal of reflection and sadness in his voice he said, "Go ahead Ira, read the statement."

In the period between April 30 and graduation on June 4, the office returned to its normal routines, although there were two additional disturbances necessitating the calling of the New York City police back to the campus. At the beginning of June, I was informed that every student employee would be receiving a check for approximately $3,000 for the work we had done during the previous weeks. (To put that into perspective, tuition at Columbia College for the 1967–68 school year was $1,900 and a typical dormitory room cost about $400 per year.) I graduated with my class on June 4, 1968. Since I had been a member of the Naval Reserve Officers Training Corps, I was commissioned an ensign in the US Navy that morning. Two weeks later, I was an officer aboard a destroyer with the Sixth Fleet in the Mediterranean.

Ira Goldberg *('68CC, '75SIPA) spent four years as an officer in the Navy, after which he returned to school and received a master of international affairs from the School of International and Public Affairs and a law degree from Fordham. His career has included working with major financial institutions and law firms. He has two adult daughters and currently resides in the Bronx. He continues to practice law.*

KEN GREENBERG

Graduate student, Architecture/Avery Hall occupier

THE JOLT OF RADICALIZATION

n April 1968, I was a second-year architecture student primed and ready for the events that were about to engulf Avery Hall into the tumultuous Columbia University strike. I had just discovered *The Death and Life of Great American Cities* by Jane Jacobs, which touched a nerve and confirmed my counterculture intuition that things were amiss in the ham-fisted ways we were abusing cities.[1] And from a completely different vantage point, my first experiences in architecture were provoking a highly critical rethink of the way the profession operated.

We had just completed an intense introductory design studio whose approach to pedagogy had forced us to dig deeply into personal, first-hand observations of the way we viscerally experienced buildings and the spaces they form that echoed the unfiltered observations so integral to Jane Jacobs's critique. The premise was that the design of buildings as places for people was not just a matter of manipulating form or aesthetics but was a potent way to make things more or less possible in accommodating the people who lived or worked in them or who encountered them from the outside. It was about what was public and what was private and what lay in between.

---

1. Jane Jacobs, *The Death and Life of Great American Cities* (New York: Random House, 1961).

The values fostered in the Columbia curriculum were focused more on relationships than on eye-catching building elevations or a "look," and my own focus had forever shifted from architecture in isolation to the architecture of the city. This "architectural" voyage of self-discovery was deeply moving and affecting—raising basic questions about our place in the world. Although it was rooted in the physical world and not overtly political, by obvious implication, it was raising fundamental questions about who was the real client: he or she who pays, or the ultimate users of the places we create?

Meanwhile, outside the walls of the academy, New York City was experiencing major turbulence. Close to home, the depredations of "urban renewal" and incursions into low-income neighborhoods near Columbia were being hotly contested, with obvious implications for aspiring young architects. The blending and merging of all the big issues of the moment—civil rights, the women's movement, the environmental movement, growing resistance to the war in Vietnam—formed a highly charged and poignant backdrop to our own mounting questions about the role and relevance of our profession. The deeper we delved into the root causes of these injustices, the more we saw consequences for architecture and city design, and the more out of touch the mainstream practice of architecture seemed to us. Our chosen profession was part of the problem, not the solution, and we very much felt the need to challenge that.

My classmates and I had collaborated to produce several editions of a small publication we called *Touchstone*, our own urgent manifesto and attempt to reach out to others in search of a grammar, syntax, and vocabulary for responsive and humane city design. We championed a strong critique of current professional practice, based on our increasing awareness of the world beyond the drawing board, and called for a rejection of the self-referential—and self-serving—ambitions of architecture evinced in high-profile signature buildings by the "starchitects" of the day.

This growing frustration with the profession was in some ways an amplification of tensions that had been growing between architects who wanted to continue designing the city at the "commissioned" formal and symbolic or strictly commercial level and those who wanted to engage with real conditions on the street. We were uncomfortable with the unbridled ambition of capital "D" design to repress the city's lively dynamics in aid of what we saw as empty and leaden plans. We were also contemptu-ous of the limp rationalizations of architects and urban designers in more corporate and commercial practice who claimed that they were operating as service providers outside the fray and unwilling to participate in the self-critique of current practices. In the place of these aloof professional stances, we were advocating an embrace of the messy, imperfect, not nec-essarily "designed" real city—and an engagement with the overtly politi-cal dimensions of all the decisions that shaped its growth.

In April 1968, Columbia University exploded when a series of inflam-matory issues—including Columbia's plan to build a gym in Morningside Park—ignited a strike. Almost instantly our internal critiques and dissat-isfactions were powerfully connected with the set of broader issues: race, gender, war, and the nature of capitalism.

It was a jolt into a larger consciousness. We were not alone but part of a much bigger struggle; others defined the issues differently, but there was a resonance. It was like a booming and insistent megaphone amplifying our more limited concerns and unheeded voices into a much larger cho-rus, with the prospect of real impacts. Under intense pressure, we tried to work out the links for ourselves. It was an intoxicating, life-altering experience.

Most of my classmates and I took over and occupied Avery Hall, the architecture building. We already practically lived in the architecture studios while working through the night on our projects, so for us, they weren't just classrooms and studios. We had developed a special kind of proprietary relationship to our "base camp," so the idea that we would join the occupation and make a stand in Avery was not such a big a step.

Each occupied building on the campus had a particular set of burn-ing issues. Not surprisingly, ours had to do with architecture and the city and the role of the university and our profession as actors shap-ing it. The Morningside Heights gym that was being aggressively shoe-horned into a public park, while offering local residents limited access, was a clear example of the institution's goals trumping those of the community. We pointed to the gym as a prime example of the kind of high-handed action our profession was widely guilty of carrying out. Furthermore, it was an example that directly implicated us in its abuse of the neighborhood.

Many of our professors and others who shared our concerns joined us. As the days unfolded, a remarkable set of impromptu seminars took place, delving deeply into what was wrong with our practice and how it could change. Sitting in the stairwells and hallways, we were hammering out manifestos and positions in marathon discussions. We were coming up with our own tailored versions of the "demands" of the general strike. Ours, seen through the lens of specific concerns about our roles as prospective architects, were as much about the physical city as they were about the broader political issues. Who would we be working for? What would their agendas be? Who would be in control? Was architecture a business or a profession? Did we have our own version of a Hippocratic oath—a commitment to do no harm and ideally do good?

In this struggle over values, it was hard to ignore the dissonance that was being revealed. The word on everybody's lips at that time was "radicalized." Some of those locked in these debates were not previously inclined to deeply challenge the status quo and were having unnerving new questions thrown at them that were hard to avoid. As we each brought our own baggage and histories, the intensely personal was being challenged by the terms of the larger public debates. We were being forced to sort out where we stood, weighing the individual against the collective voice, and we didn't necessarily all agree. There were intense arguments both in the building and outside about the demands of the strike, the nature of resistance, and the need for confrontation with the administration and ultimately the police. We in Avery wanted to parse all the issues and come up with our own, so we endlessly debated about how far to go in accepting party lines that were being constructed by others. What did we accept, and what did we not? Was our claimed autonomy a reactionary indulgence or a critical necessity?

Eventually, the police moved in and we were arrested. Order apparently had been restored to the campus, but the genie would not so easily go back into the bottle. As soon-to-be young architects and planners, many of us were now committed to developing a more ethical practice, in which the real client would not just be the one paying the bills.

While the world has moved on, many of the larger issues addressed during the strike remain, and it could be argued are even more urgent today: race, gender, income polarization, privatization, environmental degradation, and the erosion of the "public sphere." Still very much alive are debates about the roles and obligations of architects as city builders. Some of us have found ways to keep faith with and pass on the spirit that developed in those heady days in Avery Hall. In my case, I carried these lessons with me as I began a new life in another country.

Ken Greenberg *spent two years at Columbia (1966–1968) before receiving his degree from the University of Toronto. He is an architect and urban designer, living in Toronto. A former director of urban design and architecture for the City of Toronto and principal of Greenberg Consultants, he is the recipient of the 2010 American Institute of Architects Thomas Jefferson Award for public design excellence and the author of* Walking Home: The Life and Lessons of a City Builder.

LOIS-ELAINE GRIFFITH

*Barnard undergraduate/Students' Afro-American Society/
Hamilton Hall occupier*

DADDY'S GIRL

n the courtroom, I am standing with fellow students before a judge. In
protest of Columbia University's policies, we have unlawfully occupied
its buildings and disrupted its functioning. I am one of several hundred students who have participated in the demonstration, were arrested,
jailed, and charged with criminal trespassing, and now stand before a
judge awaiting dispensation of our case. I see my father among those
seated observers witnessing these procedures. I see the troubled expression on his face.

My father, Seymour Oliver Griffith, has left his Caribbean homeland,
crossed oceans to arrive in the States where he births a daughter, his only
child. He works overtime as a Photostat operator to fund her education. He endures the ridicule of his peers—men like him, from Barbados,
Jamaica, Trinidad, who play cricket games on summer weekends in Van
Cortlandt Park. They tell him that girls are not worthy of such devoted
attention. Girls get married. Girls have babies and men they must look
after. Girls cannot be depended upon to further the circumstances of people of color in this country. But I am daddy's girl.

As I stand in arraignment court, one of many students of a prestigious
institution of learning who is charged with criminal trespassing, I look
around to see my father. There is disappointment in his eyes. The judge
releases all of us on our own recognizance to appear back in court at a

later time. Outside the court, my father is waiting for me, and we walk to the subway together in silence.

It's been fifty years since that big showdown in 1968, when common folk around the world grew backbones to organize a voice of dissent to question there being value to war, and notions that skin color indicates social status.

In the spring of 1968, I join with black students at Columbia University demonstrating against war and this country's policies that allow the greed of corporate interests to usurp control of real estate serving black and brown communities. I belong to these times demanding that I put my ass on the line for what I believe.

In 1968, many in this country are conflicted about the civil rights movement initiated by Afro-Americans demanding that all citizens, regardless of race or religion, be given equal rights guaranteed by the US Constitution.

In 1968, social customs and execution of law in the States reflect the dominance of white-skinned folk over people of color.

In 1968, after this country's waging fourteen years of war in Southeast Asia, many in the USA are adamant about demanding answers to the reasons for this conflict. Those controlling the military-industrial complex regulating our economy tell the populace that war in Vietnam is necessary to combat the spread of Communist and socialist ideologies. Politics controlling funding for public educational systems purposely limit the dissemination of information about world history. Many people in the United States are unaware that the people of Southeast Asia are attempting to free themselves of the same kind of Western European colonial domination that spurred the American Revolution.

In 1968, all young men, by their eighteenth birthday, are required by law to register for the draft that automatically enlists them into the army—unless they are enrolled in college. Those young males who drop out of high school or lack funds to attend college and seek time for inventing a direction in life are conscripted for two years of service into the army and sent to soldier in Vietnam.

On April 4, 1968, Martin Luther King, Jr. is assassinated on the balcony of a Memphis, Tennessee, motel as a consequence of his arriving there to support garbage men on strike for better wages.

In 1968, the violence of King's death foments civil unrest and riots throughout the nation. Rage about King's death provokes need among people of color to identify both the obvious and subtle ways that white power structures undermine the lawful rights of blacks and browns in this country.

In the late spring of 1968, Students for a Democratic Society (SDS) and Students' Afro-American Society (SAS) take a stand with the black Harlem community against the university's initiative to seize the public lands of Morningside Park to build a gym for its students.

In the late spring of 1968, student activists occupy buildings on the Columbia campus to protest the university's financial involvement with corporations given government contracts in service of the Vietnam War, and policies that would set legal precedence, using statutes of eminent domain, to validate seizure of public lands by a private corporate entity. Student activists occupy Fayerweather, Avery, Mathematics, and Hamilton Halls. They invade Low Memorial Library and the offices of Columbia President Grayson Kirk. For almost two weeks, student protests shut down all scheduled classes.

Black students occupy Hamilton Hall. I join the protest. There are a hundred or so of us whom some might consider as representing Booker T. Washington's "talented tenth." We are a handful of Afro-Americans who have demonstrated the smarts to garner admission to this prestigious institution of higher learning. It's 1968, and policies of affirmative action are enacted by public and private institutions around this country. Affirmative action—the practice of discrimination attempting to favor those who have suffered exclusion from benefits of housing, employment, and education that white people enjoy.

In 1968, I am a junior student at Barnard College, the women's undergraduate division of Columbia University. I am the daughter of West Indian parents descended from those black Africans who survived the Middle Passage and were enslaved on Caribbean islands.

I am a first-generation American of a father who immigrated to the States in the twenties, seeking to invent himself beyond the drudgery of work in the sugar cane fields of Barbados—beyond spending his literacy skills as a clerk in some colonial British government office.

I am the daughter of parents who parlay their good standing in the Anglican Church to finagle my admission with scholarship to an

Episcopalian day school in New York City. I am a black girl who appreciates how hard her father works to provide her with the education black folk need for social and economic advancement in the States. I am a black girl who understands her father is a "race man," a devotee of Marcus Garvey's philosophies.

To some, the attendance of a black girl at Columbia University might identify me as one of the "talented tenth," those who represent the "cream," those blacks who rise to distinguish themselves in their education and careers from the 90 percent of other blacks. The "talented tenth" are able to navigate successful passage through social structures of white power. I wonder if having light skin makes them more acceptable.

But as the progeny of West Indian immigrants to this country, I have not always been accepted by American blacks into their ranks—into an understanding that, as far as the white man is concerned, the "one drop rule" holds hard and fast for all blacks. As a child in public school, I am confused by my Afro-American classmates. I am confused by their calling me out for not speaking like them, by their telling me that my English has an accent. Some of them call me a monkey-chaser, as if I am derived from some ancestor newly descended from a coconut tree.

In 1968, I join with those students protesting the university's support of the Vietnam War and the attempt to disenfranchise Harlem folk from public parklands. It's ironic that those of us who enjoy the educational opportunity denied to most of our peers are willing to risk our status, biting the hand of "the man" who gives it. I join the black students who occupy Hamilton Hall. I join them because there is grief in me about the killing of Dr. King. I join them in solidarity against corporate entities in this United States that assume superiority to dominate over those lacking the economic prowess to create change.

I have neither "good hair" nor "high yella" skin color to distinguish me from multitudes of Afro-American folk. Yet my education sets me apart from most blacks and whites. I have been schooled by my Bajan father to understand that his allegiance to that outspoken Jamaican, Marcus Garvey, is about courage to step outside ways that white powers invent to tame the black spirit—ways encouraging the mimicry of whites who would exploit resources of this earth rather than discover positions of balance within it.

Cops enter Hamilton Hall through the network of tunnels under the Columbia University campus to arrest us. They round us up in the entryway of the building where men and women are separated from each other and lined up, two by two. We hear rumors that this raid is also being conducted in the other occupied buildings and that authorities are using riot tactics to rid the campus of all demonstrating students. Later, I hear that cops are using horses to run down students and beating people with billy clubs. To avoid the riot scene outside that the cops themselves created, the police lead us through the tunnels and out the building to the Amsterdam Avenue side. We are herded into paddy wagons that deliver us downtown to the Tombs, where we are photographed, fingerprinted, and jailed.

Maybe eight of us girls are packed in a cell with a toilet bowl and sink, no bed no seats. Unlike some of the other girls seeking moments of comfort, I don't sit on the ground. I don't eat the stale Wonder Bread sandwiching a slice of bologna that we are given. I don't want to touch any of the walls in the cell. I am standing against the bars in that cell when I notice flying roaches scurrying along the edges of the back wall. I stand in that cell watching two of these nut-brown creatures, each about the length of my thumb. At home, if I see a roach I have no second thoughts about stalking it, crushing it to death. But here, if I menace against one of these creatures, I am terrified it might spread its wings, lift its sizeable exoskeleton, and fly to attack me. One seems to be chasing the other. One jumps on the back of the other. I am not a student of entomology. I am a religion major. I don't know how flying roaches multiply.

Lois-Elaine Griffith *('69BC) is one of the founding members of the Nuyorican Poets Café. After graduating from Barnard College she studied at Pratt, focusing on graphic design and printmaking. In 1979, her play* White Sirens *was performed at the Public Theater, and in 1998, her novel* Among Others *was published. A graduate of NYU's Graduate School of Arts and Science, she was a professor of English at Borough of Manhattan Community College for twenty years.*

PETER HAIDU

Faculty, Department of French/Ad Hoc Faculty Group

THE COLUMBIA STIR-FRY

I enrolled in graduate school at Columbia in 1957 with vaguely social-ist leanings—normal political equipment for a young Jew, acciden-tal survivor of the Holocaust by skin-of-your-teeth emigration from Europe in 1940. Socialism acknowledged hope for universal brother-hood, for equal, universal, and joyful dignity of self-fulfillment. The notion of revolution was irrelevant to the America of the sixties, yet it recurred repeatedly. The Communist Party was riddled by Federal Bureau of Investigation infiltrators: the street figure was 75 percent. Later, the Counterintelligence Program developed a strategy of police murder and assassination of homegrown revolutionists. "Revolution" could sell sex, nail polish, culture, or books: not political change. Even neighborhood organizations and breakfast programs for kids were dangerous to the sta-bility of the white power elite.

Available forms of struggle for liberation were civil rights and opposition to the Vietnam War, both nonviolent. The Vietnam War—illegal, unjust, horrendously savage and cruel, genocidal and ecocidal—was government violence unleashed against a distant people that posed no danger whatso-ever to America. The My Lai massacre—a month before Columbia '68—revealed young Americans as capable of the worst butchery imaginable. An utterly unnecessary moral atrocity, it was a war in which America willfully assumed colonial savageries abandoned by the French.

At that time, the connection of representation between government and citizen was still organic, not yet arbitrary. The government acted in our name. Our honor—we had honor and dignity in those days—was implicated in the jungles of Vietnam, along with the deaths of thousands of Vietnamese, and hence the masses that demonstrated in ever-increasing numbers against the war. When Martin Luther King began to link the civil rights struggle and the colonialism of Vietnam in 1967, he reached an understanding normal on the Left for years: the oppressed at home and the oppressed overseas shared a single oppressor.

That left the question: what was available as a vehicle for struggle? The question involved not only personal choices, but also the fact that the political landscape was being shaped by a younger generation, with its own heritage. Columbia 1968 did not spring up out of a historical desert. Mike Flug, the student leader of Columbia's Congress of Racial Equality (CORE) chapter, pointed out to me that many of the student activists were themselves children of Jewish labor activists of the twenties and thirties, whose work sometimes shaded into the revolutionary. My own immediate political involvement, as of the mid-sixties, was in civil rights and CORE. Students for a Democratic Society (SDS) would have been a better fit, in theory: it addressed both domestic and international issues. But SDS had committed to the anti-Stalinist lesson. It refused any party organization in favor of ongoing participatory democracy. Leadership was subject to reapproval and redefinition at every meeting, and continuity was permanently in question. Alas, this continuing competition for dominance did not push the most brilliant elements into leadership, but the most vulgar. Mark Rudd was far from the best SDS had to offer: Rudd was what the best kowtowed to.

Instead, I became faculty advisor to Columbia CORE at the invitation of the student chairman, whom I knew and trusted: Mike Flug. CORE included some thirty students or so, mostly undergraduates, white and brown. Black students, concerned with reprisals for activism, stayed away: they chose Ralph Ellison's strategy of invisibility, until SDS forced their hand in 1968, selecting the gym in the park as the symbolic "black" issue woven into its anti-Vietnam protest. Earlier, CORE had offered local residents on Morningside Heights opportunities for self-organization, with legal and political help as necessary. It discovered that behind webs of shell corporations, the university and other local institutions were the real owners of local residential properties. When clearing out their rental properties, they used the most despicable tactics of slum landlords: plugged locks, turned off heat and hot water, and failed to remove garbage. That it was *our* university, our alma mater, was intolerable.

The Faculty Civil Rights Group (FCRG) initially grew out of the observation that Columbia CORE was financially hamstrung. The FCRG had some seventy members donating a small monthly amount, a steering committee that ran from Robert Fogelson to Robert Belknap, and published reports on urban renewal and institutional expansion. When Martin Luther King, Jr. linked civil rights and the Vietnam War publicly in 1967, I brought a proposal to the steering committee at the fall meeting to submit a redefinition of the FCRG to include an anticolonialist dimension to its self-definition as a civil rights organization. Members of the steering committee warmed to the idea, until Robert Belknap spoke in opposition, at which point I cut off discussion.

Belknap, a brilliant Dostoyevsky scholar, represented what no longer exists in our time: a decent, thoughtful, intelligently conservative, and entirely honorable. That was why he had been chosen for the steering committee of the FCRG. He was the right wing necessary to constitute the steering committee for the FCRG: the trusted conservative. A real conservative, he had my trust as a radical—the trust across those party lines that is lost today.

In both civil rights and antiwar activity, the student movement was impelled by fidelity to historic ideals of freedom, equality, and respect for others' dignity. Clearly, the occupation of university buildings in a student strike infringed on the normal process of education. Any labor strike disrupts normal life. Daily blanket bombings of Vietnam and Cambodia also disrupted normal life: they tore human flesh, burned hair and skin, and sundered communal societies. Secretive university agreements, not approved by the Columbia faculty according to university norms, agreements discovered by SDS, had inserted Columbia University into the government's war program through participation in the Institute for Defense Analyses.

I spent Tuesday, April 23, 1968, at home with my wife in our apartment in the Village, preparing our move to Yale that fall. The following day, I got out of the subway a stop early, at 110th Street, so as to have a short walk to

campus. As soon as I hit the sidewalk, someone rushed up to me breathlessly: "Do you know what's going on, Peter?" News of the occupation
of five buildings followed, the campus strike, the split between the black
students in Hamilton Hall and SDS—a deplorable split in solidarity. To
one whose role would be minor, that of a secondary participant and witness at most, the event was unquestionably an anti-Vietnam war demonstration with a secondary, symbolic black issue folded in. That secondary
issue gave Students' Afro-American Society (SAS) the leverage it needed
to break solidarity, claim Hamilton Hall, and demonstrate it was the can-
niest political player on campus.

That Wednesday morning, I paced up and down Broadway for twenty
minutes, trying to think through the situation. Obviously, the occupation
would end badly: that was a given. How badly was impossible to know. I
had little sympathy for SDS. But something else was at stake, a far broader
notion, that of the student movement. Outside the South and Harlem, students had inherited the leadership role in the political struggle for human
decency and social values. There could be no question of abandoning the
movement. It was a question of fidelity to a movement of history in which
I recognized myself. It was a matter of identification.

I hied myself up to campus. Philosophy Hall, occupied by the Ad
Hoc Faculty Group, was in disarray. It was packed. People milled about,
but with no sense of direction. "Membership" was entirely variable and
uncontrolled. Mediators made occasional reports at folding tables at the
east end of the room; at the west end, young assistant professors sat in bay
windows and on radiators, as well as a group of eight or ten secretaries,
patiently waiting, eager to be part of the work. As I walked into the large
meeting room, there were perhaps a hundred faculty. Even Mike Riffa-
terre was there—a great teacher, but no liberal! After a few moments, he
turned to me and said (I translate): "Don't they understand? We're being
prevented from teaching!" (*On nous empêche d'enseigner!*)

The crowd thinned out. An idea launched the previous day reached
me: a faculty presence at the occupied buildings. Turning to the secretaries, I asked, "What do you think would be a good tour of duty? Two
hours? Three? Certainly not more. Why don't you go ahead and draw up
24-hour schedules for each building that people can sign up for?" Within
half an hour, model schedules were ready. One was chosen; it was mimeographed and announced to the meeting. Members of the Ad Hoc Group

signed up for the hours and building of their choice. During the occupation, faculty presence at the occupied buildings was assured.

How did it all work? Why did individual faculty congregate in Philosophy Hall, sign up for tours of duty in front of occupied buildings to prevent a police cleanup of the occupied buildings, and regularly show up?
"How it all works" is a mystery for a generation that has lost the psychic
potential of identification: the "alienation" of Marxist thought. The faculty
understood its students because it identified with them and their humanistic and political values, as the students identified with the populations
they undertook to serve and—to the extent possible—represented, as well
as the unknown victims of their government's Vietnam aggression. That
potential for identification, which is prior to ideology, has disintegrated,
as philosophical thought shifted from class to singularity, from causation
to contingency, from the necessity of human community to the production of suspicion, resentment, and hate.

About halfway through a particularly heated debate, one of the secretaries called me to the telephone: "Professor Haidu, I think you'd better take this call." A young male voice, sounding very present, announced
police were massing in the tunnels even now: the bust was on for that
night. He brushed off my inquiry about his identity. Hanging up, I looked
for individuals I knew personally and could trust. Robert Hanning and
Nathan Gross reconnoitered the tunnels for me and reported back in
three quarters of an hour: all quiet on the tunnel front. Dirty tricks have a
long history on the Right.

Exhausted, I left Philosophy Hall and went to my office, hoping for
a nap. The office was empty, except for an unknown thirty-year-old in
blue jeans and an open shirt—definitely not a colleague. Leaning back
in a chair, his feet on a desk, hunched over a phone, he glared at me as I
walked into my own office, as if to say, "What are you doing here?" The
place crawled with undercover cops.

At one point, Immanuel Wallerstein reported to the Ad Hoc Faculty
Group. After his comments, in a personal and hesitant aside, I raised the
question of a more general uprising. He recognized the question immediately and cut through the indirection: "Peter, you can't have a revolution in
one institution alone." True enough, but that did not meet the question. It
would recur repeatedly. Terry Hopkins, a colleague of Wallerstein's, wondered about joining the radicals: I advised him to stay with the liberals.

One afternoon, I was walking with a friend on Broadway when Lew Cole of SDS came dancing out from campus—a tall, lean, agile, handsome guy, and a droll actor as well.

"Lew, what are you doing out here? You're supposed to be in Low Library." Herbert Marcuse was in town, somewhere on 72nd Street. Everyone who was anyone in the socialist register was paying his respects. Lew Cole did a stage lurch, and put on a heavy mock German movie accent: "I am going downtown to see Herr Herbert *Marcuuuse . . . und he vill tell me that this is not a prerevolutishionary situation.*"

It was a hilarious performance, but it occurred to me, even as Lew was doing it, that his fictional Herbert Marcuse was dead right, that this was not, in fact, a prerevolutionary situation, and that SDS, while a courageous and inventive student movement, represented nothing outside of itself and didn't take its own revolutionary role seriously. In traditional Marxist terms, it was what is called adventurism.

By Tuesday night, April 30, the bust, certain from the beginning, was finally on. Philosophy Hall, around 2 A.M., was empty. I took a last look around the large, elegant reception room, disheartened but also released: the pent-up frustration of operating as unofficial chief-of-staff with no voice in decision-making was finally over. The room was empty, strewn with twisted paper wrappers, chairs oddly positioned, lights illuminating nothing.

I walked back to each of the five buildings. At each building, faculty stood by choice. I discharged what I thought was my duty and made sure that everyone knew the bust was coming: everyone did know. They stood and waited. I ended up at Fayerweather. I was terrified. Gratefully, some white medical uniforms clustered against the night-dark wall of Avery: a doctor or two and some nurses. I went up to one of the nurses and handed her my glasses: "I have no idea what's going to happen. Can you hold on to these, please?" She smiled, an angel, and reassured me: "I'll keep them for you until afterward, don't worry."

Then I joined the faculty at the three or four rows of steps in front of the building, a group of thirty or forty. In the dark of 3 A.M., they suddenly crashed out before us, four or five rows of noisy, jangly, uniformed cops in full blue regalia, carrying long shields on their left arm, some kind of elongated mace in their right hands, their heads covered with tall helmets—modern police parodies of medieval knights. A budding medievalist, it was difficult for me to know whether to cower in fear or crack up laughing at how ridiculous these *Nieuw Yauwk* City Cops could be!

In fact, the uniformed cops were just a front, a make-believe distraction for the real action. Perhaps they were intended to terrorize. The real action came in the form of plainclothesmen, specialists in crowd control, superb at their job, small athletes in jeans and T-shirts who hunkered down and snuck in between the Blues. One by one, they jumped and grabbed the faculty geese standing on the Fayerweather steps, with absolutely superb execution. I was grabbed by one plainclothes cop and literally tossed one to the next, five in a row, until I found myself breathlessly standing on Amsterdam Avenue on my own two feet, totally unharmed. For people removal, there's no service like the New York City Police Department, 1968 vintage!

With one reservation: the kid-glove service provided to the faculty is to be contrasted with the removal of the students occupying the same building, in the same protest, the same night. Those students inside Fayerweather Hall were removed from the building by uniformed New York City Blues: some were dragged down a curved marbled staircase by the ankles, their heads bouncing against the marble steps, their skin cracked open, blood dripping out.

That contrast, in the bust of faculty and students, is instructive of a policy difference. If my treatment by the police was more or less typical, and most other faculty were treated similarly, someone decided to treat faculty gently and student occupiers harshly as a policy decision. It was not rogue cops going crazy on their own inside Fayerweather. It was a policy decision, in which the university probably had some participatory role, influencing the City Blues, who took orders.

As I stood on Amsterdam Avenue, catching my breath, the nurse came by. Smiling, she returned my glasses. Then suddenly, at my left, an angry shape materialized:

"This is all your fault, motherfucker."

So spoke Mark Rudd, a man I hardly knew. He had reason to be upset, the leader traditional "revolutionary" logic said should be preserved for the future action, feeling guilty at abandoning his comrades. But Mark Rudd, a leader?!

Columbia 1968 was an institutional disaster resulting from administrative incompetence: President Grayson Kirk and Vice President David

Truman were gone within a year. It has, however, had a long and continuing futurity. The innovative adaptation of the labor strike to the university campus for political purposes at Columbia in April 1968 transferred within a month to Paris in *Mai '68*, which overshadows it in cultural memory. More recently, Occupy Wall Street transferred the technique to public space. It has since spread worldwide. The process is perhaps not finished. The question—was Columbia 1968 a success or a failure?—does not have an obvious and easy answer. *Luta continua.*

Peter Haidu *('66GSAS) was born in Paris in 1931, emigrated to New York in 1940, and studied at Stuyvesant and North Hollywood high schools, the University of Chicago, and Columbia. He served in the US Army and taught at Columbia, Yale, and the Universities of Virginia, Illinois, and California. He was the author of several articles and two books,* The Subject Medieval/Modern *and* The Subject of Violence. *He retired to Brooklyn, New York, in 2008, where he died in 2017.*

ROBERT W. HANNING

Faculty, Department of English and Comparative Literature/
Ad Hoc Faculty Group

THE GREAT MORNINGSIDE RISING

Whenever I think of the tumultuous events of April 23 to 30, 1968—what I've taken to calling the Great Morningside Rising (or GMR) by analogy with England's Great Rising (formerly the Peasants' Revolt) of 1381—I tend sooner or later to focus on three incidents that touched me personally.

WHAT HAPPENED TO THAT BOY?

April 23 was sunny, and I took to lunch a young man whom the Columbia College Admissions Office had asked me to persuade to accept its offer of a place in the class of 1972. Returning to campus, we found it in an uproar, with the lobby of Hamilton Hall packed with students protesting Columbia's policies, in particular the construction of a gymnasium in Morningside Park (at the site of which, unknown to me, there had been an earlier demonstration), and preventing egress to Henry Coleman, the College's acting dean. In the mass of students, university officials and security guards that swirled in front of Hamilton, I became separated from my luncheon companion, never to see him again.

Since that day, I have often wondered about the effect on that young man of his unanticipated immersion in the opening waves of the rebellion that would soon inundate Columbia and fragment its polity: did he rush, terrified, to the subway, newly determined to choose any other college in preference to this madhouse? Or did a sudden exaltation, a vision of college life unlike, and more exciting than, any he had imagined, convince him that Columbia was *the* place to be? Alas, the press of succeeding events drove his name from my memory, so his decision must remain an insoluble mystery, one of 1968's many cold cases.

A TEARFUL PLEA ON A COLD, DARK NIGHT

It was the third or fourth night of the Rising, and as had quickly become the norm, 3 A.M. found me in 301 Philosophy Hall, the adopted "home" of the Ad Hoc Faculty Group whose attempt to mediate between the GMR's leadership and the central administration was doomed to fail. As my colleagues' discussions continued, I was unexpectedly called outside the building to meet three students, two young men and a young woman, who had asked for me. Having emerged from one of the occupied buildings, they had this urgent message for me to communicate to my colleagues: they themselves were ready to be arrested when the police came to evict the demonstrators, but the faculty must convince the administration not to let the police attempt to clear Hamilton Hall of its African American occupiers lest Harlem, in an act of righteous vengeance, burn Columbia to the ground, the prospect of which horrified them. As one of the young men made this plea, his voice quivering with chill, fear, and fatigue, the young woman began to cry, softly but uncontrollably. I promised to communicate their concern as requested, and they disappeared into the night.

I have no idea why I was chosen to receive this fateful message, nor did I ever see its bearers again and thus do not know their fate when the "bust" came. Although the university administration allowed plainclothes police—their badge numbers obscured—to use brute force to clear the other buildings, the evacuation of Hamilton Hall in fact took place without injury under the supervision of uniformed high police brass. At no point, to my knowledge, was damage to university property threatened by residents of Harlem.

BETWEEN HEDGE AND LEDGE: LOOKING BACKWARD, LOOKING FORWARD

It was quite a scene. Within Low Memorial Library a group of GMR participants were holed up, while students opposed to the occupation, calling themselves the Majority Coalition, had positioned themselves around Low's circumference in an attempt to block efforts by supporters of the GMR to supply provisions to the rebels. Tempers on both sides had grown shorter, and the potential for violence had grown accordingly greater, so the Ad Hoc committee, in keeping with its commitment to occupy middle ground, set up a cordon of faculty members, on the ledge outside the hedges surrounding Low, to keep separate the antagonistic groups.

I drew a long shift of guard duty with David Rosand, a graduate of Columbia College one year after me and an assistant professor of art history, as I was of English. We knew each other, but not well; however, as we shared stories of our Columbia education, we agreed that a high point was the "Colloquium on Important Books," a two-year seminar in which two professors guided twelve competitively chosen juniors and seniors through the canon of Western literature. Recognizing that the course appealed less to changing sixties intellectual tastes, we still felt its worth so strongly that before our tour on the barricades had ended we had decided to attempt to develop a course inspired by the Colloquium but focused on our shared interest in the art and literature of the European Renaissance. After many conversations (several in the West End bar) and much planning, we began a few years later to teach the undergraduate seminar "Themes in the Art and Literature of the Renaissance: Myths of Love" as an adventure in fully interdisciplinary instruction, and continued to do so, with some periods of hiatus, until my retirement in 2006. David, of course, went on to become the Meyer Schapiro Professor of Art History and a world-renowned specialist in the art of Renaissance Venice. Our course was my greatest undergraduate pedagogic experience; without the GMR would it ever have happened? I will never know for sure, but I doubt it.

The GMR was also a great chorus of voices, communicating its pain and desires in language often profane, always exigent. Soaring above this chorus was *liberation*, a word of broad and often paradoxical import within the GMR's social and political dynamic. During the GMR proper, "liberated" buildings were actually occupied and closed off to all but those who shared the views (and in the case of Hamilton, the ethnicity) of the "liberators." Then, during the post-bust strike, "liberated" or "liberation" classes were those that did not require crossing picket lines—I taught one—and might have their pre-GMR content modified to consider issues deemed central to the GMR (mine did not).

The embrace of "liberation" by the participants in the GMR signified their desire for freedom from what they saw as Columbia's restrictions on student power and behavior, and from its policies harmful to the surrounding community. Even more fundamentally, and most radically, "liberation" flaunted its repudiation of its evil semantic twins, liberal politics and liberal education: the former as front for a politically repressive, economically inequitable, socially unjust, and racist capitalism; the latter, supposedly a neutral haven for the free exchange of ideas, as deeply complicit in the policies and actions of a war-mongering federal government. "Liberation," from this perspective, was shorthand for a necessary reassessment and realignment of both the university and the larger society it served and mimicked.

How, then, does this many-minded term, with its status as a watchword for the GMR, also provide insight into my three personal GMR moments? As for the young man whose response to the occupation and liberation of Hamilton Hall remains a mystery to me, my recollection of him, present at the GMR's creation and choosing, like "Hercules at the Crossroads" in a Renaissance painting, to shun or embrace it, becomes a symbolic rendering of his generation's liberation from a single, preset path, eyes on the road ahead, toward a profession, a business career, or achievement in the arts or the sciences; there would now be the option of political awareness and activism integrated into one's higher education: an option that might involve pressing the university to act justly or fairly, without, one would hope, assuming the need, or grasping for the power, to shut it down or impugn its right to exist. Either path would be honorable, and now there were two.

The three young people who pleaded with me to prevent Harlem from burning down Columbia were conversely experiencing the weight of responsibility that inevitably accompanies a commitment to liberation. That they realized this responsibility more than some of their peers— who were paradoxically blinded by visions of power and triumph—and had achieved, even as they protested Columbia's policies, a sense of self-sacrifice in the face of a threat, however inaccurately conceived, to its general welfare was profoundly noble but also tragic. This was particularly so given the administration's corresponding neglect of its responsibility to protect all its students—and its faculty—from potentially baneful consequences of uncontrolled police intervention on the night of April 30.

Last but not least, my night with David Rosand between hedge and ledge outside Low initiated my personal liberation from a purely disciplinary approach to my teaching at Columbia. Indeed, the entire GMR, for all its troubles, frustrations and anguish, proved liberating for me in succeeding decades (although I would not willingly experience it again). Twenty years later, it was a vivid recollection of April 1968 that encouraged me to respond to a racial crisis on the Columbia campus by developing the undergraduate course "'Race' and Racism: Literary Representations of an American Crisis," which I taught almost every year for the past seventeen years of my Columbia career. I now know that a university, like any

Figure 17.1 Teaching an outdoor class during the Liberation School, May 1968. *Photograph by David Bogorad.*

institution, is always in need of reform. Thank you, GMR, for highlighting, however imperfectly, that need.

Robert W. Hanning *('58CC, '64GSAS), professor emeritus of English and Comparative Literature, M.A. Oxon, Ph.D. Columbia 1964. He taught at Columbia from 1961 to 2006, primarily as a medievalist, but also on issues of race and racism in American literature. The recipient of Guggenheim, American Council of Learned Society, and National Endowment for the Humanities fellowships, he now teaches pro bono in adult education.*

Graduate student, History Department and the Russian Institute

FROM COLUMBIA 1968 TO FORT LEAVENWORTH

My parents were refugees from Nazi Germany. Conversations at home were in German, something we tried to hide so that we could appear more American. We kept a clear separation between conversations within the family and our lives at school or work. That was partly a response to my parents' experience of living in Germany, in a perverted society that had tried to imprison and ultimately kill them. The wounds at home were always open though rarely discussed because it was too painful for my mother to speak about her parents, who were arrested, imprisoned for a year, and then, in 1942, murdered. My parents survived because a German soldier who had been a childhood friend of my father's knocked at the door in Cologne. My mother answered the door. After the required salute and "Heil Hitler," he told my mother that my father had to leave immediately because he was to be arrested the following day. "America was different," as my mother would point out. "In America, when there is a knock at the door, at least I know it's the milkman."

As World War II refugees, my family was helped by a relief agency, the Hebrew Immigrant Aid Society, with a loan and some training in chicken farming. That way they could start an independent life and leave New York and Philadelphia (where jobs were hard to find) and move to southern New Jersey after my father was able to make the down payment on a farm. He raised chickens, and my mother, who had been a concert violinist in Europe, cleaned about a thousand eggs each day and gave violin lessons. She was proud to carry certain traditions with her, and taught me to play the piano and my brother to play the violin. We focused on classical music, even though rock 'n' roll was the popular music among our peers, which gave me another reason to consider myself an outsider. I was a good classical musician who studied with a teacher from the Curtis Institute in Philadelphia, but I rarely performed publicly. The family *modus vivendi* was to be as inconspicuous as possible. A memoir I once wrote opened with the line: "Our family home was a bunker in New Jersey."

My parents instilled in me the importance of being aware of the political environment around us. The experience of Germany under the Nazis had made them acutely aware of the obligations of citizenship, even though, ironically, they had been deprived of their own citizenship in 1936. Human rights was an issue constantly discussed at home, with particular focus given to the treatment of African Americans, whom my parents related to because of their own treatment in their former homeland. Everyone, insisted my mother and father, was to be treated as equals. After all, the United Nations had a provision stating that it was the responsibility of every citizen to speak out if their government was acting in violation of the Universal Declaration of Human Rights.

Once I left for Douglass College (now part of Rutgers), I emerged from the bunker, joined the Student Nonviolent Coordinating Committee (SNCC) and threw myself wholeheartedly into the struggle to gain unimpeded voting rights for black people. Because students in a northern college town were geographically far from the focus of the problem, we organized an open meeting and brought in students from Americus, Georgia, to describe the conditions they had to tolerate in school. I couldn't say how much we actually helped the cause, but SNCC members at Douglass were deeply committed to spreading the word about the effects of racism. I always felt happier when I was more involved with issues I cared about and found myself surrounded by like-minded people. No longer did I feel like an outsider.

As an undergraduate, I focused on Russian language and history, and I planned to continue in area studies at Columbia University's Russian Institute, where I started in 1965. I quickly steeped myself in the history and culture of the Russian Empire, the Russian Revolutions, and the creation of the Soviet Union, and found it exciting to be studying such an important moment of civil insurrection while being simultaneously part of the Columbia University student community. The students were actively responding to issues of war and racism, as well as challenging an arbitrary and powerful university administration. As Russian Institute students, we wondered whether the protests on the streets that eventually overwhelmed Columbia were part of a broader revolution echoing in cities across the United States and Europe. Were the demonstrations going to turn into the Russian Revolution of 1905 or 1917? Of course, we didn't live in a monarchy, so our musings about a real revolution were always more fantasy than reality. The socially active students among us, however, felt an extraordinary sense of empowerment fueled by growing antiwar sentiment as well as the gnawing impatience with the painfully slow improvement in the civil rights of African Americans. We had the sense that we could and should push back against the university's plans for its gymnasium in Morningside Park and the research it was doing for war-related projects.

The year 1968 was a turning point for me. On the third day of the building occupations in April, I visited some of my fellow graduate students who had barricaded themselves inside Fayerweather Hall. Although I was excited to meet those who were committed to the issues about which I cared so deeply, I had little desire to stay and sleep in the building for a longer time. I felt compelled to help somehow, but I questioned the efficacy of protesting within the protective walls of the university. I was conflicted because I wanted to support the demonstrators and did so from outside Low Memorial Library. After the police bust, I asked myself what the demonstrations and sit-ins had accomplished. I appreciated that students closing down the university might effect a change in the university's plans for a gym in Harlem parkland, but I didn't feel that students holed up in buildings would contribute in any substantial way to changing governmental policy on the Vietnam War. The more I learned about soldiers going AWOL (absent without leave) and the stress on students fearing the draft, the farther from the real world the 1968 demonstrations at Columbia seemed. So I looked for another way to fight against the war and the endemic racism of American society.

In 1969, I began teaching European history at Bronx Community College, where the student body was at least 90 percent nonwhite. At the end of the first class, I was approached by several male students who were upset by the challenge of the course I presented on that first day. One student had tears in his eyes as he explained that if he didn't get a good grade in my class, he might be drafted into the Army. As an African American, it was also likely that if he were drafted and sent to Vietnam, he would be placed into the riskiest of battlefield positions. Among the students in the class were veterans of Vietnam who had explained the situation, so the fears of these black students were not imaginary. It was well understood that the number of black soldiers dying in Vietnam was far greater than the number of whites. No faculty member wanted to feel that a low grade could send a person to his death. This was a real crisis for us teachers, who spoke of "the insidious power of the pen." Some of the Columbia graduate students who were teaching at Bronx Community College, outraged that a poor grade might lead directly to being killed in Vietnam, gave no grades lower than A−. I didn't want to do this because I felt it might insult those students who were serious about learning and striving to better themselves, who took pride in their achievements and did not want to be given a grade that they did not earn. Instead, I explained the requirements of the course and was clear and specific about the assignments each student had to complete. I hoped that this contract between students and me would empower them, as it would give them control over how they might fare in the course, and that my way of doing things would make them feel less helpless and victimized. The next year, the lottery system— based on pure chance—was instituted, so grades no longer were the determining factor in how soon students would be drafted.

In 1968, as the war in Vietnam intensified, popular sentiment against the conflict grew, as did the G.I. antiwar movement, and reports of resistance inside the army began appearing in the underground press. There were large numbers of soldiers who went AWOL or refused battlefield orders, and so many instances of insubordination that the military administration became overwhelmed. I began learning more about the struggles of the American servicemen after the June 1969 uprising at Fort Dix, when one hundred and fifty prisoners took over three buildings. Several political organizers were arrested and charged with arson, rioting, and conspiracy. As details about the conditions in the prison were revealed by stockade prisoners in interviews with lawyers and friends, I became increasingly involved in the legal defense of the thirty-eight young men (mostly of color) who had been mistreated and sometimes beaten by the brutal guards. Racism was prevalent and the prisoners were kept hungry and thirsty. Some were tortured by having their hands and feet tied together behind their backs, then left on their stomachs for up to twelve hours at a time until the pain was unbearable. After the uprising, nineteen of the accused rioters were kept in solitary confinement for three weeks and were not permitted to contact their lawyers.

One of the first things I did after becoming involved with the support and defense of these American soldiers was to organize several fundraising evenings at the home of Barnard College Professor Peter Juviler, cofounder of the Columbia University Center for the Study of Human Rights, where I had worked. Together with Professor Juviler, I orchestrated evening events to raise money and disseminate information about the horrifying treatment of soldiers on the military base so close to New York City.

When it was possible to attend the courts-martial, I organized a class trip for my students, which was a great learning experience about the closed nature of military society. As a group, we could legally attend the courts-martial and offer support to some of the young soldiers, who had been in solitary confinement cells that measured six by four and had no friends or family to visit them or even write to them. It was horrifying to hear officers testify that they trusted the word of fellow officers over the testimony of enlisted men in the stockade. At the suggestion of the lawyer for Terry Klug, one of the soldiers I got to know, who was concerned about his isolation and state of mind during his trial, I pretended to be Terry's cousin, which meant I could write letters to him. He eventually was found not guilty of the riot and conspiracy charges associated with the Fort Dix 38 Case, but he still had to serve his prison time for being AWOL. Our correspondence continued for about a year on a daily basis, and I later traveled to Missouri to visit him in Leavenworth Military Prison. This was a frightening experience involving an incredible amount of security and hostile guards. Once there, I was troubled to learn that one of the youngest of the Fort Dix 38 soldiers had been raped. I wanted to help him, but it was impossible to help anyone inside those prisons walls.

After traveling to be part of the March on Washington in 1969, I attended a meeting with lawyers who emphasized the importance of helping soldiers protesting against the war. Several of us participating in the March met soldiers who sought help because they had escaped the stockade in Fort Benning, Georgia. We brought one of these men to New York, and I found myself involved in finding him a place to stay and locating a lawyer to defend him. Thereafter, I became an organizer of an underground network of people who helped soldiers on the run find places to live and then secure the necessary legal advice. Once we found a safe haven for each of the soldiers, I made contact with experienced civilian lawyers who knew the military justice system and could help find the right military base where each AWOL soldier might surrender. The hope was that we could find judges who would not sentence these men too harshly. In some cases, we helped soldiers leave the country, although that was not our primary goal.

The energy and commitment of the students at Columbia University in 1968 was critical in launching me into my work in the G.I. movement. I felt supportive of and connected with the student movement but distant from my fellow students who were protesting by sitting in and taking over buildings at the university. It was always important to me that I felt my actions were making a real difference to people's lives. For me, working with people who were forced to fight in an unjust war, and had to suffer the consequences of speaking out against the war while in the military, was critical. Negotiating with lawyers so they would represent young people who had overstepped the legal boundaries of the military and found themselves in trouble became a most meaningful part of my life during the American involvement in the Vietnam War.

Susan Eva Heuman *('67GSAS, '68SIPA, '77GSAS) is a visiting scholar at the Harriman Institute, Columbia University. She received an M.A. in history, a certificate from the Russian Institute, and a Ph.D. in history from Columbia University. She taught at Bronx Community College, Brooklyn College, and for three years at the University of Zambia in Southern Africa. She has taught at Pratt Institute, Manhattanville College, Baruch College, New York University, and the Center for Workers Education of CCNY. Her publications include* Kistiakovsky: The Struggle for National and Constitutional Rights in the Last Years of Tsarism *and articles on legal culture in Russia and the Soviet Union.*

NEAL H. HURWITZ

Columbia College alumnus/teaching assistant/Ad Hoc Faculty Group

THE ESSENCE OF SPIRIT IS FREEDOM

I arrived at Columbia University and Morningside Heights in the fall of '62 as a freshman in the College. I started Friends of Student Nonviolent Coordinating Committee (SNCC) at Columbia in the fall of '64, after Goodman, Chaney, and Schwerner were murdered in Mississippi. Our kick-off meeting in Hamilton Hall hosted SNCC fieldworker Marion Barry and family friend Dr. David Spain, who had performed the autopsies on the three murdered civil rights workers. We arranged speaking events with Julian Bond and James Forman, among the men and women putting their lives on the line to combat racism, and brought in Dick Gregory for a fundraiser. In the summers of '65 and '66, I worked on Project Double Discovery, a Columbia College Citizenship Council/Office of Economic Opportunity–funded program for talented but "underachieving" and "disadvantaged" New York City high school students, who lived on the Columbia campus and were tutored by undergraduates from the College and Barnard.

As a major in public law and government, I enjoyed remarkable classroom experiences and some great home visits with Julian Franklin, Herbert Deane, Alan Westin, Walter Metzger, Mark Kesselman, Allan Silver, David Sidorsky, and Joseph Rothschild. In the fall of '66, I started in the Ph.D. program at Columbia and worked for Professor Westin as a research assistant. Meanwhile away from campus, many of us were enjoying the folk music of Baez, Dylan, and the Weavers and, of course, the Beatles and Motown. I spent time at the Apollo Theater on 125th Street. "Black and white together" had long been a theme of my life. My parents, both committed to civil rights and friends with DuBois and Robeson, had sent me to P.S. 9 in Brooklyn—"The Brotherhood School"—and from the age of five in 1950 I was with them at many demonstrations and meetings.

I was twenty-three years old in 1968, one of the youngest faculty members at Columbia. I was sleeping late on April 23 when my girlfriend told me there was a big demonstration on campus and that it included members of the Students' Afro-American Society (SAS), which was unusual. We had not seen black students as a group at Columbia demonstrations before, but now, it seemed, black and white student leaders had joined to condemn university policies. I headed over to the sundial, then Hamilton, and stayed on campus until the bust.

One of the most salient features of Columbia '68 was that the occupation lasted as long as it did because of the presence of the disciplined black students in Hamilton Hall. It could be said that Columbia created the core of the black student group when, at that time, it admitted more blacks than ever into the College. The new leadership of SAS—notably Cicero Wilson—stood for a more active approach, just as did Mark Rudd, who displaced the more moderate leadership of the Columbia chapter of Students for a Democratic Society (SDS).

The Columbia administration asked Mayor Lindsay to evict the "whites" in Low, Math, Fayerweather, and Avery, but—afraid of a negative response from Harlem—to leave Hamilton alone. "All or nothing" was the response from Lindsay and the New York City Police Department (NYPD). Leaving the blacks in Hamilton but clearing out the others wasn't going to happen, so all five "liberated zones" had the freedom they needed through the weekend of April 27 and 28. The following Monday night, when the time came for the NYPD to clear the campus of protesting students (and so-called outside agitators), I was asked to be the faculty observer at Hamilton Hall. It was striking and anticlimactic to see the students line up silently in the building's basement, under the orderly control of the police and in the presence of African American attorneys who had spent days negotiating with the authorities, and exit onto Amsterdam Avenue, where police vans were waiting. No one was injured. The operation was done effectively and efficiently.

For years I have wondered whether the black student leadership ever told the Strike Steering Committee or SDS of their plans for a negotiated, peaceful departure. If not, why? And, if so, why didn't anyone let the occupiers of Low, Fayerweather, Avery, and Math know that such an arrangement had been made? This might have made the police ejection of hundreds from the four "white" buildings bloodless. It was clear from the start that Mark Rudd and the strike leadership were prepared to allow and even facilitate a violent police response on campus. I respected the decision of students to take a stand, but it was obvious that the Strike Committee was not willing to negotiate. Its leadership did not care that police on campus would be detrimental to all, something that many of us were aware of and that we on the Ad Hoc Faculty Group worked hard to avoid.

In the end, the black students of Hamilton—who had won on the issue of the gymnasium in Morningside Park—also decided that violence was not the best option. It is a great shame that President Grayson Kirk, Vice President David Truman, and the Columbia trustees failed to resolve the situation without police. We hoped for rational behavior and creativity on their part. (The faculty discussed the option of cutting off water and electricity to the occupied buildings and ending the Strike Committee's use of Ferris Booth Hall, the student center, but, instead, we had violence, including the destruction of Truman's Columbia career.)

My most important moments during those days were spent as part of the Ad Hoc Faculty Group (AHFG), which met in Philosophy Hall. After a visit from Truman, who told the assembled faculty that the police were about to be called in, the more liberal figures in the room decided they had a negotiating role to play, and so the AHFG was born, its purpose being to prevent police action on campus. Spending time in Philosophy Hall (I slept on a cot) with these dynamic and principled men—strong Columbia loyalists—was meaningful and exciting. I was awed and thrilled to be involved, serving with some of Columbia's best and brightest, almost all of whom were College teachers. As the leader, Alan Westin was formal and sharp as a tack. Manny Wallerstein would knead and then splice and dice the situation down to the essential nub. His brilliance was stunning, incisive. Walter Metzger had wide-ranging insight, and as the university expert on academic freedom, his voice was well heard and respected. Sidney Morgenbesser, the philosopher who ended up being black-jacked by police on the night of the bust, would stand behind me while addressing the group, pounding my shoulders as he made each "necessary" point.

There were no women and no blacks, if I recall correctly, on the AHFG. It did not occur to me then to think this was strange. I did note that key members of the AHFG, and a high number of the protesters, were Jewish. We knew that off somewhere else was a group of faculty "lions," men like Lionel Trilling, Fritz Stern, Daniel Bell, Eli Ginzberg, and William Leuchtenberg, an older cohort, men insistent that the university was at great risk and that the protesters must be stopped. Some of them likened the protesters to what Nazi and Communist youth had done to destroy democracies.

It was a tense and demanding time, and every moment of that week was an on-site lesson in politics, as informative and educational as anything encountered in the classroom. With neither side willing to negotiate, there was no middle ground to be found, and along with Westin, I realized our task was futile. There was also a sadness, because, as David Truman's memoir about 1968 shows, he felt betrayed by the AHFG, which positioned itself as a locus of power, as he saw it, against the administration. Most of us liked and respected Truman and expected him to succeed Kirk as president. But that was not to be.

If, as Max Weber wrote, "Politics is a strong and slow boring of hard boards,"[1] then Columbia '68 wasn't just politics. It was a protest, of course, but also a performance—a Happening, in the warm spring weather—produced out of great anger and much frustration created by the times, involving passionate and impatient young people, directed against a university seen as complicit with the evils of US policies in Vietnam and institutionalized racism. Columbia '68—mirroring national and world events—shows what an extreme situation looks and feels like: the tensions and costs, the hopes and possibilities, the interplay of personalities and roles, the dangers of extremism and complacency. (During breaks in the faculty discussions, I spoke with my dad, the poet and armchair Marxist whose brothers and friends were in the Abraham Lincoln Brigade and the US Army. "If you're going to make a revolution," he told me, "make sure you win.")

---

1. Max Weber, "Politics as a Vocation," in From *Max Weber: Essays in Sociology* (New York: Routledge, 2009), 128.

As for Columbia's proposed gymnasium in Morningside Park, which sparked so many students into action, it's worth noting that in his 2009 memoir *Underground*, a narrative of his life as an activist, Mark Rudd writes of an event held on the fortieth anniversary of the '68 protests: "Everyone present celebrated the fact that the precious Manhattan park [Morningside] had been saved from a ten-story concrete monstrosity."[2] Debatable. I have used Morningside Park since 1962, including running a softball team there, and Mark has no idea about that area (he admitted that he had never been to Morningside Park until April 23, when the crowd pulled down the fence around the gym site). There is no question that Columbia's planned athletic facility, to be constructed on public land with some percentage allocated for community use, was controversial, and that the university's poor reputation in the local community was well deserved. But to describe Morningside Park in 1968 as "precious" is a joke to people who for decades have tried to keep it safe, clean, and usable. Ask anyone who knows the park, and most will tell you that in 1968 it was a dangerous place. That "concrete monstrosity" might have been of great benefit to all, including the people of West Harlem. We'll never know.

The lessons of Columbia '68 are many, and keep on coming. At the fortieth anniversary celebrations, in 2008, certain protest veterans (most of them from SDS) claimed that the campus action had been a working-class event, that it wasn't middle-class students at the forefront. Nonsense. Certainly, plenty of students (like myself) were able to attend Columbia in 1968 because of generous financial assistance, but to call the events "working-class" is absurd. Rudd himself writes in his book that his parents paid "the whole tuition" and that they were able to afford two visits a week to the Columbia psychiatrist, Dr. Robert Liebert, a good friend of mine after the bust. In his 1971 book *Radical and Militant Youth: A Psychoanalytic Inquiry*, Bob discusses the economic background of the protesters. His analysis of arrest records led him to conclude that although 55 percent of black students had "working-class" backgrounds, only 6 percent of white students did. (The figures for middle-class students: 18 percent of

2. Mark Rudd, *Underground: My Life with SDS and the Weathermen* (New York: HarperCollins, 2009), 322.

Figure 19.1 The Ad Hoc Faculty Group meet inside Philosophy Hall. *Photograph by Gerald Adler.*

black students and 15 percent of white students; for upper-middle-class students: 28 percent of black students and 79 percent of white students.)[3]

Even something like our daily reading of the *New York Times* was instructive. It was as if the *Times* reporters were filing reports from another continent, following some party line regardless of the facts. The newspaper's view of events was refracted through a prism constructed by the trustees of Columbia University. Those intent on criticizing the self-righteousness of student activists in 1968 might also take note of the mendacity of The Establishment.

On June 4, 1968, during the university's official commencement ceremony, when Richard Hofstadter (in place of President Kirk) began to speak, several hundred students walked out of Saint John the Divine. They marched to Low Plaza, where the moderate, reformist organization I later led with Steve Silberblatt, Students for a Restructured University,

---

3. Robert Liebert, *Radical and Militant Youth: A Psychoanalytic Inquiry* (New York: Praeger, 1971), 76.

held what we called a Counter Commencement. Speaking there along with Harold Taylor, psychologist Erich Fromm told the assembled crowd that if, at some moments in human history, you aren't out of your mind, it means you don't have one. Perhaps 1968 was one of those times.

Let it be said that those participating in the political and cultural actions of 1968 were hopeful they could successfully challenge establishment conventions and so create a new, better social order, a just and sane society. For them, as for Hegel, "the substance, the essence of Spirit is Freedom."[4] Underlying the 1968 disruption at Columbia was a sense that the disgraceful status quo could be confronted and altered for the better. On a personal note, it was jarring for me that I had friends who I respected on all sides of the issues involving the occupation.

The hopes and dreams of the decade—with its participatory democracy, "black and white together," and sex, drugs and rock 'n' roll—ended for me with the violent death of Ted Gold, who had worked for me in SNCC, and the jailing for life of my College classmate Dave Gilbert. Both were very good people, smart and gentle, committed to societal betterment, but both undone by excesses of the era and, as my dad would say, their naïveté and incautious commitments.

For now, as always, regardless of setbacks, there is always hope. I have been committed to the Jewish idea of *Tikkun Olam* for a long time now. Lately it seems that we had better be so committed and work for necessary change, or face a dark night ahead.

Neal H. Hurwitz *('66CC, '77M.Phil) led the Friends of Student Nonviolent Coordinating Committee at Columbia University 1964–1965, and directed the Student Educational Exchange Roundtable at Project Double Discovery 1965–1966. He was a teaching assistant in the Graduate School of Arts and Science 1967–1969 and 1976–1977, and a leader of Students for a Restructured University 1968–1969, which helped created the Columbia University Senate. He was editor the West Side community newspaper* Wisdom's Child *and on the executive staff of the United Jewish Appeal. A father of four, Neal is a professional fundraiser for nonprofits and a new business development consultant.*

4. Horst Althaus, *Hegel: An Intellectual Biography*, trans. Michael Tarsh (Cambridge, England: Polity Press, 2000), 175.

TOM HURWITZ

Columbia College undergraduate/Mathematics Hall occupier

THE SMARTEST KIDS I'D EVER MET: MEMORIES OF A COLUMBIA REBEL

OCTOBER 1965

I was a new Columbia freshman. We wore sports jackets, even ties in those days. Standing on the corner of 116th Street and Broadway, waiting for the light, I looked down at the newsstand and saw a copy of *Viet-Report* magazine with map of Vietnam on the cover. I was happy to see a large map of the country because our commitment there was still new, and I kept confusing Vietnam with another Southeast Asian country. I didn't know much as I crossed Broadway that morning, but I knew that much was ahead of me.

Walking onto campus, I saw a large group of people gathered around the sundial in the middle of College Walk. This was a new experience for me, and I was curious to see what was going on. A young man was standing on the stone podium surrounded by a focused crowd, mainly young men in ties and jackets, and short haircuts—they turned out to be graduate students from the School of International Affairs, foreign service officers-in-training. The speaker, loose-leaf notebook in hand, was the center of their attention. Coincidently, it seemed that he had just finished making a speech about the growing conflict in Vietnam. Now he was taking questions. The crowd was hostile and vastly more informed than I was. I was sure this was about to turn into a shouting match or would lead to this guy's humiliation. The speaker, however, with his Boston accent, wind blowing his hair back, checking his loose-leaf notebook for facts, never faltered. Turning the intensity of his gaze from one grad student to another, taking each question in turn, fully in command of his facts and logic but always patient, he took each arrogant remark seriously. He carefully shot each one down, demolishing them. David Gilbert was simply the smartest kid I had ever seen.

They were all smart. That had been hammered home to me during freshman orientation, when I sat on a campus bench. The classmate to my right was a published poet, the one to my left used "mythopoeic paradigm" in his third sentence. They were all stunningly smart, and so many of them were radicals. My life at Columbia began right there.

APRIL 1967

Some of us are still in sports jackets. Several hundred are walking around the long rectangle of the John Jay Quad as Alexander Hamilton looks down on us. Shouts of "CIA must go" and "Marines must go" echo off the surrounding tall brick dorms and class buildings. Inside one of those buildings, the CIA and Marine recruiters are met with an illegal demonstration. Even more was now at stake. We knew the geography of Vietnam in detail and the faces of the residents of its destroyed villages. The war was being prosecuted on our campus.

On this spring day, the radicals were out in force, filling the quad. On South Field, the lawn that covered the lower half of the Columbia campus, were an almost equal number of students who were chanting and jeering against us. In the kind of simplified distinction that congeals in situations like this, they were the *jocks* and we were the *pukes*. They were angry and they wanted us gone. Each time I turned the corner of the short side of the rectangle, I would look through the buds of the cherry trees and see them, glowering and chanting back at us, "Pukes suck!" Our side would yell louder.

Something had sparked their furious opposition. Even a small growth in the Left had stimulated an equal and opposite reaction. Over the winter, over the previous years, Students for a Democratic Society (SDS) had been organizing in dorms, holding floor meetings, presenting information about and debating the war, trying to raise consciousness. At that point, I wanted none of SDS. As much as I agreed with them about Vietnam, organizations, radical or otherwise, felt counter to my nature. I was an anarchist. I was interested in *action*, not endless meetings and steering committee elections, *apparatchiks* always debating without actually accomplishing anything. Yet I had to admire the tenacity of their organizing.

SDS organizers were trying to get students, who were by nature apathetic, to see their stake in this war, from which they were still protected by student deferments. But no matter how many students agreed intellectually, the active Left was still tiny. When I had walked to the demonstration earlier, bunches of students were hanging out in the warm afternoon, chatting and playing catch, as the chants reverberated across the campus. Yes, we had to stand against these recruiters, but how could we turn a fringe group of demonstrators into a movement that could have some real effect? Could we be more than just a group talking to itself? I was about to find out.

Of course, jocks versus pukes was an oversimplification. There were athletes on our pukey side, and effete intellectuals on their jockey side. And there were tough kids on both sides, facing off as the yelling got louder and tempers got hotter. What did they hate about us—our shaggy hair and beards and girls versus clean-cut boys? Was it the culture clash? Was it sexual mores and drugs? They were insulted by us. They had invested their hearts and family money in getting a Columbia education—some were training for their sport, others were planning for a future in the upper-middle class. But it was something other than our style that they disliked. We had begun to believe that Columbia had to be held to more than academic standards. Not feeling isolated in our ivory tower, we had begun to live as though we were part of the whole world. Yes, youth culture—there were plenty of fringe jackets and skin jewels out that day. But we also were invading their ivy world with news of the war and its horrors, of the university's complicity in a system that led to the worst forms of injustice. We couldn't escape that knowledge. Now we were inflicting it on them, and they hated us for it.

The crowd of counterdemonstrators began to howl, then charged. Had we taunted them? I'm sure of it. Had they been working themselves into a violent mass? That was clear. Electricity shot through the demonstration. Girls, most of whom at that time could not imagine themselves fighting physically, drew back, as did many boys. But enough of us pushed forward into a wedge to stand against our enemies. Wow, I thought, this is going to be something new around here. I piled into the shoving mass. Fists began to fly. A head next to me snapped back, knees buckled. I stepped into the breach and, following through, connected. My fist on a cheek and nose above a white collar and tie. He backed off, blood flowing. I turned my head to see a bunch of big guys fighting on our side. A fist glanced off my head. Fights were breaking out all along the line. Then various university officers, deans, and coaches began working their way between us. Panting, we were pushed back. They were pushed back.

The lightning that had struck there on the east side of campus ricocheted around Columbia. The change in mood, from the Lion's Den coffee shop to the classrooms, was glorious, shining. The campus was polarized. It seemed that by the end of the day previously apathetic students were asking, "How can I join? What do we do next?"

MID-MARCH 1968

Who is going to throw the pie? I had just left the meeting, and was now standing on Washington Place, outside my building, looking for someone who could be a hitman.

Six of us had sat in my studio apartment in Greenwich Village, a point as far as we could get from Columbia campus, and planned an *attentat*. Of course, we didn't call it that—old anarchists did—but that was what it was. We called it "an action." The idea was to create an event so crystal clear, so dramatic, that it would be like the previous spring, when we had stumbled into polarizing the campus. A condition that forced people to take a stand, to move off their apathetic student asses and do something about the world outside their books and papers and grades and sex . . . or no sex.

A few weeks earlier, Mark Rudd had pulled me aside as we brushed by each other in the stairwell of Hamilton Hall. He had just returned from a leave of absence to go to Cuba, I had just returned from a leave of absence to make a film about radicals, hippies, and yippies in the East Village. He was deep in his work with SDS. I was being my individualist self. But we were both on fire.

Columbia was not. The extraordinary burst of political energy that the battles around jocks, pukes, and Marine recruiting had detonated on campus the previous spring had vaporized. Things had fallen back into the depressing routine of the Columbia winter. SDS meetings were dominated by a political tendency called the "Praxis Axis," which argued that the Left needed to do more organizing to "build the base." Mark's group, the "Action Faction," held that political action itself—demonstrations— would build the base. I had no use for either group. All that endless discussion was boring.

Mark and I, though, were both united in our furies—the war in Vietnam was proceeding, and Columbia was aiding it. Moreover, Columbia was treating the poor people of color in its surrounding neighborhoods like third-class citizens. We didn't love the alienated life on campus much either. We had both returned to find the semester starting as normal, the Left debating, and nothing and nobody changing. "I know you don't like the meetings," Mark said, "but maybe we can plan some actions outside the SDS debating society." He told me about a recent piece of political theater at Berkeley, in which a costumed character had put a pie in the face of a government official. Then he held up a printed announcement: "Draft Head to Speak on Campus." Col. Akst, the chief of Selective Service in the New York area, the head of the draft, was coming to speak to us. Wheels began to turn.

Then we were in my apartment, planning an action that we hoped would up the political ante on campus and move the movement past talk. At the meeting with us, in black beards, black jackets, and hats, were several members of Up Against the Wall Motherfuckers, an anarchist group of intellectuals and crazies. I had met them while making my film about the Lower East Side. They would create the diversion. Mark would provide the pie and safe house. Jeff would gather a few folks to help with the get-away. Stuart would work with me to build the diversion from the inside. I would recruit the pie thrower.

My idea was to find an out-of-town ringer, have him throw the pie, then blow town. I had no idea how I was going to find him, but after the meeting, I headed out into the street. It was the first warm weekend and the village was blooming with tourists and hippies, politicos, and junkies. On 8th Street I ran into a slightly wild-eyed, former Columbia student. I thought he might know someone, one of the kids who were now hitching and half-air-faring their way across country, per-haps from his home state of California, who might be crazy enough to be interested.

He didn't, but he had run into an old friend who had just given a ride to a bunch of folks from a Bay Area street theater company. A lead. He turned to leave, and around the corner came Patricia, his friend, with a bunch of San Francisco hippies in tow. Who's this? Lincoln. Would you be interested in an adventure? Maybe. Bingo.

The March 21 issue of *Spectator* told the story. Col. Akst had just begun speaking about occupational deferments to a moderately sized audi-torium in Earl Hall, the religious services building. Suddenly I and my militarily attired friends from the Lower East Side, carrying a flag, play-ing flutes, and banging drums—"Yankee Doodle Dandy"—came busting through the back door. Peter K. and a bunch of SDS-organized "defend-ers of free speech" began fighting with us. Through our pantomime, I saw all faces turned toward us. Then, while attention was on us in the back, at the front of the room there was a flash of beard darting left. Lincoln, pie already on the wind-up, took two steps and made a perfect hit. Cream pie was dripping from a military face onto a crisp uniform. The place erupted. I saw sunlight as the side door burst open and the hitman vanished, with racing comrades, onto the fire escape. My gang—both sides of the fight—also retreated into the brilliant spring day. Later, I found out that Mark had stood, allowed Akst to begin his retreat, and announced, "Colonel, you have gotten your just desserts!" Lincoln vanished into the safe house of Mark's girlfriend's apartment, and thence to New England. Neither he nor anyone else involved was ever identified.

APRIL 23, 1968

It was just before noon. As I exited the subway and crossed Broadway, I was feeling especially apprehensive because the meeting to plan the rally had been particularly dispiriting. Would we get a crowd? A lot was riding on this demonstration. Six students had been threatened with suspension for protesting inside school buildings, against the Institute for Defense Analyses (IDA), Columbia's weapons research program for the Vietnam

War. Now we were once again trying to raise the stakes, while protecting our leadership. I was a graduate of a season of street demonstrations, filming them and their planning, and then being part of them. My job was to help marshal our march, large or small, into Low Memorial Library. Another illegal indoor demonstration.

The Students' Afro-American Society (SAS) had agreed at the last minute to cosponsor the rally. Right-wing students were standing in a line across the steps directly in front of Low, protecting our target, the administration building. It was jocks versus pukes all over again. History was repeating itself, first as tragedy, then as . . . We didn't know yet.

The crowd looked big, then it became huge. I took up my position at the back of the rally with a few other marshals. The idea was that we would gather around the sundial—where I had seen David Gilbert three years before—and hear speeches from leaders of the participating student groups, and then turn and march up into Low. That was the part I was there for, when the back of the rally became the front of the march. I listened fitfully to the speakers. My mind was working on tactics for when we began to move. A head-on, jock–puke confrontation was out of the question. We had numbers on our side, by far, but they held the high ground at the top of the wide granite steps. We couldn't overwhelm them with numbers because only the first row would make contact with them as we pushed upward. Once again, I thought of a diversionary feint. There was another door into Low on the east, to the side of the steps. It was a security door and always open. I huddled with a couple of other marshal types, at the edge of the crowd of perhaps six hundred. We tried to keep out of earshot of various deans and faculty who were deployed by a fearful administration. We were figuring out who would do what when it was time for the inevitable charge.

Or was it inevitable? Some kind of conference was going on behind the sundial. Then Mark Rudd announced to the crowd that David Truman, Columbia's vice president, had sent us a letter. He told us that the doors of Low Memorial Library had been locked and proposed that we meet with him and express our grievances inside McMillan Theater. Truman would chair the gathering. The proposal, designed to waste our energy in useless controlled debate, was unacceptable. What should we do now? The speakers were arguing the question, suggesting various scenarios. Go to this building? Go to that building? Set up a picket line?

I couldn't believe it. In inimitable SDS fashion, the leaders, when presented with a vital tactical decision, reverted to type and started another boring meeting. I was walking through the crowd, pushing my way toward the sundial. We were losing the momentum of the rally. Did the Chinese People's Army hold a meeting when it had to cross the Luding Bridge? Mark actually was taking suggestions and comments from the audience. I reached the sundial and stood next to it. The entropy among the leaders was palpable; they were at a loss. Searching for an answer, Mark's eye caught mine. "Tommy, do you have a suggestion?"

Sometimes, at moments of high drama, time slows down. This time, it was as if I had pressed fast-forward. Immediately, I was on top of the sundial—the faces of the students looking up at me—and mumbling, "As far as I'm concerned we didn't come here to talk." Then loudly, "We came here to march on Low, so I think we should march on Low." That was my suggestion.

I thought I was walking back to my position between the people and Low. But I wasn't. The crowd was turning itself inside out and following me—including the leadership of SDS. We were marching on Low!

When I realized what was happening, we were already at the first set of steps. I grabbed a few other marshals. "Let's charge the jocks hard on the left side. Head everybody in that direction. When those guys move over to block us, you all take Mark and the middle of the march and sweep over to the right, around Low and into the security door."

We moved left up the steps. The jocks all raced toward us to get a punch in at the pukes. Then the march surged right, through the opening in the jock line and around Low. We had out-maneuvered them. Then, after a brief skirmish, the cops on the security door held firm. Two Barnard girls stood on a bench and shouted, "To the gym!" The Battle of Columbia had begun.

APRIL 24–30, 1968

By this time, I had gotten much better with meetings. I could even sit against a wall, put my head down on my knees, and sleep for a half hour while the talk went on. We had met all day in Hamilton, where we wound up after leaving the gym site. Then, close to dawn, we were expelled by SAS. We had met for two days in Grayson Kirk's office, into which more and more people crowded, when it became clear that we would not be immediately arrested.

Late Thursday night, JJ had led a few of us out of the huge windows, to jump into the cool night and run a hundred yards to Mathematics Hall. It was an inside job. A junior faculty member opened the door for us, just the way a security guard had gotten us into Low. Mathematics was to be the next occupied building . . . and meeting venue.

The first task was to barricade the place. We had debated for twelve hours whether to barricade Hamilton. The blacks had grown even more bored than I, kicked the white students out, and barricaded the place themselves. In Low, there was no way for us to defend the whole cavernous building, so holding the president's office was just a matter of pushing some desks against doors and bringing new communards in the windows. In Math, we built great barricades. Those who had joined together to take the building were self-selected militants. Who else would have struck out in the middle of the night to do this? Boy and girl radicals, the best of the best, flocked to us. Some would come to call it the Smolny Institute, where the Bolsheviks had their revolutionary headquarters. Now we had to make the place safe—or at least safe enough to stop the right-wingers and to slow down the cops when they came—safe for our meetings.

What in God's name were we meeting about? Aside from how to run an impromptu commune of several hundred and to feed them and keep them safe, SDS and the strike had a major problem that had haunted us from those first moments on the sundial. Remember all that organizing, educating, and base-building that the Praxis Axis loved? It turned out that even that had not been enough. The building seizure had attracted more than a thousand participants, and vastly more sympathizers, but they were neither unified nor disciplined. SAS had around a hundred black students in Hamilton Hall who agreed to follow their steering committee. SDS had only twice the members, but we had thousands of (more or less) supporters. Making decisions, negotiating, agreeing on demands, abiding by discipline, and making policies the way any leadership had to do in the midst of desperate struggle all needed the support of participants, or else people would simply leave the buildings, the picket lines, the support work, and go back home. To gather that support at each stage, we had to meet, agree, and meet some more.

And so we went to work on the barricades, quickly, with many hands. The architects and engineers among us found building materials, wedged furniture precisely. We blocked doors, tunnels, and windows, figured out a safe and sealable entrance. We all worked together. We found we had a kitchen for our food, and there was our first breakfast to make. There was a library to keep safe. Now we had a building to house our com-mune. In those first hours, certain bonds began to form between us all. We had been through three endless days, certain we would be attacked and arrested within hours, desperately holding to six demands, only four of which most of us could remember offhand: no gym, no IDA, drop the ban on indoor demonstrations, and amnesty. We also had to make lunch, keep clean, and take care of each other. Everyone's talents emerged and were utilized. You're an artist? So make some posters. A bagpiper appeared and serenaded us, the drone of his tunes echoing in our stair-well. Someone hacked the university telephone system, and we could talk to each other. Walkie-talkies appeared in all the buildings. By the time we began to make Mathematics Hall our home and fortress, we had become a form of brilliant family.

Families have histories, though. We had none. We were making history. However we had gotten there, we were boys and girls, working and living together, crying out with our bodies for humanity and for our beliefs, and for a while, we were winning. When I remember the four days at Mathe-matics, they are suffused with a certain glow, an indwelt spirit of human possibility. It was youth, freed from its ties to chronological age, from its bonds of anxiety, uniting comrades in the purity of our ideals.

There was another, more down-to-earth aspect of the time in the build-ings. Columbia was a single-sex school. I and most of my friends had seri-ous girlfriends. Barnard was across the street, and a few Barnard students always attended our classes. But aside from a few forced mixers, there were almost no places in our lives for men and women to mix casually in a shared environment. I had never met more than few Barnard women before. Here, together, we built barricades, fixed meals, sang songs, told each other sto-ries, cleaned up, danced, fucked (yes, sometimes), and of course had meet-ings. Women did not chair the meetings, but they spoke at them. Equality, even as an ideal, was blurry at best, but we were in it together.

The first day in Math was filled with preparations for the cops. We taught each other passive resistance techniques, learned years before in the civil rights movement. We found industrial quantities of green soap and deployed it to the various floors of the building, ready to pour on the steps and slow the advance of the police. Would cigarette filters pushed into our nostrils work, as Suicide Sid suggested, against tear gas? We tested and retested the barricades. We felt prepared. Then the university and the New York City Police Department obliged by not busting us on our first day. Our best days were the next ones.

It was crazy warm, and the afternoon sun was flooding the side of Math that faced Broadway. Thirty or forty of us were sitting on the stone window ledges, signs deployed, announcing our strike to the neighborhood with chants and songs. Picketers were supporting us on the street below, neighbors who had been injured by Columbia's landlord policies in the hundreds of buildings it owned. A clarinet played "Down by the Riverside." A city bus pulled over. The bus driver passed his hat among the passengers and dumped the proceeds into the bucket that we lowered thirty feet to the sidewalk. All day long, people came by to donate grocery bags of food. Far from being in an ivory tower, we felt we were speaking for the entire city. One day, crowds from a peace demonstration in Central Park marched up to cheer us. One night, I sat on the campus window ledge, doing my four hours of guard duty. A beautiful Barnard student, who later would become my girlfriend, was my guard partner in the fragrant night.

A red flag appeared on our roof, a portrait of Che in our entrance window. Over the days, new communards, several of them from beyond Columbia's borders, came through the window to join us. Tom Hayden, a writer of SDS's founding document and brilliant organizer; Bruce Spector, a graphic artist; John Sundstrom, from Up Against the Wall Motherfuckers (the group that helped me with the pie incident); Jerry Long, with a few older members of the national SDS; and several others. Without saying so to each other, we realized that we were tired of our own limited perspectives, those that had given us the sterile meetings of the old SDS. We began to look to these slightly older guys for leadership. Hayden, a master at finding consensus, began to chair our meetings. Calm, clear, and patient, Tom took the democratic helm.

We would meet for hours every day. Runners from strike headquarters in Ferris Booth Hall, the student center, came with news and the need for votes. Sometimes Mark Rudd, Juan Gonzalez, or another member of the Strike Central Steering Committee joined our meetings, somewhat deferential to the tough Math kids, to make sure we would stand firm. Fayerweather was wavering on the amnesty demand. Fayerweather was always wavering. It was the one building that had not self-selected its founding occupiers with a militant action like ours, and it also had an open-window policy. Therefore, its essence was "mass"—people with various levels of commitment, holding different reasons in their minds for why they were there. Every few hours, they seemed likely to vote to give up amnesty. How could you end a strike without amnesty? It meant we would agree that we did not have the right to do what we did. Send over a delegation. Then, another one!

One day, JJ and several other recruiters came (again) into our meeting. In the morning, the jocks—who now called themselves the Majority Coalition—at their coaches' urging decided to circle Low and blockade the windows, the gates to the commune. They were trying to starve out the Low strikers. Our people were succeeding at throwing food over them, but their presence was an insult to the strike. We stopped our meeting and sent a detachment to join in.

I was not a leader of this attack, just a foot soldier. There was no diversionary action this time. About fifty of us, feeling way too powerful, ran in a circle around Low, getting our momentum going, and giving the front line of the football team plenty of warning to deploy themselves defensively. Then, we turned and charged into a place where reinforcements quickly could gather. I ran full tilt into a guy with a blazer (I am six foot two, he was four feet wide). I bounced off him. After a few minutes of pushing, punching, and bellowing, they fought us off and we retreated, rubbing our bruises. Was food even ready to rush to our people if we did break their line? I never found out.

Let me tell you a secret. In insurrectionary events, there is a kind of bipolar mass personality disorder. I understood this finally when I was in Cairo during the failed revolution, filming in Tahrir Square. Every day, the news came rattling through the crowds on campus, the sectors of the square, the breakfast tables in the press hotel, the buildings of Columbia: "the bust is going to come tonight," "Mubarak is going to resign tonight," "Kirk and Truman are going to negotiate and agree to our amnesty," "the tanks are beginning to move," "the Tactical Patrol Force is outside," "those crazy guys on camels are coming back." Our moods changed according to each whispered bulletin.

Our particular mood swings started with the ecstasy of being inside a new world. How to describe it? If you haven't felt it, I can only allude to it. For these minutes, hours, and days in our struggle, the pettiness of our normal personal strivings dissolved. In Tahrir, the Christians defended the Muslims in prayer. The Muslims carried crosses tied to their crescent flags. In Math and the other buildings, the cold alienation of life on campus vanished in creative friendship. Behind our barricades in both places, we defended ourselves from an enemy with vastly superior force, but over which we had moral superiority. We both provided medical care. And always we fed each other. I can only say that anyone who was there, at either place, will never be the same, because we glimpsed the promised land of *caritas*, of true brotherly-sisterly love.

The other end of the pendulum swing is abject fear and despair. An ultimatum was passed down, a deadline was set, and the end of our ecstasy was sure. We were splitting apart.

In Mathematics, we started the last day on a high. In our meeting, we set up a real government structure for the two hundred of us. We decided to elect our own steering committee. We voted in our elders, with Hayden leading. All necessities—food, communication, political education, joy—were provided for. We could run ourselves for the next six months. And when we were finished, we danced. To whom? The Temptations, of course.

Then we crashed. The news we dreaded finally came . . . little things tipped us off. The cops were amassing on Broadway outside our windows, amassing and disappearing all Monday. By evening, we were sure of it. I was in charge of the defense of our commune. "Defense" is somewhat grandiose, but we had been living in a world with many threats and we kept ourselves safe. Now, as word ran back and forth across the campus ("the cops are on College Walk," "they're taking the blacks out of Hamilton Hall"), we knew it was just a matter of time. Water was turned off, phones were dead, and electricity was cut. The defense committee shut and barricaded the last window and sloshed the industrial green soap over the stairs. This bright home of ours became a kind of cave, fearful eyes shone in the flashlights. The police lights from outside made crazy shadows on the ceiling. A garbled megaphone echoed a written order.

Because we could not come to a unified position, we decided in our last sweet meeting that people would disperse around the building in groups based on how they wanted to be arrested—walk out and obey police, second floor; passive resistance, third and fourth; more physical struggle, fifth. The defense committee would face whatever the police decide to throw at us in the lobby, behind the barricade. In Math, the lobby sat below the entire staircase. Five stories of pale faces looked down on us as the doors were jimmied open.

We were singing. We were chanting our demands. Yet this was a strangely calm moment, as cops went about being moving-men, extracting the furniture, once a barricade, and passing it out, chair by desk by file cabinet. They were blue shadows, hulking back and forth as searchlights passed across their backs and into our faces. "Up against the wall, motherfucker!" (we're Math, after all). Then the first helmet appeared in the well of the entranceway. We, the defense committee, stood above them, atop a short flight of stairs. Five more helmets appeared. The last of the barricade was vanishing quickly. Suddenly, falling from five flights above, a chair crashed between us and them. "Up against the wall, motherfucker!" Then another. This was nuts! No matter what we did, we were at their mercy. Did we want to start this off by killing a cop? I put up my arms and yelled, "Stop!" Everything went silent. A *Daily News* guy took a photograph from behind twenty policemen. There I was in the paper, with my arms still raised, eyes as wide as hubcaps, scared shitless.

The irony of the night is that we who stood right in front, who expected to face the brunt of the frustrated cops as they charged into the building, were walked or carried into the night, with its headlights and spotlights, past our pile of former barricade. They had beaten the pacifists sitting in front of Mathematics, but they only held their clubs as they took us to our paddy wagons in handcuffs. As they reached the upper floors, however, away from the view of press, and even other strikers, they beat the crap out of us, dragging our people with their heads banging on each step, down the stairs made slippery by our famous green soap.

The far greater irony is that whatever the administration thought it would solve by calling the wrath of the Tactical Patrol Force down upon

Figure 20.1 Tom Hurwitz (standing) demonstrating to occupiers of Mathematics Hall how to defend themselves from the police, as Tom Hayden watches. *Photograph by Charlotte Von Segesser.*

us, the result was earth-shattering. Now, we would win all our demands in the end. The president and vice president would resign, and Columbia would be changed forever. So much of that amazing spring was yet to come, but our earthly paradise was gone.

Tom Hurwitz *('70CC) is a member of the American Society of Cinematographers, winner of two Emmy Awards, and recipient of the Sundance and Jerusalem Film Festival Awards for Best Cinematography. He is a founding member of the faculty of the MFA program in Social Documentary at New York's School of Visual Arts and a member of the Kamera Kollectiv NYC. He has photographed films that have won four Academy Awards and earned several more nominations. Tom is a seminary-trained liturgist and a verger at New York's Cathedral of St. John the Divine, helping to oversee weekly services and the great holiday liturgies of the world's largest Gothic cathedral.*

MICHAEL JOHNSON

"Outside agitator"

WHO BE THE DOMINATOR?

O n April 23, 1968, I was living on 108th Street and Broadway, just a few blocks from Columbia. One of my three roommates, Matt (not his real name), was a doctoral student at the university, and one morning he returned from class to announce: "The school's on strike. I'm going to eat something, then go back."

"I want to go with you," I immediately said, at that time a twenty-six-year-old lad who recently had exited from a Benedictine monastery, followed by an escape from the plains of Texas and Kansas. I had plenty of free time since dropping out of NYU Law School a few months earlier (after just two months of classes) and then resigning from a job in a Newark public school at the end of March.

I had arrived in New York City in September 1967, and when I went up with Matt that morning, it was the first time I ever had walked on the campus. Even so, it was immediately clear that ordinary realities had been curbed, that the school's regular culture had been interrupted, and that many people were grappling with how to come to terms with the new reality that had descended on them. Over the course of that day, I picked up many pieces of the dynamically unfolding puzzle.

Being at Columbia with all this new energy was fascinating and exhilarating. And not just for me. I wouldn't have been surprised if there were hundreds of outsiders on campus. No one was asking, "What school are you in?" Full of life on the issues that overnight had taken on such resonance, hoping to connect with anyone who might have an opinion, we all were talking about what was going on. Old rhythms and patterns had been put aside, replaced by a kind of helter-skelter scrambling to understand what was happening. It felt as if everyone—students, faculty, administration, janitors, and outsiders alike—was communicating with each other in new and honest ways. "What is education, after all?" I asked a student who was complaining that his schooling had been disrupted by protesters and building occupations. "What other event have you ever been involved in that has generated so much discussion?" It was as if classes had ended and learning had begun.

Later on that first day, I spoke out at an ad hoc meeting (the only kind that seemed to be taking place) of graduates from across the university. Eventually the group turned to the main purpose of their gathering: choosing two representatives to the newly established Strike Coordinating Committee (SCC), a group that operated out of the student center on campus and had at least nominal control over the direction in which things were flowing. The floor opened for nominations, and someone put up my name. Surprised, I rose to explain that I wasn't a student at Columbia and that it was actually my first day ever on campus. Matt jerked me back down into my seat before I could say anything. Once elected, I had a first-class ticket on an experiential learning trip into the heart of democracy-in-the-making. Or so I thought at the moment.

Students for a Democratic Society (SDS), in the weeks and months before April 23, had made several attempts to drum up protest against Columbia's expansionary—nay, "colonizing"—schemes in the neighborhood and the university's involvement with the Defense Department, but little had come of it. The coalition forged between Columbia's Students' Afro-American Society (SAS) and the campus chapter of SDS proved to be short-lived. On the first night of the protest, with Hamilton Hall seized, SAS members asked all the white students to leave and seize another building. And so it went, with the demonstrations eventually succeeding beyond SDS's wildest dreams. The taking of Hamilton and the president's office in Low Library was followed by the occupation of three other buildings, then the call for a student strike, which quickly took hold across the entire campus. It was a major coup. In a flash, they had a national, even international, event on their hands, reported daily by the *New York Times*.

But in my role as a representative to the SCC, I began to understand that SDS didn't really have a handle on the campus happenings. It was more an organization holding a tiger by the tail, which might quickly devour it whole. My reading of the situation was that SDS obviously had tapped into—and, no doubt, helped create—a spirit of creative discontent on campus, an "enough is enough" feeling that fueled an uprising that became a historical leftist event. There was, however, a fatal flaw. SDS planning—insofar as anything those days was planned—was based on righteousness as well as on unrealistic goals and expectations, not the realities of how the politics of modern-style democracy actually work. I look back from today and see that I shouldn't have been too surprised by this. There is, after all, a well-worn historical pattern that uprisings and revolutions mostly follow. First comes the overthrowing of the ruling party, then descent into chaos, followed by the creation of a new form of ruling party. It's a full turn of the wheel, rarely a breakthrough onto a new transformative path. Think the French Revolution, the Russian Revolution, Castro's Cuba, and so on. I look back and see myself at Columbia in 1968, immersed, in real time, in that pattern.

The night of the police bust, when I stood with a group outside Fayerweather Hall awaiting the cops, I was lucky to escape without serious injury. It seemed like SDS was in triumphant spirit after that night, as if they were now expecting that the strike would flourish. The masses would rise up, having finally witnessed for themselves the truth. The evil of The Establishment had been demonstrated for all to see!

Soon afterward, a meeting was held to draw up the official strike demands, which would be followed by the official assembling of the SCC. Three or four hundred protesters, maybe more, came together the evening after the violent ending of the strike. This was to be the great democratic meeting of a new populace, facilitated by SDS. The intent, I believe, was to begin the transfer of the ad hoc authority of SDS to students and their representatives, who would carry on now that a beachhead for revolution had been secured. Something like seven major demands were proposed. Six were approved, more or less unanimously. On the demand for amnesty for those provoking and actively participating in the strike, the house was split down the middle. After meeting and discussing and proposing and voting for more than two hours, our democratic forum of exhausted protesters was confronted with a profoundly divisive issue and without any kind of a "direct democracy" protocol for handling it.

We actually tried to do it by a show of hands! Picture a handful of SDS leaders on a platform in a large, poorly lit room, trying to count a milling and jabbering crowd of more than three hundred exhausted militants, eager to move on to the West End bar and other watering holes. Chaos. I was against the demand for amnesty. I was also part of a gang of five or so who realized there was no way for a coherent, much less binding, resolution to come out of this divide in such a rapidly deteriorating situation. The count the leaders came up with was something like 175 to 170. This was obviously unacceptable. If we were to come up with an acceptable outcome, there had to be another vote with much more control of the crowd and the noise. It was decided that several spokespeople who sat on the Committee would be allowed to voice the arguments for and against amnesty.

Drawing on our inner collective Machiavelli, we went backstage to plot how to prevent approval of the amnesty demand. Since two of us were on the Committee, we secured a spot to present our argument, which we wrote out in less than twenty-five words. We rehearsed our spokesperson several times, making sure he came across logically and clearly, loud but not too loud, simply but not simplistically. He did a great job. Again, the vote was too close to call, which was our immediate objective. A motion to postpone the vote until the next meeting was overwhelmingly approved, and the vast majority was gone within minutes. The next day, I attended a meeting of the SCC, in a campus classroom. We representatives were sitting on the student seats, the SDS organizers were on the dais at the head of the group. The amnesty demand came up for discussion and vote. I don't remember which way the vote went, just the final tally: 17–16, with no discernible way forward. At that moment, I realized the uprising was over and that I wouldn't be returning for any more votes. I had no expectations for anything new to emerge.

In the end, the Columbia protests were fundamentally about the politics of domination. The university administration was representative of maximal, top-down control, with elites imposing themselves on everyone else, and for years, the result on campus and in the surrounding neighborhoods had been a minimum of actual democracy—that is, people talking to each other about common concerns and resources in the hope of reaching meaningful agreements. This is what was being protested. In April and May 1968, however, clearly some devious (to my naïve eyes) political calculus was at work. I was beginning to see that what SDS and I were doing—the imposition of one agenda over another—wasn't any different from what the Columbia administration had been doing for all those years. SDS leadership felt it should be running the show and was determined to do almost anything to make that happen. I was aiding and abetting. Yet that leadership quickly reproduced—so ironically, right there in its zone of liberation—the very dynamics it was rebelling against. I watched, without really understanding but definitely feeling, this depressingly self-defeating act, being played out in bits and pieces, yet not knowing what to do about it. In the end, I came away from my experience of the Columbia student strike deeply convinced that, in spite of everything I had been told growing up, "the world doesn't work." Convinced but distraught. If the "counterculture" is, at its deepest level, as flawed as the "establishment," what are the alternatives?

Some moments in human history are explosions of raw energy, when a collective conviction arises that things can work far better than they actually do. A new situation emerges, and suddenly, we sense how enormous the possibilities are without fully understanding all that is involved. Allied to this is the myth that if we arouse the democratic passions of the masses, true liberation will follow. This, I now know, is a conviction without any historical basis and that too often blinds us, obstructing the evolution of genuine democracy in favor of an illusory, shining mirage. Beware of the rage and fervor that prevents any significant ownership of responsibility for the predicament in which we find ourselves, that leaves us desperate and grasping for a fix.

Michael Johnson *has been involved in group dynamics and community organizing since 1973. He cofounded Ganas, an intentional community in New York City, in 1980 based on cooperation produced by open communication and an empowering approach to accountability, which is thriving today. He has been researching, writing, and organizing in the cooperative–solidarity economic movement since 2007. He blogs and is published at Grassroots Economic Organizing, and is a coauthor of* Building Co-operative Power. *He is currently working on a book tentatively titled* Growing Democracy: Cultural Strategies and Transformative Processes.

Barnard undergraduate/Strike Coordinating Committee

THE MORAL OBLIGATION TO ACT

T he strike at Columbia was ignited by the proposed construction of the university's new private gymnasium in Morningside Park, but issues of racism and opposition to the war in Vietnam had been permeating campus life for years. Beginning in the mid-sixties, Students for a Democratic Society (SDS), and other antiwar groups at Columbia began organizing a student body that was becoming increasingly politicized by civil rights demonstrations and protests against US involvement in Vietnam. From 1965 on, there were teach-ins, endless nights of dorm organizing, demonstrations, speeches on the sundial at the center of campus, and marches against the Reserve Officers Training Corps. A constant stream of written material was distributed at the university gates on everything from the need for more daycare to Columbia's involvement in research that supported the war effort. Students were driven by the belief that they had a moral obligation to act. Columbia was just one of thousands of places across the country protesting our nation's priorities. One could feel the surge coming politically, culturally, and psychologically.

These strong moral beliefs that pushed the movement forward were forged from a complex weaving of strains that began in the wake of World War II. We had grown up amid discussions about the war, and many of us came from families that had been affected directly by the war and forced to flee Europe. In addition to the obvious euphoria of defeating Fascism and the bravery of American troops, there was a parallel discussion in

America and Europe about what had gone wrong. How could this have happened? Why did the world take so long to respond? How can we act as moral human beings in a world permeated by evil? What is our individual responsibility to stand up to evil? How can we ensure that such atrocities never happen again?

These discussions and the backdrop of the Nuremburg trials produced in us a razor-sharp sensitivity to moral relativism. One of the important questions raised in the wake of the war and the trials was the relationship of the individual to a government that was acting immorally. Some Fascist governments had been legitimate in the legal sense, but their activities were clearly criminal. How does the individual decide between what is legal and what is moral? How should the individual respond to an immoral but legally elected government? When is it correct to take action against a government, even one that has been legally installed? How is legitimacy defined—morally or legally?

These questions became particularly significant as we watched the McCarthy hearings and observed troops accompanying young children into Southern schoolhouses because whites did not want to be educated alongside blacks. The same questions arose when the United States began sending its armed forces to Southeast Asia to ensure that another sovereign nation had the government we wanted them to have. We began to question the moral nature of our government, wondering what our role and responsibility was in the face of injustice, and considering how our ideas about legitimacy applied to the United States.

The philosophical issues surrounding morality and the role of the individual were not only discussed at dinner tables but also were very much a part of cultural discussions both here and in Europe, and increasingly in Africa, Asia, and Latin America, from Algeria to India to Cuba, where colonialism was being challenged. Existentialist writers like Sartre, Gide, and de Beauvoir dissected human nature and individual freedom. Frantz Fanon wrote about the psychological effects of racism and colonialism. Aimé Césaire looked at moral behavior in the supposedly "civilized" world. James Baldwin brought the argument home to the United States in his searing portrayals of racism. Brecht thrust moral dilemmas onto the stage. Each of these authors wrote not passively about the human condition but demanded that the reader or audience engage and actively take a side.

In the United States, debates that both educated and mobilized flowed through a variety of cultural forms. Music became a vehicle for moral confrontation. John Coltrane wrote *Alabama*, one of the greatest of all jazz compositions, while listening to a speech by Martin Luther King. Bob Dylan educated a generation with musical poetry that captured the crimes and hypocrisy through which we were living. Pete Seeger, Nina Simone, and Peter, Paul and Mary were our resistance fighters. A large part of the culture in the sixties demanded an examination of what we were as country and a people, and urged citizens to stand up for what we believed in. It brought a generation together and reinforced the idea of collective action and individual responsibility. It urged us to be our best and do our best.

This was the cultural background to what we witnessed on television as we reached adolescence. I was in junior high school when we first saw images of dogs attacking black people who just wanted to sit and eat at a public lunch counter. I was in high school when the church in Birmingham was blown up, killing four young girls just because they were black. I was in high school when three young civil rights workers who had gone to Mississippi to register black voters were murdered, and we waited every night as their bodies were searched for and finally found in a ditch. I was in high school when the Gulf of Tonkin incident was used as an excuse for US intervention in Vietnam. And I was in college when Martin Luther King was assassinated.

What could a young person take away from these events? Many of us absorbed the fact that racism still very much existed in this country and affected every aspect of society. We also understood that there were plenty of people willing to fight to maintain the present system, with all its inequality. The initial activity of the civil rights movement—people sitting at lunch counters and on buses, or peaceably marching—was a model of how change could be brought about in a democracy, while going South, to work in places where only a tiny percentage of the black population was registered to vote, was the essence of peaceful democratic action. Yet such activities were met with murder. The killing of Chaney, Goodman, and Schwerner in 1964 was a turning point in the civil rights movement and for those who supported it. Even though the impetus of the sixties generation to fight for progress in black and white communities was enormous, the path of peaceful change was becoming narrower and more difficult. As millions marched on Washington, Martin Luther King and

Muhammed Ali were tying together the issues of racism at home and the war in Vietnam. By the mid-sixties, the Black Panther Party had begun organizing around conditions in black communities. Their struggle and insistence that blacks had the right to defend themselves against oppression was a challenge to the old civil rights movement, the logical next step following the deaths in Mississippi.

The war in Vietnam was another mobilizing issue, one we witnessed in much the same way as we did the struggle for civil rights, watching as napalm was dropped on villages, as women and children fled villages set on fire by US troops. Beyond television, we began reading. Columbia was a highly engaged place, and we students were determined to understand everything we could about the issues that were beginning to tear the nation apart. For many of us, at least as much education took place outside the classroom as it did inside. Reliable information on Vietnam was increasingly available as more reporters, and delegations from the antiwar movement, visited the country, all providing additional insights about how the Vietnamese saw the war. Every lunch hour became a learning or organizing opportunity about Vietnam, Latin America, and Africa. The prominence of Cuba in the news, combined with information about the perspective of the Vietnamese, forced us to delve deeper into the concept of self-determination. Again the questions at the forefront were about democracy, morality, and legitimacy.

Over time we came to understand that action, in fact, could bring about change. Organizing people around shared beliefs and taking a stand together was having concrete results and propelling the student movement forward. By 1968, millions were demonstrating, alternative newspapers were everywhere, and peace groups had formed vast coalitions that included women's groups, church activists, business people, and activists from all sides. There existed not only a culture that questioned everything from a moral perspective, but also a "movement"—a community of people who took buses to Washington together and protested, who worked to bring children free breakfasts, and who gathered in churches and public spaces to stand up for what they believed was just. All this was making it harder for the government to execute the war and enforce segregation. We had not yet won, but our populist form of power was beginning to make an impact. We had no standing in the Democratic Party, yet our energy forced Lyndon Johnson to withdraw from running for another term. We were not in Congress, but questions about the war were being raised there. Mainstream media increasingly was listening to alternate viewpoints, and every now and then it would challenge the government line on the war.

At the same time, the government chose to confront, rather than engage with, its opposition. The Federal Bureau of Investigation created files on antiwar protesters and civil rights leaders as police forces around the nation attacked demonstrators. The White House lied about military involvement in Vietnam, thus delegitimizing itself in the eyes of the public and eradicating any potential space for a national debate. As the government lost credibility, more people became politicized. The two sides were hardening, and dug in ever deeper.

The pace of organizing at Columbia was driven forward within this context. By 1967, as images of carpet-bombing in Vietnam filled television screens and riots engulfed Harlem, Watts, Detroit, and Washington, D.C., the need to make changes felt enormously urgent. As both the black and antiwar movements became more militant, we Columbia students felt we also needed to push forward. With the world around us moving so quickly and violently, it was clear that action was needed to confront the university on the issues we saw as critical to its operating as a moral institution. In the spring of 1968, all that anger and moral outrage exploded as we stood in Morningside Park, confronted by the New York City Police Department, before it spilled back onto campus and into five buildings. After years of peaceful demonstrations and political organizing, it felt legitimate to fight against a gym with a backdoor for the black community. Occupying buildings seemed absolutely the correct thing to do. It put us on the side of justice.

The university administration would not accept the student demand for amnesty, which was a reflection of our insistence that what we were doing was morally correct, that we were raising the right issues and asking the right questions. Columbia's response was startling. Here was an Ivy League university that could find no way to resolve the challenge of hundreds of its own students except by calling in riot police. Looking back, it was clear that the tone of the university had been set by the national response to challenges on the same issues. There was no serious discussion, and until we closed down the campus there was no admission from Columbia that it had done anything wrong (at which point construction of the gym was suspended). Another important similarity between Columbia and the US government was how both hierarchies turned protest over very real and substantive issues into questions of civil unrest. "Law and order" was an attempt to erase content and focus attention away from an immoral war to smashed windows. Instead of a national debate, it all became about whether or not the law was being broken. The same poignant questions inevitably came up again, about how a government should respond to calls for change and about how it should engage when so many are opposed to its policies.

The 1968 Columbia strike turned out to have a profound effect on universities across the country, inspiring protests and strikes by students on similar issues. It also had a profound effect on the students who were involved. Three years earlier, many of us had been idealistic and optimistic. Through engagement and protest, we were trying to understand the world we had inherited and figure out how we could be moral individuals in those complex social and political situations. We had lived through the assassinations, bloody riots, and a war with which we profoundly disagreed. We saw and felt the consequences of racism in our own cities. We had grown up together, arguing about how to become part of the struggle for justice. A joy and connectedness existed in our joint exploration.

Much of that changed after 1968. The already narrow road of change became almost invisible. It was no longer just an issue of what our moral obligations were, but how far we would go to meet those obligations. The same questions emerged, this time even more urgent and soul-searching. When does a government become illegitimate? What is the level and nature of resistance to that illegitimacy? For those who were committed to change, the choices became stark, and for those who had been part of the strike at Columbia, these questions would define the period from 1969 into the seventies, when many deep relationships were torn apart. It even led some to the townhouse in Greenwich Village and the tragedy of the Brinks robbery in Nyack. Marcus Garvey's "Look for me in the whirlwind" was no longer just a quote—it became some people's actual existence.[1] In many ways, I felt we had entered a state of war. And, in fact, some people had. This was a war for equality and justice, a war to end

---

1.   Marcus Garvey, *The Philosophy and Opinions of Marcus Garvey: Africa for the Africans*, comp. Amy Jacques Garvey, 2nd ed. (Oxford: Routledge, 2013), 239.

another war that was far away. Perspective sometimes became lost in righteousness, and for some who had been at Columbia in 1968, the next years were spent trying to figure out how to be morally relevant in a world that was becoming highly polarized.

Some historians and commentators look at the period and focus on what they see as the big issue: how did a group of privileged young men and women veer into such violent action? There are at least two problems with that analysis. First, there were years of peaceful activity and demonstrations and marches and singing and support of rent strikes and working in the community that preceded the action at Columbia in 1968 and everything that came afterward. Second, that viewpoint puts the responsibility fully on the students, not the events and situations to which they were reacting. The violence did not begin with the students, it began when people working to register voters were murdered, when Martin Luther King was assassinated, when the might of the American military began killing thousands of people every week in Vietnam, and when the government created "enemy lists" and relied on police brutality instead of discourse. The society in which we were raised was rooted in the violence of impending nuclear war and of assassinations and carpet bombings, the violence stemming from poor educational opportunities and from a lack of decent housing and jobs, and the violence of inequality. There is a collective responsibility that any society must bear. The sixties were a reaction to the world that we inherited. The cynicism and rage of our generation was spawned from the society in which we lived.

Today, we run the risk of creating an even more intense atmosphere of racism and hatred; of prejudice against other people's religions, antagonism against those who, like most of our families, come from other countries; of disrespect for women; and of a not-so-subtle acceptance of the underlying racism that we have never quite managed to put behind us. This is a dangerous road to go down. It is the world in which our children and their children will grow up. It is the opposite of what we hoped to build in 1968. Once again, the country seems split between those who want to create a more just world and those who want to retain power by fueling racism and prejudice. As I write this, the United States seems almost as torn as it was in the sixties and faced with many of the same moral and substantive issues. Perhaps understanding more about the past will help the next generation learn from our mistakes.

Susan Kahn *('69BC) worked after graduation for the North American Congress on Latin America, which published* Who Rules Columbia?, *and did research on relations between the United States and Latin America. She did investigative reporting for network news and taught in the New York area, and currently works to bring arts programming to the Bronx Academy of Letters, a public school in the South Bronx.*

THOMAS M. H. KAPPNER

Columbia College alumnus/Morningside Heights resident

COLUMBIA IN THE COMMUNITY

I arrived in Morningside Heights in the fall of 1962, having grown up in Latin America, and chose Columbia because it had a campus in a city that was surrounded by a real community and a real neighborhood.

In that era, Morningside Heights was a fantastic, vibrant blend of people from all around the world. Ethnically and economically it was a real mix. We had doctors and lawyers, Wall Street brokers, hospital and postal workers, people who worked at the university, and its facilities and janitorial staff. Everybody lived side by side. That kind of mix you found very rarely in the city. What made it special was that people intermingled on a daily basis. I immediately fell in love with Morningside Heights.

But I soon realized that the neighborhood was in transition. Beginning a decade before and continuing into the sixties, Columbia and the Rockefeller-funded Morningside Heights Incorporated was engaged in a massive campaign of evictions that was transforming a viable and healthy mixed community into a sterile institutional enclave. The university was buying up all the properties it could, a total of 168 residential buildings, more than half of those between 110th and 125th Streets, and practically all the single-room occupancy hotels in the area, which were the cheapest housing for transient-type people. Thousands of Irish-working class, people of color, and low-income residents were evicted, dozens of whom I knew as friends and neighbors. Columbia hired social workers who would go in and pick out the most vulnerable people, often those who didn't speak English or distressed older people who didn't know their rights.

The neighborhood began to change. As Jacques Barzun, iconic Columbia provost put it, the university's mission was to rid the neighborhood of "undesirables." But for every drug dealer ejected from the community, there were many honest, hardworking people who were painted by the university with the brush of an "undesirable." Even I was considered as such: Columbia wanted my apartment so it could be given to faculty and students.

The brutality with which this neighborhood transformation was being carried out played a pivotal role in the events of 1968. But to fully understand what happened that year, one has to realize that the protests were preceded by years of organizing, at times with great intensity, by Columbia students who were keenly aware of the issues of the day, by SDS and black student groups, and also community activists. As the neighborhood was being reconstructed along ethnic and economic lines, there was a growing resistance on the part of community residents. These were men and women of all stripes—old-time leftists, middle-class social justice activists, and young people like me—deeply involved in civil rights and antiwar organizing, and who were working to build as broad a base as possible. I was part of the generation that saw the post–World War II order crumbling and dramatically reshaped. I had worked on a voter registration project in the South during Freedom Summer 1964 and brought back to Morningside Heights the lessons I had learned. I had seen poor black sharecroppers stand up to seemingly insurmountable odds, in situations in which Mr. Charlie controlled literally everything, and in the process retain their dignity and humanity.

In my case, faced with eviction and having no money and no alternative source of housing, I applied my civil rights organizing experience and became a dedicated community activist. We organized tenants (those who had not yet been pushed out) in the ten residential buildings on the square block I lived on. About 179 apartments remained occupied. We had an active tenants' organization in every building, with captains for each floor, and a steering committee with representatives for each building. We swore a blood oath that we would not move unless carried out horizontally, and we applied every legal and extralegal trick to save our homes. Fortunately for us, the student protests of 1968 were just around the corner.

The crackdown by police on April 30 unified what had been a polarized campus. Everything shut down for the rest of the semester, and the strike organized in solidarity with those arrested and beaten was 100 percent effective. It was proof—if we needed it—that severe repression is often counterproductive. In the aftermath of the police bust, Columbia's expansionary drive into the neighborhood slowed considerably for twenty years or so. Our Block Association organized a neighborhood-wide federation of tenant organizations and was able to negotiate a policy of grandfathering tenants who had been in occupancy when Columbia acquired a building. We won a significant victory saving our homes but lost the war in that we were unable to save the community. Although evictions ceased, apartments still were converted to university housing when the tenant died or moved out. A company town came into being through the death by attrition of a wonderful neighborhood.

Columbia, unfortunately, has resumed its destructive incursion into the community. History is being repeated with the Manhattanville expansion. Gentrification—the ethnic cleansing and economic homogenization of the area north of the "new campus"—is occurring at a rapidly accelerating pace. And although Columbia is not yet engaged in the massive acquisition of residential buildings, its landlords are using every harassing trick in the book to convert them into co-ops, condominiums, and luxury rentals for which they see a growing market as Columbia moves in.

When we heard of Columbia's plans to create a new campus in Manhattanville, several of us who had survived the Morningside expansion and were determined to prevent a repetition of what we had experienced founded the Coalition to Preserve Community. We held dozens of meetings, which were attended by hundreds of residents, and worked with consultants from the Pratt Institute for Community and Environmental Development to develop an alternative plan that would meet Columbia's needs as well as incorporate the community's concerns. We used a clause in the City Charter (197A) that allowed communities to formulate their vision for the future as an advisory document. The idea was to share the space and not achieve one set of goals at the expense of the other. The City Planning Commission told us they had never seen such a comprehensive and well-thought-out 197A plan. Columbia's response was to line up local Harlem politicians behind the university's plans and undermine the unanimous support gathered at every public meeting for the 197A plan.

Few of us who were active in 1968 pursued self-serving careers to gain wealth and status. Most of the people I know who were involved became activists for the rest of their lives, whether in teachers' unions, civil rights organizations, the medical professions, or, in my case, housing. We community veterans of 1968 learned our lessons. Columbia did not.

Thomas M. H. Kappner *('66CC). In 1964 he participated in Freedom Summer doing voter registration in Fayette County, Tennessee. From 1980 to 1990, he chaired the 121st–122nd Streets Block Association. He negotiated the right of tenants in ten residential buildings acquired by Columbia University to retain rent regulations. In 1985, he earned a Ph.D. from CUNY in political science, focusing on development issues in Latin America. From 1985 to 1986, he did consulting work for the United Nations Development Programme, evaluating development projects in Latin America. He taught Latin American Politics and History at CCNY until retirement in 2004. He worked with Community Board 9 on the 197A plan, outlining a mutually beneficial development for Columbia and the community.*

TED KAPTCHUK

Columbia College undergraduate/Students for a Democratic Society

MUTINY IN THE AIR

A s a red-diaper baby, Columbia 1968 began in my mother's womb. My father trained to be a rabbi in Eastern Europe but became a life-long Communist who was decorated for his actions in the partisan movement and the Red Army during World War II. My mother survived the worst of the Holocaust and eventually worked in the underground resistance until the end of the war. I was always aware of horrific injustice and was politically "conscious." I was active in my high school's civil rights and antiwar movements, and when I started Columbia, the events of Berkeley's Free Speech Movement were inspirational. I was a founding member of the Students for a Democratic Society (SDS) chapter at Columbia and served as its chairman from 1967 to early 1968. Ted Gold, my Stuyvesant High School buddy, was cochairman. We worked hard to support civil rights and end the Vietnam War. Time was filled with passion: talking, leafleting, debating, demonstrating, marching, picketing, teach-ins, and sit-ins. Our frustration and anger increased month to month, year to year. Political institutions were perceived as hypocritical and rotten.

Other upheavals were significantly feeding the cultural cauldron and making the world less stable. Sexual revolution accompanied drugs and rock 'n' roll. Dylan prophesized, Ginsberg chanted, the Beatles serenaded with "Lucy in the Sky with Diamonds." New religious commitments were

proclaimed. Ram Dass declared "Be Here Now,"[1] Jews who didn't journey to the East were joining chavurahs, and Jesus freaks, especially on
the West Coast, were creating a new Christianity. Women and gays were
already stirring. On every level, supposedly solid and normative conventions and institutions were shifting or crumbling. A generation was
defecting. Mutiny was in the air.

The year 1968 brought earthquakes: the Tet Offensive, the assassinations
of King and Kennedy, race riots and upheavals in Paris, Berlin, Prague,
and Mexico City. Things had to change. The decisive occupation of black
students in Hamilton Hall galvanized the micro-upheaval at Columbia.
Students and people of all persuasions entered the buildings—politicos,
hippies, liberals, Communist factions, druggies, yogis, poets, mathematicians, street people, physicists, proto-geeks, premeds, and ordinary folks
somehow banded together. Regular existence was left behind. The passage
of time was suspended; we occupied a different space. Our highest moral
aspirations fused with the moment to moment of the mundane. It was
totally real and totally surreal. Things were upside down. Nothing made
sense; finally, everything made sense. The world was totally transformed.
We cried with happiness and joy; fear and uncertainty were pushed aside.
Nothing was the same. It was breathtaking, it was unbelievable, and it was
beyond words. The revolution happened.

Just before the uprising, SDS made its annual change of officers and
steering committee. Not being part of the new leadership did not prevent
me from putting my heart and soul into the rebellion. During the uprising, I used my connections and experience to get essential things done:
food, health care, bedding, talking, and, most important, listening to and
holding hands with all kinds of people. On the night of the bust, sens-
ing that police brutality was imminent, I worked with Ted Gold's physi-
cian father, Hy Gold, who was always available to treat members of the
Black Panther Party, to gather doctors and nurses to treat the wounded
on campus. Later, our graduation ceremony was to be held in St. John
the Divine Cathedral. Ted Gold and I built a radio transmitter on a roof
across the street and arranged to have Country Joe and the Fish's "I Feel
Like I'm Fixin' to Die" (with its chorus "And it's one, two, three, what are

---

1. Ram Dass, *Be Here Now* (New York: Crown, 1971).

Figure 24.1 Stokely Carmichael, former chairman of the Student Nonviolent Coordinating Committing and coauthor of the book *Black Power*, leaves Hamilton Hall, a.k.a. Malcolm X University, April 26, 1968. *Photograph by Carl Gryte.*

we fightin' for?"[2]) and Dylan's "The Times They Are a-Changin'" broadcast to seventy-five radios hidden under the gowns of many of the graduates who walked out.

On March 6, 1970, I was shaken by Ted Gold's death at an explosion in a townhouse in Greenwich Village. After overcoming disbelief, I cried with grief. Besides losing a brother, I realized I also had lost my moral compass. I couldn't tell when our commitments to improve the world had become self-righteous and destructive. The revolution was eating its children, helping people by killing them. I am still haunted by the question of how good becomes evil, compassion becomes intolerance, and the revolution becomes murderous rage. Already in 1968, some people couldn't accept anyone who wasn't like them. When did Stalin get back in the picture? I wanted out, so I fled "back to the land" and vanished in the lower Sierras of California.

---

2. "The 'Fish' Cheer/I-Feel-Like-I'm-Fixin'-to-Die Rag," on *I-Feel-Like-I'm-Fixin'-to-Die*, performed by Country Joe and the Fish, Vanguard Records, 1967, LP.

Eventually, feeling insufficiently useful, I decided to move to China to study Chinese medicine. It was a way to avoid working for "the man." After returning home, I helped establish the profession of East Asian medicine in the West. I eventually was recruited to Harvard and have mostly worked researching placebo effects. I became a professor of medicine. I have been blessed with family, friends, and colleagues, and I have been a trustee of my synagogue for thirty years. I survived.

Columbia 1968 remains an insight and a feeling woven into my life, not least because the issues of the sixties reappear in new forms. All have left a deep footprint and hopefully made a difference in terms of racism, feminism, gay rights, patient rights, American imperial designs, social justice, and countless cultural mores. Important personally, the decade allowed me to experience that the "given" can always be different. The status quo is impermanent. What The Doors sang—"Break on through to the other side"[3]—applies anywhere. The visionary and possible can turn into the concrete and real. Risk-taking is part of life. I hope that the Columbia uprising made a contribution, however small, to positive change. The importance of questioning and examining all forms of authority was a big part of my life. Grateful am I for having been there.

Ted Kaptchuk *('68CC) studied Asian medicine in China after Columbia and subsequently helped create the profession of Chinese medicine in the West. Harvard University later recruited him to research alternative medicine, but Ted switched to investigating placebo effects. Today, he is both professor of medicine and professor of global health and social medicine at Harvard.*

---

3. "Break On Through (To the Other Side)," recorded August 1966, on *The Doors*, performed by The Doors, Elektra Records, 1967, LP.

FRANK KEHL

Graduate student, Anthropology/Fayerweather Hall occupier

LIBERATED FAYERWEATHER: AGONY AND ECSTASY WHILE AWAITING THE NYPD

"I 'm hungry," said one of the Fayerweather occupiers I didn't know. "We're going to have to eat, right? Let's take up a collection. I'll go out and buy us some sandwich fixings. Maybe they'll even give us something for free."

In truth, I was hungry, too. I hadn't had anything to eat since arriving at a partially liberated Fayerweather early that morning. The suggestion of food was reasonable, welcome even. It dawned dimly that we probably would have to solve this problem on a more long-range basis. It also occurred to me that I didn't know this guy who was asking for my money. Could I trust him? First with my money, second not to buy junk food (he was an undergrad . . . who knew what they ate when on their own?), and third to buy enough for all of us. Had he done a head count? I hated it any time that well-intentioned people offered to take on a responsibility but didn't do the numbers. Conversely, he had come up with a good idea just when it was needed. The added concept that local merchants might throw in something for free seemed a little far-fetched, but worth a try. That was two points in his favor. I gave him some money and didn't ask for a receipt.

Some time later he came back through the little window. He had recruited someone, and they both carried big boxes of food and drinks. As we set about preparing our sandwiches, he announced: "All the fruit in the boxes was given for free." This was the first indication that at some level people beyond the university supported what we students were doing. I mentally scored two more points for this unknown undergrad: he did what he said he would do. He recruited someone to help and to join the Strike. (Also, there was no junk food.)

We were a motley crew in Fayerweather. In the wee hours of the morning of the first day, the earliest occupiers were grad students from the sociology department, which—along with Political Science and Economics—was one of the departments housed in the building. There were other grad students from Anthropology and East Asian Studies, including me, and overnight, I had recruited one of my fellow grad students from each of those departments. A number of black students, I believe the only ones in the liberated buildings other than those in Hamilton, had made their way to Fayerweather. A few I had seen around campus at earlier antiwar or antigym demonstrations, and I surmised that they operated on a different wavelength socially and culturally from the Hamilton crowd. The Fayerweather commune also housed at least one black foreign student, a petite, light-skinned young man from Cape Verde or Guinea Bissau who had a slight Portuguese accent. I came to greatly respect him. He was always ready to help, always even-tempered, thoughtful. He would see a need and go fill it without fuss. (When days later we finally learned that the police bust was imminent, I urged him to leave so as not to jeopardize his visa status in the United States: "You've done more than your share." His response, "No, I'll stay with the rest of you.")

Then there were undergrads from Columbia and Barnard. They were by far the most numerous, and aside from the several teenagers from Harlem who roamed Fayerweather, the youngest. These teenagers came upon framed photos of the professorial ancestors of Columbia Economics professors that lined the walls of the balcony dissertation defense room above the lounge. The kids took all the white professors off their perches and put them on the floor, leaning face-in against the wall. They left only one photo up where it had been. It was of Dr. Wellington Koo, who before he had become a Columbia professor was an official in the Chinese Nationalist government under Chiang Kai-shek. I smiled at the irony of their apparent logic: white, bad; nonwhite, good. Koo had served Chiang, archenemy of Mao, who was regarded as a global beacon by political radicals.

Already on the evening of the first day of the Fayerweather occupation I came to feel increasingly uneasy. We didn't know when the Columbia authorities would call in the cops. It could be tonight, or tomorrow, or the day after. And we didn't know with what level of violence the police attack would come. Billy clubs? Tear gas? Or would the university acquiesce to our demands and allow us to walk out victorious? I gave that outcome a less than 10 percent likelihood. I felt that we occupiers needed to establish routines and follow some conventions of civilization, so I decided to scout out the building, do a count of the students, and canvass the more awake students as to next steps. In the process, I would learn the layout of the building.

I proceeded floor to floor, receiving mixed reactions and levels of responsiveness as to the urgency of getting organized. When I reached the basement, I pushed open a slightly ajar door to discover, in the shadows, five or six grad students. I told them of my building survey and raised the issue of what would be needed. We talked and came up with the barest sense of a plan to implement the following morning. I then found an unlocked classroom with a relatively clean floor, and crashed.

The next morning, while most of the occupiers of Fayerweather were still asleep, I heard someone calling down the corridors: "We need to meet. We need to organize ourselves. We've got to create committees—food, security—and liaise with the other buildings and Strike Central. Let's go around the building and tell everyone we're going to meet at 8 A.M." Who was this guy telling us we needed to get organized? I agreed with the thrust of what he was proposing but was quietly miffed that it was he who was asserting leadership. By what right did he feel he could enter the leadership vacuum? After all, he wasn't one of the original occupiers. Yet I knew that my days as leader—my hours, in fact—were over, that there was a new reality and quickly concluded that this new reality was actually what we had all been working toward. We had fought for the beachhead, chained the doors, and occupied Fayerweather, after which scores of new students flowed in. Or, rather, crawled through the one unlocked, open window on the northwest side of Fayerweather. That's what we wanted: more students mobilized, more students politicized. The comrades who came crawling through the window represented every kind of politics: hippie, Christian social gospel, antiwar, antiracist, antiuniversity (and maybe their parents), and, of course, those with no politics at all, the "just curious."

Unsurprisingly, never again in the coming week would I be president, chair, or leader. That role would cycle through a half dozen individuals as newer constituencies came in through the open window. They would reject whoever was chair and vote in someone more eloquent, or a better parliamentarian, or better at composing differences among the many tendencies, or better at navigating a course between those who stressed solidarity with the other liberated buildings and Strike Central, and those who wanted to explore separate negotiations with the university administration.

We roused people, got them into the Lecture Hall in the basement, and began our collective life together. It was centered on this room, complete with rows of fixed wooden chairs with wide armrests. The people in the chairs changed; the population grew tenfold over the course of the week. The people chairing the meetings changed; a half dozen were elected for half a day, a day or two, then superseded. The chairs and walls were the only fixed things. All else seemed to be in flux.

Participatory democracy was the order of the day. This was perhaps a dual reflection: (a) the *zeitgeist* and (b) the fact that no one constituency or political tendency had a clear-cut plurality. Some people, myself included, were content to let Strike Central (essentially Students for a Democratic Society [SDS]) negotiate with the administration, if that's what was happening. I saw my job inside Fayerweather as holding the building, maintaining solidarity with other liberated buildings, not diluting the original demands, and facilitating the political education of newcomers. They were unhappy with the proposed gym and university ties to the Pentagon's Institute for Defense Analyses, but weren't so sure about the SDS call for amnesty for students involved in the building occupations. Moreover, SDS's in-your-face style rubbed some people the wrong way.

Inside Fayerweather, we experienced a beautiful, magnetizing, communal life, but also fear and paranoia, and we learned to live with each other in a cloud of stress that, as the cliché has it, you could cut with a knife. One cause for tension was fears about what the police might do. For many students, this was their first political act. They had skipped over voting, or campaigning for Eugene McCarthy, and jumped directly into civil disobedience: trespassing on university property. For some of us, Fayerweather was "liberated" territory. For those students new to activism, it was *terra incognita*, both tempting and scary.

Each new day, and with each new wave of students crawling through the window, the same questions arose: "If there's a bust, what will it be like?

Will we be hurt? How do we protect ourselves?" Sometimes these questions were posed in keening tones. The anxiety came from the heart, and the anguished tone permeated any meeting in which these issues were raised (which was most of them). With everybody's anxiety ratcheted up, even the relatively clear-eyed and worldly wise, like me, were affected. Although we tried—relatively unsuccessfully—to get student "experts" from Strike Central to come in and explain what you do if sprayed with mace vs. if there was a tear gas attack, the thing that seemed to calm people most was pitching in with the work of daily living. There were committees to get food, cook food, serve food, and clean up after; committees to sweep and mop, including toilets; and a security committee to stand shifts guarding the window against intruders but allowing in curious visitors and would-be supporters. Mike Wallace, a history grad student and eventual Pulitzer Prize winner, was a kind of committee of one: he controlled the sole telephone connected to the outside. That connection was crucial in communicating with Strike Central and combating the rumors that would periodically circulate about this or that anxiety-producing news.

As for the glories of communal life, one day, drawn to the lounge by the sound of drumbeats, I encountered a line of people dressed in loose-fitting burlap, their faces chalked white. They moved toward me in deliberation. Some held near-life-size puppets. On some of the puppets were signs scrawled with "Landlord" and "Peon," or signs on sticks: "$" and "1 cent." These were the Pageant Players. Who invited them? Who let them in? I smiled. Whoever had invited or acquiesced in a self-invitation, should get a high five. This kind of diversion, whatever it turned out to be, was just what was desperately needed after days of intense, sometimes-acrimonious debate and the paranoia of the possible mace and tear gas threat. The actors, maintaining their solemn, dirge-like beat and walk, said nothing and made no attempt at eye contact. I fell in behind the line, adopted the same slow, lumbering gait to match the hypnotic drumbeats. More and more comrades did the same, joining the cortege. Once an audience was assembled, the actors found their voices. We were told in brief that we were about to see a fairy tale: Columbia, the evil landlord, made the peons work the land, took the fruits of their labors, and then charged them to live in their huts. The audience roared its approval. Fairy tale? At the end, the peons rose up and sent landlord Columbia packing. The audience, by now just about all those in the building, roared and whistled and applauded their approval. Then came a spontaneous chant: "Strike! Strike!" The performance had the effect of a summer storm that breaks a heat wave, cooling and clarifying the humid air, allowing normal breathing again. Politics and paranoia temporarily evaporated.

The comrades drifted back to the lounge. One black student took a classroom garbage pail, turned it upside down, and began drumming. The beat was catchy, danceable. Other garbage pails were found, and other comrades joined in the drumming. People began to dance. By now it was dark outside, but someone turned off the lights. An inaudible announcement was made. Then the lights over the balcony to the dissertation defense room were turned on, and I saw three people I knew. To the left stood Rev. Bill Starr, Columbia's Episcopalian chaplain and a longtime supporter of SDS, Students' Afro-American Society (SAS), and women from Barnard who wanted the right, like the Columbia men, to live off campus. Was he wearing his Roman collar, to prove that what was about to happen was kosher? Or was he explicitly not wearing his Roman collar, to prove that what was about to happen would be a break with tradition? My memory fails. Beside him were two undergrads I had come to know and like, Andrea and Richard. Richard was wearing a neat Nehru jacket, Andrea was wearing white. She carried flowers, picked from somewhere on College Walk, I suppose. The drumming stopped. Near total silence. All eyes were on the balcony as the couple exchanged marriage vows. Then, in his most authoritative voice, Bill Starr intoned, "I now pronounce you . . . Children of the New Age." Cheers, whoops, whistles, and a resumption of rhythmic drumming from multiple garbage cans.

Someone shouted to the newlyweds, "Tell the other buildings. Visit the other buildings!" Whether or not it was already planned, Richard and Andrea came down from the balcony, climbed outside, accumulated an entourage from inside Fayerweather and some who were on campus, and began visiting the other buildings. Some of the drummers had come along, and the noise drew people to the windows. The affirmation of life, of love, of continuity, of comradeship, of shared joy in the midst of this tense, righteous struggle, touched all who saw Andrea and Richard, arm in arm, themselves combining a formal, serious posture with faces that glowed.

As I inhaled the night, I realized what it was like to breathe fresh air. I hadn't been outside Fayerweather in a day and a half, hadn't lived my normal routine in almost a week. The intensity of the self-contained world within had blocked out everything except the other liberated buildings, the Columbia administration, the New York City Police Department. Outside, the smell of spring was in the air. There were breezes. There were stars in the sky. It was almost a revelation. As our parade made its way around the campus, the campus itself, which I had walked across thousands of times since arriving as a grad student four years ago, took on a different look. It was familiar yet new. All my other walks in this space, among these buildings, had had a purpose, a destination, usually attending someone's lecture or seminar. Now, I was just enjoying the moment in this space in the shared glow of my comrades' joy. I had a renewed sense that what we were doing, whatever the outcome with the police, was right. We were affirming life and hope. Richard and Andrea were the proof. As we came to College Walk, a *New York Times* reporter asked a friend in the procession, "What are their names?" Without skipping a beat he responded, "Richard and Andrea Fayerweather."

Back inside Fayerweather, a party had started in the lounge. The room was dark, the furniture had been pushed back to the walls, and the floor was packed with gyrating or swaying figures. A relentless, ecstatic beat emanated from the garbage cans. In the darkness, I saw a little flame but couldn't make out what it was. Then, in another corner of the room, another flame. Soon there were a half dozen little flames in different parts of the densely packed room. I was roused from my near-reverie and watched as the dancers surrounding these little flames almost ritually created a small space for each person who was holding aloft, with one hand, a burning object. The beat continued. The dancing continued. They were burning their draft cards.

Frank Kehl *enrolled in the Ph.D. program of the Department of Anthropology in 1964. He was later cofounder of the Committee of Returned Volunteers, the Committee of Concerned Asia Scholars, and Columbia Radical Anthropologists. In 1967, he was co-organizer of a Students for a Democratic Society (SDS) Radical Education Project on China's Cultural Revolution at Riverside Church. Soon after the student strike at Columbia, he began squatter shantytown field research in Hong Kong for his Ph.D., which he received in 1981.*

WILLIAM KEYLOR

Graduate student, History/Fayerweather Hall occupier

THE SPECIAL CASE OF THE FAYERWEATHER OCCUPATION

As a second-year graduate student in Columbia University's History Department during the spring of 1968, I heard the daily speeches reverberating from the sundial by Students for a Democratic Society (SDS) militants with a mixture of approval and dismay: approval of the ardent denunciations of the war in Vietnam and the demand that the university sever its connections to a think tank that conducted weapons research for the Pentagon; dismay at the inflammatory revolutionary verbiage that accompanied what I considered that eminently reasonable demand.

The occupation of Low Memorial Library in the early hours of April 24 by SDS students—after they had been gently evicted by the Students' Afro-American Society (SAS) from their joint occupation of Hamilton Hall—filled me with the same feelings of ambivalence. On the one hand, my deeply felt opposition to America's war in Southeast Asia prompted me to support the Low occupation as an appropriate gesture of condemnation directed at our university's complicity, however indirect, in the conduct of that war. On the other hand, I was disconcerted by the stream of diatribes emanating from Low Memorial Library that revealed SDS regarded opposition to this particular war as merely a pretext for a full-scale ideological indictment of "Amerika." I was an enthusiastic supporter of the antiwar campaign of Sen. Eugene McCarthy, whose strong showing in the New Hampshire Democratic primary a few months earlier had precipitated the withdrawal of President Lyndon Johnson from and the entrance of Sen. Robert Kennedy into the race for the party's presidential nomination. I was convinced that this type of pragmatic political activism was a much more effective means of promoting social and political change than seizing university buildings and issuing a wholesale condemnation of the entire American political system as rotten to the core.

But I would soon have a change of heart as I was swept up in the fervor that surged through the campus in the waning days of April. Inspired by the undergraduate militants ensconced in Low and Hamilton Hall, I joined a contingent of graduate students in the social sciences and humanities who established residence in Fayerweather Hall, the site of the history department's offices. Over the next several days, we formed a kind of intellectual commune where ideas about how to combat militarism, racism, and other social ills were freely exchanged. Liaison was established with a contingent of sympathetic professors called the Ad Hoc Faculty Group that met periodically to seek a just and peaceful solution to the crisis. At one point, I was designated to present to the faculty group a hastily drafted statement announcing that, unlike SDS and the other firebrands in Low, we Fayerweather folks were not revolutionaries intent on destroying the existing order but reformist progressives committed to the goals of ending the war in Vietnam and combating racism at home.

Amid the spirited debates in Fayerweather about the war, racism, and the university's alleged complicity in both, a new set of issues more directly connected to our daily lives as graduate students began to enter the conversations. What is the purpose of this graduate education in which we all were engaged? Why do so many of us feel disconnected from the faculty who were supposed to be our mentors and advisers as we prepare for careers as scholars and teachers of history? Why do we feel so alienated and powerless in a rigid, hierarchical education environment? Whatever happened to the august conception of graduate education—borrowed from Germany and transplanted to Columbia and other American universities—as a collaborative enterprise of master-teachers passing on their wisdom to student-apprentices?

After the forcible removal of students from the campus buildings by the New York City Police Department on April 30, a large portion of the student body responded favorably to the appeal for a campus-wide strike in protest. On May 6, more than a hundred history graduate students crammed into a lecture hall to express their support for the campus-wide shutdown, to record their particular grievances about their education experiences in their own department, and to demand remedial action from its faculty. The student assembly elected six student representatives— of whom I was one—to participate in a proposed student–faculty committee to negotiate reforms in the department. After the department chair acceded to our request to designate six faculty representatives to meet with the six student representatives, a twelve-person student–faculty committee spent the next several months in intense discussion of the students' complaints and how they might be addressed.

The six student members of the committee kept in close touch with our constituency through periodic meetings in the crypt of the Cathedral of St. John the Divine on Amsterdam Avenue. We circulated questionnaires on a wide range of graduate student grievances and solicited suggestions for reform. On the afternoon of May 17, we six appeared before the Executive Committee of the History Department, which consisted of its thirty-two tenured members (only one of whom was a woman), to present our "Proposals for Structural Reforms of the Department." We prefaced our remarks with the solemn warning that "the affairs of this department will not return to normal until the reforms [proposed by] this committee are implemented" and then read the list of proposals that had been approved by the graduate students assembled in the crypt of the cathedral.

Although the Columbia History Department, we declared, should be (after the title of a 1962 book by radical social theorist Paul Goodman that bemoaned the bureaucratic nature of higher education) "a community of scholars,"[1] its current structure was "hierarchical and undemocratic." To remedy this defect, we proposed a drastic procedural reform: graduate students must share "equal roles in the decision-making process of the department" with the faculty, through 50 percent graduate student representation on all standing subcommittees of the Executive Committee, the department's decision-making body. (An exception was made for the Personnel Committee, which dealt with matters of appointment, promotion, and tenure, but with the proviso that a parallel personnel committee composed of graduate students be empowered to convey student

---

1. Paul Goodman, *Compulsory Mis-Education and the Community of Scholars* (New York: Vintage Books, 1966).

Figure 26.1 Demonstrating on campus, April 1968. *Photograph by David Finck.*

recommendations on all appointment, tenure, and promotion cases.) Our audacious proposition was followed by a long list of substantive proposals concerning student access to personnel files, prior notification of faculty leaves, and the like.

It will come as no surprise that the many months of these student–faculty negotiations, which continued into the late fall, did not result in the implantation of any of the proposed reforms. After the end of the campus-wide strike and the intense agitation that accompanied it, the history graduate students returned to the two main tasks at hand: preparation for qualifying examinations and the selection of topics for doctoral dissertations.

In the years after I began my teaching career at Boston University, which included a twelve-year stint as History Department chair, an attitude of deference and respect toward the faculty replaced the fiery spirit of condemnation and defiance that briefly had engulfed us on Morningside Heights in the intoxicating spring and summer of 1968. At no time did the graduate students in my department evince the slightest inclination to confront the faculty with such audacious demands for the improvement of their education experience as we had dared to do. But I like to think that those of us at Columbia who later would become professors retained an acute sensitivity to the anxieties and concerns of graduate students that we had experienced there in 1968.

William R. Keylor *('71GSAS) is professor of history and international relations in the Pardee School of Global Studies at Boston University. His books include* Academy and Community: The Foundation of the French Historical Profession, From Parnassus: Essays in Honor of Jacques Barzun, *and* The Twentieth-Century World and Beyond: An International History Since 1900.

Graduate student, Art History and Archeology/Fayerweather Hall occupier

A TIME FOR REVOLT

ometime in the spring of 1968, I had a dream in which students at Columbia University staged a revolution. In my faint memories of the dream, students converged on the plaza in front of Low Memorial Library, waving flags and placards—much like scenes I had witnessed in Eisenstein's famous 1928 movie *October*, about the Russian Revolution of 1917. Today, if I told friends about such a dream, they would say I was crazy, or under the influence of some substance. Back then, however, it hardly seemed strange, given the mood on campus at the time. Antiwar demonstrations were occurring all the time, the draft and service in Vietnam were the subject of endless discussions, and campus radicals were meeting daily in the West End bar to plot future actions and debate revolutionary politics. Moreover, on April 4, Martin Luther King, Jr. was assassinated in Memphis, sparking bloody riots all across the United States—riots whose images of burning neighborhoods and National Guard soldiers patrolling with fixed bayonets filled the nightly TV news. Revolution, you could say, was in the air.

At that time, I was a twenty-five-year-old graduate student, studying the history of art while devoting most of my spare time to antiwar research and activism. I had studied at Columbia College as an undergraduate, receiving my B.A. in 1963, and returned to the graduate school as a Ph.D. candidate in 1965 after an unsatisfactory two-year stint as an architecture student at Yale. In those years, before the institution of the lottery system, enrollment in college or graduate school was essential to avoid being drafted and sent to Vietnam. So while I enjoyed the study of art, my burning passion was opposition to the war in Vietnam.

During my previous years at Columbia, from 1959 to 1963, fraternities dominated campus life, and instructors (they were almost all male) wore tweed jackets to class. It still felt like the fifties, and the legacy of McCarthyism remained palpable. By the end of my undergraduate years, however, the atmosphere had begun to change. I can remember participating in a Ban the Bomb demonstration on Low Plaza in defiance of laws requiring New Yorkers to descend into underground bomb shelters during an air raid drill (what stupidity to think that going underground would save us when Columbia was located just a few miles north of Times Square, the presumed Ground Zero for Soviet H-bombs!) and picketing the local Woolworth's in support of student protesters seeking to desegregate lunch counters in the South.

When I returned to Columbia in 1965, the sixties had fully arrived and student activism had become far more prevalent. Most conspicuous, of course, was opposition to the Vietnam War, which then was becoming a daily staple on the evening news and a constant source of anxiety for every young male who potentially faced conscription (myself included). Soon after arriving back on campus, I joined the Independent Committee on Vietnam (ICV)—"independent," to distinguish it from established left-wing political organizations for which Vietnam was a side issue—and became one of its leaders. I also was associated with the antiwar journal *Viet-Report* and was influenced by articles that appeared there and in *Ramparts* (the forerunner of *Mother Jones*) about several universities that had been found by student activists to be performing Vietnam-related research for the Department of Defense.

Spurred by a call in *Viet-Report* for students everywhere to investigate such ties on their own campus, I decided to investigate Columbia's links to the military-industrial complex. Conducting this sort of research meant digging in obscure government publications and research journals to find evidence of such links. As a result of one such foray in Butler Library, it became clear that Columbia was an institutional sponsor of the Institute for Defense Analyses (IDA), a military think tank engaged in classified research for the Pentagon. Together with other students, I set out to highlight Columbia's "complicity" with the war machine (as we said in those days) as a way of bringing the war home. For many of us, stopping the Vietnam War appeared an impossible proposition, but ending campus complicity seemed an achievable—and symbolically significant—objective.

As student activism blossomed at Columbia, many leftist organizations (mostly representatives of what we called the Old Left, purveyors of assorted Marxist and Maoist ideologies) gravitated to the campus, seeking recruits. But I was attracted to what was becoming known as the New Left—groups influenced by the libertarian ideas of Herbert Marcuse and the participatory activism of the civil rights movement. Of these, the most notable was Students for a Democratic Society (SDS), and I became an active member in the Columbia branch in around 1966.

The student members of SDS were motivated by many concerns, including outrage over the unending war in Vietnam, disgust at the rampant hypocrisy in American society (especially regarding the treatment of black Americans, who lived just down the hill from Columbia), and resentment over the paternalism, authoritarianism, and Victorian social mores that still pervaded student life at Columbia. What's more, the university's top leadership, led by President Grayson Kirk, had no clue that times were changing, and their indifference to students' concerns only amplified our anger. For example, in an interview for the *Columbia Daily Spectator* newspaper, a vice dean was quoted as saying that he cared no more about student opinion on the running of the university than he cared whether or not we liked strawberries. This response became known as "the Strawberry Statement," later the name of a book and movie.

I was not engaged in the ongoing fight over the university gymnasium in Morningside Park (a conspicuous affront to the African Americans who lived on the other side of the park), but the picture there was the same: administration indifference to the legitimate concerns of students and community members.

A week or so after I had that extraordinary dream, my premonitions became reality. Although the actual sequence of events turned out differently from the way I had envisioned them, the essence of the experience was the same: a spontaneous revolt against illegitimate authority. Yes, the leaders of SDS had been strategizing about major protests for some time, but no one planned the events of April 23, 1968. Rather, the student population had become so alienated by the war fever in Washington and the moral blindness of Columbia's leaders that it took very little to spark a popular uprising. I have attended many rallies and protests since that time, but rarely have I felt the electrifying sense of mass outrage that fueled the Columbia Strike of 1968.

Michael Klare *is the Five College Professor of Peace and World Security Studies, a joint appointment at Amherst, Hampshire, Mount Holyoke, and Smith Colleges, and the University of Massachusetts, Amherst. He studied art history and architecture at Columbia University, receiving a B.A. in 1963 and an M.A. in 1968, but switched subjects after the 1968 Columbia Strike to concentrate on international peace and security, receiving a Ph.D. in that field from the Union Graduate School in 1976. He has written or edited many books, including* Resource Wars, Blood and Oil, *and* The Race for What's Left.

JAY KRIEGEL

Office of the New York City Mayor

GETTING BACK TO "LIFE AS NORMAL"

O n April 4, 1968, Martin Luther King, Jr. was assassinated in Memphis. While other cities across the country erupted, New York remained relatively calm, in part because John Lindsay, in his third year as mayor, quickly headed to Harlem to walk on 125th Street, mingling with the crowd and expressing his sympathies. A bold move, it was a continuation of his personal outreach to alienated minority communities that began in the summer of 1966, when he raced out to East New York to defuse an outbreak of racial troubles. His visit to Harlem was impactful because he had been there so many times before, when it was calm, giving his presence now a legitimacy and credibility with those grieving over Dr. King. It was in sharp contrast to the approach of Mayor Richard Daley of Chicago. In the aftermath of King's death, Daley had instructed police to stop arsonists and looters by issuing a "shoot to kill" directive. Lindsay's response to Daley was simple: "In times of trouble . . . we are not going to shoot children in New York."[1]

Weeks later, when students occupied five buildings on the Columbia campus, the university administration seemed to be looking for a magic solution. Because Lindsay's walks in Harlem and elsewhere had had such a calming effect, they thought he could quickly defuse their situation

---

1. Sara Davidson, "Lindsay Disagrees with Daley," *Boston Globe* (Boston), April 17, 1968.

if he just came to the campus. But their assumptions were misguided. In troubled neighborhoods, the mayor could reach out to disaffected residents—community leaders, ministers, militants, parents, and street kids—and patiently listen to their grievances. He could then call on an array of commissioners and government representatives—the people responsible for things like substandard housing, schools, and social services—to respond, so that those aggrieved and skeptical residents could feel that some kind of action was being taken.

But the issues at Columbia were different. This community wasn't boiling over because of perceived grievances, nor was it seeking access to senior government officials to air their concerns. This was not a civil disorder with fires, looting of stores, and people being attacked. On the contrary, Columbia was a calm, static, and deadlocked situation, without serious risk to life and property. The presence of the mayor would bring neither relief nor resolution. This was, for the most part, middle-class students, peacefully sitting-in over an odd combination of two unrelated issues: a gym Columbia was building in Harlem, and the Vietnam War. In response, the mayor sent three aides to Columbia, each of whom locked onto different campus groups. Barry Gottehrer, our leader, worked the black Columbia students inside Hamilton Hall and Harlem community leaders; Sid Davidoff spent time with the Columbia students who were vehemently against their fellow students occupying buildings (the so-called jocks, a conservative element); and I liaised with the activist contingent, the Strike Coordinating Committee, which was dominated by the militant SDS.

Lindsay was sympathetic to the overall demands of the student protesters and vocal in his long-standing opposition to the war in Vietnam. A month before the protests at Columbia, he spoke on campus at the Law School, suggesting that urban violence at home was strongly connected to the war in Southeast Asia. And as he put it some months later in December 1968, in a speech also made on the Columbia campus, as student protests were spreading at colleges across the country:

> [T]he last year has taught us . . . that your effort and your energy may not be sufficient to build a better America, but it is necessary to that effort. I do not come to promise you that all we seek will be won if you continue speaking and acting for these goals—but I do come to say that

without you, we cannot win. You have seen how much is at stake. You have reminded us of the work to be done. Now help us to do it.[2]

But at the same time, Lindsay—whose record in Congress made clear his deep respect for the First Amendment—was troubled by the disruption being caused by this small group of radical Columbia students. As a fellow of the Yale Corporation, he was acutely sensitive to the pressures on university presidents and the difficulty of managing a college in the late sixties, as he made clear in a statement printed in the *New York Times*:

Students have a right to protest, to dissent, to demonstrate. That right is basic, but not supreme. It cannot be allowed to supersede equally important individuals' rights and privileges, among them the right of a university to teach and grant degrees, and the right of students to learn.

The demonstration by a group of Columbia University students during the past several days clearly exceeded even the most liberal perimeters of the right to assemble and dissent. The demonstrators, comprising less than 5 percent of the student body, ransacked the office of the university president, held a dean prisoner and forced the administration to suspend classes.

Regardless of the merits of their cause, the few hundred students cannot be allowed to impose their will on a university of some 20,000 students through destructive, illegal tactics.[3]

Just as the mayor's presence was unlikely to bring about some meaningful resolution of the situation at Columbia, bringing in the New York City Police Department (NYPD) also was unlikely to be helpful. The police are essential to stabilizing situations of urban unrest where domestic tranquility is being disturbed, where a community is being pulled apart, where people are endangered and property is threatened.

But Columbia—with its middle-class students who had isolated themselves from the community, deep within the ivory tower—was a very

2. John V. Lindsay, "Address by the Honorable John V. Lindsay, Mayor of the City of New York before the Student Body of Columbia University" (speech transcript, Dodge Hall, Columbia University, December 12, 1968).
3. Richard Reeves, "Lindsay Is Critical of Columbia Sit-ins, but Backs Dissent," *New York Times* (New York), May 1, 1968.

different situation. It was readily apparent that the hundreds of students now occupying buildings weren't interested in negotiating. (I was only a few years older than these students but found most of the SDS leadership, and especially Columbia chapter chairman Mark Rudd, quite unappealing, stubbornly rigid, and self-centered.) Moreover, the police would have virtually no sympathy for these students who were far better off economically and whose protests against the war, and ability to avoid military service, highlighted how the burden in Vietnam was being borne largely by the less fortunate, including the police, their families, and friends. To the cops, these kids seemed both spoiled and unpatriotic. In reality, introducing the police into Morningside Heights became a clash of social and economic classes.

Ultimately, if the university decided to enforce its private property rights and eject trespassers, the NYPD would have to be called into action. But the last thing that the police wanted to do was to get involved in this multisided and impossibly complicated conflict, in which it was obvious they would please no one.

We were not unsympathetic to the situation that the Columbia administration found itself in. As they got worn down, tired, and frustrated, and with no end in sight, they wanted nothing more than to go back to running their sacred educational establishment. Faced with this intransigent, highly vocal group that was disrupting the university, with mounting counterpressure from other students, faculty, and outside commentators urging that the disorder end, that classes resume immediately, and that the values of the academy be restored, they were desperate to end the crisis. And while President Grayson Kirk and his board of trustees were convinced—erroneously, we believed—that these campus protests were somehow infecting Harlem and exacerbating community tensions, and sought to use this to justify their call for police action, we had no doubt that the Columbia protests were self-contained.

We had been through two summers of community confrontations and eruptions, and felt battle hardened. After the dangerous and inflammatory conflicts we had been dealing with, we recognized the perils of introducing police into this unusual situation. As Barry Gottehrer wrote in his book *The Mayor's Man*, any police action would probably "result in a massacre."[4]

---

4. Barry Gottehrer, *The Mayor's Man: One Man's Struggle to Save Our Cities* (New York: Knopf Doubleday, 1975), 169.

During our regular meetings with the university administration, we patiently explained that police would only inflame the situation if they were brought on campus. So we were startled when David Truman, Columbia's vice president, finally told us, with some exasperation, "Let's just get this over with. It's inevitable. Let's bring in the cops, end this once and for all, and the next day we'll go back to life as normal."

We tried to make clear that we didn't think anything would be normal the day after a thousand angry students confronted a thousand hostile cops.

Figure 28.1 Faculty, wearing white armbands, consult with occupiers of Low Library. *Photograph by Barney Edmonds.*

Jay Kriegel *was chief of staff and special counsel to Mayor John V. Lindsay from 1966 to 1973, including overseeing the city's offices in Washington and Albany and liaison with the nation's mayors and the Kerner Commission. He was founder and publisher of the* American Lawyer Magazine *(1979–1982), senior vice president of CBS Inc. (1987–1994), and a consultant to the prime minister of Turkey and the president of Kazakhstan (1995–1998). From 1998 until 2005, he ran New York City's campaign to host the Olympic Games of 2012. He now serves as a senior advisor of The Related Companies, one of America's largest multiuse real estate developers.*

North American Congress on Latin America

THE POWER OF POWER STRUCTURE RESEARCH

I grew up in New York, the child of liberal parents—my father was staunchly anti-Communist and read *The New Leader*—and after attending Brooklyn Tech High School decided I needed to see a different side of the country. The Ku Klux Klan was still running around Richmond, Indiana, when I arrived at Earlham College in 1960, a place where all my liberal values were challenged (many of the locals considered public housing and unemployment insurance as being dangerously left wing) and where I became quickly politicized. Then, in 1962, at the age of twenty, I spent a transformative six months in Russia and Finland, where I studied the workings of the Finnish Communist Party.

Back home, Students for a Democratic Society (SDS) was developing as a campus organization, but Earlham was such a reactionary environment that we decided not to formally affiliate as an SDS chapter. Instead we established our own group, Earlham Politics Issues Committee (EPIC), and initiated debates on campus about town and gown issues (Richmond was still largely segregated), *in loco parentis*, and civil liberties. The most radical group in town was the National Association for the Advancement of Colored People, which we worked with.

Clearly, I was moving in a political direction and decided I wanted to do graduate work in sociology at Berkeley with Seymour Martin Lipset. But before heading out west, I ran into Tom Hayden, one of the founders of SDS, in New York, who suggested I go work with him in Michigan—a meeting that literally changed my life.

I was attracted to SDS because of its ability to intelligently confront power on campuses and offer students a progressive political position, to say nothing of its specific strategies and tactics. Like many of my generation, it was what I needed to hear. While in Michigan, I studied political sociology and did extensive research with Tom and Marc Pilisuk at the Mental Health Research Institute on the military-industrial complex. Next I looked at the 1965 US invasion of the Dominican Republic (DR), which we saw as a logical extension of America's imperialist ambitions. I zeroed in on the sugar industry and how this powerful business lobby used the fig leaf of anti-Communism to protect its assets in the DR.

Also, while in Michigan, in part because of my continued reading of C. Wright Mills, I was exposed to power structure research, which changed the way I looked at the world—it was eye-opening to identify all the pockets of secrecy, to peel back the skin of institutions and organizations and see what really drove them, to discover the full truth about the concentration of corporate power in the United States and the manipulation that went on. We wanted to explore the political reality around us and see how democracy truly worked. Finding out how things really functioned became a driving force in my life, no matter how subversive. Mills—along with Weber and Marx—was asking questions that the consensus rule of the United States in the fifties and early sixties did not allow room for.

Importantly, as power researchers, we were not ideologically driven. That kind of approach to change had not proven itself sufficiently adroit to deal seriously with the big issues of the day. We wanted to *challenge* power at its core and knew that the most efficient way of doing this was by understanding it, which meant rigorous documentation, and then giving people all the facts so they could continue their own investigations and take action. From the very start, an empirical analysis of what made things happen was our method. In other words, we looked at things not from a theoretical point of view but from an operational standpoint, and we never published anything that we didn't know could be fully documented.

Around this time, I joined the SDS chapter that held a sit-in at the Ann Arbor Selective Service Office in October 1965. We took the authorities by surprise (in those days they had little intelligence on our activities) and were arrested. All the men immediately received draft reclassifications, as well as sentences of thirty days in jail. With our lawyers, we developed a "Nuremberg Defense" when it came to our opposition to the Vietnam War. If the United States was committing acts of unjustified terror on the Vietnamese people, surely the Nuremberg Convention, which after World War II made certain activities illegal, was applicable. If the US government was committing crimes against humanity and violating certain standards, it had to be held accountable. We were not the exception. *There are no exceptions.* (Our appeal went all the way up to the Michigan Supreme Court, where we lost 3–2.) From there, I worked with Todd Gitlin, Al Haber, and others to establish SDS's Radical Education Project, to provide the growing influx of new members with detailed educational materials to orient them about what was going on in the world.

After Fred Goff read the paper I wrote on the DR, we met with Edie Black and Proctor Lippencott in 1966 at Princeton University and founded the North American Congress on Latin America (NACLA), to continue researching the power structures of the United States and its relations with Latin America. I knew almost nothing about Latin America but realized that politically it was as important a job to take on as Vietnam. Fred, who had a strong background in Latin American affairs, had some contacts at the Interchurch Center near Columbia University, and so we ended up with free office space inside the "God Box" at 475 Riverside Drive.

NACLA was the perfect organization for me to develop the research analysis I had started in Michigan. The first NACLA newsletter was published in February 1967. That same year we issued NACLA's first research paper, which Fred Goff and I wrote, called "The Violence of Domination: US Power and the Dominican Republic." It examined certain realities as we understood them, notably that the base of Dominican power rested on economic, political, military and social structures within the United States, not in the DR. Also in 1967, NACLA planned a "Conference on Campus Military and Paramilitary Research." I wrote in our newsletter of August that year:

The base of power for US domination overseas lies so close to our lives that we can't even see it, let alone attack it effectively. Research essential to military and civilian programs designed to insure US control over the Third World has saturated the American campus. The university budget floats on subsidies geared toward national security. Research grants permit on-site investigations for basic intelligence. Quasi-governmental institutes and centers provide extra facilities and legitimate off-campus roles as well as secrecy. Out of such "academic and scholarly" activity spring the mechanisms of domination and oppression. It is the role of the student radicals to expose the sociologists, physicists and engineers who claim academic immunity and hide behind apolitical disguises.[1]

In NACLA's October 1968 issue, Michael Klare, a Columbia graduate student, published a long article entitled "The Changing Nature of American Military Aid," which discussed the postwar rearmament of Latin American armies as being a US policy objective, and the following year a NACLA pamphlet, "The University-Military Complex," appeared. Then in 1970, NACLA published its groundbreaking *Research Methodology Guide*, which is split into two parts: (1) "Researching the Empire" (by Edie Black and Lois Reivich) and (2) "Campus Reconnaissance." In the latter section I wrote:

On all counter-revolutionary fronts—infiltration, manipulation, indirect and direct armed confrontation—universities have provided essential resources for waging more effective battles . . . The university setting is an attractive cover that eliminates conscience and maintains high productivity. The military-industrial complex is relying heavily on the innovative abilities of the academic world for defeating revolutionary solutions to the increasing exploitation and misery of the Third World.[2]

The twenty pages of the *Research Methodology Guide* contain lists of books, periodicals, libraries, and directories to prepare anyone seeking to do their own power structure research, plus details like the dollar value of contracts between the Department of Defense and various universities (Columbia: $16,203,000). We believed crimes were being committed in our name by the US government in Vietnam (and elsewhere) and that it was our obligation under certain international standards to actively intervene and object. Power structure research was our way of fighting back. Anything else meant we were complicit.

---

1. Michael Locker, "Conference on Campus Military and Paramilitary Research," *NACLA Newsletter*, August 1967.
2. Michael Locker, "Campus Reconnaissance," in *Research Methodology Guide* (New York: NACLA, 1970).

In May 1968, NACLA published *Who Rules Columbia?* Because our office was so close to campus, we were aware of various demonstrations and rallies taking place, but the building occupations came as a surprise to us. A few hours after a group of students took control of offices in Low Memorial Library, we got a call: someone let us know that all the documents from Grayson Kirk's filing cabinets had been liberated. A group from NACLA walked over to campus, not knowing whether we would be able to make sense of all that paperwork, but soon realized that what had been pulled from Kirk's office would help us construct a map of all the interlocking relationships between Columbia's board of trustees and the mass media, multinational firms (some funded by the Central Intelligence Agency), the military-industrial complex, and the New York real estate industry (a vital component of the university's business model). As we wrote in *Who Rules Columbia?*:

> This pamphlet . . . will attempt to show concretely how Columbia University is set up not to service the needs of its own constituency—faculty and students—but rather to service outside interests which, by controlling Columbia finances, effectively control its policy. These outside interests, represented on the Board of Trustees, have organized the university as a "factory" designed to produce the skilled technicians and management personnel which the US industrial and defense apparatus needs. The millions channeled into the university coffers by the agents of these interests are, for them, essentially an investment in people, which, like any investment, is expected to yield certain returns.[3]

Contained within *Who Rules Columbia?* is a folded insert entitled "The 22: Columbia's Ruling Elite," which charts the twenty-two men who made up the university's board of trustees in 1968, alongside all the other organizations, institutions, and companies they controlled. Some of the better-known examples:

Walter N. Thayer, director of Banker's Trust Co.
Arthur B. Krim, president of United Artists

---

3. *Who Rules Columbia?* (New York: NACLA, 1968).

William A. M. Burden, director of Lockheed Aircraft, chairman of the
board of the Institute for Defense Analyses

John R. Dunning, advisor to the US Defense Department and the US
Army, director of the Atomic Energy Office (US Navy)

Harold F. McGuire, director of Shell Oil

Frank S. Hogan, district attorney of New York County

Percy Uris, chairman of the board of the Uris Buildings Corp.

William S. Paley, chairman of the board of Columbia Broadcasting System
(CBS)

Arthur Hays Sulzberger, chairman of the board of the *New York Times*

Charles F. Luce, chairman of the board of Consolidated Edison

It was exactly as Mills had laid out in his book *The Power Elite*.[4] Columbia
turned out to be fully integrated into the corporate world, even though
it had a thoroughly liberal façade. We set out to reveal to students the
framework of their university from a wholly new angle, to show them
where the levers of power at Columbia really were. After all, you can't
challenge the power base of an institution if you don't know precisely
who owns what.

Michael Klare, who had studied architecture at Yale, was a great layout artist and designed each page. The team worked night and day to
have *Who Rules Columbia?* ready for early June, and it was on sale during Columbia's commencement ceremony. Our research gave a whole
new perspective and meaning to those Columbia students who had spent
years confronting the power structure of the university.

After NACLA, I went on to consult with several US labor unions,
helping them analyze some powerful corporations. With this detailed
information, we were able to develop sophisticated corporate campaign
strategies that helped unions challenge corporate power and even the
playing field.

When I look back on the past fifty years, one central theme emerges:
power structure research is an essential component for developing an
effective strategy to confront injustice and change our broken economic
and political system.

---

4. C. Wright Mills, *The Power Elite* (New York: Oxford University Press, 1956).

Michael Locker *is founder and president of Locker Associates, Inc., a New York City business consulting firm that specializes in corporate restructuring, buyouts, feasibility studies, developing business plans, and performing due diligence. In addition, over the last thirty-five years he has helped several trade unions deal with difficult business issues and corporate power.*

PHILLIP LOPATE

Columbia College alumnus/Alumni for a New Columbia

DAYS OF WHINE AND RUSES

uch as I shy away from the very notion of generational identity, I must own to being a creature of the sixties. Born in 1943, I entered Columbia as an undergraduate in 1960, graduated in 1964, and was influenced unsystematically by that period's anti-Establishment attitudes. The sixties have been so mocked, caricatured, or flattered by later generations that anyone who lived through that era sometimes seemed to have had only two choices: loyal defender or turncoat. What often is missing, which I would like to propose, is a middle path: critiquing our mistakes and misconceptions while remaining sympathetic to the era's spirit of idealism and experimentation.

"The personal is the political" was a slogan back then. I would not go so far as to equate the two, but I would argue that one's private circumstances do have a bearing on one's political views. So here are a few personal facts: in my senior year at Columbia, I had gotten married, we had lived abroad for a year and then returned, my wife supporting me while I tried to write a novel. Ultimately, I managed to eke out a tiny living ghostwriting and working for an antipoverty program. By 1968, our marriage was in serious trouble. We had moved from secluded middle-class Inwood, the upper tip of Manhattan, down to West 103rd Street, a dozen or so blocks south of Columbia, to be closer to the action, and suddenly there was plenty of action. Student protesters had occupied five buildings on campus in April 1968. It seemed worth checking out.

Having graduated four years earlier from Columbia College, I was drawn to the student rebellion for several reasons: (1) opposed as I was to the Vietnam War, I had been participating in marches in New York and Washington, D.C., distributing flyers to unsuspecting pedestrians, and generally answering the call; (2) having spent several years in writerly isolation, I was looking for excitement, communal and erotic (file under: "the personal is political"), and (3) I envied the students their fun. The Columbia I had gone to at the beginning of the sixties was a staid, tweedy place. We had aspired or pretended to be sober, mature grownups, and in consequence, I felt I was missing out on my youth. As a late-comer to the bacchanal, I wanted to protest and to party.

I visited the first floor of the student center at Ferris Booth Hall (since torn down), which had been taken over as strike headquarters. Before we could enter, we had to be vetted by somber student guards wearing Che berets. I was immediately struck by the theatrical mise-en-scène of it, the air of dress-up, a militancy pastiche thrown together from Ho Chi Minh's North Vietnam, Fidel's Cuba, and Mao's China. Card tables carrying pamphlets, posters, radical literature, buttons, and other revolutionary paraphernalia lined the room. The atmosphere was, despite a certain grim determination—the frustrated feelings that *something* had to be done about the war, that we had to *act*, not simply stand by—like a street fair.

A few days later, I was given a tour of Fayerweather and Avery, two of the occupied buildings, and I saw the dishabille of sleeping bags and blankets, book bags, and portable typewriters. It looked like a pajama party, it looked jolly, with the exception of interminable meetings at which everyone who wanted to speak could. Direct democracy notwithstanding, I already had been tipped off that the Students for a Democratic Society (SDS) leaders would manipulate the outcome by holding off votes until early morning, when they could be assured a majority. Still, I was impressed with the practical arrangements being made for daily operations, food delivery, and chores. It did not occur to me to join the occupying students, especially with my apartment's warm bed close by. It was enough just to have seen the sleep-ins to feel part of history in the making.

Much was made later of the cavalier way the students mistreated university property, smoking the president's cigars and turning hallowed classrooms into messy dorm pads. Certainly, some hostility was being expressed toward this institution of higher learning; but the occupations also may have signified an affection for the university, or a longing to know it with greater intimacy, by snoozing on its floorboards. I understood this ambivalence, having, on the one hand, fallen in love with Columbia, ever grateful for the fine education it had given me, and on the other hand, put off by its chilly impersonality and clubby exclusions. Despite my high grades, I had been passed over for various fellowships abroad because, as a friendly faculty member clued me in, some professors had disapproved of my less than deferential attitude and found me to be not one of their own. In retrospect, I see they were right: they perceived I wasn't cut out to be a scholar-academic moving compliantly through the ranks. But at the time, I felt unjustly spurned and resentful enough to share the student activists' animus.

Those tensions had been brewing for some time. In the early sixties, I had been largely apolitical, as was the campus, but when the administration censored the literary magazine, *Columbia Review*, I enthusiastically joined the protest. The college was still all male, and the hottest political issue at the time was whether women should be allowed to visit the dorms. (I was all for it.) The paternalistic, *in loco parentis* attitude on the part of the university administration rankled deeply. The fact that then-president of Columbia, Grayson Kirk, was known to be resistant to women faculty only intensified our opposition to this patriarchal authority figure. You could never admit aloud that the students' rebellion was partly Oedipal, but you could think it. And so what if it was? I was too young then to put in a word on behalf of fathers.

I don't recall how I received notice that some graduates were forming an organization in support of the student protests, but I went to the first meeting. Out of it came Alumni for a New Columbia (ALFONECO). We fancied ourselves the progressive, pro-youth alternative to the official, conservative alumni association, which supported President Kirk and the antiprotest students to the hilt. As with many New Left organizations, our members ran the gamut from mildly liberal to revolutionary, a confusion which would have to be sorted out later. For the moment, we were united by goodwill toward the strikers and a desire to support them. My own political position at the time might be best defined as social democratic, more in sympathy with Sweden's social welfare state than Maoist China, but I felt guilty about my wishy-washy politics and was open to persuasion by the more militant stance of the SDS radicals who were spearheading the unrest, should historical events move in a more extreme direction.

Tom Hayden, who had helped found SDS in 1962, remembered the chairman of Columbia SDS, Mark Rudd, as "absolutely committed to an impossible yet galvanizing dream: that of transforming the entire student movement, through this particular student revolt, into a successful effort to bring down the system."[1] It's hard to credit now the gullible belief that such an overthrow of the government and the whole capitalist system was even in the offing. I remember going during this time to a reading at St. Mark's Church, and the poet Anne Waldman whispering in my ear: the word on the street was that *it* was going down this summer. "It" being the revolution. I very much doubted that, but was intrigued that there even existed rumors about the possibility. One day, during the strike, I was on an uptown bus going past Columbia toward Harlem and saw sidewalk demonstrators yelling up to the passengers, "Join us! Join us!" From the baffled looks on the face of my fellow riders, mostly black, I could tell they had not the slightest idea what they were being asked to join. Ten blocks away from campus and, moreover, throughout the city, the disturbances had caused not a ripple. Yet in my progressive circle, the sentiment was growing that one should "organize," at least enlist in a like-minded crew to prepare for a general strike or some sort of insurrection that might break out. And so I joined ALFONECO.

About fifty of us were at that first meeting, mostly in our twenties and early thirties: psychotherapists, medical students, and writers, as well as a smattering of older people, lawyers whose children were among the protesters, and ex-Communist (maybe not "ex") organizers from the Maritime Union who had come out of the woodwork. Michael Nolan, a documentary filmmaker for PBS, chaired the meeting. I sat in the back, raising various objections, as I would in subsequent meetings. It is a truth universally acknowledged that whoever speaks up and challenges a group with irritating questions eventually will be asked to lead it. That is how I became in short order the president of ALFONECO.

By that time, the students had been evacuated from the buildings by the police, who forcibly dragged them out and pummeled them and many bystanders bloody with nightsticks. I was not a witness to this shameful

---

1.   Tom Hayden, *Rebel: A Personal History of the 1960s* (Los Angeles: Red Hen Press, 2003), 254.

event, but it became the dividing line in the protests, a scandal which the Kirk administration would never live down and which solidified sympathy for the student radicals (within hours a university-wide strike was called). During the bust, several hundred protesters had been arrested, and ALFONECO quickly got to work, its lawyers filing *amici curiae* briefs in court and its polemicists (the group was rich in writers) turning out statements for the press about how "shocked and appalled" we were at the university administration's latest clumsy maneuvers.

President Kirk and Provost/Vice President David Truman both seemed to possess tin ears, granting us much insensitive fodder to work with. We were hoping local newspapers would at least include a line or two from these "shocked and appalled" press releases, in the interest of balanced coverage. We also hoped the stream of press statements would disguise how small we were: I doubt if our membership ever exceeded two hundred in the mailing list. We engaged in public debate with the official alumni organization, men in business suits who deplored what they saw as longhair anarchists spoiling the college experience for more serious students. I went on the Barry Gray radio show and argued with someone from the official alumni group. By this time, I had all the talking points down pat: the university was engaging in military research, ripping off the Harlem community, and so on. It was easy to stay outraged after the police bust. But looking back, I wonder how much I actually accepted the logic of the strike demands.

For instance, one of the chief demands was that the university sever its ties from the Institute for Defense Analyses (IDA). Although Columbia initially had been an institutional sponsor of IDA, the university had no outstanding contracts to do military research at the time of the Columbia protests. Some individual faculty members did have dealings with the government, but the traffic was minimal: IDA served more as a conveniently symbolic focus for student outrage against the Vietnam War than an actual player on campus. Of course, in a larger sense, the university was thoroughly integrated into the "military-industrial complex," as Columbia's former president, Dwight D. Eisenhower, had termed it: how could it not be? SDS researchers were busy charting the overlapping elite who sat on the boards of banks, corporations, newspapers, government agencies, and universities. Was this a genuine conspiracy or the logical outgrowth of a corporate society? Even at the time, I was not shocked at the information in these charts. But I had a role to play, knew my lines, and relished the spotlight.

As for the gymnasium that Columbia had wanted to build in nearby Morningside Park, in retrospect it might not have been such a bad thing; the park was a shabby, neglected amenity that could have used some traffic. The bulk of the building would have been allocated to the university, while a smaller section with a separate entrance, occupying some miniscule percent of square footage, would have served the community. That the entrance to this proposed community facility was located below, in the park, had unfortunate connotations of a tradesmen's or servants' entrance, which the protesters fastened upon, although the reason for that arrangement had more to do with topography than racial prejudice. The Harlem community leaders, originally in support of the gym, had grown mistrustful, rightfully suspicious of a Columbia land grab. The university has had a long history as an acquisitive neighbor: witness its recent expansion into Manhattanville. Still, the upside was that the community would have gotten much needed recreational facilities, including a swimming pool. But its elected officials, State Sen. Basil Paterson and Assemblyman Charles Rangel, had both come out against the gym construction, while firebrand H. Rap Brown had said if it were built it should be torched to the ground. In essence, the strikers' demand to stop the gym's construction was largely symbolic, a way for SDS to link the antiwar protest to civil rights and to defer to the black students who were occupying Hamilton Hall and who themselves were deferring to the Harlem community.

A third demand was amnesty for the six SDS student leaders who had led a march inside Low Memorial Library earlier in the year, in violation of the rule against indoor demonstrations. I had no problem at the time agreeing with this demand, although when I think about it now, I am less certain that self-proclaimed revolutionaries who hope to overthrow the government and in the short term bring their university to a halt should not be prepared to pay the consequences. Under normal circumstances, they might have faced academic suspension for a term. It seems hypocritical to argue that the university is morally bankrupt, on the one hand, and to cling to enrollment in said institution, on the other. But perhaps not: in armed rebellions, amnesty often is made a precondition to peaceful settlement. Interestingly, the university administration and the faculty were much more willing to compromise on demands involving external matters, such as the IDA and the gym, but the one demand they resisted strenuously was amnesty: they seemed averse to ceding the right to discipline students who had broken their rules.

As it turned out, Columbia, having spent millions on preliminary planning for the gymnasium in Morningside Park, gave it up, severed its formal connection with IDA, and suspended punishment for almost all student infractions. The criminal cases against the arrested students also were dropped. So in that sense, perhaps the demands were shrewdly conceived as practical and achievable, and their having been met in the end constituted a victory for the strike. Conversely, because they were largely symbolic, their accomplishment changed little of substance. The faculty had taken the demands quite seriously, and tried to negotiate on each item to bring about a peaceful resolution, using their (excessive) faith in the powers of reason to avoid a police bust. The student protest leaders did not, I think, take the demands as seriously. Mark Rudd himself later boasted to a reporter that "we [SDS] manufactured the issues. The Institute for Defense Analyses is nothing at Columbia. Just three professors. . . . And the gym is bull. It doesn't mean anything to anybody."[2] But whether or not the demands were serious, SDS dug in, refusing to compromise on them, so as to compel exactly the theatrical, bloody denouement that occurred when police ousted the students. It was this very outcome the professors acting as go-betweens had dreaded: some faculty even volunteered to interpose themselves in front of the buildings if the police moved to clear them. In short, the faculty cared more about protecting the students from physical harm than the students themselves did. Youth believes itself immortal; those who have attained middle-age know otherwise.

What puzzles me now is why I gave so little thought to the validity of the demands. I seem to have been closer to the militants' viewpoint, that it was all a pretext to confront the university as a surrogate for The Establishment, so who cared if the demands were manufactured? The point was to show our opposition to the Vietnam War and racial injustice—and to stick it to Columbia.

---

2. "A Campus Rebel's Confession," *Boston Globe* (Boston), October 1, 1968.

In my current thinking, I regard the American university as a soft tar-get. Politically engaged students are in school; hence, they commence their political struggle where they are, using the university administration as a convenient though often misplaced opponent. I suppose it could be argued from a Marxist perspective that the university indoctrinates false consciousness, or, as Pierre Bourdieu maintains, that higher education reinforces the rigid hierarchical class structure. But colleges, I can't help thinking, are not primarily responsible for the ills of society, and to the extent that they provoke critical thinking, they offer a line of resistance. True, my changed perspective may have something to do with having become a faculty member at Columbia, co-opted by the academic mind-set and paycheck that lures me to identify more closely with the institu-tion. William Blake said, "The tigers of wrath are wiser than the horses of instruction."[3] I wonder whether I understood this Blakean adage in 1968, and now that I've become one of the faculty nags or ponies, have forgotten it. But no, I don't believe that righteous wrath necessarily trumps every other kind of moral authority.

ALFONECO set about raising money for the legal defense of the several hundred students who had been arrested. Our main fundrais-ing event was a benefit featuring several radical theater groups, among them the Living Theater and the Open Theater, who donated their per-formances. We held the benefit at Bill Graham's Fillmore East, usually a venue for rock groups, on Second Avenue in the East Village. The evening was well attended, we raked in lots of money for the cause, the first few acts had performed on cue and everything seemed to be going fine. The Living Theater had taken the stage while members of their troupe were roaming the aisles, muttering "I can't go anywhere without a passport." Suddenly, a gaggle of crazed-looking hippies, male and female, marched onstage, shooing the Living Theater off, and announced that they were hijacking the event for their group, Up Against the Wall Motherfuckers, a radical anarchist gang known to be amphetamine-heads. They certainly appeared high on speed as they set up a typewriter, churning out man-ifestos while haranguing the audience. One of the women pulled out a breast and started nursing, looking like a sans-culotte from the French

3. William Blake, "Proverbs of Hell," in *The Marriage of Heaven and Hell* (Boston: John W. Luce, 1906), 17.

Revolution. I retreated next door to Ratner's Dairy Restaurant, commiserating with fellow organizers. At one point I looked up to see the legendary founders of the Living Theater, Julian Beck and Judith Malina, at a nearby table, munching reflectively on onion rolls. The Becks seemed to have taken the disruption in stride, as if to say: *What are you gonna do? These things happen in revolutions.* Indeed, worst things had happened to them: at one of their local performances of *Paradise Now*, when they invited the audience members to come onstage for the big free-love finale, Judith Malina had been raped. Strange times.

An outgrowth of the strike against academic classes at Columbia was the formation of the Liberation School, whose lectures and seminars were meant to correct the dominant capitalist ideology. Out of curiosity, I attended several of these offerings. The problem with my seeking to be instructed by younger radicals was that, at twenty-five, I knew more history than they did at eighteen, and had to keep that greater sophistication on hold. The radicals, looking far and wide for exemplary militant models, were not only worshipful of Lenin but also half-willing to rehabilitate Stalin and to swallow the most far-fetched claims of Maoists. (For instance, that no one was ever executed in Communist China; enemies of the state were only "re-educated.")

The student radicals were drawn to whatever felt severe or uncompromising, like guerrilla warfare strategy manuals. The Liberation School invited all the Left splinter groups—the Spartacist League, the Socialist Workers Party—to duke it out for the correct political line. Thus, I heard Lyndon LaRouche, then calling himself Lyn Marcus, a thin man with a Lenin goatee, put forward the National Council of Labor Committee's (NCLC) position, harsh but not having yet diverged into paranoid claims that Queen Elizabeth was a Zionist agent trying to assassinate him. I listened to Paul Rockwell, of Progressive Labor, advocate that we go downtown and try to raise the consciousness of the token-selling clerks by standing beside their booths and engaging them in political discussion. I heard proposals for students to make alliances with street gangs. Criminals were seen as proto-revolutionaries, acting out against the System.

If there was anything nonnegotiable in my political beliefs, it was freedom of artistic expression. Any pressure to dilute difficult art or make it more responsive to the masses, agitprop, or social-realist should be resisted, I thought. I knew full well the fate of Babel, Mayakovsky, and Mandelstam,

writers ground up in the Soviet machine. Hence, I was especially interested in Liberation School sessions on literature. There I heard that we
would need to jettison Dostoevsky, the writer who had meant the most to
me in my teenage years, because he was reactionary; Céline, being a Nazi
sympathizer, would of course have to go, although I loved his novels; and
Yeats—my beloved Yeats—wasn't he also right wing? Over the side of the
boat with him. Freud was discredited because he emphasized individual
neurosis and not social pathology. With the literary ranks denuded, who
was left? Victor Serge, maybe. Eventually they even banished the seemingly inoffensive psychologist Erich Fromm as a liberal reformer. "Reform"
had become such a dirty word. I remember a headline in the Progressive
Labor newspaper: "The Struggle Against Reformism Is the Struggle to the
Death!" I dared not let on that many reformers were still heroes in my eyes.

There was another difference I had with the student radicals, one I would
have been too ashamed to admit: I did not hate America. (Or Amerika,
as it was styled, to conflate it with the Ku Klux Klan.) For all its faults,
and there were many, I could not see the United States as Fascist or even
verging on Fascism. I had already spent a year abroad in Spain, France, and
Morocco, and had seen that other countries could be as screwed-up as the
United States, possibly more so. Without being able to articulate it as well
as the philosopher Richard Rorty, I shared his feeling that the Left would
never succeed here until it learned to express some love for this country.

Although I had no intention of following the student radicals' reading proscriptions or accepting their more nutty ideas, I kept being drawn
back to their discourse, beguiled by its tone of certainty. It struck me as
Dostoevskian, like a chapter out of *The Possessed*. It may very well be
that I understand very little about political theory: my mind works in
another way, let's call it literary. What intrigued me, besides the radicals'
unruffled conviction, was their encoded language, rife with ritual phrases
and demythologizing tricks. At the time, I even wrote a short story entitled "Basic Facts Leading to an Analysis," which mocked this language
through a series of fragments, portentous pronouncements, vignettes,
and found texts. Underneath this pastiche lay my confession that, despite
of my efforts to imbibe Marx, Gramsci, Marcuse, and Fanon, I was still
reading them for the occasional uncanny phrase, like poetry.

I would have been happy to give up my doubts and surrender to the
correct party line: a whack on the head by a police nightstick might have

done the trick of radicalizing me, but I was not lucky enough to have been so anointed. One of our ALFONECO members, a tall, beautiful, red-headed medical student who always came to meetings wearing camouflage jackets, reported exuberantly that she had been in Chicago for the demonstrations around the Democratic National Convention and had mixed it up with Daley's police. She I would have gladly followed into street-fighting action. As it was, I managed to get myself arrested one night at City College, where a mass gathering of students was giving sanctuary to a soldier who was absent without official leave. I was standing between a Columbia chaplain, Rev. William Starr, and a kid from the War Resister's League, all of us doing exactly the same thing (nothing) at the time the police swooped us up and herded us into paddy wagons. Thrown into a Tombs cell along with twenty others, with one toilet bowl and nothing to eat for twenty-four hours but bologna sandwiches, I decided the light bulbs were too weak to write my literary opus in prison, like Wilde or Pound, and resolved to try to stay out of jail henceforth. I made the one allowed phone call to my wife, who came and bailed me out. My mother-in-law happened to be in town, and Carol commented ruefully that I would do anything to avoid her mother—even get arrested. When our case came to trial after several months' delays, the judge pronounced Rev. Starr innocent, me guilty (sentence suspended), and sentenced the boy who slept on the floor of the War Resister's League to thirty days in jail, he having demonstrated insufficient "roots in the community." A more elegant demonstration of selective justice could hardly be imagined.

I still hadn't gotten over the urge for baptism by nightstick when that summer I found myself in Mexico City, marching in a vast antigovernment demonstration, fortunately not in the same segment in which several students were shot dead. The chances I took that year make me shudder. Was I suicidal or just hungry for adventure?

After the student radicals occupied Hamilton Hall a second time, on May 21, this time without the support of the black students, there was a turning away from SDS leadership, a feeling that they had overplayed their hand. By this time a more moderate protest group, Students for a Restructured University (SRU), had come into being, whose stated purpose was to bring about a more democratic, demilitarized, and community-sensitive Columbia. The SDS leadership had total contempt for this reformist group. They insisted they were not fighting the university to improve their own environment (God forbid!), but only the lot of Vietnamese and Third World peasants and oppressed blacks in the United States. This lofty refusal to issue demands in their own self-interest (with the all-important exception of amnesty) struck me as reflecting the noblesse oblige, the entitlement, of middle-class youth. I, on the other hand, having come from a poor ghetto background and attended Columbia on scholarship, had wanted above all, someday, to climb into the middle class, and was dismayed to find its dormitory rooms shockingly dingy, its WASPy snobbish atmosphere alienating. I would have liked to have seen my alma mater improved—restructured, if necessary.

When a fact-finding commission formed to investigate the disturbances at Columbia University, chaired by Archibald Cox, ex-solicitor general of the United States and a Harvard law professor, issued its report, *Crisis at Columbia*, it found that the quality of student life did leave much to be desired:

> On a tour of inspection of all the campus dormitories with the Director of Men's Residence Halls . . . the actual residence facilities for the men were appallingly restricted. . . . Naked light bulbs in corridors, scarred and battered furniture, walls, and floors gave the older dormitories the general atmosphere of a run-down boarding house . . . [A]s we know where there is a social *esprit de corps*, University facilities *per se* are not terribly important. However, at Columbia there was neither group feeling nor individual comfort. Frequently students reported a sense that they were being exploited for the financial profit of the University.[4]

The Cox Commission added: "Certainly loneliness, isolation, and social awkwardness are not ordinarily strangers to people of college age. However, it was my impression that the Columbia experience fostered rather than ameliorated such experiences."[5] This had been quite true of my undergraduate years. SDS derided the Cox Commission report's conclusions: as if they had gone on strike to protest naked light bulbs! But I

---

4. *Crisis at Columbia: Report of the Fact-Finding Commission Appointed to Investigate the Disturbances at Columbia University in April and May 1968* (New York: Random House, 1968), 31.
5. *Crisis at Columbia*, 32.

did not see why a deteriorated environment, low group morale, and psychological malaise could not play a part in one's politics.

So I crossed over from the Liberation School and began attending meetings at SRU. The group, which had some funding, hired me as a researcher and writer. The pay may have been low, but it was much appreciated, as I was then cobbling together a scant living from freelance ghostwriting jobs. SRU seemed to be composed largely of social science graduate students, veterans of the Fayerweather occupation who were distressed by the dubious pacification uses to which their anthropological or sociological researches might be put. The organization was chaired by John Thoms, a graduate student, who sent us out as a team to gather information about various academic disciplines. We interviewed Paul Lazarsfeld, a sociology professor and pioneer in the field of survey research, and this Viennese émigré who had fled the Nazis responded to our questions politely, no doubt thinking us babes in the woods. We listened to Basil Paterson, the dignified black assemblyman, who briefed us on the Harlem community's worries about Columbia. I wrote up reports on all these encounters, which then got filed and forgotten, as was proper. If I was skeptical of the paranoid claims of SDS, I was equally dubious of the efficacy of SRU. In a sense, I agreed with that old veteran of radicalism, my ex-drama professor, Eric Bentley, who, in a speech at the sundial, commented drily that you don't try to reform a university, you bring down the government and then the university falls in your lap. Still, I had to hand it to SRU that at least they were considering ways to augment student power and make the university more democratic. SDS, on the other hand, insisted on fighting against Columbia but showing no interest in working from within to improve it. As the historian Robert A. McCaughey wrote in Stand, Columbia, "those in SDS and the Strike Coordinating Committee did not care if Columbia went under and were, as SDSer Lewis Cole put it, 'way beyond that.'"[6] They were content to expose the university as corrupt: were they to participate in future academic governance, they too would be tainted, they seemed to be saying.

By attending meetings and rallies, I got to know some of the SDS leaders, such as Mark Rudd, Lewis Cole, and Ted Gold. Mark was charmingly

6. Robert A. McCaughey, *Stand, Columbia: A History of Columbia University* (New York: Columbia University Press, 2003), 470.

bluff and always friendly to me. He would listen patiently to my caveats about the fate of poets in the Soviet era. There is a time-honored role for the poetic conscience in revolutionary struggles, and Mark seemed to regard me as his literary mascot. Mark seemed to be always surrounded by several women. Even at the time, he was criticized as a male chauvinist and the strike leadership itself characterized as male-dominated. The key to Rudd's charismatic popularity was that he spoke the colloquial language of youth, never deigning to moderate a brash style in public. When he denounced a senior faculty report that failed to grant amnesty as "bullshit," the swear word was regarded by many as shockingly rude and disrespectful (as though they'd never heard the word before). But Rudd knew what he was doing. He embodied the generation gap's slogan "Never trust anyone over thirty." His truculent speaking style enabled him to hold onto his base and show he was not about to give in, even as it negated his utility as a negotiator.

In January 1969, I shared a van with Rudd and several of his female SDS supporters to Washington, D.C., to protest Nixon's inauguration. It was snowing on the trip down, the day before the inauguration, and Mark seemed in a relaxed, playful mood, as though we were all going to a fraternity party instead of a confrontation with the police and National Guard. When we arrived at the church that would put up the demonstrators overnight, I saw to my alarm that most of the protesters who would be thrown into street fighting the next day were young high school students. Cannon fodder. I asked Mark how he expected these inexperienced kids to take on the fuzz. He said it was simple: after one day of taunting, running, and being chased, you become an old pro at street fighting. I shook my head in disbelief. As the evening meeting progressed, with the gathered youth sitting on the hard wooden church floor they would be sleeping on that night and listening in awe to Mark and other movement organizers lay out the strategic plans for the next day's counterinaugural action, I started to get a bad feeling in the pit of my stomach. I suddenly felt I didn't belong there. Having made prior arrangements to sleep at a D.C. friend's house, after an hour, I got up and started heading for the door. As I passed by Mark, he looked up and said to me, "How does it look?" I answered, "Not good." He seemed startled, nodded, and then thrust forward his hand for a *Venceremos* fist-pound. "Goodbye, Mark," I said wearily, offering my more traditional handshake. And that was the last time I saw Mark Rudd.

The next day I shivered on the sidewalk as the National Guard tanks massed and the dignitaries' limousines rolled by. We demonstrators were spread out thinly over a large parade line. Every so often, we would yell our slogans and shake our fists, and then retreat when the police advanced on us. It seemed a fairly pointless protest—not the first I had participated in, nor the last. I learned later that some of the young demonstrators had engaged more directly with the police and were roughed up. When it came down to it, I had no intentions of getting beaten silly: I was either too prudent or cowardly for that.

Back in New York, I started my first job as a poet in the schools. ALFONECO had been losing momentum, soon to disband. By the summer of '69, my marriage definitively over, I left for California and one last stab at being young. I was never much good at it.

The corollary to "the personal is political" is that one's involvements in politics may have a private as well as a public motive. In my case, I seem to have been trying to enact a youth that was fast escaping my grasp. What I did not realize was that it was not only five or so years that separated me from the student rebels. During that historical juncture there had been a sea change: thanks in part to the demographic bulge denoted by the term "baby boom" and in part to the marketing of youth culture, the students felt themselves part of a separate tribe, their age-group serving as sufficient identity, one radically different from grownups. By contrast, I and those on my side of the divide had prematurely yearned to be adult; it was too late for us to learn the siren song of youth. I could not dismiss so easily my elders' hesitations as "bullshit": if anything, I felt a twinge of pity for and identification with those professors shuttling between the benighted university administration and the recalcitrant students.

The legacy of the '68 strike was both positive and negative. Vaclav Havel said that the Columbia student actions had emboldened the Czech rebels and inspired dissidents around the world. In France, the May uprising, *les evenements du mai*, took the protest baton and ran it much further, even bringing down the de Gaulle government. A Paris student leader reported breathlessly to our Liberation School the fast-moving events; it made us giddy to think we were part of a worldwide movement. At Columbia, Grayson Kirk was replaced by ex–United Nations diplomat Andrew Cordier. Modest steps began to be taken to increase the diversity and gender balance of the student body, the faculty and the board of trustees.

Figure 30.1 Members of the steering committee hold their last meeting in Hamilton Hall before the black–white split in the early hours of April 24, 1968. From left to right: Unknown, Juan Gonzalez, Nick Freudenberg, Ted Gold, Mark Rudd (back to camera), unknown, Jonathan Shils, Ray Brown, and Cicero Wilson. *Photograph by David Finck.*

On the negative side, Ted Gold—whom I had heard deliver a humorous, self-deprecating speech at a street-corner rally: the rebel as nebbish—was blown up on March 6, 1970, by a homemade bomb in the West 11th Street townhouse. That such a sweet, gentle guy's life should end so violently testified to the runaway-train logic of revolutionary militancy. David Gilbert, another SDS organizer, was involved in an armed robbery of a Brinks truck during which two policemen and a security guard were killed. Mark Rudd joined Weatherman, which vowed to overthrow the government by violent or other means, he participated in the "Days of Rage" in Chicago, and then went underground, working at odd jobs. When he came out of hiding decades later, he, practically alone of the Weather Underground veterans, confessed to regrets for making mistakes. He was particularly ashamed of having given the okay to JJ (John Jacobs) during the second occupation of Hamilton Hall to burn papers belonging to Professor Orest Ranum. Had I known of this at the time I would have been horrified.

Most movement stalwarts never second-guessed their more questionable acts. In a recent *New York Times* follow-up article about the kidnapping of an NYU computer in 1970—a computer, by the way, that had nothing to do with military uses—one of the perpetrators, Nicholas Unger, was tracked down and interviewed. "'What do I say about being part of a generation of protests?' Mr. Unger said last week. 'The war was wrong, and people who tried to stop it were doing the right thing.'"[7] It must be good to have such a Manichean conscience. Still, one must remember that whatever was done, valid or preposterous, emerged out of the frustrated feeling that you had to do *something* about the war, you just had to *act*, not simply stand by. And in fact, the cumulative effect of all that protest activity did help bring an end to the Vietnam War. The feminist activist Ann Snitow has written wisely: "No activism is possible without naiveté, some faith in action in spite of rational assessments of what can actually be done. And, also, no activism without some grandiosity, some earnest belief in the value of making an unseemly display."[8] I should keep reminding myself of that, as I think back with bemusement to the unseemly if lively posturing, naiveté, and grandiose play-acting in which I and my confederates indulged during that time a half-century ago.

Phillip Lopate *('64CC) has written more than a dozen books, including* Waterfront, Portrait of My Body, *and* The Rug Merchant, *has edited several anthologies, among them* Art of the Personal Essay, *and is a professor and former director of nonfiction in the Columbia University graduate writing program.*

---

7. James Barron, "The Mathematicians Who Ended the Kidnapping of an N.Y.U. Computer," *New York Times* (New York), December 6, 2015.
8. Ann Snitow, *The Feminism of Uncertainty: A Gender Diary* (Durham, NC: Duke University Press, 2015), 4.

FREDERICK K. LOWELL

Columbia College undergraduate/Majority Coalition

A TIME TO STIR . . . UP TROUBLE

Much has been written about the political earthquake that became the Columbia riots of 1968 (whose aftershocks, in fact, continued to ferment unrest at Columbia through 1970). From the vantage point of fifty years, how effective were the protesters in changing the American "establishment" they so detested? What positive things emerged from that period in the university's history, and, in particular, is the Columbia of today a better place for having gone through that experience?

To begin with, a freshman at Columbia in the spring of 1968 lived in a chaotic time in the history of the United States. The country was bogged down in an unpopular war in Asia, with the specter of the military draft hanging over students' heads, President Lyndon Johnson dropped his reelection bid in the face of antiwar Democrat insurgents Sen. Eugene McCarthy and Sen. Robert Kennedy, and the political system was going through unprecedented stress, culminating with Martin Luther King's assassination in April. The riots that followed in America's cities added to the chaos. The thunder on the political Left through McCarthy and Kennedy was soon to be matched with the independent candidacy of George C. Wallace, governor of Alabama on the Right.

Many students at Columbia that spring were "clean for Gene." They dressed conservatively as they campaigned door to door for Sen. McCarthy in the early primary states and were easily recognizable by their

McCarthy political buttons. Others joined the Kennedy effort, which ended with Sen. Kennedy's assassination after the California primary in June. The dominant political leaning among Columbia students was probably Center Left; among the faculty, particularly junior faculty, it was just plain Left.

It was in this setting that a group of fringe radicals, organized as Students for a Democratic Society (SDS), tried to create an opportunity to politicize the university in a way they thought would be helpful to their cause.

Their vision of Columbia was an institution at odds with the principles of academic freedom. The radicals felt that the university should become a political weapon to be wielded by them in support of a "just" or "socialist" society; this was justified by their view that the American university already was politicized because of its ties to the government. They sought to change its politics to make it an effective tool for their "revolution," and they were willing to use force, which made universities like Columbia a soft target.

But how to accomplish that kind of change? At Columbia in 1968, you manufacture a confrontation over some bogus campus issues and hope it will attract enough support to create a hardcore and effective leftist faction on campus that will displace the liberal McCarthy and Kennedy democrats, whom SDS despised as part of the hated establishment. And, with a little luck, the university administration will make tactical mistakes, which will further drive support to your cause. And that is what happened, with amazing success. Probably no one was more surprised than SDS itself.

I wrote, nearly fifty years ago, about these events and the rather unlikely groups that sprang up, from the Majority Coalition, a student group (of which I was a member) opposed to the use of force and intimidation on campus, to the Ad Hoc Faculty Group (AHFG), to the involvement of the Students' Afro-American Society in the occupation of Hamilton Hall. Highlights were the incompetence of the administration in waiting a week to call in the police, the existence of a fifth column in the faculty that was happy to throw academic freedom out the window (even though their own existence depended on it), and the complete deprivation of the civil rights of the vast majority of students and faculty by mostly middle-class students playing at "revolution."

Columbia University in the sixties generally was regarded as a haven for leftist political thinking, and its faculty reflected this bias. In the context of both the national and parochial events of 1968, that bias became more pronounced. However, many college campuses in the United States at the time were on the left side of the political spectrum, and their faculties had a similar bias. What made Columbia unique was its taste for intolerance.

An incoming freshman in the fall of 1967 was greeted by College Dean Henry Coleman, who painted a picture of a melting pot of ideas propelled by academic freedom with words to the effect that everything a freshman might believe in would be challenged at Columbia. He wasn't kidding, and any traditional notions he may have held on academic freedom at Columbia were no doubt cast aside while he was being held prisoner in his office the following spring.

The principles of academic freedom connote a variety of different concepts, but at the very least, they include respect for the views of other people; the right to study, write, and speak according to one's convictions without interference from governments or a mob; in short, underlying academic freedom are the guarantees afforded by the Bill of Rights. These were denied the majority of Columbia students in the spring of 1968.

That speakers were shouted down, access to buildings blocked, and classes forced to be held off campus were understandable products of SDS and its supporters, whose interest in the democratic process was nil. But it was the behavior of the faculty and the administration that strains credibility.

Professor of Political Science Herbert A. Deane saw the faculty's overwhelming capacity to tolerate radical politics as a "no enemies to the Left syndrome." In 1970, he explained this in an interview conducted by a fellow student and me:

> Suppose any time in the last two or three years I went before a Columbia College Faculty Meeting and described myself or anybody else engaged in teaching a class.
>
> The door bursts open, there are four members of the John Birch Society and three YAFers [members of the right-wing group Young Americans for Freedom], and they come pouring into this classroom and say, "Don't pay any attention to this character; this is creeping socialism, you're being brainwashed, etc." I swear to you that within a half hour, the faculty of Columbia College, by a vote of 147 to 0, would have condemned that action, absolutely and totally, with no trouble at all in making up their minds about this.

But if I repeat the whole story, the same action, the same disruption of a class . . . and this time it comes from the Left, they'll fall apart into 22 groups. They just cannot bring themselves to condemn the same actions which they would cheerfully and easily condemn from the extreme Right, coming from a group which calls itself Left . . .

And this is the tragedy that they could not see, and can still not see, that you judge the actions, you don't judge the sponsor.

The faculty stake in the future of a university is a long-term one; generations of students come and go, but the professional academic lives and dies within the protective walls of the university. Thus, in 1968, when the walls around Columbia began to crack, the lack of effort on the part of the university professors and instructors to prevent a total rupture was, to SDS, at least, a welcome surprise.

The role of the faculty might have been extremely significant. As a group, the faculties of Columbia University had both the respect and the ability to exercise leadership in a time of crisis. They were, and are, after all, leaders in their respective fields, and as such were the single most important ingredient in the academic standing of the institution. Yet somehow, as a group, they never were able to take a decisive role in challenging the unfolding threat to the university.

Thus, in 1968, after the buildings had been seized, the first (and most important) manifestation of faculty organization emerged in the form of the AHFG. This "group" was truly unique, because its membership was never the same at any given moment. The AHFG was an ever-changing gathering of faculty members who met on campus, in Philosophy Hall, throughout the crisis to discuss what might be done to ease tensions. Although the AHFG began as an attempt by moderate to liberal faculty members to try to find a constructive resolution of the crisis, the informal nature of this group gave the more radical faculty members an advantage because the makeup of the group depended on who happened to have just walked in or out of the door. Not surprisingly, the AHFG lost no time in making gestures to SDS, the most significant of which was its pledge to stand before the occupied buildings to prevent the forcible entry by police and others.

By contrast, a university-wide faculty meeting held on April 28 passed a resolution by a vote of 466 to 40, which condemned the students who were holding the buildings and warned that their continued occupation might result in "irreparable damage" to the university.

The AHFG made good its promise to stop the police. Two days after the beginning of the takeover, President Grayson Kirk called the New York City Police Department. They came onto the campus, were met by a cordon of faculty members, a scuffle ensued, and a junior faculty member was clubbed. After pleas from professors and others to call off the police so that a settlement could be negotiated, the police were withdrawn. As the week of confrontation progressed, the AHFG, informal as it was, had grown into a political force.

There are two reasons for the success of SDS's counterparts on the faculty. The first was their obvious skill in manipulating the group's lack of structure to their benefit.

Second, if the radicals in the group were skillful, then most of the rest of the faculty was either uncommitted or incompetent. Like most faculty members, they also had a weakness for oratory and debate, and they believed there was no issue that could not be resolved through peaceful negotiation. Thus, a great many faculty members divided their time between trying to prevent violence and talking to the radicals in the buildings. Most faculty members claimed to deplore the seizure of the buildings. Yet they also deplored the possibility of police coming on campus. They felt that the only way to resolve the problem was to talk the occupiers out of the buildings.

Meanwhile, the university administration, now locked out of the president's office in Low Memorial Library, was in chaos.

Between 1967 and 1972, the Columbia administration was besieged. During the years of crisis, the men in Low were attacked (verbally and physically), tested, and condemned for their actions (or inactions) by all segments of the university community. Two presidents and scores of administrators came and went. Rarely has a university faced such overwhelming odds against its continued preeminence. Some observers may feel that it is to the credit of the Kirk administration, and especially the successor Cordier administration, that Columbia survived at all. Conversely, others might argue that Columbia's administrators, like nearly every other group in the university, deserve a share of the blame for the years of unrest. For it often was due to administration error, indecision, and weakness that the Columbia tumult became so severe and that the radicals managed to damage the university with so few consequences to themselves. The administration's decision to wait so long to end the occupations was a costly mistake, as it allowed SDS to dig in and seize more buildings. The delay, however, was not President Kirk's preference. His instinct from the outset of the April 23 demonstration was to crack down immediately. However, he quickly came under intense pressure from internal elements, which hampered his efforts to resolve the crisis. On the first day that Dean Coleman was being held in his office, Kirk himself remembered: "I was convinced at the outset, when I learned about the occupation of Hamilton Hall, that we should call the police immediately, and in retrospect, I think it would have been better if we had. . . . I said over and over again that we'll never solve this problem except by calling in outside force" (interview with Grayson Kirk, 1970).

Kirk believed from the beginning that the protesters were not interested in compromise and craved confrontation. Nonetheless, Dean Coleman and others apparently convinced Kirk not to call in the police, at least until the following morning. Coleman, in his testimony before the Cox Commission, tells why:

> [T]he president felt he should bring police in to get me out of the building. And I disagreed with this.
>
> My reason for disagreeing with it was a very simple one . . . one of the reasons we had tried to prevent violence between two groups [i.e., demonstrators and counterdemonstrators] on the campus is that if that got out of hand the police would get on campus if we called them or not . . .
>
> I had hoped we could have a year at Columbia without either the violence between students or the necessity of bringing the police on campus and . . . I didn't want to be the cause of it.[1]

As the week progressed, counterdemonstrators began to organize in the form of the Majority Coalition, which cordoned off the ground outside of the occupied president's office. The administration feared violence both among students and potential violence from the Harlem community (which, as it turned out, had very little interest in the Columbia saga). When the final police "bust" finally came, with its ensuing violence

---

1. "Proceedings of the Fact-Finding Commission," Columbia University, June 26, 1968, pp. 2835–36.

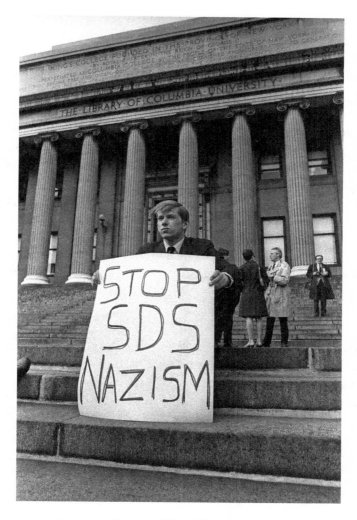

Figure 31.1 A student sit on the steps of Low Library, protesting the building occupations, April 1968. *Photograph by Gerry Upham.*

(some of it caused by students resisting and even attacking police), the
resulting injuries and chaos caused the campus to settle into an SDS-led
strike for the remainder of the academic year. The spectacle of middle-
class Columbia students clashing with police officers, whose own kids
could never afford to go Columbia, was an ironic lesson in the "class
struggle" that SDS pretended to champion.

In the ensuing four years, more conflicts occurred between radical students and the university, but with much less success for SDS, thanks to a much more effective and adept university administration.

The effect of the 1968 Columbia student riots on national politics was nil, as is evidenced by two Nixon victories in 1968 and 1972; the Reagan revolution in 1980; and the victories in New York by James Buckley, Nelson Rockefeller, and former Majority Coalition member George Pataki.

The effect on Columbia itself was hugely negative, as the university instantly acquired a national reputation for being a haven for political extremism.

The story of 1968 was not about some constructive spiritual awakening among idealistic and well-meaning students and faculty members. The legacy of 1968 is the spectacle created from an attack by political extremists on a great academic institution and the utter failure of its leaders to stand up to it. If, as a rule, history does indeed repeat itself, one hopes that this chapter will not.

Frederick K. Lowell ('71CC) is a San Francisco–based political lawyer. He was a member of the Majority Coalition in 1968 and later became chairman of Students for Columbia University, a student group opposed to any group or faction seeking to impose its point of view on the university community by force or intimidation.

Columbia College undergraduate/Majority Coalition

THE PRIMARY SHADES OF OPPOSITION TO THE COLUMBIA OCCUPATION

othing could make the meaning of Columbia's alma mater clearer than to see her suddenly attacked and so weakened that she could no longer nurture or protect her children. Students for a Democratic Society (SDS), Students' Afro-American Society (SAS), and their sympathizers were standing on her windpipe. Classes were halted. Columbia was essentially shut down. Until this incident, virtually every student assumed Columbia to be inviolate and eternal, so it was a paralyzing shock to witness this potentially mortal attack. For some, it was a galvanizing event: the Majority Coalition was born to physically oppose her tormentors. This is my personal observation of a short-lived organization that wholeheartedly rejected the strong-arm tactics of SDS and SAS and its sobering immersion into a deadly serious political confrontation.

The campus of Columbia is a blend of urban hurly-burly and scholastic asceticism in a highly stylized park setting. The university has distinct borders with imposing gates. They are high, solid, and, importantly, deeply symbolic. On the urban side of them is a cosmopolitan essence that gives Columbia its unique aura: the rhythms, sounds, and smells of the world's capital city, New York. Inside the gates is an academic refuge from a real-world caldron. Myth had it that if you were a Columbia College student and had committed a crime outside the gates, and if you could make it back inside the gates, you were safe even from the police, as Columbia was private property. Alma mater would protect you. Putting aside this myth, the sense of refuge was truly palpable. It conspicuously flowed from the temple-like architecture and serene, ivy-covered walls of its structures that invoked the gods of intellectual achievement on their friezes. Gigantic stone letters on Butler Library, visible from anywhere on the main campus, spelled out the names of Plato, Homer, Aristotle, Virgil, Shakespeare, Dante, and their ilk as an antidote to that which was base, uncritical, or irrational. Columbia was a safe house, where the dog-eat-dog of reality was held at bay just outside the gates.

This two-hundred-year-old institution began to wobble Tuesday, April 23, as the Visigoths—in the form of SDS and SAS—seized venerable teaching buildings. With each passing hour, their death grip on Columbia became more obvious and inescapable. The essence of her mission—to educate—was being erased. A flash flood of alarm began to form, fed by several disparate tributaries, an array of cultural subgroups and cohorts arrayed against SDS and SAS, all actively or tacitly in support of the thrust of the Majority Coalition. These subsidiary combinations, although unorganized, have sufficient definition and identity cohesion to deserve historic attention, because taken together, they formed a mandate for the Majority Coalition. This was a wide and variegated spectrum of people who came together because of their values and interests, which did not square with the violent and dictatorial tactics of the occupiers. Here are the outlines of the main cultural elements opposed to SDS and SAS tactics.

1. *Pragmatic Faction*

The news media gave the impression to the world that the student uprising reflected mainstream campus opinion. The journalistic ethos of "If it bleeds, it leads" ruled, with newspapers and TV news full of images of the five occupied campus buildings and the chaos caused by protesters who had forcibly stopped the daily life of the university. Yet out of the approximately seventeen-thousand-strong student population, only a few hundred were occupiers and vociferous demonstrators who actually closed down Columbia. There were plenty of onlookers and passersby, but no mass rallies attended by thousands of supporters. It was the unilateral and strong-arm tactics employed by SDS and SAS that were rejected wholesale by the great majority of the community, because they were inimical to the self-interest of the community. Many thousands of people did not believe that the protesters' grievances warranted the rupture of degree matriculation. Delay of degrees could increase tuition and loan costs, halt careers based on the award of those degrees, and interfere with continuing advanced education, especially at unrelated institutions that would not guarantee places without grades issued or degrees granted. Thousands of employee livelihoods, those of the faculty, administrative, and operational personnel, were on the line. Add to this number the great apathetic mass who saw the interruption of their regular lives as an unnecessary burden. Taken together, this spectrum of resistance, from those who had vital interests at heart to those who simply were annoyed by the inconvenience, represented the deep level of antagonism to the closure of Columbia.

2. *First Amendment Faction*

To facilitate violent action and so achieve their ends, SDS and SAS were adjudged by many to have highjacked the constitutional right of assembly and freedom of speech. From a purely politically philosophical position, this was anathema to ardent First Amendment advocates. The occupiers used the cherished academic freedom of Columbia as a stage to gain attention, and then shut down that stage (the normal classroom operation of the university), therefore denying to those who disagreed with them the very same stage. By shuttering the university and its classrooms, and instilling fear of increasing violence, the natural forums for debate and discussion—those hundreds of classrooms and related informal venues—were eliminated, and only the occupiers' message was broadcast (via banners and megaphones, which were in turn amplified by the media). This patent hypocrisy of the occupiers was deeply objected to by First Amendment advocates, a disparate, cross-cultural but nonetheless fervent cohort, to which I belonged.

3. *The Family Feud and No-Police Faction*

For many, Columbia was a family united by common goals of scholarly pursuits, academic and institutional traditions, and the pervasive myth that the campus was off-limits to the police or any state action. The Vietnam War and the civil rights struggle strengthened the resolve of this faction because the government was proven to be craven and untrustworthy. Thus, the Columbia problem, as seen by this cohort, was perceived as being better handled as a strictly internal matter, one to be somehow resolved by the disputants via discussion, accommodation, or even intramural physical action, but never by state action. This cohort believed the police to be the enemy of students, and citizens in general, because the police were the puppets of the power elite that was prosecuting the Vietnam War and stymying civil rights at every turn. This group therefore naturally supported the Majority Coalition's approach of self-help to avoid reliance on the police.

4. *Athletic Faction*

This athlete element of the Majority Coalition is instructive because it describes the most tribal element of the community. By their nature, participants in college sports are loyal to the institution for which they are carrying a pennant. They have uniforms with lions (Columbia's symbol) on them, they have marching songs, and they are on the battlefield of sports against those with battle regalia of other colleges. Flowing from this competitive environment is naturally an institutional loyalty, not all that dissimilar to the esprit de corps of armies to their country, analogous to patriotism. It is a logical step from this sense of institutional loyalty for athletes to oppose any group that is seriously at odds with the institution for which they regularly "fight" in sports. Therefore, those linked to alma mater by a sports commitment naturally would be the first to come to her aid.

The river of opposition to SDS and SAS that grew over the days finally swept me up. I was known both to the athletic cohort because of my early shared dormitory room with two athletes, Paul Vilardi and Bruce Bono, and to a wider audience because of my earlier active working relationship with the campus radio station, WKCR, where I had two "on-air" programs and participated in news and management. As a result of these connections, I was asked to give a keynote address on Sunday, April 28, before some five hundred Columbia students, of which a sizable share, but not all by any means, were athletes and related fraternity members. This audience was energized to find a way to actively resist the occupations. The purpose of my address was to recommend action. But which action? There were two choices.

One: To treat the occupation as an internal problem, a family feud, and to resolve it by employing not the police but other students to physically remove the occupiers. The law calls such action "self-help," and it is a venerable doctrine. This latter point was in keeping with the myth that

Columbia was inviolate even to the police. This internal option of removal had the perceived advantage that the occupation would be over without the use of deadly force (synonymous with the police) because the Majority Coalition (fellow students, after all) would be unarmed, as was presumed of the protesters. This approach to ending the occupation had the comforting, albeit simplistic and perhaps delusional, quality of a family squabble that afterward would find everyone able to exist together in a fully functioning collegiate environment.

Two: To place the occupiers under siege and starve them out of the buildings. The siege would be effected by forming a human cordon around Low Memorial Library, the dramatic epicenter of the occupation. The obvious advantage of this route was that it avoided direct hand-to-hand violence and yet gave those who rejected the SDS and SAS approach (for whatever reason) an active and coordinated way to voice that opposition.

In accord with my initial ambivalence over the methodology of action, I wrote two speeches on yellow legal paper, each promoting one or the other proposition. After laboring over them, I found myself emotionally torn over the decision. The physical extraction by our own students of the occupiers possessed equal dignity to the SDS and SAS physical occupation and might end it as rapidly as it had begun, without the dreaded intervention of the police. The Majority Coalition had, as said, a large number of athletic students who were physically capable of the task. Yes, it could be a melee, but it might be brief, restricted to fistfights and brawling, nothing more serious. Of course, imagining that the physical removal of students could be contained to gentlemanly brawling, and that violence would not escalate, was naïve and wishful thinking.

As the actual moment of the speech approached, the weight of recommending violence became oppressively heavy. I became fearful of the consequences for everyone and the weight I might bear for injuries or worse. I reached an almost choking awareness of the enormity of the personal responsibility of unleashing violence against anyone. No amount of rationalization could, to my mind, justify possible bloodshed. I also sensed that there was the aroma of bloodlust in the student-on-student solution, and this appalled me. Thus, I abandoned the speech advocating that the Majority Coalition themselves remove the protesters. Instead, I would advocate that a cordon around Low be established to starve out the protesters.

At about the same instant of this decision to recommend a cordon and moments before giving my speech, I received a telephone call, backstage at Ferris Booth Hall, from President Grayson Kirk. This was the first time I had ever spoken to him. He spoke firmly and directly, stating that if I recommended physical violence of any sort, I would be expelled from the university. After this conversation, I stared at the telephone in bemusement. Columbia had been brought to its knees by other students, but it was I who was being threatened with expulsion for attempting to rescue her. It was neither the first nor the last time during those days that events took on an absurdist quality.

Humbled and frightened, I took to the lectern and faced the audience. All were standing. The room was filled to capacity with males (Columbia College was not yet co-ed). A decision had been made that whatever action was taken, the implementation would be immediate and conducted with maximum dignity. A curious but profoundly meaningful aspect of the Majority Coalition action was that everyone wore a jacket and tie. We had decided to sharply distinguish ourselves from the protesters with a uniform that was clearly different from that of our generally disheveled adversary. Like any combative enterprise, one needs to be able to tell the sides apart.

Upon finishing the speech, which laid out why we were taking the action of a cordon and siege of Low, six hundred men filed out of the hall, deliberately walked slowly across campus in a long line, and took up their positions surrounding Low, standing on the inside of the hedges which bordered the building. Our job was simple: not to permit any food or water to enter the building. We thought that it was only a matter of time, a few days, a week at most, before the protesters would be forced to leave, and we were prepared to wait them out.

People on the outside began throwing food and bottles of water over our heads to their compatriots standing at the windows. We were effective in knocking many of these items out of the air and to the ground, which elevated the anger of the outside protesters, prompting them to loudly taunt and harass the cordon. Phalanxes of them charged the cordon at different places in an attempt to physically break it. Hand-to-hand fighting broke out sporadically, but the line held. Fear and tensions mounted on all sides as the hours and days wore on. Desperation on the part of the occupiers and their compatriots dramatically increased as it became clear

Figure 32.1 Members of the Majority Coalition surround Low Library to prevent food from entering, April 28, 1968. *Photograph by David Finck.*

that the cordon was tough and would not be broken by intimidation or force. Yet we on the line felt fear, too, more so as darkness fell. We knew that there would be stronger attempts to break the cordon at night, when darkness could obscure uglier tactics. Rumors circulated that acid would be thrown at us. That never happened, but the fear of possible permanent disfigurement or blindness was palpable, and defensive strategies were actively discussed. Strangely enough, the use of guns against us, or their use by us, was never feared or discussed. Guns were thought to be the province of the police, and that was a good part of the reason we rejected police involvement.

Was the Majority Coalition's reaction reasonably justified? Was Columbia College, and the university, truly at risk of annihilation? The answer turns on whether you view the academy practically or spiritually. If one sees it as an agglomeration of buildings where knowledge is passed from the learned to the initiates, then probably not. Once the protesters withdrew, the machinery would start again and roll on. Conversely, if one sees the academy as the *sanctum sanctorum* of uncensored thought and unfettered exploration of understanding, then forcibly closing the temple was a betrayal of American civilization itself, and therefore a real and deadly threat to what mattered most at Columbia and to the country.

Vaud E. Massarsky *('69CC) is the producer of seventy plays and musicals, author of short stories, publisher and editor of strategic business reports, marketing consultant, financier, entrepreneur, and research law clerk to the San Francisco Superior Court. Married to Felicia Kasputis, he has two children, Tara and Kurtlan.*

MICHAEL NEUMANN

Columbia College undergraduate/Students for a Democratic Society

NO MORE ANTIWAR! THE RISE OF THE THERAPEUTIC LEFT

T he 1968 Columbia "student revolt" doesn't rate as history. What matters about it is why it fails to do so.

1968 marks the year when the American Left ceased to matter. The reason is simple: the Left moved from addressing real issues to hyping fake causes. The causes were fake because they either were unformed and hysterically grandiose—"smash imperialism"—or tiny, yet purportedly fraught with significance, like Columbia University's development plans for the neighborhood.

Just what was fake about these causes? Whether grandiose or absurdly modest, they offered no realistic prospect of social or political change. This doesn't mean the '68 radicals were irrational, or that rationality is essential for good politics. Successful, valuable political movements haven't always had some elaborate ideology and they haven't always followed reason more than instinct. Besides, the most fake-extreme of sixties radicals always had some ponderously rational "theory" stashed away somewhere, built on whatever assumptions pleased them. What I mean by a "fake cause" is "no cause at all," no attempt to achieve anything—only a successful attempt to *feel* like an achiever.

The fakery comes out in high relief against the background of the times. The hippie movement was large and real; the lifestyle changes left their mark. The antiwar movement, too, was large and real. Wives of navy officers looked for antiwar speakers and someone wrote to the *San Diego Union*: my son just died in Vietnam and I want to say that he did die in vain. There was a real surge of social and political opposition. Its misfortune was that it came a bit later than the student Left, which therefore was awarded a kind of leadership of the whole show.

In 1968, the student movement abandoned the antiwar cause, and so, of course, the Vietnamese people. There was no more talk of actions that made any effort, no matter how small, to actually affect the prosecution of the war: no plans to stop troop trains, to disrupt the draft, or to agitate within America's armed forces. The student Left had acquired another interest: therapy through "radicalism." It sought cosmetically extreme actions as a means of transcending its middle-class hang-ups. Students became fighters—"warriors" they would be called today. They felt braver, purer, cooler. This was an end, not some means to some end; indeed, it confined itself to efforts ostensibly aimed at ends never on the horizon. It "demanded" not the sort of cultural change that hippies went some distance to effect, but a profound, deeply radical and structural transformation of society erected on the thorough destruction of the Western political and social order.

Some will tell you this was an ideal, a wild dream, a courageous and noble enterprise. There's nothing wrong with ideals and wild dreams; sometimes they have helped to sustain successful political movements. But the oracular rhetoric of the '68 radicals doesn't strike me as the innocent expression of an ideal. I believed, and still believe, it was a massive outpouring of bad faith and, despite itself, it was quintessentially American. Although I can't even speculate on the real causes of 1968, I know that "the kids" got tired of paying attention to little foreigners fighting their faraway war. If "the kids" didn't know that their grand agenda was bullshit, it was because they didn't want to know. They had become more interested in themselves, in their psychology, their theorizing, and their antagonism to mainstream America. They also loved the rush of "street fighting."

They became entranced, not with violence, but with the boisterous drama on the streets. These "battles" diminished into oblivion beside the realities of subsequent revolutions and failed revolts around the globe. Today, white-haired ex-student "radicals" still take that "violence" seriously. Others take it as a wild, irrational outpouring of "extremism." But it wasn't irrational, and it wasn't particularly extreme. It wasn't in the self-interest of the "rebels" to try and stop the war. The war did them no harm and the Vietnamese did them no good. And it *was* in their self-interest to play at revolution; it, too, did them no harm and brought them a lot of satisfaction. Their posture offended me, not because they were "radical," let alone too radical, but because they destroyed an antiwar movement that might have helped the Vietnamese. They cloaked their egotism in altruism. They pretended to fight for the oppressed of the world. In reality, they did not fight at all. They performed.

Sixties radicals often told themselves that these performances had *symbolic* value. They got *attention* in the media or elsewhere. This wasn't a craving for celebrity; it was, on the contrary, another step away from the political arena into the wonderful world of the self. Symbols *express* or *represent* things—in this case, the attitudes, the commitment, and the joyous transformation of the radicals themselves. So much the better if the world should see their inner progress. This was the modern counterpart of the Christian idea that you *bear witness* to the wrongs of the world: both attitudes help no one, but display the righteousness of your soul. No wonder student radicals were so comfortable abandoning Vietnam for the familiar confines of the university campus, where so many emotional dramas play out.

The "Columbia Revolt" was one episode in Leftism's rush to insignificance. Its precursor, earlier in the year, was the disintegration of the student Left, both on and off campuses. SDS, the chief student-radical organization, fragmented into a sort of stodgy old guard, some pseudo-Communists, and some pseudo-crazies. At Columbia, both SDS and antiwar leaders had been chosen by default for some time, and preoccupations such as penetration by "the Trots" replaced serious concerns. The new leadership decided to smash capitalism by opposing Columbia's development plans. This cause, but also the stylized and generalized outrage that adorned it, became a hit with the student body, by a process as mysterious as what makes for a hit single in the music business. The revolt, the explosion, was possible because the authorities, city, and university, never seriously opposed it—that is, they never employed the sort of violent response with which states meet actual revolts.

If there was any strategy to Columbia-style radicalism, it was appropriately psychological. Like the Days of Rage in Chicago the following year, emotion would carry the day, just as the generals of World War I thought their troops' élan vital, an intense acceleration driven by a force at life's core, would do so. Political action was purely a source of the uplifting thrill that would turn wimps into invincibles.

Much had to do with style. I had an Ethiopian friend, a talented graduate student in political theory. He wanted to enter Hamilton Hall, in mild solidarity with the black students occupying it. They wouldn't let him; he wasn't American and he was, in manner and aspect, too foreign. This is one little incident, but it sheds some light on the concern of the "revolutionaries" to maintain a certain appearance. We now might call it a brand, something that would resonate among the American people. Certainly it wasn't going to resonate with the Vietnamese.

Today, most of the revolutionaries are doing fine. Things are better in Vietnam, too, but not because of their efforts.

Michael Neumann *('68CC) was a founding member of Columbia Students for a Democratic Society. He was for many years a professor of philosophy at Trent University in Ontario, Canada. His books include* What's Left? Radical Politics and the Radical Psyche *and* The Rule of Law: Politicizing Ethics.

HILTON OBENZINGER

Columbia College undergraduate/Low Library occupier

ALREADY DEAD: INSIDE LOW LIBRARY COMMUNE

T he newspapers—and many of the faculty—thought we were simply in it for "the kicks," college pranksters out on an overblown panty-raid, or drug-crazed hippies simply tripped out of our minds. Above all, especially to the *Daily News*, we were the Ivy League; we were elite spoiled brats intent on soiling our own sheets, pampered kids, Human Be-In monsters of a permissive Dr. Spock.

Although we laughed all the time, we were totally serious. We met and talked nonstop, weighing every twist and turn in the negotiations.

We had learned that thousands of people in the neighborhood had been evicted or otherwise forced to move in the previous eight years—poor folks, colored people, the elderly—and the university was slated to push out ten thousand more in their plans to create their all-white, middle-class enclave. We knew all the lies, about the university's collaboration with the Pentagon and their plans to build their Jim Crow gym, the same as we knew with such bitterness and sense of betrayal all the lies about Vietnam, all the phony body counts, kill ratios, Gulf of Tonkin incidents, all the tumbling dominoes.

We laughed and played, but we were on no panty-raid.

Early on, we decided on a policy of no grass, no beer, just so the administration couldn't dismiss us with a cheap drug bust—although some people objected that life without a joint was just another way of caving in to the straight Establishment.

But, really, life in Low Commune was already an incredible high. For the first time, students were working together instead of trying to cut each other's throats in class. No more competitive, masculine, intellectual one-upmanship egged on by professors. For the first time, we had a real feeling of mutual aid, of group yearning and learning, and of one-mind determination and compassion. We were bound together, girls and boys, no longer isolated in girls' or boys' schools, alienated, stuffed into narrow dorm rooms or dark apartments by ourselves. Now we were a group of intersecting obligations to each other and to the world, sharing blankets and peanut butter, and we were set to overturn the System, and the discovery of that power kept us cool, kept us deliberate, filled us with joy.

Early on we had felt that high, but after the bust scare Thursday night, it became a palpable, overarching, living thing. Once we had decided that we would barricade, that we would allow ourselves to be arrested, and that we would offer nonviolent resistance in the face of cop terror, we knew we had crossed some kind of Rubicon.

Having made that choice, it was as if we were already busted, as if we were living already knowing that we were dead, so the fear of death could not sway us. Faculty, liberals, administrators, and everyone else were hollering at us that we were ruining our academic careers, wrecking our lives. And they were right; we were. But we knew that our old lives didn't matter anymore. None of us would take our expected place in the corporate war machine; none of us would allow ourselves to be used again, even though it would be "for our own benefit," no less.

The most horrible genocide was being committed right before our very eyes, and none of us would be Good Germans. A whole generation said, "No," no matter what the consequences.

Afterward, I realized it was that sensibility—that terrible Treblinka feeling—that drove me to my "already-dead" sensibility. Sure, this time it wasn't the Jews, my entire family, being slaughtered, but it was the same thing. But, unlike the Germans, our great "*Hell, No, We Won't Go!*" in fact would gum up the works. Our spoiled-brat refusal, that was life, real life— we knew we were catching a peek at another universe, and that glimpse would keep us solid, whole, honest—and that vision turned us into a commune.

It's not as if I really got to know anyone in the usual sense of collecting details about someone's past, what they majored in, or where they came from. I don't even remember a lot of people's names. We were so busy meeting over one negotiating ploy after another, deciding how to resist, fending off attacks, that anyone's individual ambitions or their past didn't seem to matter much anymore.

Some politicians said that Communists manipulated us and that we were brainwashed or coerced into staying, which only made us laugh. After all the lies, no one could manipulate us. Robbie Roth chaired one meeting (before he left and the faculty prevented him from getting back in), and when he hadn't called on everyone who had their hands up, we went up to him afterward and told him he couldn't pass over people like that, and he reconvened the meeting. After that, nothing was decided, no action taken, until everyone got their chance to speak.

Later, Tony Papert would chair the meetings. Tony was from the Maoist Progressive Labor Party, but he scrupulously encouraged every point of view, never quashed or silenced anyone, always in his soft voice reasoning everything out. Maybe it was our insistence on participatory democracy—that those who act must decide, and those who decide must act—that made him fair-minded. He respected us, no matter his dogmatic Maoist bent. No, the invisible force that held me captive was something too powerful to be wielded by one guy.

Mark Rudd was the leader of the Strike, and he became the "student radical," a certified "star" in the eyes of *Time* and David Susskind and Walter Cronkite, which we found nothing but wickedly amusing: no one occupying Kirk's office in Low Memorial Library made Rudd out to be anything too special because he was only a *schlemiel* like the rest of us. He knew it, and all his friends knew it, no matter how much day-glow the media might have dripped on his aura. Still, he had a way, a manner, a style of low-key, participatory, anti-uptight goofiness that made him not just "represent" us but "be" us. I suppose that meant real leadership qualities—just so long as he wouldn't try to be "a leader" in the traditional sense of the word.

After a few days of negotiations it became clear that, no matter what Grayson Kirk said, the gym was dead, and he and his cohorts would even have to disentangle from their Pentagon deals. So, out of our six demands, the one demanding amnesty for those in the buildings became the crux of the struggle. The administration adamantly refused, declaring, in their own game of falling dominoes, that if Columbia students went unpunished, then campuses across the country would capitulate to the forces of darkness.

Giving in on amnesty was never a question for Low Commune. How could we allow ourselves to be expelled or otherwise punished—by an arrogant administration that held its own students in contempt, no less, for doing what was right? Sure, they could call in the cops, they could even expel us, but why the fuck would we agree to *let* them? Liberals thought giving in made sense: we broke the rules, so we had to pay, even if we had just faced down imperialist genocide and racism. After all, that's all part of fair play: the faculty would pat us on the back and then sell us down the river.

"Bullshit!" was our response, which was exactly what Rudd said, thus freaking out the faculty at their meeting Friday night, but we knew he was right.

Maybe because we had that life-after-death feeling, Low just sat serenely, never budging for an instant. Intractable, we developed a reputation for being militant, although we were never the banner-waving guerrilla types like those who occupied Math. We considered every deal carefully, every proposal that was floated to us; we rejected each one point by point; and then we just stayed put, watching all hell break loose from out of the windows of Kirk's cockpit.

On the lawn and sidewalk below the windows of Low there were different roiling crowds—some in support of us, some in support but that didn't like what we were doing, faculty with their attempts to keep the warring factions separate, and jocks and the Majority Coalition wanting to beat the crap out of us pukes—with scuffles, surging crowds, fistfights, attempts to crash through the blockade, and other attempts to bring us food and supplies.

On Monday, the university stayed shut while the faculty tried to negotiate one last deal. Meanwhile, our supporters kept on trying to run the blockade. I stood on the ledge—we each took turns at the post to ward off jock attacks, to help anyone who made it through, and to show that we were the ones who had command of the heights.

We decided to wield the long poles with small metal hooks used for opening the window tops to push back any jock who might try to climb up the ledge, although we mostly kept the poles hidden, not wanting to provoke an unwarranted escalation. So when it came time to stand on the ledge, I only had my hands to ward off whatever bottle or spit or giant linebacker would come my way.

About a hundred of our friends marched around Low with boxes of food. Around and around they paraded, chanting, "Food! Food!" Suddenly the crowd veered toward Low and charged into the jock line. Fists flew, our people sprayed ammonia, I saw a knife glinting in the sun, a soda bottle swung up high above the boiling heads then dashed down, and I hollered from my position on the ledge. The professors broke up the melee, no one seriously injured, and our contingent backed up, unloading the goods in the boxes to throw their contents piece by piece at those of us doing guard duty on the ledges.

I teetered, I lunged, and I even caught a few grapefruits as they hurled over the heads of the blue and white armbands. Strikers cheered as each sardine can or loaf of bread was caught. Jocks jeered when salamis or oranges went wild or fell short or when I, the puke poet, bobbled and dropped them. Soon the jocks were waving blankets and frying pans trying to block each flight, they began flinging eggs and grapefruits and rocks at us, and I had to dodge or try to catch each missile or simply allow myself to be hit as I focused on catching the goods.

Friends told me I looked very grim on that ledge. I know I didn't smile as I concentrated intently at the fierce barrage coming at me. By the time it was all over, I had avoided most of the eggs and even managed to haul in a decent catch of groceries.

In response to that brawl, Kirk and Truman sent a squad of cops to form yet one more line, this time in front of the jocks, to keep the warring sides apart. Now we had three cordons around us, and while still we held the heights on the ledge, we could only wonder how long this *dance macabre* could go on.

Not long, as it turned out.

That night Low voted unanimously to reject the faculty's last deal, their "bitter pill," the compromise that would be hard for all sides to swallow.

Now the bust would surely come.

We met for hours deciding how we would make our last stand. One suggestion even floated around that we should all strip and resist nonviolently while stark naked. This tactic had its charms, but it was dismissed as too dangerous—who knows how the cops might react to a bunch of girls and boys in the buff?

At 2 A.M. the water was shut off, while word came over the walkie-talkie that cops were massing on Amsterdam Avenue.

This was it, no more false alarms; the bust was on.

Crowded into the largest room of the suite, we stood with our arms linked in a series of concentric circles, singing "We Shall Not Be Moved" and other civil rights songs. Axes and hatchets began chopping through the barricade of desks and bookcases and nailed-up boards, the rhythmic thuds playing counterpoint to our hymns.

Suddenly, a swath of blue uniform could be seen through the rubble, then a blue arm. A girl screamed, and we sang even louder to drown out the fear.

By chance the literary crowd from the *Columbia Review* had formed the smallest orbit at the very center of Low's concentric circles. I clutched Alan Senauke's arm tighter when the cops broke through, I looked at Les Gottesman's eyes, at Kathy Knowles and Nancy Werner's pale faces, and we howled "We Shall Overcome," knowing our time had really come when the first cop stepped through the hole.

That's when I noticed David Anderson.

David stood by himself in the very core of our most central circle.

There, in the very heart of Low Commune, was David, an open paperback book in his hands. Arms linked to no one else's, he clutched his book, his eyes steadily moving along the type.

I did a double take, but there he stood, reading with unaccountable serenity, his glasses teetering on his nose.

So intent on finishing the book, invisible in his wry, unassuming manner, no one else even noticed him. Despite the rising panic, despite the smell of violence in our nostrils, despite our straining voices, he kept on reading, unperturbed.

I gaped at him as he turned the last page, catching his eye as he looked up.

"Gotta finish the book, you know," he answered my astonished look with a wisp of a smile. He tilted it up to show the cover—Raymond Chandler's *The Big Sleep*—as if that were explanation enough, then he stuffed it into his back pocket.

How could he read a book, even a Chandler book, at a time like this? David simply offered his wry, asthmatic smile.

All the cops—dozens—shoved their way through the cleared barricade to take their positions, the final, blue concentric circle surrounding ours. Some officer blared through a megaphone—probably the official announcement that we were trespassing, would be arrested, and so on—although exactly what he said was unintelligible above the din of our chorus.

Then one cop, anonymous in his helmet, sauntered up to a girl on the very outermost circle—he seemed casual, almost nonchalant, a slight, fixed grin pasted to his lips as he sidled up to her.

He grabbed her shoulder with one hand, and then with his other, he raised one of those extra-long, aluminum utility flashlights high up over her head.

For a moment time stood still, the silvery flashlight suspended above her.

I stared at the frozen glitter of light on the long metallic tube, and even now I can see it glinting, forever poised above her head.

Then in a slow, heavy arc the cop brought the flashlight down on her skull.

Raising it up and swinging it down. Up and down, again, then again, repeatedly he pounded the girl's head, methodically clobbering her, the ghastly grin never leaving his lips.

She shrieked in pain, fell to the floor, yet he kept on swinging.

We howled in horror and rage, clutching ourselves more tightly, singing even more loudly.

Maybe they had drawn straws, and he would be first. Once that cop began battering the girl with his silvery flashlight, the rest of the horde as if on cue descended upon us from all sides. Yanking each circle of arms apart, they beat us wildly with their fists, their clubs, their flashlights.

Long talks on whether to accept arrest or go limp had meant nothing: the cops had made up their minds to beat the shit out of all of us, no matter what we did.

One by one our concentric circles were pulled apart and battered. I had hoped they would have shot their load before reaching us at the very core, but their fury raged unabated.

Out of the corner of my eye I could see one cop crack Nancy's skull open, blood quickly gushing over her eyes.

Alan yelled, "Hey, don't . . ." But before he could even finish, he was thrown down on top of one of the desks, a half dozen cops working him over, fists and clubs pumping like high-speed pistons.

When I turned back David Anderson had disappeared, swallowed up, only his book had been left behind, torn and tossed on the floor.

I stood by myself then. Trying to be very small, very quiet, I inched my way toward the other rooms and the door to the rotunda.

Suddenly, I was hit from behind and shoved through a gauntlet of cops.

Wallops, blows, jabs, a swirl of fists—I tried to keep my eyes open wide, watching the nightstick as it formed a crescent slicing into my gut.

After I was bailed out from the Tombs I slept for a day, smoked a joint, and scarfed down a greasy burger in the West End while reading A. M. Rosenthal in the *New York Times* dish out hideous jumbo lies. To Rosenthal, we were nothing but barbaric nihilists who took a shit on the very seat of civilization, which so happened to be Kirk's inner sanctum, although we had taken great pains not to wreck the place, and we had done a pretty good job, when you consider that about a hundred and fifty people had camped out in the president's suite for a week. Naturally, there was some mess, and someone did smoke the creep's cigars, but the vases, the books, the equipment, the furniture, everything was kept as tidy as possible. Nonetheless, the photos, augmented by Rosenthal's mendacious

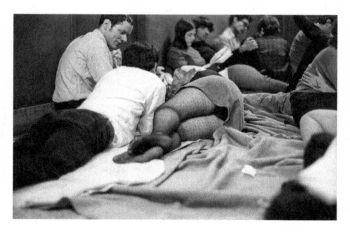

Figure 34.1 Students on the upper floors of Hamilton Hall, April 23, 1968. *Photograph by Peter Chartrand.*

bullshit, told otherwise: ink splattered on walls, idiotic graffiti, everything torn up, shredded, wrecked. I suppose the police, wanting to smear us, had mauled the premises as hard as they had pounded our skulls, while Rosenthal gleefully joined the melee with his wrecking-ball pen.

It was yet another Gulf of Tonkin frame-up, but I was not shocked, not even outraged, and I sat reading the *Times* in a kind of calm, come-down daze of worn-to-the-bone, expanded consciousness. I no longer believed nor concerned myself with the pronouncements of bombastic A. M. Rosenthals, certain as never before that The Establishment was held together by nothing but napalm, cops, and lies—and the lies were the most insidious and therefore most dangerous of the trio.

This, I thought, was my true Columbia education.

Hilton Obenzinger *('69CC) is the author of several books, including* Treyf Pesach; Cannibal Eliot and the Lost Histories of San Francisco; American Palestine: Melville, Twain, and the Holy Land Mania; New York on Fire; This Passover or the Next I Will Never Be in Jerusalem, *which received the American Book Award; and his autobiographical novel* Busy Dying, *which takes in the Columbia protests and from which this essay is adapted. Born in Brooklyn, he graduated Columbia in 1969, has taught on the Yurok Indian Reservation, and worked as part of a collective to operate a community printing press in San Francisco's Mission District. He received his doctorate at Stanford University, where he has taught writing, literature, and American Studies, and is currently Associate Director of the Chinese Railroad Workers in North America project.*

Columbia College undergraduate/WKCR

A NIGHT TO REMEMBER

riday, April 26, 1968. I was twenty years old, a junior at Columbia College, and the newly installed program director of WKCR, Columbia's student-run radio station. WKCR was (and still is) a serious station. At 89.9 on the FM dial, we could be heard in a radius of about thirty miles from Manhattan, encompassing more than ten million people. We also had a "carrier current" AM station that could be heard only on the campus. Our programming was a mix of music, culture and foreign languages, Columbia sports, news, and broadcasts of actual classroom sessions. Typically, our listenership was quite small, but because of the disturbances at Columbia that spring, we had a much larger audience than usual.

We were only young college students, but we took our role as journalists seriously. To cover as much of the action as possible, we dispatched staffers with portable equipment to various locations throughout the campus to report. Importantly, for us at WKCR the station was pretty much a "politics-free zone." Some of our people might have been in favor of the protesters and others opposed to them, but everyone understood the gravity of the protests and the role that had been thrust upon us undergraduates, we who ran the radio station. We were now journalists and had to behave as such. And so, someone who until the previous day hosted a weekly program about Polish language and culture, or was an engineer in control of the signal going to the transmitter, now found him or herself out on the campus speaking into a microphone, watching opposing groups of students jostling and sometimes fighting near the occupied buildings, with the faculty nervously interposed between everyone. Ordinarily we ceased broadcasting at midnight, but during the protests, we were running twenty-four hours per day. Staffers were perpetually tired, and I recall giving a talk to everyone about the obvious need for sleep. (I learned this wisdom from one of my government professors who had worked at the State Department during the Cuban missile crisis. He described "macho" diplomats who never went home to sleep and, after a few days, lost their judgment.)

WKCR was housed in Ferris Booth Hall, the student activities center, at the heart of the campus. We had a suite of about ten rooms, including offices, broadcast studios, storage, engineering workrooms, and a master control room. Master control wasn't large, and much of its floor space was occupied by equipment. That night it was crowded with people and was noisy—so noisy that when the call came in and I was given the telephone, I couldn't hear the person on the other end, so I stepped into the engineering closet and shut the soundproof door behind me. Frank Safran, a member of Columbia's administration and in charge of student activities, told me that Vice President David Truman had ordered WKCR to cease broadcasting news about the protests on our FM station because, in his opinion, we were contributing to the disturbances. Perhaps Truman thought that our broadcasts were encouraging "outside agitators" to come onto campus or that the residents of Harlem might come and invade Morningside Heights. Perhaps the administration wanted us off the air simply because we were shining a spotlight on the disaster that they themselves had created for all the world to see. There was no accusation of bias or of presenting incorrect information, and Safran added that we could play whatever music we wanted. I told him that we would comply.

I really had no choice. For one thing, every staffer knew the "O&O statement," which we broadcast every day, explaining that WKCR was owned and operated by the trustees of Columbia University in the City of New York. Legally, the trustees were in charge, and they had the authority to tell us to stop broadcasting the news. Additionally, I realized that if we didn't comply, the administration would surely instruct the phone company to shut off the line connecting our studios to the transmitter located in midtown, about four miles away.

In a flash, I figured out what the only moral, practical and sensible solution was. We couldn't continue with the news on FM, but I wasn't going to pretend that we weren't in the midst of a cataclysm and resume our normal evening music programming. Furthermore, I hadn't been ordered to play music. I had simply been authorized to play music. It struck me that a Ghandi-esque passive resistance gesture was the answer. I left master control, entered one of the studios, and went on the air. I explained to listeners that WKCR had been laboring to its best ability to present accurate news to the community, but that the administration felt we were making matters worse by doing so. We had been forbidden to continue with our news coverage and encouraged to play music instead. As program director, I couldn't countenance that directive, and so I had decided we would go off the air. I then left the studio, returned to master control, and threw the switch, shutting off both the FM and AM transmitters.

I hadn't planned any of this. It all happened so quickly that I had no time to think, much less to plan. I wasn't plotting out my moves in an attempt to aggrandize WKCR's role in the Columbia protests, but that was indeed the outcome. And the administration definitely hadn't planned their moves, because they got the worst outcome imaginable. As soon as we went off the air, students who had been following the action on their radios in the dorms flooded out onto the campus, making the scene even more chaotic than before. To my great surprise, it turned out that much of the media in the media capital of the world had been listening to WKCR, and they very much wanted the story of why we had gone off the air. Within a few minutes the *New York Times,* WCBS, WOR, *Time* magazine, and others were all requesting interviews with me. Similar calls must have been going to the administration because about half an hour later, we got another call telling us that if we wanted to, we could resume our news coverage. We did, of course, and WKCR immediately became a player in the activities of those days.

Fred Pack *('69CC) received an MBA from NYU Graduate School of Business in 1980. He was founder of UniPress Software in 1983, from which he retired in 2007, and now spends much of his time in Colorado doing outdoor activities.*

DAN PELLEGROM

*Graduate student, Union Theological Seminary/Columbia
University Student Council*

SILENCE IS COMPLIANCE

The first people arrested by the New York City Police Department in the early morning of April 30, 1968 were students, faculty, and a sprinkling of neighborhood residents who had locked arms in front of the five occupied buildings to deter the police action. I took my place in the line before encouraging others on campus to come stand with us, as a column of twenty or so police quickly gathered to face us. The commanding officer explained that he would count to ten. If we did not move, we would be arrested and booked, our records permanently blemished. The burly men a few feet from us began shaking their arms. I watched with bemusement until I saw a blackjack fall out of each officer's sleeve. Within seconds, I had been hit from all directions, knocked to the ground, and herded in the direction of paddy wagons parked at the foot of the Low Memorial Library steps. I was surprised when we were pushed past them, off campus, into the New York night. Relieved, I quickly crossed to the west side of Broadway and headed to a building just off Broadway that housed the office of the Columbia University Student Council (CUSC), an organization of which I as a graduate student at Union Theological Seminary had been elected president.

As I entered the building, I looked over my shoulder and recognized Nick von Hoffman, the respected *Washington Post* reporter, who for several days had been covering events for his newspaper. He was running from a policeman who was swinging a menacing nightstick in the air.

I yelled and signaled for von Hoffman to dart into the foyer of the building I had just entered. He seized the opportunity, and we quickly closed and locked the door. A naïve act, perhaps, because the policeman easily could have chosen to smash the window and continue his pursuit. Nick had interviewed me twice in the two days leading up to the police bust that night, but now all he was eager to do was find a telephone. He had picked a willing partner in me, and naturally I couldn't resist listening to the telephone conversation he made. Between a few expletives, I vividly recall Nick saying, "I covered the riots in Watts and I covered last summer's riots in Detroit and Newark, and I have never seen the police riot like they are rioting right now on the campus of Columbia University." Several more times during the phone call, he used that phrase: "police rioting." After von Hoffman left the offices, I assembled a makeshift collection of Student Council members and assorted other student leaders, and decided that the CUSC should now call for a campus-wide strike. After all, by sunrise, on April 30, many students and faculty, including those who had openly opposed the occupation of the buildings, were among those gathering on campus holding picket signs.

With delegates elected from every one of the seventeen schools across campus, the Student Council was probably the most representative body of students in operation, and my time with the organization gave me something of a unique perspective on the events of 1968. In hindsight, because I knew that student access to the Columbia administration was routinely blocked, and that attempts to discuss some of the key issues of concern to students were regularly dismissed by the administration, I looked back even a few weeks after the police bust and saw that the protests of April, in fact, had been inevitable for years. Columbia President Grayson Kirk had systematically ignored moderate and liberal student representatives, consequently rendering those students and their organizations ineffective and irrelevant. This neglect of student interests appeared to be an intentional strategy on the part of the administration, and over a period of years, it resulted in a tremendously disaffected student body. Depriving students of any opportunity for compromise or accommodation with their university set the stage not only for distrust but also for explicit dissent. As I wrote in a letter to Grayson Kirk, dated April 23, 1968, "The current confrontation would be less likely to occur if some of the major decisions being contested had been made with student participation on decision-making committees." Two cases in point, as described by me in a 1969 article entitled "Dissent in the University," published in *Social Action*:

On March 9, 1966, the Student Council, after joint meetings with the Morningside Renewal Council, whose membership consists of delegates from all the institutions and many of the community organizations in the area, adopted a resolution requesting that Columbia "suspend all efforts to construct a gymnasium in Morningside Park, and that discussions with community groups be instituted immediately, in order that any deci- sion on the site and functions of the gymnasium be the joint agreement of institutions and community groups." In communicating our views to the administration, the CUSC stressed the need for cooperation between community and University and the mutually beneficial results of coop- erative planning. The CUSC was disheartened by the administration's response to the community turmoil and distrust. President Grayson Kirk indicated that the University felt no further responsibility to "reopen consideration" of the project or to secure the assent of local residents. After the recommendation had been flatly turned down by the adminis- tration, the Student Council joined other students and community rep- resentatives in a public protest rally in Morningside Park on March 28, 1966. In this instance, the exercise by the CUSC of its advisory powers led to a blank wall of rejection. It is public knowledge that similar efforts by community representatives over the past few years have also failed.

In 1964, the CUSC president requested the creation of a student-faculty- administration committee on student affairs. His request was denied because, as the President's rather terse letter indicated, "administrators did not have enough time." In May 1965 a campus demonstration against the Naval ROTC became disorderly, and police were called onto the campus to disperse the demonstrators. Shortly thereafter, a committee of administrators recommended the creation of a Committee on Student Life. After discussions between the administration and the Student Council, a student-faculty-administration committee was established in November 1965 with four senior deans, the chaplain, five senior fac- ulty members, and five students nominated by the Student Council. This committee was given a broad mandate to examine any matter that might concern "student rights and responsibilities." In August 1967 the report was submitted. The administration refused to release the report.

Not until April 1968 was the report finally released by President Kirk. After consultation with student members of the President's Committee on Student Life, I decided to ask once more for the release of the report by the president. He refused, claiming that time had not permitted his study of the issues involved. In a meeting with the Student Council and the student members of the Student Life Committee, four of whom were former CUSC officers, I wrote the president stating that in ten days I would personally release the report as directed by CUSC. Only after I had displayed to the president's secretary the copy I was going to give to the press did the president allow publication of the report. He had prepared letters and addressed envelopes personally to several students but still would not release the report until his secretary was sure that I did, in fact, intend personally to make the report public.

We negotiated with his secretary that afternoon. I was never allowed to meet President Kirk, even as the spokesman for the officially recognized voice of the students. This does not mean that he was meeting with groups other than CUSC. It simply means that the president of Columbia University had no contact with the student body. On a few rare occasions previous Student Council presidents had been given an audience by Dr. Kirk, but this had been done coolly and without apparent administrative interest—until dialogue finally had dwindled into nonexistence.[1]

In the spring of 1969, with my degree completed, I began a career that centered on one of America's most divisive social issues and went to work at the national offices of Planned Parenthood. Family planning hardly seemed controversial to me in 1969, but the Supreme Court *Roe v. Wade* decision was looming, and by 1971, I had moved from New York to Memphis, Tennessee. Under my leadership, Memphis Planned Parenthood became the first affiliate in the South to add abortion services after the Court's 1973 decision. Four years after moving to Memphis and two years after *Roe v. Wade*, I became CEO of Planned Parenthood in Maryland, headquartered in Baltimore. Our clinic in Annapolis, Maryland, was firebombed in 1984 and I received death threats, ironically from people who called themselves "right-to-lifers." In 1985, after sixteen years of domestic family planning, I started work at Pathfinder International,

---

1.   Daniel Pellegrom, "Dissent in the University," *Social Action* 35, no. 5 (January 1969): 19–21.

a nongovernmental and nonprofit organization that provides reproduc-
tive health services and HIV/AIDS assistance in nearly thirty developing countries.

Standing outside Low Memorial Library on April 30, 1968, enabled me
to discover something about myself I never previously had put to the test.
I was clearly at my best when faced with controversy and conflict, and
April 1968, when I locked arms with like-minded people in front of Low,
turned out to be the first of many instances when I consciously placed
myself between authorities and the unprotected. Standing there that night
helped me discover where I belonged.

Dan Pellegrom *('69 UTS) was president and CEO of the nongovernmental organization Pathfinder International during which time he served as the board chair
of Inter Action, the largest coalition of US-based organizations providing human-
itarian services overseas. In 2011, he was the recipient of the Union Medal from
Union Theological Seminary.*

JON PERELSTEIN

Columbia College undergraduate/WKCR

ON THE AIR: A VIEW FROM WKCR

I t was the best of times. It was the worst of times.

For us at the WKCR radio station, it was the best of times. The members of the station were out there doing real, live, important news. And we were doing a damned good job of it—without training, without prior experience, without a single "professional" to lead us. We were developing style, developing procedure, and developing technique as we went. We felt that our heroes—giants of journalism, such as Edward R. Murrow, Fred Friendly, and Walter Cronkite—would be pleased with our work. A number of them eventually had good things to say about us in public.

I was an engineer in the station and also a news editor. During the protests, I was mostly assigned to remote coverage locations (anything outside the studio, making use of telephone lines). Each day was the same, but totally different. Roll out of bed and head over to the station. Get an assignment from one of the senior people. Go out and do your assignment (which could be an hour or two, or eight or twelve hours). Then come back and wait for the next assignment. Or work in one of our control rooms putting together material for a show. Maybe get to sleep by 1 A.M.

Most of the assignments were a blur and individually not terribly memorable. Sit outside one of the occupied buildings and occasionally report on what was happening—not much. Except at Low Memorial Library, where an increasing counterprotest by the Majority Coalition got really interesting really fast (interesting enough that some of us bought construction helmets to wear when out there). Sometimes we would interview a professor or community leader (often self-alleged) or member of the occupation leadership. We would record or air live meetings of different groups, such as the Ad Hoc Faculty Group.

Often we would try to talk through open windows to people inside the buildings. Except for Hamilton Hall (occupied by the black students), those interviews tended to result in almost canned responses about the evils of the war and the evils of Capitalist Society with almost no mention of racism, the Morningside Park gym, or the fact that Columbia was one of the biggest slumlords in the city. Apparently, the Students' Afro-American Society (SAS) knew what it was doing when it separated itself from Students for a Democratic Society (SDS).

One event does stand out in my mind—one in which I had neither tape recorder nor telephone line because it happened while I was coming back from retrieving some personal property from the engineering school. It was an SDS rally at which "the people" were being exhorted to take another building. The speeches can best be described as "Marxist Dialectic 101"—incredibly boring, simplistic stuff. Suddenly the "leader" of the rally (more like the emcee) called for a voice vote to see if "the people" wanted to give SDS a "mandate." The "ayes" were drowned out in a tidal wave of "nays." A couple of people pulled the "leader" behind a building and chewed him out. Snatches of the conversation still stick in my mind.

"What kind of idiot lets the people have any say in these things?"

"What kind of an idiot calls for a vote before knowing that the right people are in place?"

"Now we're going to have to bring in a lot of people we didn't want to bring in to get the vote we need."

Trusted people were sent out to round up those who would support a takeover. A few others quietly circulated through the crowd to talk with the "ayes"—after which those "ayes" slowly, casually, moved closer to the front of the crowd. More boring speeches and more boring speeches and more boring speeches—some of the "nays" could be seen leaving. After some interminable amount of time, another vote was taken. Definitely sounded more in favor—especially from the solid block up front—but apparently it was not good enough. More supporters were sent for, more concentration of the "ayes," another interminable period of speeches, more "nays" walking away in boredom. Another vote, and this time the "ayes" were loud enough to be taken as a mandate. Scratch another building.

The radio station itself had the feel of a three-ring circus without a ringmaster—but in fact the station leadership mostly had it under control (I'm not sure they thought they had it under control, but they did). And it could be interesting back at the station—like when journalism school professors would come over and pick *our* brains. Or when Mark Rudd of SDS showed up to volunteer his services because SDS had kicked him out of the occupied buildings for fear that he would be "disappeared" by the police (we politely declined his offer).

Or when there was talk of the university wanting to shut us down, which led to deep soul-searching as to whether we would essentially do what the demonstrators were doing—take over control of university property (the station). Most of us were of the understanding that it was a theoretical discussion and were of course bravely ready to keep the station on the air no matter what. There had been a brief interruption in our broadcasting, but our understanding was that it was due to some sort of mix up in communications with the university. It wasn't until later that we found out that it was a very real threat, but that station leadership had convinced them to leave us running.

The sundial was a particularly galling place because so much happened there, and we couldn't cover any of it live because it was too far from any building to just run a line along the ground (too much foot traffic, the line would have been trampled and destroyed). So one day a bunch of people sitting around the station decided on their own that we would lay a line from the journalism building to the sundial by burying the line along the hedges that formed the perimeter of South Lawn. For cover, both Security and Buildings and Grounds (B&G) were told that we would be *repairing* our line to the sundial. Neither organization batted an eye, so there we were about 2 A.M. digging a trench along the hedges when a bunch of drunk fraternity guys came along and asked what we were doing. Somebody decided to be a wise-ass and said, "We're burying the primacord." The frat boys laughed and went on their way. Thirty minutes later we were surrounded by a bunch of people in suits—clearly New York City Police Department (NYPD) detectives.

"Watcha doing?"

"Just the radio station repairing our telephone line to the sundial. There's a big speech tomorrow and we want to cover it."

Both Security and B&G confirmed our bona fides, and we let the detectives test the line. "Sorry to have bothered you guys, but we got a report of someone claiming a bomb was being planted."

"Ohhh, probably those drunk frat guys from Sigma Alpha Mu (SAM)— they thought it would be a funny idea if that's what we were doing." By 8 A.M. the next morning four or five NYPD cars were parked in front of the SAM house.

WKCR had some interesting "special operations" groups. It was nothing formal, nothing particularly planned by the station's leadership (more like despite the station leadership), more a reflection of the kind of crazy people the station attracted. We had people who were experts on telephone systems, people who were experts on locks and keys, and people who were experts in acquiring equipment (especially telephone company equipment) that a college radio station probably shouldn't have had. And we had a world-class intelligence analyst with his own mini-Central Intelligence Agency (mostly station freshmen who thought he was Sherlock Holmes and referred to themselves as the WKCR Irregulars). These special groups came together perfectly.

Our lock-and-key group wasn't a bunch of lock pickers so much as they were key collectors (although they were good lock pickers). Basically, we had a key to every single lock on campus. We could move through the tunnel system and enter any building we wanted. We had access to pretty much every room and office on campus, including the telephone distribution panels (when we needed to run a telephone line for a remote). Our telephone group could connect up any telephone communications we needed. The combo was so good that we had direct phone communications with our people who had decided to report from inside the occupied buildings. They didn't have to dial—all they had to do was pick up certain phones and they would be directly connected to our master control room.

There is a story, never confirmed, that when the police busted Low, our reporter in there picked up one of the phones and started reporting on what was happening. Some cop came up to him and smashed the phone he was using. Our guy simply stepped over to the next desk, picked up that phone, and continued reporting. The cop followed him and smashed that phone in turn. Our guy simply stepped over to the next desk, picked up the phone, and continued reporting. Unfortunately, that's when the cop got tired of the game and smashed him instead of the phone.

The talk of the university possibly shutting us down had gotten us paranoid. So one night our telephone group went down and rewired the distribution panel serving Ferris Booth Hall. Any line that was marked as ours was changed to indicate that it belonged to someone else and their lines were changed to show as our lines—plus some additional hidden lines were put in just in case someone killed the distribution panel itself. Thus, if someone went down to the distribution panel and tried to cut our lines, they would instead be cutting lines for the Chess Club, the Student Activities office, and others. We briefly toyed with the idea of switching our lines with those of *Spectator* (our frenemy), but decided not to—if only because someone sent to cut our lines would probably also cut theirs.

The morning after the bust, we went down to check the patch panels and found that every one of our lines had in fact been cut. Cut repeatedly and thoroughly so that it took about a week for New York Telephone technicians to repair all them. Well, every line *marked* as ours. The lines we actually were using were intact, but the poor Chess Club suffered, as did a number of other organizations in Ferris Booth.

One time we got word that David Truman was going to move through one of the tunnels to be interviewed by a *New York Times* reporter. So a couple of people, including me, were sent down to intercept him and ask questions. The next morning, I woke up to a phone call from my parents wanting to know why my photo was in the *Times*. There I was, holding a microphone in the very surprised face of Truman with a not very happy *Times* reporter standing nearby trying to ask his own questions.

NYPD ran lines from the telephone distribution panel in a university building to a command vehicle that fairly early on was moved to Amsterdam Avenue, just outside of campus. It may or may not have happened that some of our telephone group—without the knowledge of the station leadership—tapped the police phone lines. And whoever did it was good—not just a simple tap but some sophisticated stuff using some of the equipment that a college radio station wouldn't have had so that NYPD wouldn't be able to detect the taps with normal detection equipment.

Our intelligence guy spent hours listening to tapes that may or may not have been recorded from a tap that may or may not have been in place on the police communications van. He expected that they would start using more code phrases and circumlocution as things moved closer to a showdown. By Monday, the NYPD sounded like Mafia members caught on wiretaps.

"You know the guy, that guy with the thing? Well, he's going to be going to the place, you know the place I mean . . ."

At one point Monday afternoon, the circumlocutions got so bad that someone on the other end of the line blew a gasket and ordered the senior person from the command post down to police headquarters because "I can't understand a damned thing you idiots up there are saying."

Through the university's ham radio club, we got our hands on some radios that could be used to monitor the frequencies that NYPD was known to use when mounting big operations, mostly unencrypted frequencies used for logistics and transportation (back then NYPD was not sophisticated when it came to radio security). WKCR Irregulars maintained a vigil on those radios. The demonstrators, who had citizen band radios that we also were monitoring, had much better radio communications security than the NYPD.

WKCR Irregulars were watching for people leaving Low with rolled-up documents or extra-large briefcases that would indicate building plans for the occupied buildings. By Saturday, a steady stream of those documents was leaving Low and heading over to the police command post.

At some point, WKCR Irregulars were sent out to watch NYPD facilities that were known to be used for staging large operations.

By Monday, there were those on campus who suspected that things were soon going to come to a head. We didn't suspect, we knew. No, we never heard anybody say the words, but all the intelligence was there: Increased chatter from the command post. Repeated telephone calls between university administration and the command post. Radio chatter of NYPD troops coming in from the outer boroughs ("Okay, van #3456, I want you on 31st Street parked behind van #4567"). Sightings of large numbers of vans and buses full of riot gear–equipped police at some of the known NYPD staging points. Phone booths near and on campus put out of commission, along with open campus phones.

The sudden departure of the Majority Coalition left many people wondering, but not us. To us, it was just final confirmation of the pending operation.

A lot of the police radio chatter was cops talking about how they were going to bust heads, no matter what the demonstrators did or didn't do.

Then there was my undercover cop "buddy."

Soon after the April 30 bust, I was in the lounge in Ferris Booth Hall listening to a group of strangers rehash events. Something about one of the participants got my Spidey senses tingling. The extent to which he was asking questions and sucking up information just felt "wrong" in some way. I saw him a number of times over the following two weeks and realized that he was working his way up the food chain by using his initial contacts to get introductions to people who were more involved in the takeovers, which in turn he used to get introductions to the next person up the line. He wasn't in any way inciting anything, rather he was focused on gathering information about the people involved. Because I was a member of WKCR, he somewhat glommed onto me and we spent some time talking. I got to know him a bit—a pharmacy school student, a little bit older because he had spent a couple of years in the Army after high school, somewhat radicalized after a tour in Vietnam. We shared stories about our respective campuses (including one about a hated assistant professor of math). I called the pharmacy school, and they confirmed that he was a student there. Nice guy, but I continued feeling uncomfortable about him. Finally, I challenged him—told him I thought he was

Figure 37.1 The Columbia student radio station WKCR broadcasts from the steps of Earl Hall, overlooking the west side of Low Library, April 1968. *Image from University Archives, Rare Book and Manuscript Library, Columbia University in the City of New York.*

an undercover cop. He denied it. I basically told him I wasn't going to openly accuse him unless I saw him continuing to work his way up the food chain. He disappeared from campus.

Fast forward to the Hamilton Hall bust on May 21. I was on the South Lawn with WKCR press credentials (but not NYPD press credentials) when three big cops surrounded me. "Uh-oh," I thought, "I'm in for a beating." But no, it was just an invitation to come talk with their boss. Guess who? Yep, he was not just a cop, but a lieutenant in the Bureau of Special Services (NYPD's Red Squad). He gave me a warm greeting and introduced me to his captain as the guy who "made him" as an undercover. The captain and I had a pleasant conversation about how I had come to identify my buddy as an undercover, which culminated in the captain offering me a job in NYPD ("We can use someone with your talent."). Then he asked me whether I knew who it was who had tapped their command post on Amsterdam Avenue during the first bust.

I replied, "Tap? What tap? I don't know anything about any tap."

"You misunderstand me," he said, "I'm not looking to jam them up, I want to hire them." He thought they were good—better than NYPD's people—and even gave me a couple of his business cards in case I "found out" who they were.

My buddy detailed an officer to escort me across campus so I wouldn't "get hurt," then suddenly pointed at a figure crossing South Lawn. "Isn't that [the hated math professor] you were telling me about?" Why, yes, it was. He signaled two other officers and pointed at the professor. A day or two later, I saw the professor—he had been smacked around by two cops and was sporting a bandaged head and a bruised rib. I think, in his own way, my buddy had just thanked me for having not outed him publicly.

It still feels vaguely "wrong" to admit that it was the best of times. But it was.

Jon Perelstein *('70CC) arrived in Morningside Heights in the fall of 1966 as a dorky nerd from a "typical" sixties American suburban middle-class upbringing. Four years made him slightly less dorky but didn't change much beyond that. He completed two years at Columbia Graduate Business School and then pursued the world's second-oldest profession (systems consulting) for more than forty years. Now semiretired, he takes on only projects that sound like fun, with clients who will listen.*

DAVID F. PHILLIPS

Columbia College undergraduate/Student Draft Information Center

COLUMBIA AND THE DRAFT

entered Columbia College in the fall of 1963. While Kennedy was president, the war in Vietnam did not seem like that big a deal. The prevailing strategy of containment implied a need to support the anti-Communist government in South Vietnam against what were seen as encroachments from the Communist north. This strategy didn't seem out of line to me then. I was a cradle Democrat, a liberal, a supporter of Stevenson and Kennedy, and an anti-Communist. I supported the war at that point, because I believed the rhetoric that was used to justify our involvement. Today, everybody understands that as applied to Vietnam, containment was a deceptively simplistic view of the situation, badly misconceived and deliberately misrepresented. This was not so at the time.

In the summer of 1964, I had a dialogue on the war with a college classmate, a pacifist, who was convinced the war was wrong politically and morally. I remember spending a long time trying to write a letter to him justifying the war, but no matter how hard I tried, I couldn't write a convincing argument for it. So I concluded that he was right and changed my position. I supported President Johnson, the "peace candidate" in the election that year. He promised we were "not about to send American boys nine or ten thousand miles away from home to do what Asian boys ought to be doing for themselves."[1] In August 1964, Johnson had used the

---

1. Jeffrey W. Helsing, *Johnson's War/Johnson's Great Society: The Guns and Butter Trap* (Westport, CT: Praeger, 2000), 37.

Gulf of Tonkin incident to get a resolution from Congress allowing him to do pretty much as he liked in Vietnam. But I did not expect the treachery to come, and neither did most Americans. As we saw it, Johnson was going to avoid the massive American involvement that Barry Goldwater would have launched.

Johnson was elected in a landslide in November 1964 and immediately began ramping up the American role in Vietnam to previously unimagined levels, in terms of the number of Americans in action, our role in the war, and the ferocity with which we were fighting (defoliation, napalm, burning villages). The bombing of North Vietnam was sharply escalated just after the election. By March 1965, we had nearly thirty thousand soldiers in Vietnam, including some in combat rather than advisory roles. By July, the number was one hundred and twenty-five thousand. In November 1965, it was announced that troop levels would rise to four hundred thousand, and eventually it would go significantly higher. Most of these soldiers were draftees.

Meanwhile, it was becoming increasingly clear that the South Vietnamese government was a corrupt cabal basically incapable of defending its regime on its own. What we really were doing was intervening in a civil war on the inevitably losing side. And many people were beginning to realize we were being lied to—about the Gulf of Tonkin incident, the progress of the war, and the reasons for fighting it. Nowadays, we *expect* the government to lie to us, but in 1965, this was an enormous shock, and it undermined the basis for acceptance of the war.

At eighteen, in September 1962, I registered with the Selective Service System in the ordinary way. I was glad to do it, in a sense, as it was a rite of passage. I thought student deferments would place me at least five years away from draft eligibility and that there was no prospect of my being involved in the war. In 1966, both of those things changed. My student deferment ended when I was suspended from the college for a year, for reasons unrelated to the war. And the war had gone into high gear and was soaking up draftees at a rapid rate (almost two million conscripts were inducted between August 1964 and February 1973). Even if I had not been suspended, I would have been exposed on graduation the following year. I was clear that I was unwilling to go to Vietnam. My case was typical of many for whom the draft, and the real threat of induction, forced a decision on the morality of the war; this, in turn, required an encounter with larger political issues. The war was no longer an abstract political question when it *really could be you* forced into the jungle with a rifle.

I decided I was a conscientious objector (CO), which meant that my conscience wouldn't allow me to serve in the war. To qualify as a CO you had to be opposed to participating in *all wars*, to war in any form—a conscientious objection just to the war in Vietnam (even on a religious basis like the Catholic Just War Doctrine) was not enough. Also, the objection had to be *religious*. It used to be thought that this meant membership in a "peace church" like the Mennonites or the Quakers, or at least a belief in a Supreme Being. But the Supreme Court had recently decided (in *United States v. Seeger*, 380 U.S. 163, 176 [1965]) that belief in a Supreme Being was not required, but that the law had to recognize a "sincere and meaningful belief which occupies in the life of its possessor a place parallel to that filled by the God of those admittedly qualifying for the exemption."[2]

During World War I, COs were allowed to serve in the army in noncombatant roles, typically as medics, but those who could not conscientiously do that were imprisoned. In World War II, the government took a different approach, and allowed COs who could not serve in the military to be drafted into civilian work "of national importance." The draft ended after the war but was soon revived under a new law, the Selective Service Act of 1948, which continued more or less the same policy toward COs. I wrote to my local draft board and told them that I was no longer a student but that I was a CO, and asked for the necessary form (Form 150) to make my claim.

Returning (or maybe even requesting) the CO form legally prevented the local board from drafting me until my application had been acted on. The board responded quickly, reclassifying me I-A (available for induction) and providing a copy of Form 150. When I got the form the first thing I saw, and it was a shock, was that I had to complete it and return it within ten days. Some of the questions were very hard—for example "Under what circumstances, if any, do you believe in the use of force?" I was not really prepared to answer these questions immediately, so I called the Central Committee for Conscientious Objectors (CCCO) in Philadelphia, at that time almost the only resource available to give serious, well-informed advice to men preparing to claim CO status, and asked them if ten days really meant ten days. Yes, it did.

---

2.   "Welsh v. United States, 1970," in *Constitutional Debates on Freedom of Religion: A Documentary History*, ed. John J. Patrick and Gerald P. Long (Westport, CT: Greenwood, 1999), 105.

My objection to the war in Vietnam preceded my objection to all wars, and if the question had not been forced by my having been suspended from school, I doubt I would have taken a comprehensively pacifist position. But thinking it through, I honestly could not justify participating in war in any form. I feel quite differently now, but that was then. This meant I could not accept the noncombatant medic role either, because the role of the medics was clearly stated in the Army Field Manual as supporting the army's military mission. So I thought and thought, and I wrote and wrote, and made one draft after another, and by the time of the deadline, I had written a document sixty-four pages long. I had never written anything close to this long before, and I did it all pretty much on my own. CCCO sent me their Handbook for Conscientious Objectors, which was very helpful, but they were in Philadelphia. The American Friends Service Committee (AFSC) in New York had a staff member who worked part time on draft issues, but he was not equipped to help me work through Form 150, and neither was the War Resisters' League.

I sent in the form on July 5, 1966. Then I started thinking about doing something about the lack of help that had been available to me. It had taken me nine days of heavy full-time work, and I'd had numerous advantages (including most of a Columbia education and an air-conditioned town house to write in) that most people didn't have. Clearly some kind of help was needed for CO applicants on a general basis, so I went back to AFSC to discuss this with Jim Knapp of their staff, and later with Dan Seeger (the defendant in *United States v. Seeger* and director of the AFSC's New York regional office). We decided, with AFSC's unhesitating support, to establish a Committee on Conscience and the Draft. I became the chairman and Jim was the staff person.

The first thing we did was get a copy of the Selective Service Act and Regulations and read them through. We decided that we would counsel men not only on CO status but on other classifications, on the grounds that keeping unwilling conscripts out of the Army was a good thing whatever the basis.

The classification system worked like this. A man of draft age was classified I-A (available for induction) unless the local board placed him in a lower classification instead. In theory, the burden was on the registrants (as we were called) to prove their entitlement to a lower classification. I-A-O was for COs who would serve as noncombatants; I-O was for those who wouldn't. Men in all three of these classifications were equally subject to being drafted; the difference for I-Os was that they would be drafted into alternative rather than military service.

Other classifications would defer or avoid draft eligibility, the most relevant for us being II-S (student deferment). The rules for this kept shifting. Undergraduates had to be on schedule—that is, a quarter of the way through after one year. At one time class standings were also relevant: under student pressure, Columbia avoided cooperating with this by refusing to compute class standings. Originally graduate students were deferred, but this was phased out. There was no draft lottery yet.

IV-F, another popular classification, meant "mentally, morally or physically unfit" for service. "Morally unfit" could mean a prison record, drug use, subversive politics, or homosexuality. "Physically unfit" did not necessarily require a serious illness or disability—back or knee problems, bad enough eyesight, and even (in theory) the traditional flat feet could make a person IV-F. A registrant could ask for IV-F, or it could be given after an Army physical examination. I-Y meant unfit at the moment, but maybe not later if the need for soldiers grew acute enough, or if the disqualifying condition improved or responded to treatment.

Then there was a long list of other classifications, most of which we seldom saw. II-A was for essential civilian employment. Until 1968 this included not only war-related work, such as that in defense plants, but teachers in areas of teacher shortage and service in the Peace Corps (while actually serving). A lot of people did become teachers to get a II-A deferment, but in 1968, the rules for this became much more discretionary. II-C was for essential agricultural employment—there wasn't much of that in New York City. III-A was the hardship deferment—sole surviving sons, some fathers and "Kennedy husbands" who got this classification during Kennedy's presidency while it was still available, and special cases decided on an individual basis. IV-C were nonresident aliens, but if you took the IV-C you couldn't become a citizen later on. Resident aliens could be drafted. IV-D were ministers and seminarians. II-D was for National Guard and reserves—we didn't see a lot of those, but many men did join these units to avoid being drafted into the "real" Army.

Once Jim and I and a few volunteers understood the statutory and regulatory system, we opened for business as draft counselors. We were immediately overwhelmed by the demand, and soon concluded that our primary role should not be to do the actual counseling (although we continued to do it to maintain our skills) but to train counselors so there would be enough of them to meet the need. I developed a curriculum and a set of materials for training volunteer draft counselors. By the time I returned to Columbia College, the AFSC Committee was training counselors and counseling draft-age men in fair numbers.

I decided to establish a similar project at Columbia, which was full of men of draft age. The University Chaplain's office sponsored us as a student activity. We were not allowed to use the Columbia name, so I called it the Student Draft Information Center (SDIC) instead, and Chaplain John Cannon gave us a small office in St. Paul's Chapel on campus. We set about helping students who didn't want to get drafted avoid being drafted; we worked with many of them to figure out if they were COs (and if so, helped them apply for CO status). We also trained counselors. A flyer that we printed at the time read:

> No one is permitted to counsel with the SDIC unless he is committed to total objectivity in counseling, and until he has completed all of a sixteen-hour course of lectures, discussion, and role-playing, supplemented by extensive reading and written work. After that he must himself be counseled, and complete a two-stage apprenticeship, before we feel he is ready to begin on his own. He is expected to remain familiar with the SDIC library, and to use the local and national sources of specialized and general information with which the SDIC maintains close contact. There are now about two dozen SDIC counselors; their backgrounds range from non-cooperator to veteran. So far they have assisted close to five hundred men; by our first anniversary that figure is expected at the least to quadruple.

We maintained a comprehensive collection of Selective Service material, issued bulletins, wrote a few articles in the *Columbia Daily Spectator*, and brought speakers to campus. I spoke on the radio and at events focused on the war or draft issues.

I took a lot of people through the CO process and was fairly rigorous in exploring the issues. You say you don't believe in the use of force? How about using force to open a window? Does objection to war necessarily imply objection to self-defense or personal defense of others?

And so on by Socratic method until we got to what the man *really believed*. In many cases, he was not quite sure what he believed. We were careful not to maneuver people into positions that satisfied the law if those positions did not truly reflect their beliefs. A lot of what I did in CO counseling was help people, who may not have been any more certain than I was when I filled out my own form, figure out just what they really did believe.

We were very good at technical details. Don't ask for the CO form until you have prepared your answers to the questions. A teaching job will (or won't) get you a II-A. You're too old for a statutory II-S, you need local board permission, and given your circumstances here's what you might say in your request. This I-A may look scary, but it doesn't mean you're about to be drafted, only reclassified. And lots more of the same.

We also counseled people who wanted to break the law—by not registering, by refusing induction, by burning their draft cards, or by fleeing to Canada. We were scrupulous not to advise people to break the law, but we did tell them specifically what was involved, what was legal and what was not, and what they could expect if they did what they were planning to do. We urged people at least to consider using lawful methods first—do you need to ignore the classification process and get prosecuted if you can qualify as a CO or get a deferment or an exemption?

After a while we outgrew the office in the Chapel, and Chaplain Cannon arranged for a larger suite in the appropriately named Dodge Hall. There we had an impressive suite, fully fitted out with phones and carpets and offices and counseling rooms—we could run as many as twenty counseling sessions at once if we had to. The more I did, the more I learned. I specialized in taking exceptionally difficult cases. It was all great training for a lawyer, and I think it is the reason I was later admitted to a famous law school despite a very spotty academic record.

Antidraft work merged seamlessly with antiwar work. But even at the time, we had our doubts about how much good it was doing. We got thousands of men out of the draft one way or another—incredibly, I can't recall a single one who tried to get out but eventually went in anyway. And I suppose it did some good in raising awareness and in helping some genuine pacifists crystallize their thinking and avoid impossible conflicts. But for every college student we helped get out of the draft, the Army (or the

Marines, who drafted too in those days) just drafted someone else. We may have made more work for Selective Service, but we didn't slow the war down for a minute, and we may have diverted attention from substantive protest into procedural issues.

The draft was related to the protests and the strike of 1968 meaningfully but only tangentially. It was catalytic in forcing individuals to make a personal assessment of the morality of the war beyond received ideology and patriotic platitudes. Those against the war were driven to ask further questions about the processes that brought us into it, the arguments and claims used to justify it, the means and weapons used to fight it, and the conscription necessary to maintain it. Questioning authority on such topics was a novel and emboldening experience. Objections to the war opened minds to broader critiques of political, economic, and social conditions and gained a sympathetic hearing for radical voices like Students for a Democratic Society (SDS). And the parallel struggle over civil rights led many to apply the ethic and methods of resistance used there to the war as well.

The draft was therefore instrumental in forming the attitudes that made student opinion receptive to the protests and the strike. But neither the draft nor the war was directly at issue. Everyone recognized that the university had no control over the war or the draft. It already had refused to furnish Selective Service with class standings. The only war-related element among the six demands was that the university withdraw from the Institute for Defense Analyses. This demand was related only marginally and symbolically to the war and had no connection to the draft.

I think that Columbia 1968 was not really about either the war or the draft, but that *both in combination* were essential to the volatile mix of resentment, disillusionment, and outrage that allowed the protests and strike to find support. The draft without the war wouldn't have done it: there had not been any widespread resistance to the draft in the seventeen years before President Johnson escalated the war in 1965. And the war without the draft wouldn't have done it: there has been no significant domestic resistance to any American military action since the draft was abandoned in 1973. And *even the war and the draft together* probably would not have done it without the disciplined and determined leadership of SDS.

David F. Phillips *('68CC, '74SLS), a retired lawyer and librarian, is a heraldic scholar in San Francisco who was elected to the Strike Committee after the bust. He graduated from Columbia College (1968) and from the Columbia School of Library Service (1974), and from the University of Pennsylvania Law School (J.D. 1971). He is the author of* Emblems of the Indian States *and* The Double Eagle *as well as other heraldic works.*

JOHN POKA

New York City Police Department, Tactical Patrol Force

IMPRESSIONS OF A ROOKIE COP

I joined the New York City Police Department's (NYPD) Tactical Patrol Force (TPF) in 1967 and have vivid memories of the following year, when I sat for days on a bus with other officers, all highly motivated and ambitious, on streets adjacent to the Columbia campus, feeling gung-ho, pumped up on adrenaline, testosterone charged, and preparing to mount an offensive against a band of activists and their supporters. I believe it's fair to say that no matter how vocal people are who say otherwise, we young policemen and women—defenders of the status quo—were more reflective of the views of the majority of Americans than the small group of dissident and anarchist anti–Vietnam War Columbia students inside the occupied buildings just a few feet away.

At Columbia, members of Students for a Democratic Society (SDS), and their protests against the war, were gaining no public traction or support. SDS then hijacked a local cause (Harlem's African American community was angry at Columbia's proposed gymnasium, which was to be built on public parkland adjacent to campus) and combined this with their anger over the university's apparent associations with the Department of Defense. But their arguments, often reduced to a series of questionable facts, were devoid of critical thinking and analysis. Worse still, SDS members lacked worldly experience and believed in their own intellectual superiority and righteousness. Such self-serving and simplistic rationalizations made it clear to me, and many defenders of the status quo, that their decision-making was based on flawed reasoning. What also must not be forgotten are the actions of Columbia's Students' Afro-American Society (SAS), which initially joined with but quickly turned its back on SDS because it did not want to associate itself ideologically with violence and the destruction of property. As a representative of the NYPD who firmly believed he served as a protector of society, I perceived the obsessive young men and women of SDS as immature. When it came to achieving purposeful change in society through peaceful means, these were people who didn't know the difference between radicalism and fanaticism, whose activities—so divorced from lawful behavior—led directly to socially unacceptable disorder and chaos.

Too many of the protestors appeared to be immune to a certain understanding of the world, believing in the tragic notion that the forces of law and order existed not as a protective shield but as a sword designed to subjugate and control. Columbia was being led by inept and arrogant administrators who committed one colossal blunder after another, including the gym in Morningside Park, which was a brazen example of their invading, intruding, and infringing on the West Harlem community. But the student movement, I felt, lacked a viable moral compass, and I could find no commonsense rationale for the rebelliousness and disillusionment of the Columbia radicals. Their violent behavior was indefensible and ultimately escalated because their frenzy went unchecked. (No one can dispute that the leadership of SDS in those days was in tune with the authoritarian teachings of Mao and Lenin. The evolution of SDS into the Weatherman faction subsequently crystallized these extremist political views.)

This was an era notable not only for the losses of Martin Luther King, Jr. and Robert Kennedy but also for the loss of many police officers. No one but members of the force today remembers that fifty years ago it was open season on the police, that we couldn't walk down the street without looking over our shoulder. Objects were regularly thrown down on officers from rooftops, and the number of police deaths and casualties significantly increased during these years. Also to be taken into consideration was the oftentimes skewed public understanding of our role in society (prone, as always, to manipulation by the media), which resulted in many people always managing to find fault with the police, and the belief of many members of the NYPD that Mayor John Lindsay, at the helm of the New York City government, was providing neither the strong leadership the city needed nor the support we needed as the enforcement agent of the law (a case in point was his attempted expansion of the Civilian Complaint Review Board, which we felt needlessly tied our hands and restricted our ability to do our job). Nonetheless, by the sixties, the NYPD was expert at handling the kind of urban violence that was overwhelming some American cities in the second half of that decade, an era in which young people were advocating the violent overthrow of the system and calling for insurrection and "death to pigs." The TPF, the police equivalent of the Marine Corps, an elite group of one thousand in a police department of around thirty-six thousand men and women, embodied a new kind of policing (disbanded in 1984, its motto was "Our like will never be seen again"). We were the flying squad, all at least six feet tall, specially trained then dropped in, at locations around the city, as crime fighters. Wherever the criminals went, we followed, taking a different kind of fight to the streets, one that local precincts had never seen before. It is important to know that the TPF was composed of people who, as statistics will show, were highly educated and who, as a group, successfully avoided the stigma of an occupying army.

When tasked with clearing the occupied campus buildings at Columbia, we members of the TPF had no idea what we were being asked to deal with. What was happening on campus appeared, at first sight, quite different from the kind of violence we so often were confronted with in other parts of the city, but it didn't mean we felt no fear when preparing to face Columbia students. We had been trained to expect the unexpected, and each of us predicated present experience on past experience, which in our line of work rarely involved individuals and groups that observed established rules of order. Quite the opposite. No matter how peaceful we might have thought the majority of book-learning students, it was known that a group of diehard activists—so-called "outside agitators"— were also in those buildings. They had, for some time, been fueling the fire, leading to a gradual but noticeable escalation of violence within the increasingly emboldened antiwar movement. When sitting on that bus, awaiting a political decision to be made as to whether we should empty out the buildings, I recalled something my company instructor had told me during training, about confronting an adversary. "If you need to pull your revolver," he explained, "you aren't expected to engage in a duel. You, with superior resources, are expected to prevail." This philosophy, to me at least, was as relevant when dealing with middle-class students who might employ deathly force in their resistance as it was when engaging with knife-wielding drug dealers on the Lower East Side. Simply stated: "You can never underestimate the enemy."

For many police officers, whether present at Columbia or not, the student takeover in 1968 shattered the image that the student protest movement could be dealt with summarily. No understanding of those events, that conflagration of disorder, can be complete if the framework with which we members of the TPF (an apolitical group that only ever followed orders) had to wrestle is not taken into consideration. We were there to do our job: to return control of the university to those lawfully charged with its operation so that those students seeking an education (the majority on campus) could be so provided. There is no question that we all believed in the right of peaceful protest, but our duty was to protect those endangered or facing possible harm. Because the Columbia administration wanted police assistance in removing people who were criminally trespassing on university property, the NYPD had a duty to fulfill. It's worth stating here that while Columbia was a place of learning that some of my colleagues and their children undoubtedly one day aspired to attend, none of us looked at our arrival on campus in 1968 as part of what might be described as a "class struggle." This was about law and order, plain and simple. We had a job to do, and we didn't have the luxury of framing those events philosophically or ideologically.

Let me close by stating a few facts that no reader will know, but that might offer a deeper understanding of this particular police officer in late-sixties New York. I was born in what at the time was Hungary (now the Czech Republic), and as a child, I spent time in Austria and France, picking up languages as I went along. (Years later, when on the police force, I served as an interpreter for the Hassidic community in New York.) With the Nazi occupation of Hungary, my parents—who had a flourishing textile business and were able to afford an excellent education for me—left for southern France, then after the war, we returned home, only to be confronted by Stalin's Iron Curtain. I arrived in the United States at the age of eight, with my parents, at a time when immigrants were expected to be more American than the Americans themselves. Taken in from the dangerous storms of Europe, the joy I felt at being here, the drive I had to improve myself and the community around me, is hard to express.

With only a hundred dollars in his pocket and an imitation alligator suit-case in hand, my father proved to be an immediate success in the real estate business, even with his broken English. I would practice speaking my new language in front of a mirror, determined to fit in and be useful to the country that had given me a new home. My parents never wanted me to become a cop, but after my mother was mugged twice on the streets of our Bronx neighborhood, I joined up, as idealistic as any American ever was, proud to devote my life to public service, to protecting and serving. Since leaving the NYPD, I have worked as an attorney with two law degrees, practicing in two states, defending and protecting the rights and liberties of the community.

I respectfully ask readers to consider the events at Columbia in 1968 from a different—and probably quite novel—perspective. Think about how we policemen and women were feeling during those days, a period when law-breaking was becoming socially acceptable, certainly if it was dubbed "civil disobedience." We remained steadfast in our belief that one cannot reasonably object to certain laws by exhibiting disorder and breaking other laws, and we were acutely aware that we couldn't be certain

Figure 39.1 New York City Police on campus. *Photograph by Gerald Adler.*

about what we might find behind the locked doors and hiding in the dark corners of those five occupied buildings.

John Poka *graduated from the Dwight School, where he was poetry editor, and from the City University of New York, where he was news editor of the college newspaper. He has a law degree from CUNY, Queens College, and an LLM from Temple University, and today works as an arbitrator and litigator. As a former YMCA director, he created an adult education program in the South Bronx. During his tenure with the New York City Police Department, he was awarded more than fifteen medals, acted as an interpreter for the Corporation Counsel, and was on special assignment protecting diplomats and persons threatened by organized crime.*

HENRY REICHMAN

Columbia College undergraduate

THE SOUND OF BREAKING GLASS

Years after the events of 1968, as a historian researching the Russian revolutionary movement, I came upon a memoir written by a railroad employee about the experience of activism during the general strikes that swept Russia in late 1905, precursors of the more profound transformations of 1917. "Only yesterday a drunken Makar Mikhailovich was . . . demanding 'more vodka on credit': today he is a delegate to the Liubotin railroad congress, a top-notch speaker, and the first to sing the Marseillaise," the writer recalled. "It is difficult to convey the joyous agitation with which we greeted our entry into social affairs," he continued. "In the first days of the strike everyone felt not quite himself: the institutional structure of everyday life that had existed for years was broken at the root."[1]

Those words struck a chord with me that I doubt they would with most other historians. For it seemed to me that the experience recounted in this yellowed memoir from an obscure publication of the twenties was eerily similar to what I lived so many years afterward as a twenty-one-year-old student at Columbia. To be sure, the Columbia rebellion was hardly a revolution, even a failed one. And most of my fellow students were more likely to abuse marijuana than vodka. But the sense that events were compelling us to abandon the distractions and frivolities of everyday life and

---

1. Henry Reichman, *Railwaymen and Revolution: Russia, 1905* (Berkeley: University of California Press, 1987), 231.

to "enter social affairs" was equivalent. And in those days, I also felt "not quite myself," or, to be more precise, I discovered something more about who I really was and might become.

When I entered Hamilton Hall on April 23, 1968, it was not the first time I had participated in a sit-in. The preceding October I had been arrested for blocking entry to the New York City draft office, briefly sharing a jail cell with, among others, the poets Robert Lowell and Allen Ginsberg, and Dr. Benjamin Spock, the famed pediatrician. So I was no stranger to antiwar civil disobedience. Nevertheless, as events developed that evening and the "institutional structure of daily life" began to give way around me, my commitment was challenged.

In my memory, the critical moment is most closely associated with the sound of breaking glass. It was early on the morning of April 24, after the white students left Hamilton Hall. A dwindling group of exhausted and demoralized protesters was milling about wondering what to do next when Mark Rudd led a small group of no more than fifty, perhaps fewer, toward Low Memorial Library. I followed in the rear, not certain of what would happen or even what I wanted to happen, when someone broke through the glass window of a door to that imposing building to gain entry and begin a second occupation.

In the weeks to come at Columbia and later at Berkeley, where I went to graduate school, I would grow accustomed to the sound of windows shattering, as young people took to the streets in growing numbers and with intensifying anger to "bring the war home." But that morning, the sound seemed to smash more than glass; it seemed to herald the shattering of a once-sheltered existence and the beginning of a new and frightening phase, not only in the movement at Columbia but in my own life. My first reaction was to flee. Returning to my apartment, tired, confused, and uncertain, I fell asleep. A few hours later I returned to campus to learn that the occupation had spread. I rejoined the rebellion, ending up in Mathematics Hall, later deemed the most militant of the buildings.

I was never the strongest advocate for militancy, but days into the rebellion, I found myself committed to a movement that would shape the rest of my life. One morning, Tom Hurwitz was guarding the window through which people entered and left the occupied building. Suddenly I heard his voice boom, "Hank Reichman! Your father's here." Of course, I heard this as dripping with sarcasm. Here I am—the tough, now-embarrassed revolutionary youth with the concerned father. (Later I would learn that my wife, also in Mathematics but who I did not yet know, had the same expe-rience with her dad.) My father arrived in his suit and tie. He had been a radical and student rebel at City College in the thirties. He invited me to breakfast and tried to convince me to leave the building.

"You've made your point," he said. "Everything after this will be destructive."

I replied, "No dad, we have to stick it out," which is what, I'm now cer-tain, he expected to hear from me. Years later, as a historian, I would study the generational conflict paradigmatically evoked in Turgenev's classic *Fathers and Sons,* but that day I lived it. I went back into the building.

Sometimes it seems I never left. For what that building and the broader events of that incredible spring have come to mean for me is a lifetime's commitment to the fight for social change and justice. But I need to won-der whether in some ways I ultimately haven't embraced my father's outlook. For as rebels always do, we students at Columbia in 1968 shat-tered more than glass in our efforts to end the war and defeat Columbia's ill-conceived plan (that's putting it far too mildly) to build a segregated gym on public land. I can recall how some militants in Mathematics voiced the opinion that we should "destroy the university," at least as it currently existed. I remember timidly approaching Tom Hayden, who masterfully chaired discussions in Mathematics, to let him know that I didn't fully agree with that approach. I didn't want to destroy the university; indeed, I loved it. But I wanted, so to speak, to save it from itself.

And in a sense, that's what I'm still doing. Eventually I earned a Ph.D. and taught for more than thirty years at multiple universities. During that time, I took to faculty governance, became active in my union, and ended up a national officer of the American Association of University Professors and chair of its hallowed Committee A on Academic Freedom and Tenure. I therefore have thought much about the role of the faculty at Columbia and in student movements generally. And I have grown more sensitive to the threat to academic freedom and to the autonomous university that militant student rebellions can pose. Were something like the Columbia strike to happen now, I would be one of the active faculty thrust into the middle. I know what my position would be and it would not be the posi-tion that the young, rebellious me wanted the faculty to take. Having said that, I still think that too many of the faculty abdicated responsibility, and I think they did so not through their often hostile response to the strike but through their lack of response to what caused the strike. In retrospect, it seems to me that Columbia's faculty basically never stood up. Why was it left to students to demand that the Institute for Defense Analyses get off campus? That should have been a *faculty demand*. Faculty should have been saying, "We do not do secret war research on this campus. This is not academic freedom." But did they? By and large, I think they didn't. Only a tiny minority, mainly junior faculty and mainly on the far Left, did so. Too many were simply silent.

The memory and lessons of Columbia were therefore much on my mind in the fall of 2015, when a new wave of student unrest swept American universities, focusing on demands for racial justice. As at Columbia and other universities in the late sixties and early seventies, the students frequently were condemned by the media—the *Wall Street Journal* called Yale protesters "little Robespierres"[2]—and by many faculty members, too, for allegedly threatening free expression and seeking to impose their demands undemocratically. But it seemed to me that the students were doing what we did at Columbia; they were and are raising issues that their elders—their professors and the administrators of their institutions—were all too often eager to dodge.

And so, taking to the virtual pages of one of the preeminent online publications about higher education, I wrote in 2015:

> [I]t's necessary to credit the students for their courage and determination in addressing the sometimes unconscious but nonetheless real and persistent racism that infects our society and our campuses. In doing so, they have made and will again make mistakes. They will offend others even as they respond to deeper offenses against their own dignity. They may demonstrate indifference to the rights of others, as protesters everywhere always have. But, in doing so, they will learn. And that, it seems to me, is the essential point. Student academic freedom, in the final analysis, is about the freedom to learn. And learning is impossible without error. . . .
>
> Faculty members should welcome the challenges the protesting students have posed. Student movements offer countless opportunities for students—as well as their teachers—to learn. To approach them in this way . . . is therefore simply to fulfill our responsibility as educators.[3]

2. "Yale's Little Robespierres," *Wall Street Journal* (New York), November 9, 2015.
3. Henry Reichman, "On Student Academic Freedom," *Inside Higher Ed*, December 4, 2015.

I hope the young man of twenty-one, who at Columbia in 1968 found his life transformed by the sound of breaking glass, would understand and, perhaps, even approve.

Henry Reichman *('69CC) earned a Ph.D. from the University of California, Berkeley. Professor emeritus of history at California State University, East Bay, he serves as first vice president and chair of the Committee on Academic Freedom and Tenure for the American Association of University Professors.*

MIKE REYNOLDS

New York City Police Department, Tactical Patrol Force

HATS AND BATS

T he Tactical Patrol Force (TPF), part of the New York City Police Department (NYPD), was formed in 1959. It was an all-volunteer group of cops all over six feet tall who had shown their capacity for tough policing. These were cops who liked being cops, liked being active, and liked making arrests. TPF cops patrolled high crime areas and were called to respond to crowd control duties. It was, in effect, the NYPD's riot squad. Trained in crowd control, TPF could turn on the force quickly, and just as quickly turn it off.

I had come from a fairly well-off family and had two years of college. All in all, I completed seven years of Jesuit education. I knew the theory of policing and was about to learn the reality of policing in the sixties. I joined the police department in February 1968. When Martin Luther King, Jr. was killed, all training was halted and we went straight out into the street. My company was sent to TPF. It was months before we would see a classroom again.

Fifty years can wreak havoc on memories. The 1968 Columbia business takes on a surreal image. Flashes of yelling students and swinging night-sticks mix with images of card games and coffee on the buses as we waited for the university administration, the police brass, and city officials to decide just what to do about the student takeover.

We spent several days and nights on buses parked on streets in Morn-ingside Heights before we actually walked onto campus, which gave the working-class cops a good opportunity to build up resentment against the elite students who were running amok and pissing away their shot at a fine education and a future that the cops would have liked to see their own children get. When the order "hats and bats" (helmets and night-sticks) finally came, there was no doubt in any cop's mind about what was about to happen. The ungrateful elites were going to get the spanking they so richly deserved.

There is an aphorism that there is more law in the end of a nightstick than in a Supreme Court decision. That night at Columbia showed that no matter what, all law ultimately rests on force, which can be obvious, as it was at Columbia, or subtle, as used in business. Advertisers tell consumers they absolutely must have this product instead of that product or their neighbors will laugh at them. Fear of ridicule is not the same as a nightstick on the head, but the principle is the same: buy our product or else.

If the students at Columbia learned anything about the real-world use of law, the cops learned a lot about mob psychology. I remember this one kid. He was one of the students we had arrested. He had been pulled—not too gently—from a building, and now he was about to be put in the police

Figure 41.1 Members of the NYPD Tactical Patrol Force. *Photograph by Peter Chartrand.*

wagon to be taken to be booked. The kid was trembling and had pissed himself. As I helped him into the van, I asked what the matter was.

He said, "You're going to kill us."

I asked what the hell he was talking about.

He replied, "You're going to take us up to 125th Street, shoot us, and throw us into the river."

I told him he was nuts, that he had gotten his lumps and was now being taken to be booked, given a summons, and made to go to court a week or two later where he probably would have to pay a fine, but maybe not. He was having none of it. He was convinced.

TPF had a reputation for being tough, but mass executions were considered bad form. Where this kid got the idea remains a mystery to me, as we didn't have time for a chat. I assumed he had been brainwashed by the radicals leading the whole business. Nobody had gotten much sleep in the days and nights before the removal. Fast talkers and sleep deprivation might have been able to get these people to believe just about anything. Hallucinogens were popular back then, and maybe he had taken some acid. What it showed to me was that under the right circumstances even the best and the brightest could get their brains scrambled.

Looking back, Columbia was basically no different than any other mob confrontation we had. The only real difference became apparent in hindsight. It was one of the few times this kind of force was used on a white crowd. And not only were these kids white, they were far from working class, being the children of upper-middle and upper-class parents who were attending an Ivy League university. But as far as us TPF cops were concerned, it was just another confrontation involving the use of force.

Mike Reynolds *was a member of the New York City Police Department from 1968 to 1976. After the Tactical Patrol Force, he was an instructor at the Police Academy and then a beat cop in the South Bronx. He left the job and went into the family real estate business. Three of his sons were on the job in September 2001 and were first responders to the World Trade Center. Reynolds has received numerous awards for his service as a volunteer emergency medical technician in his community and is on the board of directors of an agency that cares for people with developmental disabilities.*

Barnard undergraduate/Avery Hall occupier

STOPPING THE MACHINE

I had just turned seventeen when the Columbia revolt broke out. It was a set of events that changed me, clearly shaping the direction of the rest of my life. In fact, I spent the next twenty-plus years self-identifying as a full-time revolutionary, radical, anti-imperialist, and I have remained a part-time social justice activist.

Although I am reflective when I talk with friends about my history, I have taken few opportunities to think or write about it in a disciplined way. Nor is my memory objective. Even if I hadn't learned a lot as a criminal defense attorney about the complexity of witnessing, and even if others hadn't written compellingly about the pitfalls of memoir, I would have little trust in my memories or in those of others—not from intentional dishonesty but rather emotional necessity. There are T-shirts that read: "If you remember the sixties you weren't there." I would say instead: "If you remember the sixties, it will most likely be in a manner that makes your life choices look good."

Having said that, my memories of the strike and the months leading up to it are clear as day. I arrived at Barnard the previous September, a timid, young, socially awkward commuter student, in thrall of the professors I encountered and exhilarated to be in the world of academia. My plan was to major in English and become a professor. I was going to live the life of the mind. At the same time, I had attended antiwar demonstrations in high school and was looking for activism, so I chose Barnard because

Columbia University was already identified as having a strong antiwar movement. I was thrilled when women from Students for a Democratic Society (SDS) came to my dormitory during Orientation Week and talked about their recent trip to Cuba and the war in Vietnam. That semester, however, I didn't do much other than study intensively, read the political leaflets that came my way, and negotiate the difficulties of being seventeen.

And then came March 20, 1968. The pie. I read about it in *Spectator*, the campus newspaper.

> The director of the New York City headquarters of the Selective Service System was struck in the face with a lemon meringue pie yesterday during a talk at Earl Hall. . . . Witnesses stated that Colonel Akst, who had been invited to speak at Columbia by the Earl Hall religious counselors, the Chaplain's office and the Student Draft Information Center, was answering a question about occupational deferments when eight or ten people entered the rear of the auditorium.
>
> The demonstrators, garbed in Army fatigues, began to disrupt the meeting, playing a flute and waving toy firearms. A scuffle reportedly broke out when several people at the back of the hall left their seats and began to push the demonstrators. The audience of 150 turned around to see the disturbance and when they looked back to the speaker's podium, Colonel Akst's face was covered with pie.[1]

It seemed perfect to me: a humorous challenge to authority and a clear statement that the US military was not welcome at Columbia.

A few days later, the *Spectator* published an article about the research of students and SDS member Bob Feldman, who had discovered institutional connections between Columbia and the Institute for Defense Analyses, a military research branch of the US government. My view of the university as a scholarly refuge was finally and irrevocably shaken from its foundations. "Academic freedom," I learned, was a shield for Vietnam War research, and a sword against students who tried to hold the university to account. It would only be years later, with the post-Watergate hearings of the US Senate Church Commission and other investigations, that

---

1. Robert B. Stulberg, "Draft Official Hit in Face with Pie during Talk Here," *Columbia Daily Spectator* (New York), March 21, 1968.

we were to learn how thoroughly every major American university was targeted with clandestine Central Intelligence Agency infusions of money and personnel, and how willingly they participated in Federal Bureau of Investigation repression of the student movement.

And a few days after that came the walk-out of several dozen students from the campus memorial for Dr. Martin Luther King, following Columbia SDS chairman Mark Rudd's interruption of the service and denunciation of what he called Columbia's "policy of racism." I was too young for Freedom Summer '64 but was a strong supporter of civil rights and, at age twelve, with the blessing of my left-liberal parents, had taken part in the 1964 boycott of New York public schools to protest segregation. Like many students, I was well aware of Columbia's activities in Harlem and the community's protests against the substandard housing maintained by the university, as well as Columbia's attempted expansion into Morningside Park. As such, I considered a memorial to Dr. King conducted by an expansionist slumlord to be the worst of hypocrisy. That outrage and, fundamentally, the shock of Dr. King's assassination, propelled me to the April 23 demonstration. I spent those days reading and talking with friends about the strike, but I didn't make the decision to go into a building until Friday, April 26, when word was put out that the bust would probably come over the weekend.

I considered carefully which building to enter, and chose Avery Hall, home to the architectural and urban planning graduate students. Inside, I was largely in silent awe and confess that it was only years later that I came to appreciate the significance of the passionate discussions I was on the periphery of for so many hours each day. But what exhilaration! With all those endless meetings, I felt part of a national, even international, student resistance. One moment in particular has remained with me, a heated debate about *who* should decide which way we might move forward. Someone explained that David Gilbert, one of the SDS leaders on campus, said he would accept the results of a referendum on the strike if the votes of the Vietnamese and the people of Harlem were taken into consideration. Even more than Columbia students, they were affected most by Columbia policies. I understood that instantly. The strike and buildings occupations weren't about us students so much as an entire movement coming together in solidarity. It was probably with the visit of Kwame Ture (then Stokely Carmichael) and Jamil al-Amin (then H. Rap Brown) to Hamilton Hall that I began to recognize that the black student occupiers represented the black community, and that supporting their goals was a crucial aspect of the solidarity I knew was so necessary. I entered Avery as a leftish Democrat and departed as a devoted student radical.

Today, I'm not sure what I think is the proper intersection of democracy and activism. I certainly have changed my thinking from the dualist dogma that I held for years following the Columbia strike to a more nuanced view of society. But who gets to decide when to disrupt the institutions and daily lives of others within the United States? Who votes on whether Black Lives Matter or climate change activists get to gum up an institution, or even the traffic? A favorite song recorded back then by Judy Collins had the lines: "It isn't nice to block the doorway / It isn't nice to go to jail / There are nicer ways to do it / But the nice ways always fail."[2] In retrospect, mainstream neoliberal historians view the civil disobedience of the civil rights movement as moral and appropriately defiant of state power. Today, that's how I see myself—someone who, as Mario Savio put it, fifty years ago placed my body against the apparatus to disrupt the operation of the machine.

Eve Rosahn *dropped out of Barnard in 1970, did support work for the Black Panther Party, came out as a lesbian, and organized against the Federal Bureau of Investigation's Counterintelligence Program. In 1981, she was jailed for sixteen months for refusing to cooperate with a federal grand jury investigating the Brink's robbery. Despite her legal travails, she was finally admitted to the bar in 1994 and recently retired from directing the Parole Revocation Defense Unit of the Legal Aid Society of New York.*

---

2. "It Isn't Nice," on *Fifth Album*, performed by Judy Collins, Elektra Records, 1965, LP.

MICHAEL ROSENTHAL

Faculty, Department of English and Comparative Literature/Ad Hoc Faculty Group

LIFE ON THE LEDGE

"Garbage, faculty!"

This cry, repeated several times a day, emanated from the second-floor window of the southwestern side of Low Memorial Library, otherwise known as President Grayson Kirk's office, currently being occupied by angry Columbia students. Eager to humiliate the faculty who were standing guard on the ledge surrounding the library, protecting their right to protest, the students summoned them to receive the large plastic bags of garbage generated by life in the presidential suite. Answering the call, the younger teachers—preceptors, instructors, assistant professors—clambered up the metal grill on the first-floor windows, extended one arm upward while clinging to the bars with the other, and dutifully accepted the garbage offering. The students were delighted. The faculty, earnest in defense of their students, seemed happy to be playing a role. The garbage, after all, had to be removed.

Our presence on the ledge (I was an instructor in the English Department, lithe enough to climb up the windows but unwilling to do so) came about through endless deliberations conducted by the faculty, attempting to find a negotiated peace to the crisis. The lounge in Philosophy Hall became the site of all-day discussions about the occupation and what to do about it. That the students had little interest in our philosophical anguish did not seem to occur to anybody immersed in the lounge debates. But if talk failed to provide a solution, the least we could do was

provide our bodies to demonstrate our allegiance to those undergraduates in Kirk's office, keep them from harm, and generally bear witness to
what was going on. The administration couldn't pull a fast one—like trying to slip in the police to clear out the office—if we were on guard. To
this end it was agreed that faculty, identified by white handkerchiefs tied
around our arms, would occupy the ledge.

Once on the ledge, things got complicated, as rules of engagement
had to be established so that faculty would understand their duties. Not
a problem for professors, of course; the day after we took to the ledge, a
flyer was distributed, authorship unknown, outlining our responsibilities.

The most important clause had to do with turf ownership: it was made
absolutely clear that only authorized faculty could inhabit the ledge. This
meant that no students, either those sympathetic to the occupiers or those
against, could set foot there. Anyone attempting to do so could be physically ejected.

More elaborate were rules relating to the conveying of food to the protesters. Because no one was permitted to enter or leave Low, the sole means
of providing them with nourishment required hurling loaves of bread,
cold cuts, processed cheese, and the like from outside Low to the grateful recipients waiting in the second-floor windows for their gift packages.
This was made more difficult than it might otherwise have been when a
group of undergraduates, largely athletes, opposed to the strike and eager
to get in on some kind of action, formed themselves into the so-called
Majority Coalition, by all odds the smallest organization of students. In
addition to marching around the campus, protesting the protesters, they
established as their territory the ground between the faculty-patrolled
ledge and a hedge, fifteen feet or so to the west of the library, facing the
ledge. Their mission was twofold: to ensure that no supporter try to get
into the building, and to force those attempting to supply those within to
fling their packages from outside the hedge, maximizing the possibility of
errant throws.

Our published instructions tried to account for all exigencies. The
most important stipulation had to do with food that missed its target and
fell to the ledge. To protect our professorial neutrality, under no circumstances were we permitted to throw it back up to the window. At that
point the supplies belonged to us, not the students, and could not be given
to them. The rule was absolute. Any violation of this restriction would be

punishable by expulsion from the ledge. Food that bounced off the library but did not land on the ledge, however, was not ours, but the Majority Coalition's, and we were not expected to contest ownership. We were charged with making sure that neither Majority Coalitionists nor colleagues of the strikers gained access to the ledge. Garbage removal remained a voluntary activity, not covered in our guidelines.

Although I found our position as guardians of the ledge to be fairly absurd, two particular moments stood out for me. The first occurred when a professor of philosophy, perhaps more sympathetic to those inside Kirk's office than his fellows, did the unthinkable. When an errant loaf of bread found its way to the ledge and landed at his feet, he bent down and, with due deliberateness, picked it up and threw it to the waiting students in the window. We were all dumbfounded. A chorus of cheers burst out from beyond the hedge, in praise of his courageous behavior. Cries of execration were showered upon him from the outraged Majority Coalition. The response was swift. He was escorted from the ledge in disgrace, amid healthy booing. I wondered whether he would be permitted to return the next day, but I noticed he never came back. I suspect he would not have been allowed to, even if he had appealed for redemption.

The second incident involved a breaching of the faculty's control of the ledge by the Majority Coalition. Although I was standing right there, I was unaware of why it happened. All I know is that without warning or any clear motivation, several students popped onto the ledge. Perhaps they were testing our resolve, or were simply eager for some physical confrontation, as hanging around between hedge and ledge, insulting the strike's supporters, was not an entirely fulfilling activity. Whatever the reason for the encroachment, we responded magnificently. We promptly surrounded the trespassers and not particularly gently wrestled them off the ledge.

Although this event was surprising, nothing was particularly astonishing about it. The astonishing part followed. Apparently in the brief tussle, one of the intruders got scratched and began bleeding slightly. As we reestablished our decorum on the ledge, we found ourselves being excoriated by the Coalition's leader, a college senior. I remember his words exactly: "One of my men is bleeding, a man who had never done anything wrong in his life is bleeding, and it's your fault!" I was mesmerized by the claims of purity regarding the injured student, his instant rhetorical transforma-tion from student to man, the moral haranguing we, the august faculty, were receiving at the hands of someone who several days before we were teaching in our classrooms.

The lunacy of life on the ledge—fetching bags of garbage, dismissing faculty in shame for improper behavior, fighting off interlopers, being upbraided by self-appointed student leaders—served as a neat microcosm of the madness that engulfed the campus that week in April. Perhaps the best analysis of what was going on at Columbia is not to be found in *The Strawberry Statement* or *Up Against the Ivy Wall* but rather in a book written several thousand years earlier, Thucydides's *History of the Peloponnesian War*. His brilliant examination of how the revolution in Corcyra changed language itself speaks also to the dynamics of the Columbia revolution:

> To fit in with the change of events, words, too, had to change their usual meanings. What used to be described as a thoughtless act of aggression was now regarded as the courage one would expect to find in a party member; to think of the future and wait was merely another way of say-ing one was a coward; any idea of moderation was just an attempt to disguise one's unmanly character; ability to understand a question from all sides meant that one was totally unfitted for action.[1]

The word that disappeared entirely during the student uprising was "student." In the new world that no longer was willing to accept tradi-tional power roles, there were no students. There were protesters, strik-ers, steering committee members, negotiators, runners (to carry messages between buildings), and Majority Coalition members. And lest anyone think that classroom buildings were being illegally occupied, they became communes, and those staying within them, communards.

In pointing out the absurdity of much that was going on around us, I don't mean to trivialize the events of '68. There was genuine anger, there were real issues (some), and there were committed students (some). But the experience has become so entombed in solemnity that it is useful to

---

1. Thucydides, *History of the Peloponnesian War*, trans. Rex Warner (New York: Penguin Books, 1954), 242–43.

remember that while serious things were happening, some students also were having a very good time: the subjects of intense media attention, self-important in their deliberations, excited by their power in closing down the university. A candlelit procession around the campus celebrated a New Age marriage. Postrevolutionary curricular guidelines were formulated to replace traditional, no longer relevant, ones. Now anybody could teach anything. Courses would no longer be the prerogative of stuffy types with Ph.Ds.

The flight to fantasy was not just appealing to students. But the fantasies pursued by the faculty had to do not with remaking the university in a more democratic model but in asserting the power of rational discourse to solve problems. The faculty counted on its stock in trade—talk, subtle, compelling, earnest—to bridge the gulf between administration and students. That neither faction particularly cared what solutions the faculty were capable of devising didn't affect the torrent of talk that filled 301 Philosophy Hall from morning to night. You could stop by any time you wanted to hear why amnesty was wrong, why it was right, why black students had to be treated differently from white, why the police should be permitted to clear the buildings, or why they shouldn't be allowed on the campus.

The Philosophy Hall lounge also served as the place where the administration would communicate its thinking to the faculty. A senior dean, elevated to emissary-in-chief, would periodically appear before the assembled faculty to explain what the president and vice president wanted us to know. It was not a pleasant job. The facts he shared remained scanty, and the faculty, disgruntled at being kept out of the highest level of deliberations, did not receive his briefings cordially. I witnessed one of the more terrible moments of this interaction. The dean was being harshly questioned by faculty who were outraged by his uninformative report. He was clearly exhausted; he might well have been drunk. Suddenly he snarled at one relentless professor, "All right, I'll tell you what's happening," and then began mumbling, making very little sense. The embarrassment was palpable; the solution unclear. I was sitting next to two departmental administrative assistants, who were horrified: "We've got to get him out of here." They conspired together, and then one of them went outside the lounge. A few seconds later she reentered, walked up to the dean, who was struggling unsuccessfully to be coherent, and whispered in his ear.

"I'm sorry, I have to stop. The president needs to see me," he announced to us, and left.

I spent the days leading up to the bust doing my duty on the ledge and trying to fathom what might be happening by listening intently to the interminable talk in the lounge. As no one had access to any real information, our questions couldn't be answered. We had no idea how or when the occupation would end.

In retrospect, given the unreality of everything that was going on, it made perfect sense that I would learn in the early hours of April 30 from the bartender at the West End, on 114th Street and Broadway, that the police were coming to clear the buildings. If President Kirk wouldn't tell us, at least we could count on the bartenders. I finished my beer and immediately returned to the campus. Looking for a strategic place to plant myself, I headed for the south door of Fayerweather, where faculty were gathering. Passing in front of the security entrance of Low Library, I beheld a chilling, somewhat surreal sight: large numbers of thick-necked men, clearly not students, came flowing out of the building, all disguised in sweatshirts from different colleges—Adelphi, City College, NYU. The better to pretend they were not policemen but innocent college students? Who knows? Colored buttons worn near the neck ensured that when they set about beating up students who got close to them they wouldn't be fighting with each other. I have never understood to this day whom they thought they were fooling with their various sweatshirts.

As the uniformed police faced us in front of Fayerweather, I spotted F. W. Dupee, a marvelous professor of English whom I revered. I resolved that whatever happened I would stick with him and try to prevent him from getting hurt. He alarmed me when he admitted that he regretted wearing his expensive new dentures before the upcoming police action, but I felt this was no time to confess fear. Not to an older man I admired. The police, clenching small blackjacks, urged those of us in front of the building, now some twenty or twenty-five strong, to disband, but we hardly could just go away. Instead we burst into "We Shall Overcome" and waited for the police to come at us, which they promptly did. Having exhibited our courage, we were then free to scatter. I pushed Fred ahead of me toward the St. Paul campus exit, receiving a few indifferent punches on my back and shoulders in the process. But Fred, eager not to miss the action, looked back over my shoulder, earning a majestic left black

Figure 43.1 Rock band the Grateful Dead play a concert on campus in support of protesting students, May 3, 1968. *Photograph by Peter Chartrand.*

eye for his efforts. The next day, Jimmy Wechsler, the Columbia alumnus and feisty editor of the *New York Post*, condemned the police for manhandling the distinguished literary critic (as if they had even the slightest idea of the elegant grey-haired gentleman's identity). As Fred received congratulations for his heroism and toughness, only the two of us knew that he had not been manhandled by vengeful cops but hit by a wild punch that he never should have turned around to receive in the first place.

The police were efficient in emptying the buildings. They were also violent—unnecessarily so. After a week of being insulted by students, who delighted in calling them "pigs," it would be unreasonable to assume they would opt for gentle behavior. They didn't appreciate being treated with contempt by those they considered spoiled kids, who were trashing an institution they would have loved their own children to be able to attend. Clearing the campus was payback time, and the police made sure to deliver their message unambiguously. If not defensible, it was at least understandable.

The consequences of the "revolution" were all too real for the institution: seven hundred students arrested, the president and vice president losing their jobs, and alumni financial support severely damaged. It would take years, a new administration, new governing structures, like a university senate, and overhauled disciplinary procedures, for it to recover. I personally was stunned by the mass craziness that had swept over Columbia, by the ease with which people fled from reality in illustrating Thucydides's insights into the frailties of human nature. If one wanted the perfect conclusion to the week's madness, it was provided not by the students or faculty or administrators or police but by Dr. Frode Jensen, a Columbia trustee, who had not been on the campus for the bust and had no direct experience of it. When asked by the *Spectator* about the allegations of police brutality, a subject not dear to the heart of any trustee, he took refuge in his own alternative reality in which it was easier to live: "I refuse to accept the fact that there was any brutality. There was not."[2]

Michael Rosenthal, *who retired from the English Department several years ago as the first Roberta and William Campbell Professor of the Humanities, served as Columbia College's associate dean from 1972 to 1989. Recipient of Guggenheim and Rockefeller Fellowships, he also was given the Alexander Hamilton Medal, the College's highest award. He is the author of four books, including* Nicholas Miraculous, *a biography of Columbia's president from 1902 to 1945. His most recent publication is* Barney, *the story of Barney Rosset's Grove Press and his successful battle to break down the censorship laws of America in the 1960s.*

---

2. Oren Root Jr., "Brutality on Tuesday Denied, Police Praised by Trustees," *Columbia Daily Spectator* (New York), May 2, 1968.

JOSHUA RUBENSTEIN

Columbia College undergraduate/Fayerweather Hall occupier

HOW I LEARNED I WAS A MENSHEVIK

learned I was a Menshevik during the Columbia strike. The irony is that I have spent the last forty-five years of my life as a student of Soviet history.

That spring of 1968, when I was in the second semester of my freshman year, I had yet to study Russian language or have any particular knowledge of how the Bolsheviks differed from the Mensheviks. I had not been politically active on campus, let alone a member of Students for a Democratic Society (SDS). But as with so many other students, undergraduates and graduate students alike, I hovered on the margins of events. I participated in the Vietnam Moratorium Day on campus in the fall, attended the memorial service for Martin Luther King, Jr. in St. Paul's Chapel on April 9 and watched as Mark Rudd, wearing a tie and jacket, commanded the platform away from President Grayson Kirk and led the crowd in singing "We Shall Overcome," his arms entwined with others as Kirk, looking awkward and out of place, stood nearby, alone, untouched, barely moving his lips as he struggled to keep his composure.

I was on College Walk near the sundial that Tuesday, April 23, when SDS and Students' Afro-American Society (SAS) leaders urged the crowd to follow them into Morningside Park to tear down the fence surrounding the construction site for the controversial gymnasium. I joined the crowd and watched as others, gleefully and with no resistance from the forces of order, pulled down the chain-link fence and stomped on the twisted metal—a blow, I'm sure they believed, against institutional racism, against The Establishment, against the Vietnam War. I was in the crowd as we walked back to campus, assembled on the steps in front of Low Memorial Library, and heard the first calls to take over buildings. The strike was under way. I had no intention of joining the demonstrators inside.

Within a day or two, as hundreds of students settled into five campus buildings, members of the faculty began meeting in Philosophy Hall. Along with many others, I pressed my nose against the large windows on the side of the building as they debated over how to bring the administration and the demonstrating students to the negotiating table, how to avoid violence, how to avoid the call for police to clear the campus. I was at the window when David Truman came into the hall in the very early hours of Friday, April 26, and alerted them that the police were being summoned onto campus. The crowd of professors, almost to a man (I doubt there were many women among them), loudly protested and then and there, with no formal debate or vote, made clear they would stand in front of the buildings to protest the summons to police. If that was their decision, I told myself, then I belonged inside the buildings, too, come what may.

Fayerweather Hall was nearby. I had no idea how the makeup of one group of demonstrators in one hall differed from another, at least not yet—except, of course, for Hamilton Hall, which the black student demonstrators were now occupying. I went into Fayerweather and quickly understood that I was among hundreds of others, mostly if not entirely graduate students, who were, as a group, like myself, unaffiliated with SDS but fed up with the university administration over the gym issue, the disciplining of six students for an earlier demonstration against university involvement in military-related research (the IDA 6, as we called them), and, of course, with the Vietnam War and the draft—all of which fueled our common frustration with The Establishment. But who could take over the Pentagon? Fayerweather Hall would have to do.

I found myself sitting on a hard marble floor. Someone gave us instructions about how to cover our eyes, nose, and mouth with a damp cloth when the police started lobbing tear gas into the building. But then they didn't storm the campus after all. The administration backed down, no doubt because faculty members now were "standing witness" in front of each building, a rebuke to Grayson Kirk for failing to negotiate a way out of the crisis, preferring instead to summon the police. He was playing into the hands of SDS. As I understood their logic: "Nothing radicalizes like the Cossack's whip."

We all settled into an uncertain few days. Gradually, our mornings and afternoons turned into hours of debate, among ourselves and often with SDS leaders, over how to proceed, how or even whether to engage with the administration. The issues seem so shallow and insignificant today, but for us, with our future as students and the fate of the university—if not the universe—in our hands, we came to understand how much SDS wanted to prolong the strike, goad the administration into clearing the buildings with force, and thereby expose its authoritarian and illegitimate status, much like the government in Washington, D.C., whose Vietnam War seemed to us the same thing but on a much larger scale.

Still a freshman, I began to speak up. If we could not withdraw until the university granted us amnesty, weren't we implicitly recognizing its legitimacy? I threw Lenin back at them. "Did Lenin take over the Winter Palace and then ask the Tsar for amnesty? No, he wanted to replace the Tsar, to see the autocracy crumble and be replaced with a more just order."

Figure 44.1 Mark Rudd (checkered shirt) and William Sales (with microphone) surrounded by protesting students in the lobby of Hamilton Hall, April 23, 1968. *Photograph by Gerald Adler.*

By that logic, I argued, we should be willing to leave the buildings if the administration was willing to establish a more transparent and more sensible disciplinary procedure that recognized our rights and relinquished their arbitrary privileges. Many of us in Fayerweather grew to distrust how SDS was leading the strike, ignoring our pleas to negotiate in good faith, insisting that they, and they alone, should be allowed to interact with the administration. This was the origin of the Fayerweather Statement. A group of us tried to reach out on our own, to go around SDS to establish a channel of communication with the administration, even speak with reporters at WKCR and let them know that at least in Fayerweather Hall, a group of students was open to negotiating an end to the takeover.

SDS got wind of our efforts and identified me as a chief instigator. It was early on Tuesday evening, April 30. They sought me out in Fayerweather and gave me a stark choice. I could leave the building by the ground-floor door or exit out a window. At least they gave me a choice. Several hours later the police stormed the campus. The Cossacks used their whips. They cleared the buildings; beat up students, faculty, and bystanders; and arrested seven hundred. The campus grew more angry and polarized. The strike persisted. SDS had their way.

A hundred years ago, the Mensheviks joined the Bolsheviks in opposing the Russian autocracy, but they remained committed to more conciliatory policies, to work with liberal parties, and to sustain respect for civil liberties and democratic procedures once the Tsar abdicated. In that little piece of the world called Fayerweather Hall, it was easy to recognize how strident politics could overwhelm more principled but less determined opponents. A Menshevik, indeed!

Joshua Rubenstein *('71CC) was an organizer and regional director of Amnesty International USA for thirty-seven years. He is also a longtime associate of Harvard's Davis Center for Russian and Eurasian Studies and the author and editor of several books on Soviet history, including the first history of the Soviet human rights movement, biographies of Leon Trotsky and the writer Ilya Ehrenburg, and books about the Holocaust in German-occupied Soviet territory. He is currently associate director of Major Gifts at Harvard Law School.*

Columbia College undergraduate/Students for a Democratic Society/Strike Coordinating Committee

WHAT IT TAKES TO BUILD A MOVEMENT

uture students of popular organizing—whose numbers, hopefully, will swell into the millions in coming years—will find a rich mine of case studies in the Columbia strike of 1968. At the center of the organizing that built the strike (or rebellion, as many of us still call it) were two organizations: the Columbia chapter of Students for a Democratic Society (SDS) and Columbia Students' Afro-American Society (SAS). I'm not competent to comment on strategy or internal arguments of the latter, but for the past fifty years, I have thought and written about SDS's goals, strategy, and tactics, trying to pick apart the successful from the unsuccessful. By a strange stroke of fate, I happen to have been at the center of these debates on how best to build our movement, often taking the form, characteristically enough, of intense faction fights. Permit me to tell you a story of one such faction fight.

The antiwar movement at Columbia was begun by a small number of people (not including myself—I was still in high school) in the spring of 1965, just as the war in Vietnam, which had been brewing at a low intensity, jumped up to the level of American main force involvement. Between that time and the strike of 1968, SDS and its predecessor, the Columbia Independent Committee on Vietnam, was engaged in a process of *strategic organizing* on campus. Our goal was the "politicization" of the student body, which we hoped would produce the mobilization of thousands of students and others into the antiwar and antiracism movements. The word "organizing" at that time had a precise and technical meaning, the process of building mass movements, and was inherited intact from the labor movement of the thirties to the sixties and from the classic black civil rights movement in the South from 1945 to 1965. For these life-and-death struggles, and for us, "organizing" had a much more robust and consequential meaning than, say, making physical arrangements for an event.

As an eighteen-year-old freshman from Maplewood, New Jersey, a then all-white upper-middle-class suburb of Newark and New York City, I wouldn't have known "organizing" if it hit me in the face. But that's exactly what happened when I fell in at Columbia with my new gang, by far the coolest kids around, the ones already learning about the war and beginning to protest it. Many were, unlike me, red-diaper babies, meaning they had grown up in labor, socialist, or Communist families. Several had been volunteers in the South or had grown up supporting the civil rights movement in the North. Organizing was in their blood.

They taught me that the Vietnamese and the Chinese and the Cubans had organized revolutionary movements to throw the imperialists out of their countries; the Student Nonviolent Organizing Committee (there's that word again) had built a successful voting rights movement in Mississippi and other racist bastions of segregation, despite massive legal and extralegal terrorism. Our job, these more experienced radicals told me, was to organize at Columbia. Build the movement! That was the acknowledged goal of every meeting we held over a period of four years.

(Back then I didn't stop to define what "movement" meant because it was always linked to a crystal-clear adjective in the phrase "mass movement." I knew it involved lots of people; what it took me years to realize was that "movement" means a movement of history. In other words, it takes millions of people to move history. It's the ultimate democratic concept).

The strategy we adopted was to build protests against the Vietnam War and racism at the university, the institution we found ourselves in. The term "build the base" was used constantly to warn against getting too far ahead of our fellow students—which would mean isolation and failure—so education and talk were the primary means of recruitment. For years, SDSers knocked on freshman dorm doors, just as David Gilbert, a senior, had knocked on mine. We set up literature tables several times a week on College Walk, the center of campus, where brilliant debaters, like David Gilbert, often could be found arguing with prowar Reserve Officers Training Corps guys. We held teach-ins on the war and meetings on Columbia's racist labor practices. When a recruiter for the Marines or the Central Intelligence Agency showed up on campus, we would hold spirited demonstrations—with much yelling and occasional shoving matches with prowar students. Over the years, as the war grew in size, these public actions seemed to be growing steadily larger, too. Our organizing was paying off.

By the fall of 1967, a new wind was blowing through national SDS, and we felt it strongly at Columbia. The organization had, over the previous two years, quite brilliantly analyzed the nature of the war, concluding that it wasn't a well-intentioned mistake, but rather part of our country's continual drive toward global control. We called it, rightly, "imperialism," and its cause was the capitalist economic system, with its constant drive for more land, labor, and markets. The allegedly defensive Cold War against Communism was in fact an aggressive war to control the planet. Arrayed against the empire (Star Wars would emerge a decade later out of this milieu) were Third World national liberation struggles. Attacks on dozens of democratically elected governments around the world, as well as against the Cuban revolution and Vietnam, were intended to destroy socialist models of Third World development before they could become attractive to other developing nations. According to our radical anti-imperialist analysis, the US empire was on the decline, as signified by the emerging defeat in Vietnam. As early as 1965, we recognized that the American war was doomed.

Given an understanding of this global situation, which side would you be on? We asked ourselves this question over and over, and we decided that we would never be Good Germans, looking the other way.

In February 1968, while the Tet Offensive in Vietnam was raging— which gave the lie to the US government's claims to be winning the war— I visited revolutionary Cuba and fell in love with the idea of socialism and the "heroic guerilla," Che Guevara. My group, drawn from SDS chapters around the country, met Vietnamese who had already been fighting the Saigon puppet government for years—some living in underground tunnels, far from their families. They told us that there was no way they were going anywhere and that the US people eventually would get tired of the war and demand to bring the troops home. That, of course, is precisely what happened, although it would take seven more years and millions more casualties.

Returning to Columbia fired up to fight the war and to work for socialist revolution, I found a changed situation: the Tet Offensive had flipped public opinion from 60 percent prowar to 60 percent antiwar, and propeace challengers to President Johnson's renomination appeared in the Democratic Party primaries. Community people, backed by a few students, had blocked bulldozers breaking ground for a new student gym in the public Morningside Park between Harlem below and Columbia above. Best of all, a so-called Sophomore Caucus of younger SDSers was demanding direct action, and less talk, believing that now was the opportune moment to mobilize students to act against the war and racism. In this atmosphere, I was elected chairman of the chapter, replacing the older, steadier, "build the base" leaders. We wanted *action*, so naturally we became known as the "Action Faction." Those who continued the cautious, go-slow, "organizing" approach, schooled in Marxist social theory, adopted the name "Praxis Axis," "praxis" being a German word for unity of theory and practice.

In a brief period of a few weeks in March and April, the Action Faction organized a number of provocative actions, such as hitting the director of the New York City Selective Service Office (the draft) with a pie when he spoke at Columbia, and an unauthorized "illegal" indoor demonstration against Columbia's research for the war. But on April 4, 1968, the campus and the entire country came to a complete and total halt when Dr. Martin Luther King, Jr. was assassinated in Memphis. SDS decided to organize a walkout of the hypocritical "memorial" that Columbia administrators held for Dr. King a few days later.

Now the most assiduously apolitical students and faculty at Columbia could no longer sit on the sidelines, avoiding the war and racism. Dr. King, it must be noted, had spoken out against the war a few blocks from campus, in Riverside Church, exactly one year to the day that he was murdered. The only logical strategy, we of the Action Faction thought, was to be bolder, more aggressive, and confrontational, which would attract more people to join us. Elders like David Gilbert and Ted Gold of the Praxis Axis kept asking us, "Have you built the base?"

SDS had had little contact with the SAS. At that time, Columbia was at least 95 percent white, and the few black students on campus felt isolated and under attack. But since 1964, there had been a small but significant increase in the number of African Americans who had been accepted into Columbia College and Barnard as freshman. They banded together in SAS, led by politically cautious students who didn't feel confident in rocking the boat. But in April, after King's murder, younger, more militant, and radical students came to the fore, believing that they should act as representatives of the larger black community of Harlem fighting Columbia's institutionalized racism. An SDS member, Paul Berman, had played in a funk band with several of these new SAS leaders. He arranged a meeting between myself and Cicero Wilson, the incoming chairman of SAS, at which we discussed an alliance between our two organizations, which became, only a few days later, the occupation of five buildings and the largest student rebellion up to that point in US history. We had accomplished our strategic goal: "to politicize the campus."

The details of that rebellion are well known, but one point is salient: without the action of the SAS students holding Hamilton Hall for seven days, the other four buildings would not have been occupied, the Harlem community would not have been mobilized to defend us, and the strike that followed the police bust never would have materialized. It is that coalition that made all the difference.

After the strike and the summer break, Columbia SDS, now intoxicated with its success and dominated by Action Faction mentality, failed to reignite the rebellion. Their tactics escalated in militancy, and by the end of the school year, SDS became isolated on campus. Having been thrown out of Columbia during the strike, I was by then working as a regional and national traveler for SDS, helping local chapters organize, spreading the gospel of anti-imperialist rebellion and militancy. My watchword was action; I even went so far as to proclaim in articles and speeches that "organizing is another word for going slow." Traveling the country, I encountered other SDS organizers and members who were thinking the same, and together we formed what eventually would become the Weatherman faction of SDS. In June 1969, just one year after the Columbia rebellion, my group was elected to run the SDS National Office in Chicago. I was the national secretary.

And that's the moment when things began to fall apart. We were so sure of the lessons of Columbia—that militancy would lead to victory—that we completely forgot about organizing, the hard work of education, gaining people's trust, building relationships, forming alliances, and "building the base." Arrogantly, we set out to build a revolutionary army, a "white fighting force to ally with the people of the world." Our goal, for example, was to bring thousands of "revolutionary youth" to Chicago in October 1969 to "Fight the Pigs." Instead, we wound up with a few hundred people, fewer than we had started with in June. But no matter, we still knew we were right. So we doubled down and decided to build a revolutionary guerrilla army, following the model of Che Guevara and Fidel Castro. The result was the ill-fated and tragic Weather Underground, which over the next seven years became smaller and smaller, more and more isolated.

What became of the Praxis Axis? Most were older graduate students or upperclassmen who went on to become valued and respected left-wing writers, academics, journalists, editors, and doctors. A few former Praxis Axis leaders, such as Ted Gold, the previous vice chairman of the Columbia SDS chapter, and David Gilbert, my mentor, joined the Weatherman faction, and by the spring of 1970 eventually went underground with us. They had been won over to the Action Faction, probably for the same reason as the rest of us, that they thought Columbia was a model for militancy. Ted Gold died with two other comrades in March 1970 in an accidental explosion in Greenwich Village while making bombs to be detonated at Fort Dix, New Jersey. He was twenty-two years old. David Gilbert stayed underground until 1981, four years after I turned myself in. He was arrested in the Brink's armored car robbery, as a getaway driver, working with the Black Liberation Army, a remnant of the New York Black Panther Party. A Brink's driver and two police were killed in that robbery. David is in state penitentiary to this day, on a seventy-five-years-to-life sentence for felony murder.

David Gilbert's incarceration and Ted Gold's death haunt me as the embodiment of the Action Faction error. It wasn't our militancy that made the difference, it was the persistent, long-term organizing work that indeed "built the base," that convinced Columbia students (and some faculty) that they needed to act against the war and racism. Circumstances in the spring of 1968 created a perfect storm in which people chose to participate, but without that long-term organizing, we would have had nothing. Indeed, after that moment passed, all our ultraradical ultramilitant self-expression—bombings, communiqués, underground infrastructure—came to naught.

There doesn't seem to be an alternative to strategic organizing. It's the only thing that will get us out of our present mess.

Mark Rudd, *a lifelong peace and social justice organizer and student of organizing, was the chairman of the Columbia Chapter of Students for a Democratic Society in the spring of 1968. Kicked out of Columbia, he was drafted and announced that he wanted to go into the US Army to organize fellow soldiers against the war, which resulted in his being granted a mental illness deferment. He became a full-time organizer for SDS and helped form the Weatherman faction and subsequently the Weather Underground. He was the last national secretary of SDS. A federal fugitive for seven and a half years, he surrendered in 1977, and then moved to Albuquerque, New Mexico, where he became a basic skills instructor at the local community college, teaching fractions and algebra for thirty years.*

WILLIAM W. SALES, JR.

Graduate student, Political Science/Students' Afro-American Society/
Hamilton Hall occupier

SELF-DETERMINATION AND SELF-RESPECT:
HAMILTON HALL, FIFTY YEARS LATER

T he Columbia insurgency occurred within the opening decades of the
postindustrial period. Major universities like Columbia were in the
forefront of adopting a corporate-business as opposed to a collegiate
model of structure and administration. By the late sixties, behind a facade
of being an oasis of thought and free expression, Columbia had become
an important component of the war-making and urban renewal machinery of contemporary America. This metamorphosis was not unchallenged
inside of Columbia, but increasingly, the administration and the board
of trustees were unresponsive to those students and faculty who feared
that the institution was coming up on the wrong side of the struggle for
human rights and social justice.

Columbia students were changing as well, and especially its black
students. In the mid-sixties, the class character of the majority of black
undergraduates shifted from the upper levels of a prep-school-educated
black bourgeoisie to a more unequivocal background in the working
class and the public school system. When we got to Columbia, most of
us were laboring over a false dichotomy, which characterized the "house
Negro" understanding of white people. According to this schema, there
were "good" white people and "bad" white people. "Good" white people were middle-class whites who were in the professions or business and
employed black servants as part of their lifestyle. They were viewed by
many blacks as kindly, generous with their gifts, and protective of their

servants over and against the depredations of "bad" whites. The latter were white lower-class bigots prone to mediate their relations with black folks through gratuitous and copious racist violence. Knowing how to act around "good" whites (cultural assimilation) and avoiding those places habituated by lower-class bigots was the key to successfully negotiating the racial divide in America. Education became the key to salvation, as it was the most rapid venue for racial and cultural assimilation. This was seen as especially true at private, elite, Ivy League institutions like Columbia. At the same time, we thought that it would be a sure refuge from the oppression and violence of bigots.

For many of us, Columbia turned out to be a bitter disappointment. We saw the university as a community of "good" elite white folks and assumed we were safe from racial bigots there. We were wrong, for some of the "good" white folks were as bigoted as their poorer counterparts. Those who were not personally racial bigots supported policies of institutional racism that did harm to black folks and people of color. Under these circumstances, the assimilationist model of the black bourgeoisie was inconsistent with the growing self-recognition of our intrinsic worth as human beings and our possession of fundamental human rights. Thus, we increasingly were alienated from Columbia. This alienation, however, led us to search for a more satisfying mission to promote human rights and social change. An older group of conservative black student assimilationists and gradualists were nervous about challenging the racial status quo on campus. These two groups struggled for influence and leadership within the Students' Afro-American Society (SAS), with the conservatives winning out initially over a more activist minority. The essence of that conflict was encapsulated in a debate that took place in March 1969 in the pages of the campus student newspaper *Spectator*, between black conservative Oliver Henry and me as a spokesperson for movement activism. This internecine struggle was largely limited to undergraduate black students, until the 1968 takeovers, which initiated a dynamic that transformed the conservatives represented by Henry's position from a majority of black students to a distinct minority. Between September 1964 and April 1968, black student activism developed outside of SAS and then reemerged as the dominant force inside SAS with the ascendency of Cicero Wilson to the chairpersonship, backed by the considerable numbers and influence of a politicized Omega Psi Phi Fraternity.

In much of the literature on the Columbia protest of 1968, organized black students in Hamilton Hall are identified as SAS. This is inaccurate. SAS as a body never endorsed participation in the takeover. Members of SAS certainly were present, as was its chairman Cicero Wilson, but so were other significant organizations of black Columbia and Barnard students. To highlight the breadth of our support among that black student community, our press releases and other material we issued while in the buildings used the phrase the "Black Students of Hamilton Hall," which quickly morphed into "Black Students in Nat Turner Hall of Malcolm X Liberation University." We discussed in our earliest meetings in Hamilton Hall how we should identify ourselves. We knew a conservative bloc within SAS would not endorse cooperation with Students for a Democratic Society (SDS), let alone a building takeover. Given the lack of an organizational meeting and the experience of decision-making within the organization on controversial issues, we picked a name that reflected the reality on the ground.

White students were also changing. White participation in the civil rights movement had created a space for the children of the Old Left to find their own radical roots in a New Left insurgency. Especially through participation in Student Nonviolent Coordinating Committee (SNCC) or in support of its white student activists, white radical students became more critical of the American status quo of the fifties and early sixties. SDS represented the cutting edge of this new white militancy, but it was apparent to some degree in large numbers of white students. This radicalization accelerated with increasing US involvement in Vietnam. As with all wars, Vietnam had become not only a rich man's war and a poor man's fight but also an old man's war and a young man's fight.

Increasingly, black students could find allies within the white student body. This alliance was not formed easily, however. Black students had been immersed in the anti-Communism of the postwar period. Our radical leadership—W. E. B. DuBois, Paul Robeson, and Claudia Jones—had been decimated by the impact of McCarthyism. Non-Communist but progressive black leadership also had been redbaited and stigmatized. The Federal Bureau of Investigation had put both Martin Luther King, Jr. and Malcolm X on the Security Index because of their alleged Communism or Communist affiliations. There persisted in American society the feeling that black people who challenged the racial status quo were either

Communist dupes or Communist themselves. The New Left orientation of SDS clashed with the feeling among black students that we should avoid being perceived as Reds.

At the same time there was a debate within the Black Freedom movement on the role of the Communist Party USA and Old Left Communism in our struggle. Writers like Harold Cruse accused the party of elitism and paternalism in its relations to its black members. In the behavior of white radical student leaders, there was enough elitism and paternalism to support these black misgivings. These white leaders tended to dismiss our misgivings about using extreme Left rhetoric in media interviews and broader community forums. On our part, we always emphasized our relationship to local black struggles in language already prevalent in our struggle. We called for a new relationship between Columbia and the community, not the overthrow of capitalism. To the extent that SDS leadership was committed to this stance, it created difficulties in establishing and maintaining an alliance with black students as it opened our leadership up to the claim that we were mere dupes of whites who were not really committed to black liberation.

An example of these difficulties occurred outside Hamilton Hall on the first day of the demonstration, April 23. Cicero Wilson addressed the crowd and admonished the students. His stance was one of racial mistrust and his comments were not appropriate to the facilitation of a measure of racial unity already achieved. Cicero, while not a black student conservative like Oliver Henry or former SAS head Bob Belt, was quite the anti-Communist and never really trusted SDS leadership on that account. I spoke immediately after Cicero. My focus was to see whether we could salvage black–white student action against the gym. I knew that black activists could accept many Communist principles if presented in the context of the ideology of Third World liberation. If one used the words of Fanon, Cabral, Mao, or Nkrumah or made references to the movements they led, many blacks willingly would endorse your position, especially when combined with major references to Black Nationalism. I offered up to the integrated crowd of students a quick speech that had strong elements of Third World Left rhetoric and an acknowledgment that white students thus far had done well in manifesting solidarity with the struggles of the black community. We quickly got back on the right track working together to take over Hamilton Hall.

Black students in Hamilton Hall did not "split" with the agenda of white students. We endorsed the demands of the strike and never wavered from that position. There were, however, important tactical considerations that could not be ignored. We felt that white students underestimated the violence that the system was capable of directing at its own citizens when challenged. Black students knew this from the beginning. As a small minority of the student body, blacks did not want mere numbers to swallow up their presence in the demonstration. In addition, our smaller numbers and stronger mutual familiarity allowed us to arrive at firm consensus significantly quicker than our white counterparts. Stylistically, the ultrademocracy of SDS with the amorphous, fluctuating white membership in the strike was a protest style we wanted no part of. It appeared to us anarchic. I personally respected the SDS leadership. The need to keep cohesion among their constituency was a monumental task that they should be praised for executing. Their self-sacrifice and adherence to a principled position in support of oppressed people of color, in Harlem as well as Vietnam, commanded our respect. No decision to assume separate tactical headquarters should imply that we were not comrades in the same fight.

The occupation of Hamilton Hall was a spontaneous action, but the black student activists were by then networked with each other and with numerous leaders and resources within the Black Freedom movement. This is true even with the acknowledgment that the majority of black Columbia students had not participated previously in a major civil rights protest. The richness of these previously solidified human and organizational resources was a major reason we succeeded in Hamilton Hall.

We entered Columbia during the period when the Southern civil rights movement was shifting to a northern urban focus, and all the leading civil rights figures came to Morningside Heights. Some spent considerable time with black students. SNCC, Southern Christian Leadership Conference (SCLC), and the Congress of Racial Equality (CORE) specifically targeted the more activist black students at Columbia for recruitment. Blinky Hall, James Foreman, and Michael Simmons of SNCC were well known to us. It was their hope that SNCC could harness the developing northern black student activism and use it to propel their turn to the urban North. In similar fashion, Rev. James Bevel, an aide of Dr. King, spent considerable time with our circle of black student activists. Some of us were already members of Harlem CORE's male caucus. A small group of activists had long, intimate discussions with personages like National Association for the Advancement of Colored People (NAACP) Executive Secretary Roy Wilkins, CORE head James Farmer, and Columbia law student and civil rights icon James Meredith. Black students, some of whom would later occupy Hamilton Hall, were present and involved in the urban rebellions that swept the nation between 1964 and 1968, including Harlem, Detroit, and Newark, and those sparked by the assassination of Dr. King. They had participated in the antiwar movement and joined in the Harlem contingent of the huge April 12, 1967, march, which Dr. King and Dr. Spock led to the United Nations.

Joanne Grant (*Confrontation on Campus: The Columbia Pattern for the New Protest*, 1969) interviewed some of us after the bust as part of her preparation for the book she was writing on the takeover. She was quite upset at what she perceived to be male chauvinism among the Hamilton Hall leadership. We did not understand what she was talking about. Our functioning inside Hamilton respected a traditional conception of gender roles. Women handled the food arrangements, and security was handled by men. The steering committee was all male. Indeed, as I was later to realize, there were issues of gender inequality in the leadership and style of the Hamilton occupation. It was attenuated by a kind of paternalistic approach, which informally acknowledged the need to consult with particular female students who knew how to get things done and who offered excellent advice. They were not given a position on the steering committee. They should have been. We never solicited their perspectives as women in the struggle. We should have. Barnard women in our group had organized, even before the occupation, to advance a black women's perspective on the issue of the gym. They did not raise a demand inside Hamilton for formal recognition within the leadership. Sisters inside Hamilton had access to the steering committee leadership. We were all good friends and would not have done anything without the approval of the sisters, but our stance was paternalistic. Our major concern was that we had to protect the women from harm at all costs. The notion that they might be able to defend themselves and didn't need us was foreign to us.

Although the majority of black protesters were undergraduates, black graduate students played a catalytic role in Hamilton Hall. Of the four members of the steering committee of black students, two were graduate students—me and Andy Newton, a law student. There were at least three other black law students in Hamilton as well as a graduate of the School of International Affairs (SIA), Carolyn Anderson, who continued as a doctoral candidate in African History. Barbara Wheeler, also a SIA graduate, then working on a doctorate at Teacher's College, organized support there and through her Harlem contacts to provide meals for us during the occupation.

Our network with other students included the Black Student Congress, the emergence of which was facilitated by the Metropolitan Applied Research Center, whose director was the preeminent social psychologist Kenneth Clark, the father of Hilton Clark, founder of SAS. Vincent DeLusia, a graduate of SIA and the Columbia School of Business, spent time with us in Hamilton. He was instrumental in networking us with St. Claire Bourne, formerly of the Peace Corps and a graduate student in the School of the Arts, later an important black documentary filmmaker, and SNCC's Stokely Carmichael (Kwame Toure). Sam Anderson, Carolyn Brown's husband at the time and a graduate student in math at City College of New York, was with us in the building and brought a wealth of contacts from the movement through SNCC, the original Black Panther Party, and as a poet who participated in the Black Arts movement. Sam also linked us with important community struggles in education. Representatives of the West Harlem Community Organization, community control movements centered on Harlem's I.S. 201 and Brooklyn's Ocean Hill Brownsville districts, and students at Brandeis High School on the Upper West Side all joined the Hamilton Hall occupation.

We had excellent representation provided us by the NAACP, which included Robert F. Van Lierop of the NAACP legal staff, a former New York State policeman who would go on to become a documentary filmmaker of the Mozambique Liberation Movement and later Vanuatu's Ambassador to the United Nations. Another of our lawyers, Jay Cooper, out of NYU Law School, went on to become mayor of Pritchard, Alabama, the first black mayor elected in a major city in that state. Of course, we must note that Raymond A. Brown, one of the country's most prominent defense attorneys, represented us in court and was also the father of steering committee member Ray Brown.

Columbia University had only a miniscule number of black faculty members, so the pool of possible black faculty mentors was less than slim.

Nevertheless, among those few, several deserve mention: Preston Wilcox, on the School of Social Work faculty, helped Ray Brown and I avoid the pitfalls of opportunism around the issue of the gymnasium. We initially conceded that community folks and their student allies were too weak to oppose construction of the gym. Our position was that Columbia could be pressured to increase the size and amenities of the community portion of the gym structure, but it was too late to force them to abandon the notion of two separate gyms within one shell. Preston was adamant and won us over to the position that the struggle was against any form of Jim Crow building, not about getting a better deal within an essentially Jim Crow arrangement. Another black faculty supporter was Ambassador Elliott Skinner, later chair of the anthropology department. He was proud that his son Victor, a Columbia College undergraduate, was arrested with us in Hamilton.

Our takeover of Hamilton Hall represented a challenge for our parents. In every era of black insurgency, our people had been victimized by the violence of reactionary white supremacists and police terror. Our parents sacrificed immeasurably to see that we had the educational opportunities

Figure 46.1 Construction on the gymnasium in Morningside Park. *Image from University Archives, Rare Book and Manuscript Library, Columbia University in the City of New York.*

that might lead to the kind of economic security to protect us from this viciousness. They were all so proud of our admission to Columbia University and what that meant for the future of their children and the family name. Most black folks, even during this era of profound social change, did not directly challenge the hegemony of powerful, white-dominated institutions like Columbia. Nevertheless, on balance, most black parents of Hamilton Hall occupiers did not pressure their sons and daughters to leave the protest. The father of the playwright and poet Ntozake Shange, a medical doctor, set up a little office inside Hamilton to minister to the medical needs of students. My own father left work in another locality and came to New York to spend time with me inside Hamilton Hall. He never asked me to leave or expressed disagreement with my political choices. This was true despite his great fear of seeing directed against me the extreme violence against black people and union supporters that he had experienced as a young adult in the mills and coal mines of western Pennsylvania.

Inside Hamilton Hall, we experienced true self-determination. Everything that went on inside the building was a result of decisions we made and had to live with. It was our larger black community that literally fed us and stayed the hand of the police for a week. We ironed out disagreements and established workable protocols for maintaining the livability of the building and for democratic decision-making. Our success in remaining together under those circumstances greatly enhanced our mutual self-respect. It created for us a visceral experience of what Black Power and self-determination could be within the larger society.

William W. Sales, Jr. *is a professor emeritus and past chairperson of the Department of Africana Studies and director of the Center for African American Studies at Seton Hall University. He received a Ph.D. in political science from Columbia University and also holds a master of international affairs degree from Columbia's School of International Affairs. He is the author of two books:* From Civil Rights to Black Liberation: Malcolm X and the Organization of Afro-American Unity *and* Southern Africa/Black America: Same Struggle, Same Fight.

BILL SHARFMAN

*Graduate student, English/Preceptor, Columbia College/
Ad Hoc Faculty Group*

LONG AGO AND NOT AT ALL FAR AWAY

When the crisis at Columbia began in the spring of 1968, I was a graduate student in the Columbia University English Department, but perhaps more important to me, I was a preceptor, teaching two classes a semester at Columbia College. I was twenty-three when I first started teaching in the College in 1966, but that represented a turning point for me, because although I was a middling student, I was a committed and pretty good teacher, and that's what I really liked to do and identified myself with. As a result, I had an office in Hamilton Hall (along with three others), which put me at ground zero when the occupation of buildings started at Columbia, as it started right downstairs.

It rapidly emerged, once the occupation of Hamilton got going, and further occupation of other buildings rolled out, that there were two potentially dangerously opposed and intransigent factions: on one side, the white Students for a Democratic Society (SDS) and the black Students' Afro-American Society (SAS) who quickly wrested from the white students the first building occupied, Hamilton Hall; and the distant, unimaginative, insensitive, authoritarian university administration. It was in that gaping no-man's land in between where the Ad Hoc Faculty Group equally rapidly formed to try to bring reason to the crisis.

At the earliest meeting of the Ad Hoc Faculty Group, in the first-floor lounge of Philosophy Hall that came to be its home and headquarters (every faction had its HQ), the first discussions raised the question who legitimately should be included, allowed, and considered to be members of the group. Some of the senior faculty immediately questioned the presence of teaching staff. Debate ensued, as it did to a fare-thee-well about everything.

But being as committed to teaching as I was, and as interested in being part of the faculty as I was, it turned out very quickly that I was the one who resolved the matter of defining where and how to draw the line for those who could be included. "Why not," I shouted, "include anyone who teaches classes, with sole responsibility for giving grades to those in their classes?" That criterion seemed reasonable to me because I knew it included me, which was really all I wanted at that point. Somehow, this was almost immediately agreed to, and thus I was one of the Ad Hoc Faculty Group for the duration of the crisis at Columbia.

Had it not been for the Ad Hoc Faculty Group, I think, the occupation likely would have been over in two days. That's because the administration was led by President Grayson Kirk, with an appendage, the vice president, David Truman, who, as I imagined it, had the cops on speed dial and probably reached for the phone countless times during that protracted period of endless negotiation. Unfortunately, with two such intransigent, entrenched, self-referential sides, we were working hard and in good faith at negotiating with non-negotiable parties, so the outcome was inevitable, as it always is when one side can default to military power and the other has a role in mind to play, and won't budge from it. Kirk stuck with default. It was all he knew.

Both the immediate and longer crisis, it seemed, went on for weeks and weeks, and looking back on the entire period, it still does. The uprisings and ensuing endless discussions and further violence took place in and against the backdrop of the civil rights struggles of the sixties and the Vietnam War. Faculty or no faculty, I was as abraded by it as anyone: my own college career at Michigan began with being in charge of the luggage of John F. Kennedy's entourage the night he came to Ann Arbor and gave a speech on the steps of the Michigan Union about his idea for something called the Peace Corps, and ended with Lyndon B. Johnson as my commencement speaker, talking about the "Great Society." In New York, we were all of us saturated with an unrelenting media assault of news of Vietnam. That costly, misused authority was the backdrop for what erupted at Columbia.

In his introduction to *Up Against the Ivy Wall*, Robert Friedman uses the term "obsolete absolutism" to characterize the administration, and "the archaic power structure of the university," which was bumbling along in its own world, pressing unthinking alliances and commitments in the face of civil rights activism and antiwar rage. But, Friedman concludes: "Living through the crisis was perhaps the best education many Columbia students will ever receive, and reliving it . . . one discovers a pattern that is not only the basis of most of the world's crises today but promises to duplicate itself two, three, many times tomorrow."[1] This has been my own lifetime experience precisely. Some of the specific things I saw and heard have stayed vivid with me, and I often replay them in my mind. And as I've said every time I've had the chance from then until now, I'm not coming out until all my demands are met. Including amnesty.

I follow a rush of people to the offending gym construction site in Morningside Park, and come upon a violent mob of people in motion. Students are pushing and pulling the chain-link fence surrounding the site, trying to tear it down. Fights are breaking out and people are getting trapped inside, pinned against the fence. It's chaos, exactly the kind of scene I avoid getting close to, since there's always the danger of being sucked in or caught up in it. Suddenly, cops are trying to stop it and corral someone, anyone. But it's really an angry maelstrom. Anyone watching can see this isn't an event with a beginning and an end; it's like watching the sea. It surges, falls back, then surges again. There is no epiphany, but one feels and absorbs the immense energy being expended, endlessly. I've seen it, felt it. I work my way carefully around the main mob and make my way back to the campus, away from the eruption.

Tuesday, April 23, after lunch. I am in my office on the fourth floor of Hamilton Hall, the College English Department, with one of my office mates. There suddenly comes a great hubbub from below—loud, aggravated sounds working their way up from the building's lobby. We head downstairs to see what's going on, but remain where we have a safe overlook on the stairs from just below the second floor, because the lobby is

---

1.   Jerry L. Avorn, with Andrew Crane [and others] of the staff of the *Columbia Daily Spectator*, *Up Against the Ivy Wall* (New York: Atheneum Press, 1969), 22.

now packed with people who would be milling about if they could easily move. There are white students, black students—it's another agitated mob, and this time its focus is the office of acting dean Henry Coleman. Sure enough, Coleman's door is open and he's standing in it, confronting the mob that has pinned him in there. He's not going anywhere through the lobby. There is some attempt at communication going on between him and the students toward the front of the mob, but it's too noisy and confused to make sense of, except that it certainly is a hostile confrontation. Coleman appears to be holding his composure; the students are worked up. We watch this scene for a bit, then retreat back upstairs to the office. After a while, seeing that what's going on in the lobby is getting more heated, more charged, more crowded, we gather up our stuff and, working our way carefully around the mob, exit the building. We won't be back inside any time soon. It is April 23, 1968, and the occupation is beginning.

It's a lovely, sunny day. April 25, I think. I saunter over to Low Library, where I know at least a couple of my students are among the occupiers of Grayson Kirk's office suite, the one with the famous Rembrandt on the wall. A number of students are sitting on the window ledges above. I wave to them. It turns out one of the first things the students who have occupied Kirk's offices have done is repair the copy machine; it wasn't working when they got there, but everyone knows a revolution depends on the free flow of communications, so they got it running. My students, and the other students they are with, are feeling on top of things, obviously, in the catbird seat, so to speak. Hey, they say to me in a nearly chirpy way, guess what we found in Kirk's desk drawer? What? I say. A copy of *Naked Lunch* bought in the Omaha Airport, they report with glee.

I am in a state, a mood, some combination of sick to death of all the politicizing and posturing on both sides, the notion of SDS being revolutionaries but demanding amnesty, all the rhetoric, the rhetoric about rhetoric, the attention-getting, the aggravation, agitation, and intensified emotional density of every meaningless moment. It's one huge itch. I have already spotted Jimmy Breslin on College Walk, plying his trade in an impressive sharkskin suit, and now I spot a TV news crew from CBS, a standup guy with a soundman and cameraman, so I wander over. I tug on the Important News Correspondent's sleeve. I say, you're from CBS News, that right? Yes, he says. I say, well, you should know that I have no statement to make at this time.

I am on the upper level of the campus, in front of Mathematics Hall, and I'm fairly close behind two cops, close enough to eavesdrop, in a casual way. One cop has been there, the other, a young guy, has just come on duty, hasn't been here before. What's going on here, he wants to know. Kids are barricaded inside that building and a bunch of other ones. Like overnight? Yes. Boys and girls? Yes. I can see the dawning recognition of what this picture really is. The young cop's expression becomes one of complex incredulity, resentment, jealousy, hatred, revulsion, wonderment and possibly distant admiration, recognizing youthful criminal behavior that can only mean free love. I picked up that same recognition other times from patrolling cops, and it would be painfully acted out later. You bet it would.

April 30. The Tactical Patrol Force (TPF) is coming: the bust. I am with other Ad Hoc Faculty Group members lined up in front of Avery Hall; we have committed to interpose our bodies between the administration-ordered cops and our students. Others are positioned in front of other buildings. It's an uncomfortably tense, apprehensive, and scary time, but when the TPF attacks, it's almost instantaneous. They are paramilitary professionals—military, really—and say nothing. I am unceremoniously pitched over a hedge, and, in effect, my night is over. But the night itself is very far from over, and some of our group end up in St. Luke's Hospital across Amsterdam, as do many students.

I wander the campus, seeing what is going on, but without any plan, kind of dazed and detached, actually. A scene that has been etched in my mind forever, nowhere near any of the buildings, nothing to do with occupation or trespass: a young woman on the ground, mid-campus, curled up as close to a ball as she can get, being beaten violently, and screaming "Help, police!" It is a cop that's beating her. He's really into beating her; it's just gratuitous violence. What the hell am I doing hanging around campus with the TPF and all this police wilding going on, including an army of plainclothes cops on the attack and running after anyone they can clobber? The instinct and urge to witness, not watch, is too great to dismiss.

I am once again in front of Mathematics. The barricades have been pulled apart, the students have been dragged out. There are no students left in the building; only the cops have access now. Several of us look up and see a fire on the top floor. Smoke is pouring out of a couple of the windows. This is ended pretty quickly, but we have already seen it.

The spring siege of strike, and endless discussion of reform and politics and disruption—a siege of dysfunction that would go on and on—has settled in. I find myself meeting classes in various predetermined locations, on the grass in front of the buildings, for those who want to show up. It is hard for everyone to focus or for the discussion to stay within planned topics. Nevertheless, faculty persist in trying to hold classes and stick to assignments. One such day, a picture of me meeting a contingent from one of my classes on the grass in front of Philosophy Hall appears in the *Spectator*. Irony of ironies, we are right under the statute of The Thinker.

I run into Steven Marcus, my dissertation director, who is eager to report his latest story about teaching in these truly crazy times. He meets his class, he tells me, and immediately is confronted with drumming going on in front of Hamilton. Lots of drummers, making it hard to hear, let alone concentrate on anything. What do you think was due today? he says. Can't guess, I say. John Henry Cardinal Newman's *The Idea of a University*.

One spring evening, a beautiful warm day, relative quiet on campus. Inexplicably the jocks in the fraternities take it into their heads to stage a panty raid on Barnard. They stream across the same South Lawn that was, at an earlier time, the scene of a plainclothes riot directed at any and all students, including those very same jocks. I wander over to Barnard, and sure enough, damned if bras and panties aren't flying out the windows of one of the Barnard buildings. I find myself at the very back of the crowd, standing next to Dean Robert Belknap, Professor of Russian and a tall, thin, somewhat ascetic-looking personage. A reporter for the *Spectator* spots him and immediately asks, Dean Belknap, what are you doing here? Belknap strokes his chin, and says, oh, I'm here taking a dim view of things.

Bill Sharfman, *B.A. from the University of Michigan, M.A. and Ph.D. from Columbia University, taught in Columbia College 1966–1969, as well as at Idaho State University. He was director of judging for the PACE Awards for Innovation, contributing writer for* Automobile Magazine, *and senior vice president— strategic planning for J. Walter Thompson USA. Since 1985, he has been an independent consulting strategist in New York.*

MARVIN SIN

*Columbia College undergraduate/Students' Afro-American Society/
Hamilton Hall occupier*

COLUMBIA 1968: MY COURSE CORRECTION

B y 1968, a power shift had taken place within the larger black political movement. There was a loud call for Black Power, which proclaimed that the lives of black people would no longer be directed by white people. But at Columbia University, no matter how determined we were to challenge the hierarchy that surrounded us, assumptions of superiority confronted us at every turn.

During the sixties, Ivy League institutions like Columbia decided to diversify enrollment with nontraditional demographics. Almost every black student at Columbia before me had come through the prep school system. I arrived in the fall of 1966 as part of the first overwhelmingly public school class on campus. Many of us might have been the top students in our high schools, but we were still a totally different demographic to what Columbia's administration, faculty, and student body were used to. We were youngsters with divergent mind-sets and cultural preferences, most of whom had grown up in black communities. Simply put, we were from the hood. We were smart, but we were still from the hood.

While we were inside Hamilton Hall, behind those locked doors, as a group we rifled every office. In one drawer, in the dean's office, we found a file on each of us, which contained various details, including how the administration had profiled us. I realized, after reading a few pages of my file, that according to Columbia authorities I was not expected to graduate.

Here it was, in black and white, typed on piece of paper that was signed by a representative of the university: "UNLIKELY TO SUCCEED."

A judgment had been made before I even got there.

This affected me profoundly.

We in Hamilton Hall were all radicalized by what we encountered and uncovered during those days. It transformed our relationship with the university, and, I think it's fair to say, with America.

For some of us, there was no turning back.

In joining the crowds who move through Ivy League schools like Columbia, I was being ushered onto a stairway that would take me to another echelon of life. I was being offered a level of privilege previously unavailable to me. My freshman year was the first time I ever met people from backgrounds so different from my own. Up until that point, it had never occurred to me that this is how some people actually lived. I realized that Columbia was preparing me to play a certain role in society. I came from a world and a community, but had been pulled out of that community by Columbia because I had reached a level of academic achievement. Once on campus, I was being trained to serve a *different* community, one that was completely alien to me. I remember thinking at the time, "If I and all of my friends—we who are considered by some to be the best of *our* communities—are being extracted for the purpose of serving *other* communities, who will be left to serve at home? If there is a system in place to methodically remove all those who are capable and able to serve a machine, but that machine is oppressive, then something needs to change."

It was while inside Hamilton Hall during those days that I closed a chapter of my life and decided I would rather be a stone paved toward the success of my own community than to take possession of whatever privilege the people of Columbia were preparing me for. The illusion being offered to me by Columbia was that we were authentic participants in the system, that we could move upward through the ranks, in conjunction with everybody else. But reading my file in that office in April 1968 opened my eyes.

Everything is essentially a product of its creation. There is nothing we can do about the history that underlies modern-day institutions. Racism, the seed planted centuries ago, can never be undone. It's part of the fabric of the society we live in, part of the daily experience of millions of people in the United States. You can't fight against it and expect to win. The better course of action is to prepare yourself so that you are not adversely affected by its negative consequences.

Some people might have thought that their protests and occupation of various buildings on the Columbia campus were going to radically transform the institution. But they never could achieve anything of the sort. You can push and pull at the walls at much as you want. They might temporarily yield, but eventually, like a rubber band, they return to their regular shape, to the calcified structures that exist.

Those structures are what the powers-that-be are most comfortable with. They benefit the powerful. No one else.

The year 1968 informed my understanding of how best to move forward, and the direction in which I should focus my life's energies. From the perspective of fifty years, I understand that my Columbia experience was pivotal. I became aware of the mis-education I was being offered and so became determined to educate myself. I forged lifelong friendships with classmates that endure and sustain me to this day. My journey as an artist and leather craftsman began at Columbia. Student activities and protests infused me with a sense of agency in the "real world." They opened me to the different ways in which I could define and influence the course of events in my community. Columbia connected me to Harlem, by way of a work-study job, and opened the door to a separate reality: The Afrikan World.

The student protests of the sixties are connected to the Arab Spring, the Occupy movement, and the Black Lives Matter movement. People the world over are calling for a new social, cultural, economic, and political system that respects and elevates our collective humanity. As an artist, I understand that such universal yearnings can be satisfied only by the creation of something new, something NU. Protest and negotiation may change the face of oppression, but never its essence—although it can transform passive observers into active change agents and positive forces in their communities.

Marvin Sin *is a native of Bed-Stuy, Brooklyn, New York, and a master leather-craftsman, a creative journey the origin of which dates back to 1968. He has also been involved in cultural activism in Harlem, Washington, D.C., and Chicago through organizations such as Blackfrica Promotions, Visions Collective, Black Gold, and the NU Afrikan Vanguard.*

Columbia College undergraduate

UNITERS

olumbia, for all its faculty, administrators, and course catalogs, may never have devised a more profound learning experience than the strike itself. We didn't think of it as an educational experience at the time, but wasn't that what it was? We were learning things no professor taught, that went far beyond any upper-level class. It was a graduate seminar in psychological change and how people—including myself—are transformed under pressure. Contemporary Civilization and Humanities had only been study aids. The strike, in its infuriating, improvised way, was the free-form take-home midterm, the dry run for the real test each of us knew was coming: what our deepest truth would be in dealing with the draft. The strike didn't change the trajectory of my life, but it did force me to realize who I was. None of this was why I thought I had come to college. But in learning these things I found why I had really come. The strike didn't waste my tuition. It was what I was paying for.

If these reflections have any broader value, it might be because I was part of the largest group—or rather nongroup—on campus. These were the approximately 50 percent of students (at least in the College), who weren't part of the Students for a Democratic Society (SDS) or the Majority Coalition and who weren't deeply political, but ranged from broadly moderate to liberal to center-left. Each of us was in different stages of groping our way to oppose the war. We supported Gene McCarthy and Bobby Kennedy, not Humphrey or Nixon, and were sympathetic to the issues raised by the demonstrators. Some, like myself, who went inside the occupied buildings but didn't stay, were appalled by talk of weapons being brought onto campus by both protesters and the police, but were willing, in the end, to stand outside the buildings, arms linked, as a shield against those police.

To describe what this amorphous group had in common, I would say that in our deepest selves we were *uniters*. We wanted and hoped to change the country, but believed such change could come about only by convincing a broad majority. We believed—against odds and assassinations—in outreach, electoral politics, and nonviolent change. Most of all, we believed in the possibility of balancing social and political change with our own needs and desires as individuals. We weren't centrists; we didn't feel the current center of opinion was correct, but felt that it needed to be shifted. For some who had been at the March on the Pentagon in October 1967, confronted by troops and tear gas, that simple reminder—"Stay together!"—meant a lot more: anyone who joins us is one of us. There was no test for who was committed or pure enough. What dismayed many of us about SDS was its apparent belief in division, in being absolutely right and committed and viewing everyone else as irrelevant. What dismayed us about the Right was its active divisiveness: the use of "freedom" to limit other people's rights, to define themselves as more "American," more patriotic. We were often pessimistic in the short run, but in the long run, perhaps, we were irrationally optimistic: surely people could be persuaded to share our broad values? We felt that being willing to change your mind was a good thing. After all, we were doing it ourselves all the time! During the strike, we were called pinkos, cowards, liberals, spineless, fools, hidden racists, naïve, and unsophisticated. We worried about being each of those things, and about being nothing, because in 1968, everyone was supposed to be something. (Whether I was any or all of those things, it's probably easier for others to judge from these reflections than I can.)

But beyond being a nonmember of this nongroup, I also found myself in the strange, semihopeless role of being their interpreter. During the strike, an associate dean I knew had me come in and spend forty-five minutes every morning serving as a sounding board for what liberal-moderate-center-left students might be thinking. Erwin Glikes, who had known me from a fellowship application for a junior year abroad, would

bounce ideas off me: How would students react to various possible administration proposals? What if we offered this, what if they proposed that?
I pushed ideas for amnesty and brainstormed ways to create a broader
sense of community (not restoring one, because there had hardly been
one to begin with). "You're not going to bring in the cops, are you?" I kept
asking. In the end, such outreach proved futile. But with zero authority
and in the improvisatory spirit of those two weeks, I felt—and still feel—
good to have involved myself in those sessions with Glikes, during which
I felt in some deep way, as I did facing the cops that final night, that this
was who I needed to be. In that feeling and its seeming absurdity, I was,
without thinking about it, being, in my bones, a uniter.

In playing this odd role, I was atypical. But this only made me typical
of uniters. Each of us had reached this point in atypical ways. This may
be exactly why we didn't fit into narrower, more easily categorizable positions. We were each in transition *before* the strike, as well as during it.
Each of us had come to who and where we were in April 1968 for reasons
of our own. My reasons, the ways I was atypical, included (1) my hatred of
ideology, (2) my choice of politics as a career and my uncanny experience
of dropping out of it, and (3) my being busted as a bystander at an earlier
demonstration. These shaped why I reacted to the strike as I did.

If people believe in things because of their childhood, that explains why
I hated ideology. My family was among the very few Jews in conservative
and Scandinavian Bay Ridge, Brooklyn. Bay Ridge was the only assembly district in New York State to vote for Barry Goldwater. Our next-door
neighbor, and my surrogate father, was a member of the John Birch Society. My mother had been, although I didn't know it at the time, a member
of the Communist Party. My father had always been too much of an icon-
oclast to join any party. I would take my neighbor's arguments upstairs to
my parents, and their response back down to him. On issue after issue,
I realized that their underlying human values weren't far apart. They
agreed on many things—as long as you didn't frame them ideologically.
This led me to become a debater and to seek politics without ideology to
bring people together. As a result of growing up this way, I had a better
intuition—and perhaps a more urgent desire—than many of my liberal
friends for how to appeal to a broad majority of people. Reading each flier
handed to me during the strike, listening to each impassioned speech on
campus, arguing with others and with myself, and brainstorming with the

associate dean, I would ask myself: is this simply reaffirming those who are already convinced, or can it also be heard by the other side?

Hoping that politics could resolve conflicts instead of escalating them had led me to stay in New York and attend Columbia, but also caused me to be isolated in college as well. My views and activities had been shaped by electoral politics: overseeing student volunteers on West Side Congressional campaigns, drafting state and federal legislation, organizing rallies to defeat a referendum against the City's Civilian Police Review Board, and, in the fall of 1967, helping conduct a large voter survey to convince first Bobby Kennedy, then George McGovern, and finally Gene McCarthy to challenge Lyndon Johnson. I slept in the dorms but was hardly ever there. I was majoring in government, active with the debate team, and planning to go to the Law School. Like the five other "West Side Kids," as we were dubbed in New York Magazine, I was going to make a career in politics. We thought we were going to take over the world. (One's now a Congressman, another a state assemblyman, another became chief counsel to the Motion Picture Association and another ran Bill Clinton's reelection campaign; the one who replaced me after I dropped out ran Boris Yeltsin's campaign.)

But in the midst of all this, in late November 1967, I turned my back on electoral politics, for a reason I could hardly explain. I cared about the issues, but working in politics I didn't feel real to myself. It was as if a previously silent part of *myself* was finally speaking up. It couldn't tell me who I was, but it could tell me who I wasn't. I had that same feeling the second morning of the protests, when David Shapiro beckoned to us to follow him up into Low Memorial Library.

The first time I got busted, it happened in my usual atypical way. Although I had dropped out of politics, I had remained somewhat involved. I spent a few weekends helping my former colleagues run the student campaign for McCarthy in New Hampshire, although I still hoped Kennedy would run. On a weeknight in late January 1968, I was at Rockefeller Center to help present a petition to Kennedy from thousands of students urging him to reconsider running. The Kennedy clan was having a party on the skating rink, while a dozen of us huddled upstairs on the sidewalk, waiting. Suddenly hundreds of demonstrators ran past us, SDS protesters from a rally against Humphrey at the Plaza Hotel, chased by police. The cops started rounding up everyone. I hurried downstairs to ask what I should do.

"Find out where they're being taken and we'll get them released," an assemblyman I knew advised.

I rushed up to the police captain. "You're arresting kids who have nothing to do with the demonstration."

"Him!" he shouted, nodding to a sergeant. As two large cops banged me up against the paddy wagon, I grinned stupidly (only making them angrier, I'm sure). How could this be happening? It didn't seem real. (This should tell you how innocent and privileged I felt without being aware of it.) When I was finally loaded into the paddy wagon's cold darkness, clinging to anything I could as it rattled downtown toward the Tombs, an SDS kid lurched and pointed to me as the captain had done.

"Hey Kennedy kid," he jeered. "Haven't you given up on the system yet?" This was the question that later hovered over those like me during the Columbia strike. My experience "obstructing pedestrian traffic," in the words of the court, was a precursor to what many of us felt on campus the night the police charged us. Stupefaction at the unreality of reality. Indeed, that's perhaps what the sixties felt like overall.

Such moments distilled what much of the strike was: moments in the theater of self-radicalization. We didn't think of it as theater back then, but that's what it was, as much for conservative students who were radicalized in their own way as for liberal ones. Calling it theater isn't meant to diminish what happened, but to understand and emphasize the strike's power for us. Mark Rudd and the SDS crowd, however weak they may have been in planning and organization, turned out to be naturals at drama. To understand the strike, indeed simply to remember it, is to see it as a drama that played out not only—and not even most importantly—on the campus, but in our heads. We were all performing. We were creating roles that offered counter-roles the administration colluded in, again and again. In trying *not* to play a role, we were playing roles as well. We might have been working from a script whose pages we hadn't yet seen. It unfolded as a parent–child confrontation in which everyone felt self-justified and enraged. The strike was theatrical, in that its real transformations were psychological more than they were political.

If this seems harsh, it was true for two major reasons. First, it was theater more for its participants than for any potential audience. The broader impact of the strike—how those outside the university would react to it—never seemed to be considered. If you do things in politics, it's the counter-reactions that matter and how you build support to anticipate and resist them. No one seemed to be thinking about this. If David Shapiro is photographed in *Life* magazine, feet up on Kirk's desk, smoking the president's cigars, what impact will that have on tens of thousands of people all over? No one had any idea. No one cared. I should have had more sense of what those effects would be, from growing up in a right-wing neighborhood, from being involved in politics. But I, too, indulged in self-involvement, in playing, in having fun. I didn't think about the broader consequences—the backlash our images would propel. The media played the only role you could expect: they showed us being who we, at our most theatrical, chose to be.

The second reason the strike was theater is that whatever the dangers, everything was taking place within the safe cocoon of the university. Nor was the strike even directly about the war, which is what we most cared about. The strike's issues were surrogates, whether the gym or student power. The university was a surrogate for the government. Our anger at Grayson Kirk was our anger at Lyndon Johnson. Kirk and the university were *in loco parentis*, the pompous role they had carved out for themselves, and they were going to be tormented for it, and to show they deserved it. Our words were broad and noble, but if we didn't care about the counter-reactions to what we were doing, then, if I'm painfully honest, what we cared about most deeply was our own psychological change.

When the strike began I was aware of how much the strike was a surrogate struggle over surrogate issues. And then I forgot. That was how it swept me up, like a great wave at the beach, so that the swirling and tossing of that rushing water became all there was. And in that powerful current, all you try to do is remain standing.

The reason I wasn't interested that first morning, April 23, when demonstrators went down to the gym, was simple. The gym seemed like a stand-in for what was at stake in the country. In January 1968, the Tet Offensive had ripped apart all the propaganda for the war, Johnson had withdrawn from the race in March, King had just been assassinated, and Kennedy and McCarthy were challenging Humphrey. Everything seemed to be on the line. If the demonstration had been about Columbia's Institute for Defense Analysis and the university's ties to the war, that would have been more urgent, more relevant. I passed the gathering demonstrators on my way to music humanities, whose terrible grade I would ultimately be spared by the pass–fail grading from the strike.

When I came out of class, I saw that the protestors had returned from the gym. Fliers were pushed into my hands. I heard what seemed crazy to me: students were holding the dean hostage in his Hamilton Hall office. Why would you hold a dean hostage? What was the endgame? It sounded to me like dangerous children playing. Protestors called out to us. "Come on! Join us inside!" My back stiffened, my negative image of SDS revived. I had seen Mark Rudd around campus. He seemed clumsy, loud, and unsophisticated. Indeed, this was part of his shtick: "I'm not sophisticated, I can just be a loudmouth." I didn't take him seriously. When I later read the Port Huron Statement, I was moved and impressed. But at the time, SDS at Columbia seemed to me self-involved and self-righteous. The flier had their puritanical tone I was familiar with: "Only we are right. If you're not one of us, there's something wrong with you. You should feel guilty." To me, this was the opposite of what was needed to change the country. Bobby Kennedy was appealing to ethnic whites, to blacks, to Hispanics, both to increasingly conservative union voters and to students and liberals against the war. In my deepest nature, I felt that SDS's purist approach was wrong. Their slogan, "If you're not part of the solution, you're part of the problem," was an updating of Hitler's "If you're not with us, you're against us." That divisiveness wasn't something I wanted to be part of. I walked past Hamilton and went to lunch instead.

Later in the day, there was a call for a sit-in, with its positive echo of civil rights. The administration seemed to be clamping down on students, on dissent. This was a broader concern I could share. My best friend and I decided to join in, as a mark of solidarity. Adding to the numbers could discourage a crackdown. That's as far as our thinking went. After dinner, we grabbed sleeping bags and pillows from our John Jay dorm rooms and our girlfriends joined us to sleep over in Hamilton Hall. It felt like something out of Tom Sawyer—half-serious, not thinking about consequences, like Tom and his friends going over to the island. The assignment for next morning's political revolution class, that seemed serious. It was readings from Mao. We had only one copy so we passed it back and forth, as we lay on the floor between the wooden desks. That what we were doing might have anything to do with our reading never occurred to us. We were just protesting a little thing. This wasn't the Chinese Revolution.

At four or five in the morning, Rudd banged on the classroom door.

"We gotta leave so the blacks can have their own building."

"What time is it?" one of us groggily asked. Except for what seemed the far-off yellow lamplight from the hall, the room was in shadows.

"Come on," Rudd's voice was hoarse. "We're gonna take over Low instead. Hurry, we gotta leave."

Half-awake, I half-digested Rudd's order as we stumbled out of our sleeping bags and were herded, stumbling, down the stairwell. What kind of revolution, what kind of political movement, would begin by dividing buildings between blacks and whites? Sure, the black students might want their own building as a symbol. But that Rudd had been persuaded, or guilt-tripped into this, seemed proof of his stupidity. What kind of leader was he? How could we be stronger if we were divided? As we reached the ground floor lobby, everything seemed chaotic. All about us, people were rushing in and out. Someone spoke in a low voice: "Guys from Harlem are bringing in guns." Guns, here? What could be more of a violation to creating a community? We were shoved outside. Shivering in the early grayness, I looked up and saw students clambering into Low Library. David Shapiro was perched on a windowsill, in dark clothes, like some giant crow. His grin had never seemed sharper, or more excited. "Here," he called down to us, pointing to where to climb up.

I felt cold and surreal. What was all this for? Other than being some kind of symbol, to show you could take over a building when janitors weren't looking, what point could there be to occupying Low? I distrusted symbols as much as ideology. What did this have to do with ending the war? "Don't be a fuckin' coward!" someone shouted. I was ready to go back to the dorm, to try to go back to sleep.

Over the next few days, my distrust and distance subsided. Each day there were more revelations about the university, its ties to the war, the self-serving lies by which it felt it had to protect itself from us. A broad range of students joined in occupying other campus buildings, an occupation that came to embody the right to dissent itself. I admired the junior faculty who called for student and faculty participation and sought to reach out to students and administration in a thoughtful, disciplined way. They had more at stake than any of us. They, and the many who stood outside the buildings as sentinels, weren't members of SDS. That they were uniters was demonstrated by their reaching out to support the protesting students, to demand amnesty, and to create a broad coalition with and protect SDS. It was because they were uniters that they took these actions and these risks.

What was I willing to do, what risks was I willing to take? Being the advocate for the students with the dean's office each morning, arguing for amnesty, trying to find a peaceful solution felt right and natural to me. At night, standing with others outside the buildings to ward off the cops felt right to me as well. I, like everyone alongside me, was risking the same assault by the cops that I had experienced at Rockefeller Center. I knew what that was like. But was I a coward not to go back inside those buildings? Some part of me fantasized that I might want a career in politics after all, so I didn't want another bust on my record. But I also felt I would be lacking some deeper courage, some willingness to be myself, if I joined a building occupation whose means and ends disturbed me. For what I felt strongly about wasn't the demonstration itself, but the principle of protecting students against the police, of keeping police off-campus, of the university as a community. I couldn't name this deeper part of myself to which I needed to be true. Looking back, I can see that it was my need to be a uniter and my sense that unity was needed more outside the buildings than within. But the greatest danger to this value, I soon learned, was inside myself as well.

We huddled outside Fayerweather, a thousand students facing lines of cops, chanting, "We are not afraid! We are not afraid!"

Someone near me called out. "Bullshit!"

We laughed at ourselves, at our pretending to be fearless. Our linked arms gripped tighter. An hour later, when the police charged, a cop stomped once each on each of my wrists. I didn't feel the pain. What I felt was unreality. We were on our campus on a spring evening, we were students, this was our college. Yet this was happening. It was the shock of assumptions dissolving. It was not like a pane of glass being shattered, but of one being removed. It's the same world all around you, but the assumptions have been removed. You're in it for keeps.

A little later, I watched numbly from across Broadway, by the Chock Full O'Nuts, at students being shoved from College Walk into paddy wagons. Next to me, conservative students were cheering on the cops. They looked like guys from Bay Ridge. I glanced at them and across Broadway again. I was overwhelmed with anger. I took in the old, staid Columbia buildings across the street—big, solid, entrenched—presiding above the cops as if reinforcing them, as if the buildings, the cops, the cheering conservative students were all saying in different ways, "This is how it will always be." A thought pierced my mind. I want to burn this place down. In my zipper jacket and blue jeans, I shook slightly. I didn't do anything. Thoughts like this happen in such moments—feelings of injustice, anger, revenge and fear. Uniters aren't immune to rage or to the desire for violence or revenge. The question is: what do we do with these feelings? To what end do we enlist them?

It's tempting to share these feelings with those who agree, to amplify, to be echoed, to tighten the circle of those who are already convinced. It's tempting not to believe in having to persuade the majority. What most surprised me about the student strikes at London School of Economics (LSE) when I was there a year later, in 1968–1969, was how the Socialist Society and Conservative Student Union debated at each Friday's student body meeting. More than 90 percent of the student body came. Everyone could speak. The votes on each strike action were close—1,530 to 1,470, one way or the other—and we abided by them. I don't remember SDS ever proposing votes at Columbia. My sense was that, as a vanguard, they didn't believe in having to convince others, and nor did they believe the majority should govern. The administration at LSE was more intransigent than at Columbia, but something about the need to unite the majority of students required and created a powerful discipline of its own. This discipline—of uniting people toward seeing each other as people with the same rights— seems to me tough-minded, not soft-minded, and more essential now than it was fifty years ago. When I look back at the Columbia strike, that's the lesson I take away. The strike made me both hate Columbia for its administration and be proud of the ways we found, despite ourselves, to work together.

When I look back at the eighteen-, nineteen-, and twenty-year-olds we were, I see an extraordinary arrogance. We believed we knew how to run society and that society and politics could be changed easily and *permanently*. We were optimists because we were in an optimistic country, despite its bitter problems. We took for granted economic optimism, American optimism, a strange afterglow of John Kennedy optimism, and a belief in youth that the media helped encourage. We never doubted that there were right answers and that the most complex problems could be solved, that things could be set right. When I look now at the complexity of any issue, school systems or police or race or the Middle East, I now that these aren't things where you can just wake up the morning and expect to solve them. Today, that assumption seems simplistic to me. But what doesn't seem simplistic is the choice we made about how to see each other, about whether to be uniters. For this choice is at the heart of how we try to solve anything.

Gene Slater *('70CC) received a master's degree in city planning from Massachusetts Institute of Technology and for the past forty years has run a financial advising firm helping public agencies finance affordable housing and urban development throughout the country. Gene lives in the Bay Area and has two sons, both school teachers. He is working on a master of liberal arts from Stanford, writing about inclusive and exclusive freedom in America.*

SUSAN SLYOMOVICS

Barnard undergraduate/Fayerweather Hall occupier

A SENSE OF RIGHTNESS

"**S**hit, she's only seventeen. We can't kick a youthful offender out of the country," the New York City Police officer said while booking me for criminal trespassing plus felony class some-letter-of-the-alphabet charge. Sergeant Buckley, whose face and name I never forgot, looked pleased that I was an enemy alien and could be deported. Hadn't I signed forms swearing as a foreigner generously granted an American student visa not to overthrow the US government? I was dispatched to the New York Women's House of Detention (since razed, but then the world's only art deco prison from the outside). Transferring me to the Tombs, Sergeant Buckley fed me Hershey bars with almonds, and fretted that I was shoeless and sockless. I had lost them when I resisted arrest by going limp, shoulder-to-shoulder with fellow students crouched along the sweeping spiral staircase of Mathematics Hall. I was carried out, one man holding my feet and another grabbing both wrists, my body swinging gently in the night breeze like a hammock, while thousands outside were chanting "Strike! Strike! Strike!" At one point, some half dozen of us were handcuffed together in a vehicle. Buckley found me a pair of white socks and we kept on talking.

We were four Barnard freshmen—Anya, Janet, Caroline, and me—each having helped the other through an actual open window across a metaphoric threshold into the Fayerweather commune. We remained roommates throughout college and friends for life, enfolded within that bracing female intimacy that never lets you forget your callow seventeen-year-old self. Weeks of demonstrations, committing myself to the student uprising with my body, and the nonstop talking, flirting, and tuna fish sandwich-making, remain an ecstatic blur of happiness and adrenalin.

My parents were Czechoslovakian Jews forced from their homeland in 1938 by Fascism and again in 1948 by Communism. Arriving from an Austrian DP camp to Montreal, they had known too many Nazi slave labor camps, Vichy and Soviet prisons. A mere twenty years after they settled in North America, the year 1968 proved seismic: my family was buffeted by the longed-for return heralded by Prague Spring and their fear of Quebec nationalism advocating independence from Canada. I, in turn, embraced feminism through the Columbia Women's Liberation movement and the luminous presence of Kate Millet on campus. I imagined myself freed from the shadows of the Holocaust and first-generation immigrants by multiple moves across a border and through a window.

Two, perhaps three times, my loving parents made the nine-hour drive from Montreal to New York for the various pretrial hearings, just as they had chauffeured their only daughter to ballet and piano classes. William Kunstler defended a lot of us and Barnard paid our legal fees. When my mother asked him where she had gone wrong as a parent, she loved to remind me of his reply: "How could you say that! Your daughter was a hero. They are all heroes. You should be proud." I have vivid memories of their pride mixed with a refugee's terror that I was at the mercy of the police, of a courtroom packed with hundreds of students and DA (and Columbia trustee) Frank Hogan, as we watched the swift dismissal of charges against Columbia's star basketball players and my friend Allan, the revolutionary, red-faced, as his diminutive mother stood up and yelled at the judge, "That's my son Allan. He's a good boy—you leave him alone!" My felony was reduced to misdemeanor, then dismissed and expunged. No criminal record barred access to my American citizenship ten years later.

My abortive deportation and brief prison foray have never left me. Looking outward, I became myself. I have worked as an academic and an activist primarily in and about the Middle East and North Africa on issues of political prisoners, civil rights, and police and judicial reform. I locate that in my experiences of Columbia '68 and its aftermath. Instead of writing about my life and work, I wish I could somehow convey what

I can still call forth of 1968 from time to time: extraordinary joy, out-bursts of productive energy, the sense of rightness in the inevitability of collective action, and a commitment to nonviolence. I feel no nostalgia for my seventeen-year-old self, but Columbia '68 changed me in ways rooted in aspects of my background that emphasized teaching, justice, and dancing.

Nor can I ever forget the charismatic JJ—aka John Jacobs—so like the rabbi-intoxicated men with whom I had grown up, haranguing me from his revolutionary pulpit on the top floor of Mathematics Hall. I had followed another man from Fayerweather to Mathematics, then the bust was announced, and he jumped out the window. I stayed. As the crowds roared and the police lights flashed below, JJ assured us this was no defeat. Instead, we would retreat to the surrounding mountain enclaves and from those heights descend, encircle, and conquer the city, just like Mao. I know now that he didn't mean the actual Adirondacks and Catskill Mountains where my parents, bereft of family, spent the Jewish High Holidays. He meant keep on resisting any way I could.

Susan Slyomovics *('71BC) is professor of anthropology and Near Eastern languages and cultures at the University of California, Los Angeles. Her most recent book is* How to Accept German Reparations. *She lives with her husband and son in Los Angeles.*

Graduate student, Architecture/Avery Hall occupier

AVERY HALL TO URBAN DEADLINE

The six-day occupation of Avery Hall by the Columbia architecture students and others was an exhilarating but difficult period. Regardless of my commitment to the issues of the strike's six demands, there was a countering ambivalence. Emotion blurred insight, and doubt and fear sometimes trumped steadfastness. I feel I stumbled my way through most of those six days. That said, the Avery Commune and the strike have, to this day, shaped my professional and civic life.

I grew up in Hartford, Connecticut. I enjoyed an upbringing as a kid of privilege and went to the "best schools." I graduated from Yale in 1964 having majored in English, thinking I wanted to be a journalist. In the summer of '63, I won an internship at the *Hartford Courant* just as civil rights issues were taking hold, and became involved in the North End Community Action Project (NECAP), pushing a range of civil rights issues in that predominately black neighborhood. I met a young architect, Jack Dollard, who was building playgrounds, renovating housing, and designing a neighborhood school. That was it. Enough with struggling to be the objective journalist. I wanted to be involved in tangible change. In the fall of 1964, I was off to Columbia to become an architect.

My time at Columbia and New York City from 1964 to 1971—filled with anticipation, anxiety, exhilaration, triumphs and failures, lots of fun, and a few disasters—was transformative and defining for me. I had an emerging yet unformed sense of wanting to engage with community building.

By coincidence, when I arrived at Columbia that fall, so did Peter Prang-nell, who became our first-year design studio professor. Peter had stud-ied at the Architectural Association in London and Harvard. During our days spent in the studio, and late nights at the West End bar, Peter led us on a path of discovery. He sent us out to observe how New York City worked, starting with Jane Jacobs's West Village neighborhood. He urged us to study indigenous architecture from around the world and brought to campus various European modernists. He introduced us to a modern architecture that was socially responsible and grounded in creating a built form that enhanced human experience. Peter was also a troublemaker, challenging the administration and the pedagogy of the architecture school's curriculum, which still had a foot in its Beaux Art past.

Peter's energy and vision were embraced by a majority of my class-mates. But in 1968, Peter left Columbia to take a position at the University of Toronto's architecture school. Although he had no direct involvement in the Columbia strike, his thinking about architecture and the role of the architect in society was present in the minds of those students protesting inside Avery.

If the first two years of architecture school were filled with enthusiasm and discovery, the next semesters that led to the spring '68 strike were less than inspiring and often disheartening. In addition to the vacuum left by Peter's departure, internal and external forces took their toll. The studio projects seemed cut off from the social and political forces raging in the "real world." There was the dark cloud of the Vietnam War and the strug-gle for civil rights. I saw the Federal Urban Renewal program as a direct assault on the American city and, in particular, low-income urban neigh-borhoods. In fact, federal programs like Urban Renewal and the Inter-state Highway Act were systemically destroying urban neighborhoods and displacing the predominately low-income families who resided there. This was compounded by corporations and institutions, such as Colum-bia University, which, because of their wealth and disproportionate influ-ence over the political process, served as coconspirators in this assault on the cities. Most of all, what was being built was clearly serving the inter-ests of the "haves" at the expense of the "have-nots." In New York City, it was Robert Moses versus Jane Jacobs. With a few significant exceptions, we were not being taught an architecture that served the needs and inter-ests of those of limited means or addressed in any meaningful way the social issues of the day. Instead, we were being asked to design museums and shopping malls in our design studios. I felt the disconnect.

On campus, multiple issues were related to the actions and policies of Columbia University. The most egregious was the university's plan to build a gymnasium in Morningside Park, which would rightly become a central issue of the Avery Commune. This was linked to university policies on property acquisition in the neighborhood and the displacement of low-income tenants out of Morningside Heights. Uniquely, for architecture students, certain important questions arose: Why did the School of Architecture have no defined role in the selection of architects and the design of campus buildings or university policies as they related to campus planning and expansion? Why weren't the design studios focused on addressing these social issues?

While undergraduate campus protests and demonstrations were mounting, most of the architecture students remained focused on their work. I don't remember where I was when students occupied Hamilton Hall on April 23. The following day, Dean Smith told students in Avery that the university was closing down and that we were to leave the building by 6 P.M. I immediately returned to Avery. (The business and law schools were given a similar directive, and complied.) Upon repeated visits, Dean Smith was told that we would not be leaving and that Avery would remain "an open house," a place to discuss the issues of the strike. Subsequently, we were informed that the deadline to leave the building had been extended to Monday.

The ensuing days were filled with debates. Was there a design solution to the problem of the gym? I ended up leaving Avery on Saturday morning and went to Hartford to speak with my early mentor, Jack Dollard. I returned to the building on Sunday afternoon with a renewed determination to stick it out.

I backed the idea that Avery should remain open. While supportive of the black students in Hamilton, I opposed endorsing Students for a Democratic Society (SDS) and had a strong reaction to Mark Rudd who that first Wednesday evening came to Avery to ask/demand our support. He seemed more like a petulant kid who had problems with authority figures than a leader. I also had difficulty with the demand for amnesty. I appreciated the suggestion from Herman Hertzberger to explore designs of a gymnasium that "connected" two communities rather that split them, but it seemed gratuitous without input from the other community (West Harlem). I was moved by John Young's low-key remarks just past midnight on Monday, affirming our position, urging us to hold course, and to make our case to those outside Avery. Who was this guy, and where did he come from?

Monday was dominated by the movements and mobilization of the police, who had been caged in school buses along the campus crosswalk for days, and by increased rumors that a bust was imminent. Inside Avery, the focus was on preparing for the bust, building barricades, and discussing self-protection and conduct related to how most effectively we might resist the police.

The bust came at 2:30 A.M. on Tuesday morning. Ironically and sadly, a group of sympathetic faculty members, and those urging a nonviolent resolution of the strike, who had gathered on the steps in front of Avery, endured some of the most brutal beatings by the police. Over the ensuing hours, the police broke through the barriers and hit, shoved, dragged, carried, or otherwise emptied the building of strikers, randomly dropping them to either side of the Avery entrance, some to be handcuffed and arrested, others left staring in disbelief.

For me and my colleagues in Avery, that was it. The bust catalyzed our convictions and affirmed our determination to "strike on." Over the following days, we met to discuss and decide what to do next. There were some, particularly strikers from the classes of '69 and '70, who had to decide whether and on what terms they would return to the School of Architecture in the fall. Those who did return actively pushed curriculum-restructuring and a range of academic and administrative reforms to make the university and the school more responsive to the issues of the time. Many of these reforms were implemented under the deanship of Jim Polshek.

For another group, myself included, who were to have graduated that spring of '68, things were different. We would not be returning to Columbia, and—determined to move forward and find a way to practice architecture in a meaningful way—we founded Urban Deadline. The name intentionally expressed the urgency we all felt. Our focus was to apply our skills to the issues raised by the strike.

Any discussion of Urban Deadline must begin with the seminal and ongoing involvement of John Young, who came to the attention of most of us on the sixth day of the strike. John had come to Columbia to get a master's degree in Professor James Marston Fitch's newly established preservation program. He was older, with more work experience than most of us, and possessed an exceptional range of skills and talents. He was a licensed architect and could draw, design, and draft construction documents. John emphasized that it was people of limited means who likely lived in older, deteriorating buildings, and that this should be a focus of our work. This prompted me to recall a course I had taken from Professor Fitch, in which I had gotten a hint of his belief in a more encompassing definition of preservation. It was not just about, as he would say, "preserving places where George Washington slept." It also was about appreciating, preserving, and adapting our existing built environment.

Between 1968 and 1971, Urban Deadline intervened to prevent the demolition of historic buildings. It is safe to say that all or most of the historic mills of Paterson, New Jersey, now the Great Falls National Park, would have been demolished as part of an urban renewal project had not Urban Deadline been able to persuade the city to pursue an alternative course. The Schermerhorn Row buildings at the South Street Seaport likely would not exist today were it not for Urban Deadline. Through a city-funded program, Urban Deadline designed and constructed sixteen storefront "Street Academies" for high school dropouts in Harlem and Brooklyn. We designed and built neighborhood parks in vacant lots on the Upper West Side and Lower East Side, and we converted an abandoned firehouse into a commune and artist collective. We preferred to work in concrete so those who followed would have to struggle to demolish what we built. You might still find the remains of a basement stair at a building near 115th Street and 8th Avenue, or a concrete retaining wall in a small courtyard on East 6th Street that was once part of a generous neighborhood park.

We were advocates for low-income housing and, in the spirit of Abbie Hoffman, suggested at a public meeting with the Metropolitan Museum of Art that we could convert one of their galleries into housing if they would just relocate "the Rubens" to the basement. We wrote a housing policy for the Mailer/Breslin mayoral campaign to allow squatters to inhabit vacant buildings. And just for fun, we helped construct the second stage at Woodstock in the summer of 1969.

An interesting juxtaposition: in 1969, the Citizens Union of the City of New York presented Urban Deadline with a citation for "Promoting the City's Aesthetic Interests" for our Street Academy work. The previous year's winner of this award had been Roche and Dinkerloo, the consummate corporate architect, for the Ford Foundation Building completed in 1968.

Also in 1969, those of us from the class of '68 who had left Columbia after the strike to form Urban Deadline met with Alex Kouzmanoff, a revered professor who served as the fourth-year thesis adviser and was one of the faculty members who had been on the steps of Avery before the bust and had been beaten by the police. What to do with us had become an administrative problem for the school. We showed Alex the Street Academy projects we had designed and built over the last year. He was impressed and accepted it as our thesis submissions. We subsequently were awarded degrees as members of the class of '69.

In 1971, having acquired some applicable architectural skills, I returned to Hartford to work with Jack Dollard on a neighborhood housing project. Subsequently, I founded an activist preservation organization, the Hartford Architecture Conservancy (HAC), for which James Marston Fitch gave an inspiring inaugural talk on the power of preservation in community building. With Jared Edwards, I formed Smith Edwards Architects, now Smith Edwards McCoy Architects. As a Hartford-based firm, for the last forty years, we have provided architectural services to the Greater Hartford community. Whether it be new construction, restorations, or the adaptive reuse of an existing structure, the focus of our work has been on the civic buildings that make up this community, specifically its schools and housing. To this day, the skills I developed and the beliefs I hold as they relate to architecture, design, and community building were forged in my prestrike exposure to the thinking of Peter Prangnell and my poststrike experience with Urban Deadline.

The Columbia Strike, and the part played by the Avery Commune, led to significant reforms that otherwise could not have been achieved. The construction of the gym in Morningside Park was abandoned, the university severed its ties with the Institute for Defense Analyses, and changes in university leadership led to significant institutional reforms. These extended to the School of Architecture both internally as it related to curriculum and externally as it related to campus planning and design.

Figure 51.1 Avery Hall, home to striking Architecture and Urban Planning students. *Photograph by Gerald Adler.*

Today, issues that stoked the turmoil in 1968—war, racism, and economic disparity—are again at the fore, more virulent than ever. In our cities, this disparity in wealth and opportunity is made starkly visible by what we build and for whom. What are we teaching today's aspiring architects? Who will that architecture serve? The questions asked and debated in the Avery Commune in 1968 are as relevant today as ever. The fiftieth anniversary of the Columbia strike hopefully will prompt and warrant reflection by the university. I wonder what conclusions the Graduate School of Architecture Planning and Preservation will draw, and whether the students of Avery might be occupied with other, more disruptive thoughts?

Tyler Smith *('69GSAPP), FAIA, has been engaged in the civic life of Hartford for nearly fifty years since attending Columbia and his work with Urban Deadline. As an architect, editorialist, teacher, and participant in a host of nonprofits, he has been both a practitioner and advocate of preservation and cities.*

KARLA SPURLOCK-EVANS

Barnard undergraduate/Students' Afro-American Society/
Hamilton Hall occupier

FORMING COMMUNITY, FORGING COMMITMENT:
A HAMILTON HALL STORY

I was born in Willimantic, a Connecticut mill town, the elder of Odessa and Kelly Spurlock's two girls. My parents were Southerners who had met shortly before the United States entered World War II. They married at the end of the war and lived for several years near relatives in Philadelphia. But in 1947, drawing inspiration from the film *The Egg and I*, they struck out on a venture to start a chicken farm in eastern Connecticut. That dream was short lived, but my parents stayed on. My mother took a job as a secretary at the University of Connecticut and my father worked in local factories.

In the late forties and through the fifties, Willimantic was a town of about twelve thousand, predominantly middle and working class, and mostly white. Moving to that semirural New England town enabled my parents to escape segregation and afforded my sister and me the advantages of rock-solid, if not progressive, public schooling. My white classmates and I enjoyed enduring friendships, but around the age of puberty, a social curtain gently fell between us. That curtain was race. Recognizing that I was sidelined from the full high school social experience, I plotted my escape. I applied to and was accepted early decision at Barnard, drawn by its academic reputation but even more by its location in New York City—its cosmopolitan promise.

I jumped with both feet into life at Barnard. Classes were challenging, and outside of class, the environment was abuzz politically. I was intrigued by students passing out fliers for Students for a Democratic Society (SDS) and vendors selling pamphlets on Malcolm X published by some New Left press. Essentially, though, that academic year(1967–1968) was about self-discovery, love, friendship, racial identity, and group solidarity. That year the personal and the political converged. Coming from a small town with few African Americans, I was excited to meet other academically oriented black students, including a few who today I would call intellectual, although back then I would have called them "heavy." These were the kind of people who name-dropped Frantz Fanon and Albert Memmi and who had read beyond the first chapter of Harold Cruse's *The Crisis of the Negro Intellectual.*

In the fall semester of my first year, H. Rap Brown spoke at Dodge Hall on the Columbia campus. This tall, caramel-colored, Louisiana "brotha," sporting a big bush and dark glasses, had just succeeded Stokely Carmichael as the new chairman of the Student National Coordinating Committee (SNCC), the "N" in SNCC no longer standing for "Nonviolent." "Violence," Brother Rap proclaimed, "is as American as cherry pie." Barnard black women, who by this time were no longer Negroes but Afro-Americans, did not make it home from Rap's speech before our ten o'clock curfew. I expected the hammer to come down on us, but it never did. Only recently I learned that several of my classmates had negotiated a relaxation of the rules so that we could be fully present at this historic moment. Shortly after Rap's visit, *in loco parentis*—the curfew, parietal hours, afternoon tea—came to an unceremonious end.

The truth of H. Rap Brown's pronouncement that violence is at the core of American life became all too clear on April 4, 1968, the day Martin Luther King, Jr. was assassinated. I was home for Easter, but when I returned to school, the world I had known appeared to unravel. By mistake I took a train from Port Authority to East 116th Street instead of West 116th and came up out of the subway station in East Harlem to see police with dogs out in force, smoke wafting through the air.

Two weeks later, I was in my dorm room when word reached me that I should head over to Hamilton Hall for a demonstration. I might not have gone had I not heard that the Soul Syndicate, a Columbia student band that played covers of Smokey Robinson and the Temptations, was scheduled to perform. Soon after I arrived, the doors were locked and we were told that the building was being occupied. Panicked, thinking about my classes, I remember thinking, "My God! How am I going to get my paper in tomorrow?" My friend, who was from Detroit's black upper crust, chided me: "Certainly if I can stay in this building, you can stay!" Shamed by this former debutante into upholding my responsibilities as a child of the working class, I summoned up the courage to "stand with the people." Several hours later, when rumors began to circulate that brothers were bringing in guns from Newark, once again I nearly folded in hysteria. "I can't die! I don't want to die!" I shrieked. Once again, my friends calmed me down. (Whether or not there were actually guns, to this day I don't know.)

Later on that night, I again received a jolt when we were informed that black student leaders had asked white students to leave the building. Some, but not all, of these students were affiliated with SDS, the group that had initiated the building takeover. The decision was understandable but nevertheless unsettling. On its face, the demand that white students depart Hamilton Hall seemed to me to contradict the values of integration and equality with which I had been raised. The idea of putting white students out did not feel right to me because it seemed to mirror an all too familiar pattern of racial exclusion. Yet the winds had shifted within the old civil rights coalition, with black students asserting their right to define and lead their own movement. Undoubtedly black nationalism, ascendant at that time, shaped our response to the white activists in Hamilton Hall. We were wary of entering an alliance in which our leadership and vision might be subordinated.

Black student leaders did not feel they could predict or control the behavior of white activists. We doubted that white student activists had witnessed or directly faced the harsh and unforgiving response of entrenched power or the relentless instrumentalities of law enforcement unleashed. They did not appear as mindful of their vulnerability as we were. As black students, we understood the cruel dance of challenge and devastating response revealed so openly during the modern struggle for civil rights. Certainly, some black students in our group came from relatively privileged backgrounds, where parents' money, status, and influence empowered their sons and daughters to stand up boldly against perceived societal wrongs. But even these affluent black students understood— whether through observation, firsthand experience, or family lore—that challenges to the status quo could invite brutal reprisals.

We also felt compelled to guard our collective reputation. Most of us had been raised with the injunction "Do nothing to bring shame to your family or to the race." Black student leaders feared being yoked to students who might take actions we could not support or defend. Despite our common cause, the decision was made to separate.

Once the white student activists departed, we released Dean Coleman, who had been barricaded in his office. Relieved that now we would not likely face kidnapping charges, I began to feel much better about the occupation. By week's end, I was all in. We narrowed our grievances against Columbia largely to outrage at the university's disrespectful relationship with its Harlem neighbors, symbolized by the decision to commandeer public land in Morningside Park to build a new gymnasium. Several of our students maintained close ties to our allies in Harlem, who fed and protected us. We realized that Harlem's physical proximity to Columbia would require the university and the city to adopt a nuanced and strategic response. We hoped that community support and the presence of Harlem at our doorstep might discourage a police raid. No one, we reasoned, would want to see the rebellion that had marked the community's response to the murder of Martin Luther King spill over to the west side of 116th Street. With Harlem residents outside in the street and hot food coming in through the windows, we saw ourselves as standing up for a community that stood with us. Our Hamilton Hall community—numbering nearly a hundred—ate breakfast, lunch, and a hot dinner every day. Despite the fact that the *New York Times* did not understand or care to convey our position, we knew the people of Harlem believed our cause was just. We also took comfort in knowing that adult professionals were on the outside negotiating on our behalf. Some of these were parents who were attorneys, and some were friends and colleagues of parents, including prominent leaders such as Percy Sutton, Basil Paterson, and William Booth, New York's commissioner of human rights.

As the days passed, my admiration for our student leaders grew, and I remember with gratitude the leadership style exercised by the inner circle. I was particularly inspired by Carolyn Anderson, a graduate student at the School of International Affairs. Powerful and regal, Carolyn contributed intellectual and emotional balance. Undoubtedly, she gave coherence to the inner circle's strategy sessions. She was not seen as just a pretty face, although she was beautiful, statuesque, dignified. My sense is that

she wielded a great deal more influence than might have been acknowledged publicly. Clearly, she was a woman to be reckoned with. Her calm
demeanor and her wisdom anchored the group.

Although some in leadership positions were not necessarily nurtur-
ing or hands-on, they all clearly adhered to a political mode of organizing
based on consensus. By exercising a willingness to wait for the most reti-
cent among us to come along, everyone was kept engaged and a sense of
trust and community developed. The leadership kept a benign and watch-
ful eye out, demonstrating a kindness and patience that allowed the group
to inch toward an increasingly progressive posture. Ray Brown, a Columbia
College senior, was an intelligent, articulate spokesperson. Cicero Wilson,
a sophomore, who I perceived to be working class, was down to earth, genuine, and accessible. Bill Sales, older and a graduate student, was politically sophisticated, astute, and keenly observant. As a group, we would not
act until all agreed to act. We held interminable discussions after learning
details about the state of negotiations with the city authorities and Columbia. All voices were heard—even pusillanimous voices like mine.

For a student interested in the social sciences, Hamilton Hall provided
the best kind of experiential learning. Our constructed community was
heavily gendered, with women staffing the kitchen patrol and men controlling the clean-up brigade and the keys to the bathrooms and showers.
In establishing a rigid demarcation of roles based on sex, we capitulated
to an intentional campaign to bolster black men's standing in a patriarchal
society. Black nationalism awakened in us an awareness that black men
in America were persistently threatened with emasculation. The standard script for the righteous "sistah" would become: "Stand behind our
'brothas,' not beside them, so they can take their place as leaders of their
families, as men." At that time, there was a sense—bolstered by sociology—that the majority of black families had followed a deviant matri-
archal pattern at odds with the dominant American patriarchal norm.
Consequently, black people, male and female, needed to support black
men in their struggle to recover their rightful position in the hierarchy
established by the dominant society.

Conscious of the frequency with which black people were subjected to
racial stereotyping and our responsibility to combat it, we were also serious about performing what today would be called "the politics of respectability." Let it not be said that we trashed a building or left it dirtier than

when we found it. We wanted to make certain there could be no justification for saying we lacked respect for persons or property. We wanted to be regarded as scrupulous and disciplined—a group who, through our actions, gave voice to the concerns of a disregarded, marginalized community.

The men and women in Hamilton Hall related to one another as brothers and sisters. Although there may have been occasional flashes of irritability, there was little of the normal stress-related acting-out one might have predicted when a large group of young adults under duress must live together in makeshift circumstances for a week. In general, members of the Hamilton Hall community were kind to one another. I observed no sexual activity, no violation of social mores. It seemed to me we behaved in ways our parents would have approved of. And as each day passed, we grew closer and formed an unspoken bond. We became family.

A week after the occupation began, in the early hours of April 30, police entered Hamilton Hall to take us out. Forewarned, we lined up, men on the outside and women on the inside, and began passing around wet rags and Vaseline for the tear gas or mace we anticipated. We knew we might die. But we faced the unknown with a glint of the spirit expressed by the Jamaican-born Harlem poet, Claude McKay: "If we must die—oh let us nobly die."[1] If we were going down, we would go down with dignity.

I remember the police officers who came through the tunnels underneath Hamilton Hall to arrest us. Is it a false memory that they were black, that they were somber, even tearful? Did I conjure up this vision? Is it true that they were very quiet, almost gentle?

We were taken out through the tunnels and transported to the Tombs in lower Manhattan. By late afternoon, we were released on our own recognizance.

Is it true or a false memory that I went back to Barnard and from the roof watched that evening as fellow students were beaten and run down by mounted police?

When I finally called my parents, my father asked, "Were you mixed up in that mess at Columbia?"

I said, "Yeah, Daddy. I was in Hamilton Hall."

1. Claude McKay, "If We Must Die," in *The Book of American Negro Poetry*, ed. James Weldon Johnson (New York: Harcourt, Brace and Co., 1922), 134.

"Good!" he replied. "I thought maybe that's why we hadn't heard from you." My soft-spoken, socially conservative, politically progressive father offered his final words on the subject: "If my generation had done what we were supposed to do, you wouldn't have had to be in that building."

A week after we left Hamilton Hall, a number of us attended a political meeting in Harlem. One authoritative figure publicly issued a sobering threat against Charles 37X Kenyatta, a local community activist who was rumored to be a Rockefeller operative. The stakes suddenly skyrocketed. From that moment on, I was out. No more meetings, no more protests. Soon afterward, school ended and we left for home. Over the summer, Columbia dropped charges against most of us.

The outcome of the protest was ambiguous, our reaction to it—bittersweet. I realized that any efforts going forward must square with my identity. Although I admired activists such as Angela Davis, I had no intention of violently confronting the system, going underground and subsequently meeting my maker with guns blazing during some jailbreak, plane hijacking, or bank heist.

Figure 52.1 African American students on the balcony of Hamilton Hall, with a poster of Stokely Carmichael. *Photograph by Peter Chartrand.*

I stepped back from the edge, but set out on a path that would bind me to those with whom I share common cause—young adults—many of whom come from marginalized communities separated from the dominant group by race, by class, by gender, or by gender identity or sexual orientation, and who struggle to find themselves, their purpose, their voice. For the past forty years, I have served as a bridge, seeking to accomplish goals that will both empower students and help make the colleges where I have worked more flexible and responsive. In retrospect, my participation in the takeover of Hamilton Hall at Columbia during a time of great ferment—the swordplay between victory and sheer destruction—left me deeply convinced that all things are possible when people with pure intentions and a shared sense of purpose come together. I gained a belief in the power of listening to others, of compromise, and of politics infused with love.

Karla Spurlock-Evans *has served as dean of multicultural affairs and senior diversity officer at Trinity College (Hartford, Connecticut) since 1999. Previously, she taught or worked as a student affairs administrator at SUNY Albany, Haverford College, Lake Forest College, and Northwestern University. Karla graduated from Barnard College in 1971, Phi Beta Kappa, magna cum laude, with honors in political science, and from 1971 to 1975, she attended Emory University (Atlanta, Georgia) as a Ph.D. student in American studies.*

Columbia undergraduate/Low Library occupier

FROM COLLEGE WALK TO THE STONEWALL INN

T he reasons I chose to go to Columbia were the academic programs, the fencing team, and New York City culture. But two subtexts were probably more important components in my decision. I had been going to Student Nonviolent Coordinating Committee (SNCC) meetings and doing civil rights organizing since my early teens. When I was fourteen, in August 1963, I went to the March on Washington for Jobs and Freedom, and found myself on the Mall, a few hundred feet from Martin Luther King, Jr., as he gave his "I Have a Dream" speech. Being that political at such a young age pretty much ensured that by the time I was seventeen, social justice would be my partner for a lot of decisions. Students at Columbia seemed to be the most politically engaged of all the schools I was considering. But even more than political activism, I was wrestling with a subtext that couldn't be discussed in 1967: "the love that dare not speak its name." Coming to terms with being gay in much of the world is still an overwhelming, dangerous struggle. But for many living in this post-Stonewall culture, that struggle is now eased or gone. In pre-Stonewall times, however, the task was terrifying.

Although New York City was notoriously dangerous back then, those dangers took a backseat to the fears of being gay in the suburbs and the search for self-acceptance. In that context, New York City was potentially the safest haven. There was safety in danger for some of us.

There was also the excitement of being in New York. Within days of the Fillmore East opening in March 1968, my friends and I were there. There were nights at Gerde's Folk City, the Village Vanguard, and the Village Gate listening to Baez, Dylan, Collins, Mitchell, and Ochs. Going to 125th Street to hear Nina Simone was a little unusual for a white kid, but how fantastic it was. Everything was more accessible. The guards at the Metropolitan Museum got to know me and waved me through, a real gift to an art history major. There were no turnstiles, no crowds of people. Instead, dust bunnies blew across the gallery floors. We often had those rooms to ourselves.

In the vastness of the city, I could slip away from my Columbia friends and have another life in bohemian downtown New York. Many nights were spent at Max's Kansas City, the art and music world hangout. I was dating an older guy who was pretty well known, so I always got waved in past the velvet rope to the back room, the hangout of Warhol's gang and the rock world. Then there were the nights at the Stonewall Inn, Julius, and the Ninth Circle, gay bars in the Village where a password was needed to get in. Life wasn't dull. Through my friend David, a Julliard senior, I met Jackie Curtis and soon after found myself hanging out with three Warhol Superstars: Jackie, Holly Woodlawn, and Candy Darling. It was a walk on the wild side. We were all outlaws just by being who we were.

By day I would attend some remarkable classes: contemporary civilization with Sam Coleman, humanities with Paul Zweig, art history with David Rosand, Eugene Santamasso, and Alessandra Comini, architecture history and theory with Everard Upjohn and Eugene Raskin, and French with Scott Bratton. On top of that there was fencing practice daily and fencing meets. It was fantastic to be a part of the one sports team that Columbia could count on for the championship.

And then April 23, 1968, came around. We met at the sundial, at the center of the Columbia campus, for a rally. Dr. King had been killed a few weeks earlier. Racism was on our minds. We were protesting American involvement in Vietnam, the university's involvement in war research, and its decision to build a private gym in a public park used primarily by the neighboring black community. An attempt to enter Low Memorial Library (which isn't actually a library, rather the university's main administration building) failed when security guards locked the doors. The crowd had nowhere to go. Something clicked when the voices of two Barnard students shouted "To the gym!" A group of us charged toward the construction site in Morningside Park. Before long there were a lot more people following. It wasn't the leaders of the student political groups who led the charge, instead just a few random students who felt that this was a moment that must be seized. A chain-link fence surrounded the construction site. It was a fence waiting to be stormed, and we obliged. It didn't take long for the New York City Police Department to arrive.

We headed back to rally around the sundial. As the afternoon wore on, we moved into the lobby of Hamilton Hall and spoke passionately about why we were there and what our aims were. Hours passed. Before morning rolled in, black student leaders broke from a caucus to tell the white students that the only real issue was race. They told us that we didn't understand their struggle, that we wouldn't be in the fight for the long haul, that we should leave Hamilton. They called us a bunch of—and this is a fairly direct quote—"spoiled, white, suburban candy-asses." (Urban Dictionary: "*Candy-ass: Someone who is easily scared or avoids dangerous situations. Pansy. Sissy. Fag.*") So we left.

The Stonewall uprising, the start of my own personal civil rights movement, was still fourteen months away. The thought of speaking up about antigay rhetoric in those days was inconceivable. And yet, there it was in the air.

Having been ejected from Hamilton early on the morning of April 24, some of us regrouped around the sundial, trying to figure out what to do next. We had to show that we *did* understand, that we *were* committed, and that we were ready to prove we weren't candy-asses. As we stood there talking, a security guard approached. The security and custodial staffs at Columbia had been trying to unionize, but the administration had blocked their efforts, with the result that the security guards were as angry with the Columbia administration as we were. The guard held up a large, full key ring and nodded toward Low. "You want to get inside?" he asked. He knew that we had tried to go into Low the day before, but that it had been locked up tight. We followed the guard up the steps to Low and watched as he unlocked a door.

Again, at first just a few of us went in. We stood around in the lower floor entry for a few minutes, unsure of where to go or what to do. Then the guard led us upstairs, through the rotunda, our destination the day before. But then he kept going. He led us up to the president's office, unlocking doors as we went. Suddenly, we were in Grayson Kirk's suite of rooms. This was unprecedented. Others eventually followed, and soon a crowd was gathered inside the office.

Once we were there, the best way in and out wasn't through the whole building and unlocked doors but via the second-floor windows, climbing up and down on the bars of the offices below. It was faster, and a lot more exciting. People seemed to fly in and out. The first night, there was a fairly large group of us in Low, probably about a hundred. At one point, Prof. Orest Ranum came in through a window in his usual eccentric attire, an academic robe. Telling us that the police were on their way, he said we should all leave. Needless to say, we ignored him. Then Mark Rudd, head of Columbia Students for a Democratic Society (SDS), came flying in the window, saying the same thing. Many left. About two dozen remained. We put a sign in the window: "JOIN US." By the next morning, we were front-page news. Soon hundreds of people were occupying five buildings.

A couple of days later, inside Low we were confronted with a line of faculty around the building, a cordon which in theory would prevent violence between us inside and the right-wing students—the jocks—outside. One night, when almost everyone was asleep, I crept along the second-floor ledge to where my French professor, Scott Bratton, was on the overnight shift. Although we never would have said so out loud, Scott and I knew we were both gay. We carried the same secret. I asked, in a whisper, whether he would let me slip out so I could go back to my dorm room in Carman Hall to change my socks and underwear and then return. He agreed. This—along with a listen to the first few tracks of Simon & Garfunkel's *Bookends*, which had been released a few weeks before—became a nightly ritual.

The bust came on April 30. We knew it was coming. We were nervous but not really frightened. With all of us sitting on the floor in a circle singing "We Shall Overcome," the cops axed down the door (which we purposefully had left unlocked) and came in kicking and swinging. It was chaos, a scene from a movie, a movie you would never want to be in. One cop kicked me in the side. My motor reflex was to extend my leg up. Unfortunately for me, I extended my foot into another cop's crotch. In reprisal, I was grabbed by six cops and taken to the mimeograph room for a private beating. Then they hauled us from the building, dragging us by our feet down the concrete steps of Low, our heads hitting each step. We were being arrested by a special unit of the New York City Police Department, the Tactical Patrol Force. It was later explained to me that they had been trained to inflict maximum pain while leaving the least outward bruises and scars.

Arresting so many of us in one night, city resources were strained. Overcrowded paddy wagons had to drive around until they found jails that could handle us. We were often unsure of where we were. At one point someone looked out of the peephole and shouted, "We're passing Hong Fat." Hong Fat was a Chinese restaurant on Mott Street that a lot of us frequented. In unison, we shouted "Hong Fat!" The paddy wagon came to a quick halt. The cops drew their guns, thinking we were shouting a signal and that it could be an uprising. It took a minute or two for them to calm down after we explained what had so excited us. Eventually we arrived at the Tombs near City Hall. Each cell was filled with as many of us as could be squeezed in. Several of us were in fairly rough shape, having been beaten, kicked, and dragged down stairs.

When I was brought into the courtroom for arraignment, I was surprised to see my father there. Even more surprising was discovering that his bulging pockets were filled with cash to bail us all out. Mom and Dad had gotten what cash they could out of the bank and called their friend Sam Raskin, whose son Jonah was also involved in the strike, and some other friends to round up whatever cash they could. Sitting next to Dad was our Fire Island neighbor and friend Stanley Geller. Stanley was a distinguished lawyer who had been instrumental in the 1962 *Engel v. Vitale* Supreme Court case, which led to prayers being prohibited in public schools. Although he was a legend, I had been told that he remained behind the scenes because of the shadow that still hung over him from being blacklisted during the McCarthy era. Mom and Dad had called him to defend me. He also had been contacted by other families as well as by the Barnard administration to represent all Barnard students. Stanley was involved in getting us all released on our own recognizance. Soon after being released, I went to St. Luke's Hospital, where I was approached by the Lawyers' Guild to be the test case against the city for police brutality. Within a few days, Federal Bureau of Investigation (FBI) agents were stationed in the elevator lobby on the ninth floor of Carman Hall, right outside my dorm room. I found myself with an FBI tail, something of a badge of honor.

Somehow nothing during that week of the strike seemed frightening—not storming the fence, not going into the president's office, not the police invasion of the campus, not our arrest, and not the FBI tail. We knew that what we were doing was right. We hadn't anticipated that the bust would be violent, but it was, and I knew any wounds would quickly heal. I'll tell you what was terrifying, though. It was an evening a few months before, one of the most hair-raising of my life. After much agonizing, I had decided to go to a meeting of the Homophile League of Columbia University, one of the first ever gay activist groups on a college campus. I crossed the campus in the dark, from Carman Hall to Earl Hall, the religious studies building where the meeting was to take place. I was shaking. The campus was pretty empty, but I kept looking around to check whether anyone was watching. Would I be found out? Would my friends stop talking to me? Would I be blackmailed? Would I ever be able to have a professional life? Inside was a small group sitting in a circle.

Being beaten by the cops and being arrested for opposing the war, for opposing the university's involvement in it, and for opposing a private gym on public land were causes to be proud of. Being arrested for being gay, that would have been a disgrace. That was terrifying.

Peter Stamberg ('71CC) *attended Rhode Island School of Design (B.F.A., B.Arch.) and the Architectural Association of London (Grad. Dipl.) after Columbia. He is a partner in Stamberg Aferiat Architecture, New York City. Stamberg and Paul Aferiat have been a couple since 1976 and were married in 2004 in Massachusetts, soon after it became the first state to recognize same-sex marriage.*

ELEANOR STEIN

Graduate student, Law School

FIVE RED FLAGS

When it comes to understanding the logic behind the Columbia uprising, context is everything.

In February 1968, African American students at South Carolina State College in Orangeburg demonstrated, and police opened fire. Three were killed and more than thirty wounded. On March 19, a Howard University sit-in morphed into a campus building takeover, and on the last day of that month, Lyndon B. Johnson announced that he was not going to run for reelection. We danced in the streets.

On April 4, Rev. Dr. Martin Luther King, Jr. was assassinated in Memphis, where he had gone to support the city's striking sanitation workers. In more than one hundred cities across the country—in Chicago, Baltimore, Cincinnati, and Washington, D.C.—people took to the streets and were confronted by tanks. Seventy thousand troops were called out, and in Washington, D.C., machine guns were mounted on the Capitol balcony and the White House lawn. Forty-six people were killed. In the midst of mayhem, Oakland police shot and killed sixteen-year-old Black Panther Bobby Hutton.

Back in January had been the Tet Offensive, when North Vietnamese and National Liberation Front (NLF) forces attacked more than one hundred cities, with more than thirty uprisings in provincial capitals. Most dramatically, NLF forces temporarily occupied the American embassy in Saigon. This was the year in which more than half a million

American military personnel served in Vietnam, with more than 14,500 Americans killed in combat. We were consumed by our belief that this unjust war had to stop and that we had to stand side by side with African Americans to combat racism. And that is what we did at Columbia in April 1968.

At the time, I was completing my first year at Columbia Law School, alongside my brilliant cohorts Gus Reichbach, Michael and Bruce Ratner, Margie Leinsdorf (later Ratner), and Barry Willdorf. Despite my upbringing by Annie and Arthur Stein, former Communists, union organizers, and antiracist activists, and my teenage organizing with the student Congress of Racial Equality and National Committee for a Sane Nuclear Policy in New York City, I was determined to get law school under my belt and begin to practice. But on April 23, as students led a march off campus to Morningside Park, to protest the construction of Columbia's new gymnasium, Gus and I slipped out of the back row of class and brought up the rear. When students decided to sit-in at Hamilton Hall, and then take other buildings, as urged by the African American students, I joined in. I decided to hold on to my privilege as a lawyer-in-training, so wore an armband, which marked me as slightly apart from the rebels: legal observer. Years later, I met a then-medical student who confirmed that he, too, wore a protective armband: medical presence. But after a few days living in Fayerweather, those distinctions began to wear thin, and I was one of five law students arrested on April 30.

Retrospective cynicism is cheap. A single action, people might say, no matter how dramatic, seldom results in fundamental societal change. The university prevailed, the war bled on for another seven years. The gym was never built, but Columbia expanded in the neighborhood.

So what did we accomplish? The meaning of 1968 at Columbia remains contested ground, with a strong establishment interest in dismissing the whole project as a kid's game that threatened the city with violence and accomplished nothing. But the fact is that almost immediately, our action sparked countless student protests and takeovers all across the country. It symbolized that privileged young people were taking a stand by rejecting their inheritance of war and racism. Make no mistake: the ruling class was shook up. The successful fight against the construction of a gym for Columbia students in one of the few green spaces in West

Harlem stands as an early victory for what is now termed environmental justice. It turns out we were fighting for equitable distribution of the benefits of the environment. It's worth mentioning that a 2008 reunion of hundreds of participants, men and women who occupied those five campus buildings, made clear that almost everyone had remained in helping professions, community organizations, and advocacy.

Was Columbia purely symbolic or was it a real radical movement? The phrase "purely symbolic" misses the fact that symbolism is an enormously important, motivating, inspiring, and enraging aspect of human existence and life.

A demonstrator laying down in front of a troop train in Oakland was a symbolic action. She wasn't going to stop the transport of draftees to Vietnam. She would likely be arrested, and might even die. And yet, what a powerful symbol! What actions like that shout to the world is a simple, but powerful, message: I will give my life to stop this war or even to delay this war for a few hours by preventing the delivery of troops going—likely to their death or injury—to kill Vietnamese people in my name. People who immolated themselves, people who marched across the bridge in Selma. Each of these actions are the iconic images of that period, and each of those actions could be characterized as purely symbolic.

We didn't have the power in 1968 to physically stop the gym. We didn't have the power to remove the Institute for Defense Analyses from the campus. What did we have? We had the power to convince a sufficient number of people on that campus and even some who made the decisions at the university that these things were wrong, that they should be stopped, that they could be stopped, and that the price for not doing so was going to be high for the university and the city.

The ultimate symbolism of Columbia for me was the incomparable sight of five red flags, flying from the roofs of the five occupied buildings. That memory stirs me to this day. Even though I wrote, in a contemporaneous account of the takeover, that "we can't run a socialist communal university in a capitalist city and society,"[1] the events at Columbia remain

---

1. Eleanor Raskin, "The Occupation of Columbia University: April 1968," *Journal of American Studies* 9 (1985): 255–60.

a marker in my life. I went into Fayerweather as a legal observer before being dragged out by the police as a woman determined to transform my life and throw my body and spirit at the oppressors.

To participate in an act of liberation at the age of twenty-four was a gift. Seamus Heaney says it best, in his "The Cure at Troy":

> History says, don't hope
> On this side of the grave.
> But then, once in a lifetime
> The longed-for tidal wave
> Of justice can rise up,
> And hope and history rhyme.[2]

Eleanor Stein *(Raskin, in '68) teaches climate change at Albany Law School and SUNY Albany. From 2004 to 2015, she taught renewable energy, energy efficiency, and climate change adaptation. In 2015, she earned her master of law degree in climate change law. Currently, she teaches climate justice and El Salvador sustainability. She shares her life with Jeff Jones, their sons Thai and Arthur, their daughter-in-law Logan, and grandson Seneca.*

---

2. Seamus Heaney, *The Cure at Troy: A Version of Sophocles' Philoctetes* (New York: Farrar, Straus and Giroux, 1991), 76.

MICHAEL STEINLAUF

Graduate student, English and Comparative Literature/
Mathematics Hall occupier

NEVER AGAIN?

Twenty years, I now know, is not a long time. In 1968, World War II had ended just twenty-three years previously. But for us college students, the war seemed like ancient history. Many of our fathers had fought and defeated the enemy to win good jobs and new homes in the various Levittowns of America. Christians and Jews now lived in apparent harmony. If you stayed up late watching TV, at about 3 A.M. the stations would sign off, but not before the "sermonette"—fifteen minutes of uplift by equal turns from a priest, a minister, or a rabbi. Things occasionally broke through. Some movies: *The Pawnbroker, Judgment at Nuremberg*. Those documentaries some of us had the misfortune to watch, the ones with bulldozers shoving skeletal bodies into piles. And then there was the Eichmann trial. Eichmann was a vigorous, middle-aged man, so what he had done could not have happened so very long ago. And some of us, mainly Jewish kids, but not only, learned a phrase.

"Never again" was in some corner of our minds when years later we watched those screaming naked children running down the road fleeing napalm, or the prisoner with a gun held to his ear by a South Vietnamese official about to pull the trigger.

For me, however, World War II was much closer: it was my family. My mother, father, and I lived in a small apartment in Brighton Beach, Brooklyn. They slept in the living room on what was called a Murphy bed, a contraption hidden vertically behind great doors during the day that came down for the night. I, the hope of the future, was given the only bedroom. From my window I could hear the ocean half a block down the street past the boardwalk, while periodically from the other direction the subway rumbled by on the elevated tracks.

The neighborhood was all Jewish, mainly elderly Jews who could not afford to move to Florida and who, when the weather permitted, lined the street and the boardwalk in plastic and aluminum beach chairs. They spoke accented English and lots of Yiddish. The Russians hadn't arrived yet to turn the neighborhood into Little Odessa. There was also a sprinkling of younger families such as my own, who were known as refugees. The couples were in their late thirties and forties, considered old to be parents of young children, and typically they had one child each: my friends and me.

Often on weekend evenings, my mother would host dinner parties. The guests were all like us, refugees of a certain type: Polish-speaking Jews who had survived on false papers on the so-called Aryan side, that is, pretending to be Christian Poles. Sitting around the table after dinner, sometimes playing Polish card games, they would launch into endless stories. "I was on the tram and some Germans started looking at me funny so I jumped off and broke my arm." "Some neighbor snitched to the Germans and we had to move out fast." "Got accosted by the *shmaltzovniks* [blackmailers] and had to give them my necklace and rings, and even then they wanted to turn me in." "Two German officers sit down across from me on the train and start to stare. '*Sie sind Jude.*' What do I do? I start laughing . . . and laughing. Pretty soon they pick it up too and we're laughing together and finally one of them offers me a cigarette."

The only one who had nothing to say was Yasha. He sat on the couch after dinner and dozed. He had numbers on his arm, meaning he'd been in Auschwitz. "Him you don't ask," my mother instructed me. Yasha was married to my mother's best friend, a tiny woman who loved to recite long extracts from Mickiewicz's poetry. Yasha, who resembled a bullfrog, was uneducated. Theirs was a postwar marriage, typically mismatched, my mother explained, meaning they had lost their spouses, perhaps their children, in the war and had married to avoid being alone.

All this was what they referred to as *wojna*, pronounced *voyna*, which meant "the war." It also meant one half of my childhood, the private half. The other half was living in my all-Jewish neighborhood, where the worst persecution was noogies at the hands of the bully Buddy Eisenberg. Years later in a sociology class at Columbia, I came across a word that was just coming into use: Holocaust. An awareness of that word and what it signified flowed underground and went on to feed the fury that would shortly explode. Jewish students, after all, were everywhere at Columbia, although their connection to the recent past was often still unconscious. But for me the connection was front and center. I understood that Holocaust meant *wojna* and more. Holocaust made sense of my childhood. It hurled it into history, making me part of something huge and meaningful—and horrendous. I had been placed on earth, however, for the sake of a different history. I had been given the only bedroom in order to make the future amazing.

Only sixteen years old when I arrived at Columbia College, at first I would sit on the sundial at night and stare at the names chiseled into the façade of Butler Library: Homer, Herodotus, Sophocles, Plato. All mine, I would think. And then, there was history again, but the other kind, my kind: watching Dylan going electric at Newport, Jefferson Airplane and the Grateful Dead jamming at midnight at the Fillmore West, flowers dropped into gunbarrels at the Pentagon, Janis buried in flowers at the Fillmore East. When I wired speakers for an antiwar demo on the corner of 111th Street and Broadway, it wasn't the speeches that mattered but blasting "Masters of War" down Broadway. These moments all pointed in the same direction, and we, the longhaired kids who called ourselves freaks, who smoked pot and dropped acid instead of swilling cocktails and beer, we were the vanguard of it all.

Every generation looks out at the world and sees walls around them. The natural response is to push because the walls are really in your face. In normal times, you soon realize that the walls are stronger than you are, you make your compromises, and you opt to be a responsible individual with a career and a family. But there we all were, pushing together at the walls, and all of a sudden the walls fell. And as in Pennebaker's Dylan movie *Dont Look Back*, some guy with a microphone comes running over and demands, "What's the answer? What does it all mean?" We didn't know what to tell him. We weren't leaders. We weren't anything. We were youth. We shouldn't have had that kind of power, but suddenly we did. We were handed the ball and we had to run with it.

So, we took our demands—the Institute for Defense Analyses off campus, stop building the racist gym—and occupied Hamilton Hall. But the blacks decided they wanted Hamilton to themselves. They told the white students to go and take their own building, and thereby played out the larger dynamic of what was happening in America. The blacks called the shots; they were our vanguard, the vanguard of the vanguard. So we said thank you very much and went and took Low Library. Two days after that a bunch of us, dissatisfied with the liberals we felt were calling the shots at Low, jumped out of the windows at midnight, sprinted across the lawn, and took Mathematics Hall. I had gone home for the night and returned to find the Math Commune proclaimed. We were the ultimate militants: the vanguard of the (white) vanguard.

Proud of having become the administration's worst nightmare, we welcomed "outsiders," nonstudents, radicals from all over the city. This meant, first of all, Tom Hayden, who showed up in a white karate gi and who we immediately elected chairman. It also meant four guys dressed in black leather, one even wearing a black leather cowboy hat. These were the Motherfuckers of the Lower East Side. They carried knives. They had begun as a radical arts collective called Black Mask, and then morphed into a kind of political street gang that took their name from a line in LeRoi Jones's poem "Black People": "Up against the wall, mother fucker, this is a stick up!"[1]

The Math Commune lasted four days. Boredom, dirt, fatigue, nonstop meetings, on one hand, but on the other hand, the palpable, visceral feeling that we were making history. The boredom was the eye of the historical storm we had fomented and which now raged all around us. Inside Math, time stopped; outside, it accelerated. We chained the doors shut, piled chairs in front of them, and soaped the stairs, so that when the big bust came, and the cops finally made it in, slipping and falling on the stairs, were they ever pissed. We had scattered into offices to make it harder for them. Four of us sat on the floor with arms linked, but when a cop coaxed me up by clubbing me in the head, everyone else jumped up pretty fast. And then we were out into the night, blinded by the camera lights, hundreds of people chanting "the whole world is watching" and rocking the paddy wagons we were being crammed into. I held my head high as the blood trickled down my neck. More than seven hundred of us were busted that night.

---

1. LeRoi Jones, "Black People!" in *The Leroi Jones/Amiri Baraka Reader*, ed. William J. Harris (New York: Thunder's Mouth Press, 1991), 224.

In the aftermath, the line between liberals and radicals sharpened. Liberals had put on ties and jackets and worked for Gene McCarthy. We thought they were ridiculous, because the system of American capitalism—with all its amoral might, with what it was doing in Vietnam where it was most graphically evident—was monstrous. Moreover, it had a monopoly of violence, and no monster of this kind was going to voluntarily surrender that power—through the ballot box or anything else. We began to feel that what we were after was a lot more than votes.

Standing on the corner of 111th Street and Broadway, catty-corner from where I had strung the speakers some years earlier, I stood talking with a friend late one night. "Wouldn't it be amazing to change everything," I remember saying. Who needed career and family when you could have that! *There* was something you could dedicate your life to. It actually already *had* started to happen, and I was part of it. Very soon, I was convinced, no one would be going to college. Universities as we knew them would no longer exist. And so I dropped out of grad school and moved to the West Coast in order, finally, to "get serious."

The final flicker of Marxism-Leninism, this was a footnote to it, less revolution than its dream. We were without a party, we scorned all hierarchies, we were based only in small collectives. Our mantra was "the personal is the political," or to paraphrase the words of Henri Lefebvre's *Dialectical Materialism*, which I first read in a cabin in the Massachusetts woods: the *production* of man is the production of *man*. When I finished his little book, I put on Beethoven's Ninth and tears streamed down my face. I had become convinced that it was within the power of human beings to create a new human being. That human being would no longer be capable of building gas chambers. That human being would emerge out of arduous struggle both on the street and at home. The goal was to build a movement, one powerful enough to overthrow the capitalist system. But that movement would be of no value, indeed, it would be just an "ego trip" unless it was accompanied by a breakthrough on the individual level, unless it was able to create wholly sharing comrades, brothers and sisters who would always have your back just as you would have theirs. Every aspect of life, seen through the lens of revolution, could make sense, could be rational. Was this any different really than living according to God's law, living as a pious Jew or Muslim? Only for us—and that was quite an "only"—the authority was our comrades here on earth.

Our rulers would fight us tooth and nail, of course, and use any means at their disposal to defeat us. And therefore the need for a third arena of struggle, beside the street and the home. We had to build an underground. Violence could be met only with violence. What we needed was a clandestine armed force, what some called a people's army. Personally, I was terrified of violence. When cops were coming at us down the street, I would flee rather than engage them with clubs and belts the way my braver comrades did. This, of course, proved personally fortunate in the long run, allowed me to survive when others didn't. But back then, I considered myself a coward and a hypocrite. The best I could do was to encourage "armed struggle" by writing leaflets and articles, editing newspapers. My weapons were words.

All this vastly simplified my personal life. I didn't have to make disconcerting personal decisions, think about a profession or starting a family. Such choices were bourgeois individualism. Living underground, and for a while I had to, didn't feel like a sacrifice. It came easy. It's what all those childhood stories had prepared me for. Eva Hoffman, a writer who has wrestled with a past similar to my own, mentions a writer of her parents' generation who declared that the Holocaust was the standard by which to judge the world. To which she responds: "But I think that the paradoxical task of my generation, caught within this awful story, is to get adjusted to the ordinary world in which we actually live, to acknowledge the reality given to us."[2] I was finally able to do that, but it took quite a long time, so that today, on the threshold of old age, I'm the father of young sons.

Back then, I was reading Bertolt Brecht, not Eva Hoffman. My favorite poem was entitled "To Posterity" and my favorite line in that poem was "Oh, we / Who wanted to prepare the ground for friendliness / Could not ourselves be friendly."[3] Today, I see that line as monstrous. If we actually had gained power back then, one of two things would have happened: either I would have been murdered or I would have murdered others. Such was the merciless logic of "Up against the wall."

In reality, however, the dark pull of that poem expressed who I thought we should be rather than who we were. The comrades I was closest to

---

2. Eva Hoffman, *Lost in Translation: A Life in a New Language* (New York: E. P. Dutton, 1989), 253.
3. Bertolt Brecht, "To Those Born Later," in *Bertolt Brecht: Poems, 1913–1956*, ed. John Willett and Ralph Manheim (New York: Routledge, 1987), 320.

were generous and sweet. When the sweetest and most generous of them was killed by police in a bank holdup, doubts began to rock everything I believed. A moment some time later sealed things for me. I happened to be in Paris when little firebombs began to appear in the pockets of clothing in stores that catered to working-class people. Reach into such a pocket and you would lose fingers, perhaps a hand. Nothing on earth could possibly justify that, I decided. And I realized that from the anarchist bomb thrower through the destruction of "class enemies" through the righteous terrorists of *Battle of Algiers* and on to ISIS, I could no longer distinguish "good" violence from "bad." What then?

Today, by way of Walter Benjamin, I can only say that in the sixties we were privileged to feel the rustling of the skirts of Messiah. He came close, made his presence known, reminded us of himself with the lightest of touches. And that's it, he was gone, leaving us to do our best in this fallen world which, I now affirm, may be the only one possible. So that today, amid the renewed struggle that many of us have joined, the goal is not to replace this world, but to make it less fallen, to wrest it from those who would drag it through the mud.

Michael Steinlauf (*'67CC, '69GSAS*) *is a professor of history at Gratz College near Philadelphia. He is the author of* Bondage to the Dead: Poland and the Memory of the Holocaust *as well as numerous studies of prewar Jewish culture in Poland, and contributing editor to the* YIVO Encyclopedia of Jews in Eastern Europe. *He has been active in various kinds of Jewish memory work in Poland, including serving as chief historical advisor and curator of modern Jewish culture for the POLIN Museum of the History of Polish Jews in Warsaw.*

MICHAEL STERN

Columbia College undergraduate/Spectator *newspaper*

COVERING—AND COVERING UP—SPRING '68

The tradition of all the dead generations weighs like a nightmare on the brain of the living. And just when they seem engaged in revolutioniz-ing themselves and things, in creating something that has never before existed . . . they anxiously conjure up the spirits of the past . . . and borrow from them names, battle cries and costumes in order to present the new scene in world history in this time-honored disguise and this borrowed language. . . . In like manner a beginner who has learnt a new language always translates it back into his mother tongue, but he has assimilated the spirit of the new language and can freely express himself in it only when he finds his way in it without recalling the old and forgets his native tongue in the use of the new.

—MARX, "THE EIGHTEENTH BRUMAIRE OF LOUIS BONAPARTE"[1]

Daily journalism is inherently a conservative enterprise. The rhetoric of the "new," of scandal, foregrounds the exceptional event against the background of the unexceptional, the taken-for-granted flow of daily life. But of course the real scandal of our society is precisely the unre-ported structure of our everyday, normal existence—inequality, racism,

---

1. Karl Marx, "The Eighteenth Brumaire of Louis Bonaparte," 1852, in *Marxism and Art: Essays Classic and Contemporary*, ed. Maynard Solomon (Detroit, MI: Wayne State University Press, 1979), 54.

injustice, misogyny, discrimination, the depredations of the national security state, and the permanent war economy.

The Columbia strike happened in the media capital of the world—back when "media" meant daily newspapers with national agenda-setting scope (the *Times, Post, Daily News,* and *Wall Street Journal*), the national broadcast networks (CBS, NBC, and ABC, all headquartered in New York), and a handful of national weekly magazines (*Life, Look, Time,* and *Newsweek,* again all headquartered in New York). And these media largely covered the strike as a spectacle—a scandal (privileged, ungrateful kids trashing a venerable institution) and a police story (who got arrested where, in what numbers). The real scandal—the university's complicity in the Vietnam war machine, its structure of privilege (who got draft deferments and why, what residents got forced out of Morningside Heights by Columbia's relentless expansion, etc.), and its production of instrumental knowledge for America's owners—went mostly unreported and unexamined.

I came of age as a both a reporter and a consumer of media in '68. Arriving from a small town in Ohio, I started working for the Columbia *Daily Spectator* student newspaper as a freshman in the fall of 1966. Like everyone else on the staff, I soon was majoring in *Spec* as much as in my academic discipline (English).

The *Times* was our bible. We followed its principles in all things. We had beats (I started out on the Morningside Heights beat, and then moved on to political affairs just as Students for a Democratic Society's [SDS's] on-campus antiwar organizing was heating up). We emulated its oh-so-serious version of news judgment and layout (passionate daily conferences were held in our offices in Ferris Booth—editors squeezed onto the couch in the editor-in-chief's office, reporters hanging around the door—about what ran on page one, how many columns it got above or below the fold, etc.). And of course, most important, we carefully separated "news" from "opinion" and "reporting" from "analysis" (with those little "news analysis" boxes set into the first paragraph of our think pieces). Our heroes were the past *Spec* men (there weren't any women) who had gone on to splendid journalism careers, like Max Frankel (then the *Times*' White House reporter) and Lawrence Grossman (head of NBC News) of the celebrated 1952 editorial board. And we idolized the *Times*' "riot" team—John Kifner, Michael Kaufman, and Sylvan Fox—who we were starting to run into at demonstrations.

In class, however, I was being immersed in other perspectives on storytelling—the fulfillment of the university's classic role of humane education. These weren't based on the New Journalism—that term for the first-person, in-your-face, novelistic reporting that Hunter Thompson, Norman Mailer, Tom Wolfe, and others were doing hadn't been coined yet—but the best of the old: the great political journalism of the past two hundred years, from Defoe and Swift to Marx and Orwell. On top of that, I was being introduced to the great nineteenth-century realists like Dickens and Balzac, who laid bare the dark soul of life under capitalism, and to the theorists of revolution and reaction from Rousseau and Burke to Lenin and Debray. Meanwhile, out on the campus, and in the city around us, the world was exploding with political action as the antiwar and civil rights movements converged. The boundaries between class and street started to blur. I'll never forget one day in the fall of 1967, during an argument over the syllabus in Warner Schilling's class on American foreign relations (why wasn't William Appleton Williams's *The Tragedy of American Diplomacy* on the reading list?), when an anti–Dow Chemical recruiter demonstration swept by outside. Politics was my beat, so I jumped out of the window to cover the protest.

These multiple, mutually refracting layers of lived and reflected-upon political and social experience culminated for me in the strike—simultaneously reading about, doing, and covering politics and social action. In *Homage to Catalonia*, Orwell wrote of the "revolutionary atmosphere" in Barcelona in 1937: "General and private, peasant and militia man, still met as equals; everyone drew the same pay, wore the same clothes, ate the same food and called everyone else 'thou' and 'comrade'; there was no boss-class, no menial-class, no beggars, no prostitutes, no lawyers, no priests, no boot-licking, no cap-touching. I was breathing the air of equality."[2] Spring '68 was like that for me, both in the buildings and outside, but the intoxication of liberation was filtered and intensified by my attempts to understand and describe what was happening in my *Spectator* stories. And those stories increasingly were informed by a different standard of truth-telling than the *Times'* hallowed "objective" journalism.

---

2.   George Orwell, *Homage to Catalonia/Down and Out in Paris and London* (Boston: Houghton Mifflin, 2010), 71.

Watching the *Times* reporters write that a tiny band of hooligans had hijacked the university despite the administration's valiant efforts to address a few legitimate issues was profoundly disillusioning. From the *Times'* repeated claim that only a handful of Columbia's many thousands of students were involved in the protests to its demure description of the Institute of Defense Analyses (the architect of, among other Vietnam War strategies, the Phoenix Program of assassinating Viet Cong cadre)—as "specializ[ing] in finding answers to many of mankind's most pressing problems,"[3] its coverage was no less false or misleading than the *Daily News'* predictable redbaiting about "Red-fronter-led" conspiracies on campus.

Writing for *Spec* while reading the mainstream press was my opportunity to try to break out of the old forms and learn the new language Marx describes. I had lots of help, of course. Stephen Cohen's contemporary civilization course, for example, was teaching me to see our purported "revolution" in the light of the history of socialism. For a generation, Communists had fought with democratic socialists over "trade union consciousness"—trying to spark a working class–led revolution versus negotiating for better wages and working conditions through collective bargaining under capitalism. So, to my SDS friends' anger, I wrote that SDS's six demands were a contemporary version of the old argument. They were an attempt to prevent the strike from turning into a negotiation with the administration based on the academic equivalent of trade union consciousness. This was about bettering students' lives within the current campus structure (so-called student interests) instead of challenging the very agenda of the cold war research university.

Reading T. E. Lawrence, Conrad, Forster, and Malraux in Michael Rosenthal's and Edward Said's English classes was teaching me to put the antiwar movement into the larger context of subalterns' struggles, both armed and intellectual, against the hegemonic power of empire—which included the United States and its Cold War research universities like Columbia. Working on *Spectator's* series about life in the neighborhood's run-down single-room occupancy hotels (mostly for people on welfare),

---

3. B. Drummond Ayres, Jr., "A Target of Campus Protestors Is a 'Think Tank,'" *New York Times* (New York), April 26, 1968.

and collecting African American English dialect samples in Harlem for William Labov's sociolinguistics class, was teaching me, a white country mouse from the Midwest, about what urban poverty was like and how Columbia's real estate policies helped perpetuate it. In a more professional vein, Nat Hentoff of the *Village Voice* hung around the *Spec* office during the strike and encouraged us to find our own voice. And Nicholas von Hoffman, then of the *Washington Post*, took me under his wing a bit as a source and iconoclast-in-training. The day after the bust, when I was sporting a huge black eye and swollen temple from being blackjacked by a plainclothes cop on South Field the night before, he escorted me over to where Vice President David Truman was standing on the plaza on front of Low Memorial Library. Nick shoved my aching head in Truman's face and shouted "See what you've done?" But even Nick was unable to shake Truman's basilisk glare. Truman wouldn't give us a statement, so von Hoffman walked over to Low to see whether he could get something out of President Kirk's office. The lower-level door was locked, and Nick, wearing his trademark shit-kicker boots, just kicked it open. Nobody was home upstairs, of course, but I learned a great lesson about walking through walls to get a story. That summer, Nick went on to write *Two, Three, Many More*, his roman à clef about a student uprising at an elite college, while some of the *Spec* staff (including me) were writing *Up Against the Ivy Wall.*

In the end, I came to see the *Times*men and their mainstream colleagues as unhappy prisoners, rather than ill-intentioned tools, of the system. Traditional "news" in those days was the product of bureaucratic processes performed by political actors with complementary agendas (reporters and their sources). There was a news hole—pages or airtime—to fill and an organizational structure designed to fill it. Content was generated by the recordkeeping activities of journalists based on assumptions about what would be "newsworthy." These enabled the allocation of resources (camera crews, reporters) in advance to places (press conferences, demonstration sites) where the predictably unexpected would emerge against the background of the taken-for-granted, all in time to make deadline. Columbia was just one of innumerable such sites where a tiny proportion of potentially noticeable happenings were reduced to all-the-news-fit-to-print in a form effacing the very process of noticing and selecting.

I got my nose rubbed in this after the *Times* ran a Columbia story in the fall of 1968 about SDSers "assaulting" students and faculty, trying to keep them out of a building during a demonstration—ominous, Brown Shirt-like political "violence." I had been there, as a *Spec* reporter, and when interviewed by Sylvan Fox about what happened told him that people who stood in doorways when others were trying to pass by should expect to get shoved, and that there hadn't been any violence, just some milling around. That perspective—which suggested there actually wasn't much of a story in the first place—didn't appear in the piece that ran the next day under Fox's byline, but rather a quote from a professor about "Fascism on the Left" rearing its ugly head yet again. I later learned that the desk downtown, not Fox, had sought out and inserted that quote and edited what he had filed accordingly. "After you've been working here three days," one of his colleagues told me, "you realize that a lot of the mistakes we make are just human errors." But the important mistakes were really systemic errors, dictated by the structuring rhetoric of scandal and the ethnomethodology of news.

Figure 56.1 A layout man at work on the *Columbia Daily Spectator. Photograph by David Bogorad.*

After I graduated in 1970, I started a tryout at the *Washington Post*, but cut it short when belatedly I was awarded one of Columbia's Kellett Fellowships and went off to Cambridge University to do English for a couple of years. I ended up getting a Ph.D. and teaching at Harvey Mudd College, the engineering campus of the Claremont Colleges in California. In between my regular courses on Shakespeare, Dickens, and science fiction, I taught media sociology and tried to emulate my Columbia professors'—above all Said's—stances as public intellectuals, engaging in and reflecting on politics as a critic and reviewer, trying to keep the emancipatory spirit of '68 alive inside. I ultimately changed careers, ending up as a lawyer in a big Palo Alto firm (to what would have been Orwell's horror, I'm sure). But the technological utopianism of Silicon Valley—the belief that democratizing and personalizing access to computing power, information, and communication can be liberating—has its affinities with the more humanistic aspects of the New Left's program. So I'm still trying to pay homage to the spirit of '68 in some of my legal work, freelance journalism, and documentary film production. That still springs eternal for me.

Michael Stern *('70CC), a former journalist and English professor, practices law in Palo Alto. He is chair of the board of* The American Prospect *and executive producer of* General Magic: The Movie.

"Outside agitator"/Up Against the Wall Motherfuckers

HUNDREDS OF PAIRS OF WINGS

968—that wild year! I was a member of a group called Up Against the Wall Motherfuckers, based in the Lower East Side of New York City, which became the only nonstudent chapter of Students for a Democratic Society (SDS). The best description I ever heard of the Motherfuckers was "a street gang with an analysis." Before we went running out into the streets and causing disruption, everyone had to participate in a study group. We discussed current issues, talked through the theory, and studied Bakunin and Kropotkin and the historical conflict between the anarchists and the Communists and the socialists. The Motherfuckers ran a free store in the neighborhood that provided clothing and some food, as well as printing services (you paid whatever you could). We set up crash pads for people who needed them (runaways who ended up in New York) and published in the underground press, including local newspapers *Rat* and *East Village Other*.

Being a Motherfucker was a lifestyle. More than anything, we considered ourselves a family, with a mission to provide services for the community and to be engaged in political change. Our credo included self-defense, so we held karate classes, and whenever we went on a camping trip, we all did target practice. It was a mixture of militant politics and theater—one of the first actions we did as a group was during a New York garbage workers strike. The wealthier neighborhoods hired private contractors, but the trash and rotting garbage was piling up around the Lower East Side and

374 HUNDREDS OF PAIRS OF WINGS

other poor areas, so one night a bunch of us piled onto the subway with bags of garbage, others got in a van, and we converged on the fountain at Lincoln Center, where we ceremoniously dumped our collection of trash. It was a "cultural exchange." The Motherfuckers were accused of being all image and no content. Our response was that without an image, no one is going to pay attention to your content.

People always asked us what our demands were. In the immortal words of Janis Joplin: "We'll know we've got it when it makes us feel good."[1] *That* was our demand! Our name came from the last line of a LeRoi Jones poem: "The magic words are: Up against the wall, mother fucker, this is a stick up!"[2]

We were influenced by international groups—in England, Italy, and Germany—but most of all by the Situationists in France. Their position on the mass media was one we adopted: Don't Cooperate, to the point of smashing cameras if they got in our faces. The Situationists taught that if the bourgeois media gets hold of you, if you consent and cooperate, you'll quickly be co-opted. (Who wants to be bought and sold like a Che Guevara T-shirt?) Part of the justification for using the name Up Against the Wall Motherfuckers was that it kept the establishment media from mentioning us. They could never say exactly who we were, which was fine with us, because it meant we were insulated and protected. Our choice of name was linked to our belief that the dominant cultural paradigms had to be brought down (the Lincoln Center action: "garbage for garbage"), that a genuine, successful, and liberating revolution would tear down the walls of both politics and culture. The Establishment would crumble.

From the start, Up Against the Wall Motherfuckers was an informal collective, with no leaders or membership rolls, and small, too—maybe no more than a dozen or so that formed the core. We applied to SDS to be a street gang chapter because we felt that the student movement was weak and ineffectual and, frankly, needed our assistance. We went down to the national SDS meeting in Lexington, Kentucky, to practice

1. "Piece of My Heart," on *Piece of My Heart*, performed by Big Brother and the Holding Company, Columbia Records, 1968, LP.
2. LeRoi Jones, "Black People!" in *The Leroi Jones/Amiri Baraka Reader*, ed. William J. Harris (New York: Thunder's Mouth Press, 1991), 224.

our disruptive politics and advance our style and content. I remember Carl Oglesby, one of the theoreticians of SDS, talking brilliantly about how he saw things in the United States—a battle to the death within the ruling class between Yankees (the New England banking community) and Cowboys (Texas oil magnates), fighting for control of the country and the war in Vietnam. (That was also one explanation for Kennedy's assassination in Dallas.) I thought this was all pretty brilliant, but Ben Morea, a member of the Motherfuckers, had had enough. He ran up onto the stage, grabbed the microphone and shouted that everyone should quit this intellectualization bullshit and join us on the streets. "Fuck the Yankees and fuck the Cowboys, too!" he said. "We're the new Indians!" Crazy, I know, but it did appeal to certain segments of SDS, and we made lots of connections that weekend.

We got back to our place on the Lower East Side and kept up our work fomenting all kinds of discord on the streets of New York, staging responsive activities to police brutality, and targeting anyone who was opposed to the counterculture community that was emerging at the time. We fought back, establishing the Action Committee for Immediate Defense (ACID), which patrolled the Lower East Side and kept an eye out for the cops doing their rounds and monitoring their dirty work.

One day we got a phone call from JJ, who was always much more in tune with the Motherfuckers than he was with his fellow Columbia SDS students. "Hey! We need help. We've taken a building on campus."

"What kind of help do you need?"

"Well, it might turn into a fight."

"Wow!" I thought. "Students ready to fight?" JJ knew we had experience of dealing with the cops and what tactics could be used to combat them, and I figured we could offer the students some technical support. "Hey guys, let's get up to Columbia!"

I ended up as a liaison with the SDS folks and was sent uptown. People were standing around in a crowd outside Hamilton Hall, where inside there were still black and white students together. There wasn't much going on, so I headed back downtown. A few hours later there was another phone call.

"We got kicked out, so we took our own building. Hurry up and get back here." It seemed more interesting now that more of the campus had been occupied. This was something new, a breakthrough in both strategy and content. It wasn't just a street protest march—this was the white protest movement and the Harlem community working together.

I found Low Memorial Library and encountered two students at the door who had been given orders to let me into the building. Some of the first conversations I had inside the building were about whether breaking down a door to the president's office and sitting in would constitute violence. This continued into a debate about how militant this whole thing should be, about what the blacks were going to do in Hamilton, and how the demands of protesters might best be achieved. There was a faction inside Low insisting that the majority of the occupiers of the building weren't going to be militant enough and could never make a strong enough statement. And anyway, Low was getting crowded. The most accessible nearby building was Mathematics, which backed onto Broadway. That was seen as an advantage when it came to bringing in supplies (buckets lowered down from the windows, filled with food and medical supplies by people who wanted to offer their support) and also if there was a need to escape. Suddenly, we were inside Math.

The endless meetings inside Math were very, very boring. But that was the kind of ultrademocracy we were practicing—giving everyone the chance to weigh in, whether or not someone really knew what they were talking about. It was important that everyone have a voice. The whole point of Columbia '68 was that if you were inside one of the occupied buildings, you had just as much power as anyone else. It didn't matter who you were, what your major was, who your parents were, or whether you were on scholarship or paying your own way or not even a student. None of these things mattered when it came to our daily lives inside Mathematics. Everyone was equal. Peter Kropotkin, that turn-of-the-century Russian anarchist philosopher, once wrote about a flock of birds flying in tightly packed formations as they dived, turned, and swooped in unison with no apparent signal or leader, no confusion as to direction, all moving and acting as if they were one bird with hundreds of pairs of wings. This is an aspiration and a model for a society based on consensus, unity, and where we have become a people at home in a place. Many hearts feeling the passion of purpose, many eyes sharing a vision for action.

As a representative of the Motherfuckers, working with SDS, I was an "outside agitator," focused on logistics. As a group, we had done a lot of thinking about the question of self-defense. We were familiar with the tactics of the New York police from our many street "confrontations" on the Lower East Side and at larger antidraft, antiwar demonstrations. The key strategic question at Columbia was this: What do we do when the cops arrive? Fight back? Or give in? The Math Commune's collective thoughts on the subject alienated us from much of the Radical Left, especially students, who were reluctant to push things to the point of By Any Means Necessary. (The Motherfuckers used that phrase everywhere: BAMN!) When it came to the debate about violence and nonviolence, it was our position that the real dichotomy was not between violence and nonviolence, because that debate only served the ruling class. This discussion took people who might have agreed about everything else, and split them on that one issue, preventing them from unifying against the forces they were challenging.

The true dichotomy, in our view, was between offensive and defensive violence. Offensive violence was most often perpetrated by the state, whether imperialism abroad or suppressing its own people when they seek change. State violence is anonymous, mechanistic, political, and self-serving. If you want to achieve any meaningful change, then not resisting state violence BAMN—thereby accepting and permitting it, and hoping it will go away if you don't challenge it—was seen by us as, ultimately, suicidal. So, inside Math, we implemented our self-defensive credo and taught the students basic tactics about how to protect themselves from police aggression. Ideas and theories are vital to the struggle, but sometimes we need to actively fight to protect ourselves, our family, our community. We claimed the right to defend ourselves against any form of state-sponsored violence that came at us, a concept that shook up most of the white protesters (later we had a saying: "Armed Love").

At one point, we received inside information from a friendly newspaper reporter about the timing of the impending police action, scheduled for nighttime. Strategically, we felt it would be best if the police invasion of Math took place once the sun had come up, because the more daylight there would be, the more media would be gathered and the more protection from violence we might have. Few people in Math had experience with street fighting, and it wasn't easy to convince someone who had never been confronted by police at an antiwar demonstration of what probably was coming and how bad it could get (in nonlethal terms). I, and some others, got fed up with all that talk about the boundaries of nonviolence, so we ducked down into the basement. We checked the doors to the tunnel system we knew was spread underneath the entire campus, exploring the possibilities (based on a tip from our informant) that the cops weren't necessarily going to try and enter by Math's front door and were considering coming in underground. Blocking those tunnel doors seemed to us to be an important defensive move, so we dragged over a vending machine and some desks and chairs. But that wasn't good enough, so we tore down the one-inch-thick marble partitions between the stalls in the bathrooms between the toilets, at which point we were informed that we were way out of bounds because the group, as a whole, hadn't yet decided we should go that far. A debate ensued, about whether the cops might be even more pissed if they had to spend time busting through our barricade. In true Motherfuckers style, we began marching around the place—perhaps five or six of us—with a chant: "WE ARE ANTIPARTITIONALISTS! DOWN WITH THE PARTITIONS! FREE THE TOILETS!" Eventually the crowd was convinced of the need for a barricade, and the whole group got to work, making what turned into really sturdy blockades that we spent a lot of time on. Finally, here was something we physically could do together and into which we could channel our energies.

Then I stepped over the line again by grabbing the fire hoses. The water to the building hadn't been cut off, and I explained that we could hose the cops as they came through the door. Almost everyone in that meeting was against it. "You could hurt someone!" they all yelled at me.

I thought I was right to do what I did because I knew that the police would be coming through those doors with blood in their eyes. The only chance we had was to delay and hope the media attention would somehow temper them. Our strategy was not to hit them, but rather make it harder for them to hit us. Some people thought I was acting undemocratically, and maybe I was. Recalling my time spent in a rural volunteer fire department, I readied the hoses (which were never used).

It turned out the cops were saving Math for last. It was going to be their dessert, probably because it was known to be the most militant of the five buildings, and also the one with the most nonstudents. We could hear them coming, one building at a time, and in the lights they had set up, we could see the chaos. When they reached Math, it took the cops forty-five minutes to dismantle that barricade and get through the front door. They never did use the basement entrance. When they finally broke through, we were all sitting on the three floors of staircases, in our protective civil rights pose, arms over our heads. As they marched past us, everyone was slugged on the back of the head by a plainclothes cop with a small club. As I recall, some of them were using handcuffs as brass knuckles. Angry and pumped up, screaming and yelling, they got to the top floor and starting pushing everyone down the stairs, and then shoved us into paddy wagons.

A note about the media and Columbia. I went to college with that friendly reporter I mentioned, who in 1968 was writing for the *New York Times*. He and I had a mutual benefit policy: he would give me information on police briefings, and I would give him information so he was in the right place to get a good story that would reflect our concerns. I trusted him to write the kinds of articles we wanted the world to read, but his editors would scratch out anything that pushed up against their corporate concerns, so our side almost never got represented fairly in the pages of the *Times*.

In the days that followed, the Motherfuckers acquired two new recruits, students who dropped out after the melee and became among our best long-term members.

Several years ago, one of my young nephews said to me, "Oh Johnny! Those sixties must have been really incredible. You guys had everything! Wow!"

"Hold it just a minute," I told him. "You have to understand that for everything that was brand new and exciting, that had never been done before, there were equal parts of risk and joy."

Fear was associated with every freedom we embraced. They told us that rock 'n' roll would make us lose our hearing and send us to Hell. Were we really risking our salvation by dancing like Elvis Presley? No one knew what the side effects were going to be of those new birth control pills. Would all the women of our generation die of blood clots thirty years after our sexual revolution? Would our brain cells rot from the acid and LSD we were taking? And as far as demonstrating and fighting against the government and the Vietnam War, we never knew when The Establishment would lose patience and start shooting for real, which is exactly what happened at Jackson State and Kent State.

The sixties wasn't all fun and joy, and you would have to be ignorant not to be afraid at least part of the time. One of the Motherfuckers, a street philosopher, once said to me, "When you're living in a nightmare, paranoia is a normal response." That's something I want today's young people to know when they look back on that time. Nobody voluntarily gives up power. Freedom always comes at a cost. But it's worth it.

Johnny Sundstrom *left the cities of America in 1970 and became part owner and manager of a cooperative livestock, forestland, and garden operation in western Oregon. As founder and director of the Siuslaw Institute (since 1994), he provides natural resources consultation and administers watershed restoration and education projects; he recently retired as head track and field coach at the local high school. He has helped develop community-based organizations in pacific Russia and the western United States, and recently has been carrying on his deceased son's work in Kenya. For more than forty years, he has been visiting Arapaho relations in Wyoming and has published several novels about the settling of the American frontier.*

Graduate student, English/Students for a Restructured University

POLITICAL EDUCATION AND THE BIRTH OF STUDENTS FOR A RESTRUCTURED UNIVERSITY

April 1968. Election year.

I was working toward a Ph.D. in medieval literature in Columbia's Department of English and Comparative Literature while teaching part time at the now-defunct Columbia College of Pharmaceutical Sciences. I shared an apartment uptown with a couple of other Columbia students and was about to join a politically active neighbor in setting up a storefront office in support of Sen. Eugene McCarthy's presidential campaign. Like almost everyone I knew, I was very much against the Vietnam War. My focus was on national, not campus, politics.

I had no knowledge of the activities of Students for a Democratic Society (SDS) on the Columbia campus, nor did I know anything about the university's proposed gymnasium in Morningside Park or the Harlem community's opposition to it. In fact, in the three years I had been at Columbia, I never even dared to go down the steps into the park because of its unsavory reputation for dangerous muggings.

But I loved the cultural richness that the university had engendered in our neighborhood. Where else could I have found the actors, musicians, and artists who so willingly volunteered to help me produce a sold-out performance of the seventeenth-century poet John Milton's little-known masque, *Comus*? And who, at our cast party, uniformly agreed that we should contribute what was left of our takings to the McCarthy campaign! I went home brimming with gratitude.

Comus was performed on Saturday, April 20. Three days later, at 2 P.M., a large group of students—black and white—began a sit-in at Hamilton Hall. The next morning, my radio alarm woke me with the news that two more buildings at Columbia had been taken over. This was something I had to see. By mid-afternoon, I was on campus and found a quickly evolving situation. The black students who held Hamilton Hall were in direct contact with the Harlem community—no great friends of the university—and that situation required delicate handling. For their part, the white students were having a great time exploring President Kirk's filing cabinets and other items in his well-decorated office.

Once the Columbia building occupations began, I found myself aligned as much with faculty as with the striking students. I wandered in and out of faculty meetings and for three nights joined the vigil at Low Memorial Library, below the windows of the president's office, on a narrow ledge just deep enough to stand on, arm in arm with colleagues. During the day as well, a few faculty members were always present to protect those inside from the so-called Majority Coalition, primarily athletes, who had been massing, with some menace, in front of us, furious because of the disruption to their education. From where I stood, I could see how difficult it was for them to hold themselves back.

Because the only entrance to Low was now carefully guarded, the striking students were cut off from their usual suppliers of food, so supporters resorted to a new system of delivery. During the day, friends of the students inside Low began throwing food over our heads in the hope that the students inside would catch it. The rule was that if you didn't catch the food and it fell, then it had to lie on the lawn and nobody could claim it. It was a bizarre situation, and anyone who violated this rule faced the threat of violence.

After two nights of staying awake on the faculty line, I was really tired, so thinking the situation was stable, on the third night I left the line to go home, which meant that I missed the police bust, which became a police riot, in the middle of the night.

When I arrived back on campus, on Tuesday, April 30, not long after the sun had come up, I was confronted by the walking wounded. I learned that the sixty-five-year-old secretary of the graduate English department had been beaten so badly that her head was completely bandaged. The New York City Police Department's Tactical Patrol Force had stopped for no one. That was enough for me. I was now ready to join the strike against an administration unable or unwilling to protect its constituents.

After the bust, SDS formed a Strike Coordinating Committee (SCC) and let it be known that it was now very much open for business, and that representatives from every school on campus were needed to help determine the course of the strike. Post-bust, the plan was that if you had the backing of thirty-five students from your particular school (business, law, social work, etc.), you could represent that group on the SCC. Newly elected by members of the graduate faculties, I was surprised to discover that the SCC—some seventy people—was much bigger than I had expected.

As part of the SCC, I found myself becoming a voice for the more moderate students, who I would say constituted about a third of the SCC. We were generally those people who had not been inside the buildings and had not undergone that hothouse radicalization. One of the freshmen who had been inside a building once told me, with an absolutely straight face, that when Nixon got the nomination at the upcoming Republican Convention, disaffected Rockefeller supporters would spill out into the streets and join the revolution. He really believed it. But it was clear to us that this was not going to be the beginning of a Marxist revolution.

Meanwhile, certain members of SDS seemed resolute on ignoring the policies we were formulating, and they employed simple but effective tactics to neutralize our points of view. They were good at leaving us talking, deep into the night, debating what the SCC's position would be on some minor issue, while they set about working the mimeograph machines. By morning they would have distributed a statement as if it had been agreed on by the entire SCC.

Our frustrations mounted, and so I called a rump session, a caucus of the moderate students, and we agreed that we would have to separate from the SCC. At a meeting in the large auditorium in John Jay Hall, I stood and said something to the effect of: "the rhetoric of the Strike Committee—all this Marxist dialectic, this talk of students being at the vanguard of a revolution—is not the direction we are interested in going. We need to find our own way of expressing our ideas." About twenty-five of us left the meeting, roundly booed by the crowd, and proceeded to form our own organization, which we called Students for a Restructured

University (SRU—an awkward name, but the best we could think of on such short notice).

In a speech I gave as chairman of SRU, on May 16, 1968, at a campus meeting of General Studies students, I spoke about the split in the Columbia protest movement. What I described as "a tender and tense coalition" had been maintained to demonstrate moderate students' support for the overall aims—and even the tactics—of those who occupied the buildings. The political demands of SDS, we felt, were generally sound and worth fighting for, but a new chapter was beginning. It was clear to us that students needed a voice in the governance of their university and that we as an organization might be able to exercise some pressure on the administration and bring about meaningful student representation. This was a possibility that SDS had no apparent interest in addressing. They had bigger issues at stake. This is how I described the situation:

This evening twenty-two delegates to SCC, representing constituencies of about fifteen hundred students, formally severed ties with that body and reconstituted themselves as a new group called Students for a Restructured University. Let no hasty functionary at Low Library or overzealous agent of Sulzberger's *Times* smile at the news. The strike is not broken. Those of us who left have not broken faith with our mentors in SDS. We continue to feel a deep gratitude to the original strikers for their role in awakening us to the political realities of our common situation and we remain in admiration of the efficiency and effectiveness of the dedicated team at Strike Central. But we have reached a point now where we must require of ourselves an affirmation of our own distinct identity, our own distinct concerns.

Although the SCC has been consistently united behind the demands of the May 3 resolution—notably the demand for amnesty—there has existed a concurrent division over questions of emphasis and style. SDS has continually emphasized the necessity for viewing our political demands within a national political context; thus the political education of the community at large has assumed for them the highest priority. Their reiterated assertion has been that a free university is impossible in an unfree society. We, on the other hand, while recognizing the force of this analysis, have nevertheless been concerned with wresting from the present upheaval some constructive rebuilding of our immediate

POLITICAL EDUCATION AND THE BIRTH OF STUDENTS   385

context. Briefly, we believe that a free university can be the vanguard of a free society. We cannot view with equanimity the prospect of an indefinite future of polarization and unrest, while awaiting the total political awakening of the total society. We want amelioration of our condition, and we want it now.

We decided that our first order of business had to be organizing a Counter Commencement. Graduation day was June 4, just three weeks after SRU came into being. We let it be known that our ceremony would be held on the plaza outside Low, where the university traditionally held its commencement ceremony. To reduce chances of a clash, the university decided to move its exercises into the Cathedral of St. John the Divine, four blocks away.

Three hundred graduating SRU members and supporters entered the Cathedral, along with the other graduating students, and seated themselves among them. Then, as soon as history professor Richard Hofstadter started to speak, they rose together and quietly marched out in an orderly fashion. Their parents and families were waiting for them outside, and joined in a march up to 116th Street where they turned left and flowed onto the campus. As they began to fill the plaza, a newspaper reporter rushed up to me, and with great excitement yelled, "You did it! You did it!"

It almost didn't happen. Nigel Paneth, our emcee, was holding the only amplification device we had—a bullhorn. Seeing this, a couple of SDS members tried to wrest it away from him, but he held on. As others came to his aid, the SDS bullies retreated.

When the crowd had assembled, Nigel gave a brief speech of welcome and introduced our four main speakers. Dr. Erich Fromm, the psychoanalyst, author, educator, and humanistic philosopher, called the walkout a protest against "society . . . approaching a state of chronic low-grade schizophrenia . . . the split between thought and feeling, truth and passion, mind and heart."[1] His speech was followed by that of Alexander Erlich, professor emeritus of economics at Columbia, and writer and cultural critic Dwight McDonald. Finally, Dr. Harold Taylor, a former president

---

1. Erich Fromm, "In the Name of Life," in *Natural Enemies? Youth and the Clash of Generations,* ed. Alexander Klein (New York: J. B. Lippincott, 1969), 240.

of Sarah Lawrence College, at that time the head of the Department of Education in Washington, D.C., ended the ceremonies with the following benediction: "By virtue of the authority vested in me by the trustees of the human imagination, derived from the just powers of human nature and the constitution of mankind, I hereby confer upon all of you here present, a degree of beatification through the arts."[2] With these inspiring words, our Counter Commencement ended on a high note.

The day after our Counter Commencement, SRU was forced to move out of its offices in Lewisohn Hall by the summer dean, who held a grudge against us. Fortunately for us, the president of Teachers College, Dr. John Fischer, was sympathetic to our cause, and offered us office space in a five-room apartment on West 121st Street, which became a beehive of activity all summer long. Many reporters came from near and far trying to comprehend the upside-down situation at Columbia. My main goal was to focus attention away from SDS radicals and to put it instead on the wisdom of structural reform. SRU believed that power should not be hoarded by the central administration. Professors and students alike merited an organization that spread power more broadly and encouraged differing factions to work together.

SRU's vice president, Sandy Kayden, turned out to have a knack for finding grant money, and we ended up with $30,000 (including a grant from the Ford Foundation). This money was used to pay for our staff and to research and write a report on recommendations for university governance, giving a role to faculty and students. In the end, graduate student Neal Hurwitz wrote that report for us. In October 1968, these recommendations were published in Columbia's student newspaper *Spectator*, along with those of several other groups.

In April and May, Professor Archibald Cox of Harvard University came to Columbia with his team to try to determine what factors caused the disturbances on campus. To this end, he set up a series of small-group meetings in a well-appointed apartment nearby. I was invited to one of the last of these meetings. After an interesting exchange of ideas, Professor Cox made the observation that what had happened at Columbia could never possibly happen at Harvard and supported this statement

---

2. Mark Rudd, *Underground: My Life with SDS and the Weathermen* (New York: HarperCollins, 2009), 112.

POLITICAL EDUCATION AND THE BIRTH OF STUDENTS 387

by describing the distribution of academic buildings on the Harvard campus. In April 1969, Harvard exploded with its own version of the Columbia strike.

At some point late in the summer, I met with a graduate student who, for his master's thesis, was interviewing members of both SDS and SRU active during the strike. He had been surprised to find that nearly all the SDS students identified themselves as middle class, whereas the SRU students identified as working class. This class element was interesting to me. The wealthier kids could afford to be radical. We couldn't. I was working class and could be at Columbia only because I had a full fellowship. I valued what I was getting from the university and didn't want to jeopardize it.

It has now been fifty years since Columbia set off the dynamite that blasted away a chunk of the rock cliff that was to have been the location of its new gymnasium in Morningside Park. You can still see the scars of that blast through the water trickling down to the pleasant pool below, much used by regular flocks of migrating birds and perhaps by a turtle sunning itself on one of the larger rocks in the pool. Just south of this pool, there is a large field that might have been taken over by Columbia, but instead offers the general public baseball and softball fields and space for kite flying, picnics, calisthenics, or just hanging out.

My wife and I live on Morningside Drive, just a few blocks up from the steps down to the pool and the great field. We raised our children here, and we are continually grateful for the genius of Frederick Law Olmstead and Calvert Vaux, the original designers of Morningside Park. And we're grateful that Columbia backed away from its attempted intrusion and allowed the vision of Olmstead and Vaux to endure and flourish.

John Thoms (*'67GSAS*) *received a Ph.D. from Columbia in 1979 and has taught literature at Mannes College, Columbia College of Pharmacy, and Mercy College. He was a tenured professor of English at New York Institute of Technology. Married since 1969 to Judy Johnson, he has two children and four grandchildren.*

HAROLD S. WECHSLER

Graduate student, History

IT'S BETTER TO BUILD UP: POST-'68 GOVERNANCE AT COLUMBIA

Some time during the week of April 23, I put on a green armband, that color reserved for those Left-leaning members of the Columbia community who chose to stand in front of the occupied buildings and attempted to prevent the police from storming them. I had grown up in a Brooklyn neighborhood that included many police, firefighters, and civil servants, and knew what the police might do if called onto the Columbia campus. I still am haunted by the images of the police action. But I also was repelled by the brief triumph of "manipulatory democracy"—a riff on "participatory democracy," one of the New Left's founding principles—that resulted from the police bust that had ripped through the campus, causing many injuries to students and faculty, the night before. A gathering the next morning of Students for a Democratic Society (SDS) leaders on the balcony of the Law School building, looking like a presidium, vividly symbolized this triumph. These leaders looked down at more than a thousand demonstrators standing on 116th Street protesting the police action. As a wearer of the green armband, I felt caught between an administration with too many deaf ears on one side, and tenacious students willing to take advantage of that obstinacy on the other.

I had decided to stay at Columbia for graduate work in history after receiving a B.A. from the College in 1967. Several weeks after the bust, I joined the staff of the Project on Columbia Structure, the student–faculty research arm of the Executive Committee of the Faculty. The Project, directed by Columbia Law School professor Frank Grad, recruited about fifteen students from several Columbia divisions. I spent the summer of 1968 attending staff and committee meetings, discussing the university's past and future relationships with its students, faculty, and surrounding community, and writing about university governance.

The Project was located in an apartment house basement on Morningside Drive. The graduate student participants on the Project asked why our programs did not address the conditions of academic work, university governance, and student and faculty rights and responsibilities. Absent that instruction, for some of us, the Project—and later the Senate—was at least a crucible for campus leadership.

The Project's September 1968 report signaled the direction later taken by the Executive Committee. "Academic government has failed to keep up with contemporary needs and expectations, and has been largely unresponsive, not only at Columbia University but at universities generally," the report stated, "both to the desires of faculty and students to play a role in the shaping of the University's policies and social goals, and to the need of defining its relationship to the society of which it is a part."[1] Significant change in governance, we knew, was coming to Columbia, and we saw our research as helping that process along.

The Project continued into the 1968–1969 academic year. One highlight came when members of the Columbia College Band, dressed in their blue blazers, serenaded surprised staff members with a chorus of "Who Owns New York" during our Christmas party. That party, by the way, evolved into a characteristically intense discussion of whether black studies courses belonged in separate or established departments.

The Project produced about twenty reports, most of them related to the work on "restructuring" conducted by the Executive Committee. Others— like "Columbia and Morningside Heights: Columbia, the City, Planning, Renewal, Expansion, Acquisition, and the Community," Bill Bonvillian's report on the university's questionable community relations and housing policies, and Mark Weiss's report on "Junior Faculty at Columbia"—later enabled the new university Senate committees to define agendas and act

---

1. Executive Committee of the Faculty, "Preliminary Proposals for the Creation of a University Senate and a Student Assembly," September 10, 1968, pp. 2–3.

on concrete data. My report on methods of choosing trustees argued for Senate participation in the selection process. The final proposal included a significant consultative role for the Senate. Its participation would transform the undemocratic method of board self-perpetuation, whereby the trustees selected their own successors, into a more egalitarian process. I suspect that informal discussions among students and faculty on the Project staff and members of the Executive Committee were equally or even more influential than our formal reports. Frank Grad attended most Executive Committee meetings and its minutes show that his comments to the committee were consistent with staff consensus on many key issues. At the same time, he often guided us toward a more nuanced understanding of how universities work.

Few staff members supported a bicameral governance structure that separated students from faculty. The Executive Committee opted for a unicameral body by mid-fall 1969; its minutes quote one member as saying: "Students do not want an isolated 'Mickey Mouse' [to] play legislature of their own, where it would be easy to develop adversary attitudes." But, collectively, the staff did not see itself as an independent political force; it took no formal positions on the Senate proposals. By contrast, many other student organizations had much to say, although finding common ground among all groups proved difficult.

A year in the basement gave us time for our views to develop. Mark Weiss recalls that in February 1969, the two of us worked through the night to prepare a critique covering many technicalities of the draft proposal for a Senate. Focusing on the composition of the Senate and its committees, eligibility for Senate seats and for places on its committees, representation of constituencies, and Senate and committee powers, the critique presumed that the rules of the game helped to determine substantive outcomes and that all university constituencies therefore expected the Senate bylaws to be fair. To those reading between the lines of our report, our message was that tenured faculty and administration would have to give just a little more.

Project members were impressed by the proposed bylaw giving the Senate broad legislative powers: the enumerated powers did not limit the Senate from considering "all matters of University-wide concern, and all matters that, though not of University-wide concern, affect or relate to the interests of more than one faculty or school, or that concern the

University's relations with its affiliated institutions."[2] This was Frank Grad's position from the outset, although he and the staff knew that having broad powers did not compel their use.

Critics at the time often charged that university faculty had abandoned their teaching and institutional service obligations to pursue professional and disciplinary recognition. These criticisms echoed student complaints of neglect. Worse, so the indictment went, faculty guided their graduate students in the same direction. But the faculty members who served on the Project on Columbia Structure, the Executive Committee of the Faculty, the University Senate, and its committees refuted that charge. Many of Columbia's best and most respected faculty members invested substantial time and energy in healing a deeply wounded university. Project staff learned that lesson well. I have spent thirty-five years teaching courses on higher education administration and still apply a key lesson learned during my year on the Project: faculty, staff, and students have an institutional stake equal to trustees and administrators, so therefore must retain a voice in campus affairs—and not only during crises. In turn, those constituencies must accept their institutional responsibilities with the same dedication and commitment given to their studies and their teaching.

I take pride in the small part I played in helping the Project—and the Executive Committee through the Project—design and implement a governance mechanism that the president could consult at tense moments, that created informal connections across a university divided into many fiefdoms and vassalages, and that kept a careful eye on the university administration (as Walter Metzger emphasized in an early Senate speech), while also becoming the university's arena for resolving important disputes, for channeling potential crises into productive directions, and occasionally, as Robert Kennedy famously said, for turning problems into opportunities.

Project participation motivated and enabled me to embark on a career focused on the study and practice of higher education, a career that has offered incomparable rewards. My involvement in the protests; my work on the Project; and, later, my membership on the Senate staff and on a

2. "Executive Committee Staff Proposal," *Columbia Daily Spectator* (New York), October 10, 1968, S-6.

392 IT'S BETTER TO BUILD UP: POST-'68 GOVERNANCE AT COLUMBIA

Senate committee—one vibrant formative experience after another—taught me that it's better to build up than to tear down.

During the building occupations, Columbia sociology professor Allan Silver put a question to SDS leadership, specifically Mark Rudd: "Is there anything about Columbia University—even in its current, unreformed state, with all its imperfections on its head—which you find precious, and even indispensable?"[3] Rudd and the leadership couldn't (or wouldn't) answer the question, but fifty years later I can offer a useful response: we must complement our commitments by bringing reason and rigor to subjects about which there is all too often only heat and passion in the public square. If we don't, who will?

Harold S. Wechsler *('67CC, '69GSAS; 1946–2017) was professor of education at New York University. He received a Ph.D. from Columbia in 1974. He wrote on the history of minority access to American higher education, college governance, the formation of disciplines in American universities, and the encounter of Jews and American higher education. His books include* The Qualified Student: A History of Selective College Admission in America.

---

3. Allan Silver, "Orwell, Thou Should'st Be Living at This Hour!," *Columbia Daily Spectator* (New York), March 24, 1969.

Barnard undergraduate/Mathematics Hall occupier

A FOOT SOLDIER'S STORY OF THE SIT-INS

O ne reason I prefer writing fiction to nonfiction is that nonfiction tends toward linearity: with fiction, it seems possible to imitate the multiple layers and simultaneous truths of the real world. I have always been disappointed by the great overarching theories of history and philosophy and religion. They have an abstract loveliness and can work well as guides, but they fail to capture the lived experience of human beings.

I came to Barnard College as a transfer student in fall of 1967 after a year as a volunteer for VISTA (Volunteers in Service to America), an agency of the War on Poverty. I had been part of a tight community of young people working in a rundown neighborhood in Norfolk, Virginia. Before VISTA, I attended Bucknell University in bucolic rural Pennsylvania, and before that, lived in a coalmining town in Appalachia.

I grew up believing that human beings always are passing through a stage that leads upward to another stage. Then, at last, you do what the obituaries in my hometown newspaper call "graduating to heaven." At Bucknell, I thought I had the stages laid out: go away to college, become a professor of literature and famous writer, and eventually win the Nobel Prize. I stopped paying much attention to heaven, but it was still clear that there were stages. Around me, people were rejecting the liberal arts and talking about dropping out of college to do something relevant like join the Peace Corps or VISTA.

While with VISTA, I learned a crucial lesson about class, power, and economics. Our team conducted a survey of people in our neighborhood. They liked our playgroups for their kids, but what they really wanted was cheaper food. There were no supermarkets in the immediate area, just a lot of grungy little stores with green meat, withered carrots, and an excellent selection of cigarettes. So we organized a food-buying club to purchase meat and veggies wholesale and distribute them weekly to club members.

It seemed almost mindlessly obvious to us, but we were called on the carpet by the people running the antipoverty agency we worked for. They said a food co-op was Communistic and endangered the livelihood of the local grocers, some of whom were on the board of the antipoverty agency. The people who distributed the antipoverty money were business owners who wanted to put in place nothing that might have even minimal impact on the economic structures of the community. We VISTA volunteers were incensed and drove to Washington, D.C., to the VISTA office, where we got support for our project. The food-buying club quietly continued at a local church.

When my year in VISTA ended, I could have signed on again but wanted to go on to the next stage. I was now completely cynical about the established order and was beginning to hear opposition to the war in Vietnam. I wanted to be part of higher level change than just providing cheap pork chops, so I transferred to Barnard and arrived just in time for that *annus mirabilis* 1968.

Living off campus with two other Barnard transfer students, I studied literature during the day and cooked spaghetti and listened to The Doors at night, occasionally tinkering with grass and boyfriends. I also started going to Students for a Democratic Society (SDS) meetings at Columbia.

At Columbia, I was blown away by what seemed to me the most brilliant boys I had ever heard. Oh, how they could talk! Wondrous political motor-mouths—they seemed to have read *The Eighteenth Brumaire of Louis Bonaparte* in kindergarten. They casually distinguished Trotskyite from Trotskyist and drew analogies to the Popular Front and sneered if you didn't know the Lincoln Brigade was not part of the American Civil War but the Spanish. They seemed to know everything worth knowing, and they talked about it volubly and endlessly. My skills at writing English papers were nothing compared to this. I felt this flood of language breaking over me as the crest of history. I think I wanted to ride the wave of words more than I wanted to stop the war.

It took me a while to realize that the brilliant speakers at the SDS meetings didn't all agree, that dozens of small groups had conflicting ideas, and that some of them were part of preexisting political parties. Some of them apparently hated each other as much as they hated Lyndon B. Johnson. Others weren't even all that interested in the words but wanted militant action now. That group shouted "Fuck!" a lot.

I've often wondered, if I hadn't been a transfer student living off campus, whether I might not have ended up joining the Socialist Workers or Progressive Labor or one of the other small parties, or even going underground with Weatherman. But I was too busy putting my energy into looking for a break in the wave of words where I might dash in and get wet.

Then the sit-ins happened, and I was plunged under. I've written about much of this in my novel *Trespassers*, which has a fictional protagonist—that is to say, she isn't me—but the novel is quite accurate to my experience of the sit-ins. I was just beginning to grasp that being brilliant and reading Marx didn't stop you from romanticizing violence or from embracing style rather than substance. In particular, we embraced the style of the Black Panthers as much as we could. The Panthers, of course, had much more than style: they were deeply embedded in their communities, where they did a lot of important work—some of it the kind of thing the VISTA volunteers had tried. But a lot of our brilliant boys preferred the visuals: the raised fists and thrust jaws. The guns. When rumors went around that the black students in Hamilton Hall had weapons, there was a flashflood of testosterone at Low Memorial Library and Mathematics Hall.

I hear myself being cynical about SDS boys, but they were also right about so many things, especially how the war industry was linked to research at the university and how the university was arrogantly planning to take parkland that was used by people in Harlem. They were right, if sometimes simplistic, about the self-interest of the ruling class. And truth in advertising: I was eaten up with jealousy. I wanted to make speeches, too. I wanted to be them!

Once we took the buildings, though, I began to feel the comradeship and occasionally would take a turn speaking at the endless mass meetings. Public speaking was valued in the old-fashioned school system I attended in West Virginia, and also at the First Baptist Church of Shinnston, West

Virginia, so I would take opportunities to speak my opinion, and once or twice I got a laugh, which made me noticed but not taken seriously.

I wrote a paper on *Middlemarch* for my Victorian Novel class on a typewriter in Low. Later, after I was locked out of Low while on a message-carrying mission, I moved over to Math. There I mostly spent my time avoiding the peanut butter and jelly detail: I had a belief that if I joined the female crews of feeding and cleaning, I would be shut out of any chance of living truly politically.

During the sit-ins, I began to have some understanding of participatory democracy—we had plenty of time and acted like the kind of political entity that Rousseau imagined as the definition of democracy—one in which everyone is a decision-maker. Rousseau didn't think it was a practical system, and some of our great debates were over things like whether or not to make the toilets unisex. A more serious consensus was reached in favor of passive resistance in the event of a police bust—that we would not fight the police or build barricades to slow their progress.

This led to another lesson in politics: democracy is terribly fragile. The Action Faction of the SDS was not part of the consensus. It did its vanguard thing and filled the stairwells and halls of Math with furniture to slow the police, completely undermining our democratic decision. Then, of course, the police came, and having to get through the barricade made them really, really angry, so by the time they reached us upstairs, the worst of them punched and beat our boys.

That, however, was a high point—not the beating, but waiting for the bust. Those of us who had decided to be arrested, the great majority, sat together in darkened rooms. Not talking anymore, and increasingly frightened, but, because we were frightened, we also were brave. I remember the echoes of the bullhorns in the night, telling us to come out. I remember a feeling of exaltation because we no longer were arguing or yelling "Fuck." We were quiet and still, using our bodies to stop the draft and the bombing, to give the kids in Harlem a chance.

We also were having an adventure. This is where art works so much better than nonfiction. In real life, as in the best art, there is always more than one thing happening at a time. You can be politically aware and morally righteous and also have a rousing good time. It was a great moment, and none of us will ever forget it.

I also see a connection to what I learned about self-interest when I was in VISTA. We never would have done so much, not so many of us, without the personal fear that we, or those close to us, would be sent to Vietnam. We saw an unjust world, but it was also very personal. The women's movement articulated this for me a few years later. It said that the personal *is* the political, and another version of that idea was put out by a red-nosed Boston politico who said all politics *is* local.

Of course, our connection to history and the political is personal *and* local. We are physical beings with one particular angle of vision. This is why we need our novels, to understand others' angle of vision. This is why we need our marches and mass demonstrations, so that we can feel ourselves in context. It doesn't mean we don't analyze; it doesn't mean we don't see the big picture. Being with others in an action gives us the broader perspective.

In the end, what we need is always to expand our self-interest to embrace the interest of as many as possible, someday perhaps to the interest of all sentient beings and the earth as well.

Meredith Sue Willis *('69BC) is from West Virginia, where both of her parents were teachers. She has published more than twenty books and is a veteran writer-in-the schools. She teaches novel writing at NYU's School of Professional Studies and works with an antiracist organization in a New Jersey suburb.*

JOEL D. ZIFF

Columbia College undergraduate/Citizenship Council

FROM COMMUNITY SERVICE TO POLITICAL ACTION: THE EVOLUTION OF THE CITIZENSHIP COUNCIL

I grew up in an observant Jewish community in Minneapolis, living values of commitment to democracy and social justice. My father subscribed to *The Nation*, which I began reading in high school. My high school was a mix of Jews, blacks, and mostly Scandinavian students. Although each culture had its own social circles, North High was a diverse, integrated school where students interacted not only with their own social group but also others. When I came to Columbia, the goals and values of the civil rights movement and President Johnson's War on Poverty resonated with me, but I wasn't especially interested in going South to work on voter registration. I wanted to do something locally.

As a Columbia College freshman in 1965, I joined the Citizenship Council, which had been established in 1957 to provide students with opportunities to volunteer in a variety of social service projects. I became a tutor for the Harlem Education Program (HEP), a community-based organization founded by the Northern Student Movement, based at a storefront on 147th Street between 7th and 8th Avenues. More than a hundred Columbia students participated as tutors for HEP. Each week, I took the subway to 145th Street and met with a ten-year-old boy in his home, helping him with reading and math homework.

My experience volunteering in Harlem was fulfilling in many ways. I had the opportunity to get to know the child I tutored and was inspired by his family's determination and commitment to overcome the challenges of poverty. I valued being able to make a difference in this boy's life and knew that his family appreciated my efforts. It was thrilling to become part of the community with its unique, thriving culture. Locals were friendly and welcoming as I walked from the subway each week, and the director of HEP, Thelma Cockerham, was an energized, street-smart, caring leader who became my mentor. Without question my experiences at HEP became a formative part of my college experience, stimulating my interest in studying history, political science, and the social sciences in general.

In my sophomore year, I took on a leadership role at HEP and became responsible for recruiting, training, and supervising student volunteers. I worked closely with Thelma, gaining more understanding of the community and its challenges, and deepening my appreciation of her work. Together, we strengthened the training of volunteers, with regard to both academic and social issues related to tutoring. My experiences at HEP certainly provided a foundation for life after college, through to the present day. After graduating Columbia, I pursued a master's degree in education and taught school for several years, after which I entered a doctoral program to become a psychologist. I continue to teach at the college level, in addition to my private practice, as a senior lecturer teaching psychology courses at Cambridge College, an undergraduate school that provides nontraditional adult learners from underserved communities the opportunity to obtain a college degree.

My desk at the Citizenship Council office in Ferris Booth Hall, Columbia's student center, became my campus home. In addition to my work with HEP, I engaged with the heads of other projects, including faculty advisors and administrators, and developed deep friendships and connections with like-minded students who shared common values and interests. Because the Citizenship Council was a student-run organization, we developed ideas, created programs, and evaluated and refined them based on our experience. Faculty and administrators were available for encouragement, guidance, and support, but the initiative always came from students. The learning curve was steep and stimulating. For all of us who engaged in these efforts, we had a unique opportunity to develop our vision, skill, and self-confidence.

Epitomizing this high level of drive and enterprise was the development of various federally funded programs, developed and implemented primarily by undergraduates. With the advent of the War on Poverty, funds were available for projects focused on education and community development in disadvantaged communities. The Citizenship Council designed programs, wrote grants, received funding, and implemented two federally funded projects. The first was Project Double Discovery in 1965, led by students Steve Weinberg and Roger Lehecka, which brought students from inner-city neighborhoods to campus for a summer school program and that thrives at Columbia to this day.

The second, with which I was more deeply involved, operated summer day camps in two neighborhoods where the Citizenship Council had programs. As the student director of this program, I gained invaluable experience in developing ideas, writing proposals, and administering the project. We constantly were given opportunities to think outside the box—for example, hiring an indigenous sculptor who created amazing totem poles from dead trees in Central Harlem. One activity for the children in the day camp was simply to watch him work while he talked with them.

Another aspect of this program was our effort to create connection and dialogue among diverse subgroups of our staff, which often led to powerful and constructive outcomes. We set up weekly meetings that included black and white college students, teenagers from the community, and professional staff, facilitated by a team of therapists whose techniques included the utilization of "psychodramatic enactment." I recall one instance in which a highly competent supervisor brought in novice therapists who lacked experience and had a difficult time managing the group dynamics. In one group, the facilitator made the mistake of calling one of the neighborhood youths a "nigger" in the context of what was supposed to be a role-play. The teen was understandably upset and reacted violently.

But despite mistakes like this, for me personally, the experience with these kinds of activities was transformative. Growing up, I had a well-developed intellect but no real emotional awareness. I was always trying to figure out and analyze what I should be feeling. It was a revelation, therefore, to discover that I had within me a range of emotional reactions separate from my thinking.

In my junior year (1967–1968), I took on the leadership of the Citizenship Council. In this capacity, it was my exciting responsibility to supervise and coordinate every project, which involved administering more than a thousand volunteers. It was a role in which I took great pride. Now I had not just a desk, but a coveted (if small) office, with my own phone, in Ferris Booth. I was tasked with developing new programs, something that inevitably was shaped by trends in the wider culture, not least the deepening understanding that issues of poverty and social justice were not limited only to racism in the South. The war in Vietnam had escalated, and the government itself seemed to be a source of oppression and violence. There was an emerging awareness that every institution in society—including the universities—somehow contributed to the problems. No one who was part of the Columbia community could turn his or her back on the big issues of the day.

Students became aware that Columbia was not only an educational institution, but also a major landowner in the neighborhood, with a portfolio that included distressed properties. This was bad enough, but when Columbia announced its plans to build a gym on public land in Morningside Park, we began to feel uncomfortable with our role. While we in the Citizenship Council were working to help distressed communities by providing educational and social services, our school was contributing to the destruction of the very communities we were trying to serve. It seemed hypocritical to continue our work while ignoring what the Columbia board of trustees and administration was doing in Morningside Heights and West Harlem.

The Citizenship Council started a new project, focused on researching the real estate activities of the university, and we discovered a network of corporate entities that had extensive holdings in nearby neighborhoods. These served to hide the fact that Columbia was a powerful landlord—slumlord, actually—in the community. In an attempt to expose and ultimately curtail Columbia's expansion, in 1968, the Citizenship Council published an eighty-page report entitled "Columbia and the Community" (written by Marc Rauch, Bob Feldman, and Art Leaderman), which provided data for political action. Our members were active in opposing construction of the gym, which would have given locals greatly restricted use of the building. The project was being pushed through by the university despite the fact that no key community groups had been consulted—an indication of just how much power the university could bring to bear on city government. "Parkland should be sacrosanct," read a Citizenship Council report, "especially in an area as crowded as West Harlem ... We appeal to Columbia's administrators to reconsider the entire gym issue, both in the interest of fair policy regarding the uses of public land,

and in the interest of avoiding a dangerous clash between Columbia and West Harlem residents."

Various politicians, including Sen. Basil Paterson, fought against the building of the gym, while J. Raymond Jones, head of New York Democratic County organization, suggested the lease be renegotiated so that Columbia and Harlem would split use of the gym 50/50. I quoted him when I gave testimony to the Cox Commission (I don't now remember where this quote comes from) in July 1968: "I submit that Columbia, having received an unusually rich plum, should not retain the lion's share of the fruit while doling out to the community scarcely more than a pit-end."[1]

Many of us at the Citizenship Council decided to focus on the issue of the gym and emerged at the forefront of protests that brought a heightened awareness of Columbia's role in the community. I was part of a group of students, greatly influenced by principles of civil disobedience, who joined together in February 1968 and became part of a demonstration in Morningside Park, with the hope that we would be arrested and thus shine a light on Columbia's actions in the community. It was vital that Harlem take a closer look at the land-grab policies being implemented on its doorstep, and at Columbia's expansionist policy and its disregard for the interests of the local community. On that day we tried to block access to the construction site, but we were unable to do so. Eventually, after we began to shake the temporary fence surrounding the gym construction site, the police grabbed us for criminal mischief and disorderly conduct. Looking back, I can see how it was something of a dry run for what happened on April 23 later that year. (The *Columbia Daily Spectator* newspaper reported on February 29 that "[a] spokesman for the police department tried at one point to speak to the crowd, but his plea for attention was lost amid shouts against the 'racist gym and cops.'"[2])

That February, protest brought an important development: a convergence of concerns of the Citizenship Council and the Students for a Democratic Society (SDS). Columbia's SDS chapter, which had up to that time been focused primarily on organizing students against the war in Vietnam, was broadening its interests. Several SDS members were in Morningside Park that day and were arrested with us. Preventing construction of the

1. "Proceedings of the Fact-Finding Commission," Columbia University, July 16, 1968, p. 3378.
2. Dearing Carpenter, "Thirteen Arrested While 150 Protest Gym Construction: College Student Charged with Felonious Assault," *Columbia Daily Spectator* (New York), February 29, 1968.

gym became one of the key demands made during the student strike in April 1968. I was glad that SDS was focusing its attention on local concerns, even though my personal relationship with the organization was conflicted. I had many friends in SDS and agreed with many of their goals, but I also had difficulty with the political correctness, with the jargon, and with some of their tactics. I never officially joined the Columbia chapter, but always considered them allies. I didn't take part in the occupation of the buildings because my attorney advised me to avoid such activity while I was still involved in legal proceedings stemming from my initial arrest in Morningside Park. But when the building occupations began, the Citizenship Council became Strike Central, the administrative offices for the strike. In contrast to the illegally occupied buildings, our offices were in the student center, so SDS could use the facilities legally. Almost overnight the Citizenship Council had become not just a student volunteer organization but also a center for political activism.

The strike increased the depth of my disillusionment with the institutions of our society. I remember feeling intensely dismayed as I read daily articles in the *New York Times* about the strike. I couldn't believe that the *Times*, which I thought was an icon of objective news reporting, was so obviously distorted in its reporting. It didn't go unnoticed that the publisher of the *Times* was a Columbia trustee.

The Columbia strike reflected many changes in the national culture, most dramatically the emergence of Black Power on campus. Before April 1968, black students generally had not been so vocally involved in protests against the gym or other political activities in the local community. At the start of the protest, Hamilton Hall was occupied by both white and black students, but all whites soon were asked to vacate the building. No longer was the protest a cooperative, biracial venture. Blacks were anxious to differentiate themselves, and whites inevitably began placing more emphasis on supporting the autonomy and leadership of blacks, as well as engaging in outreach to other whites, working to confront racism in their own communities. For the Citizenship Council, this national trend, as reflected in the change in relationships between black and white Columbia students, led to a questioning and redefinition of our mission and our roles.

When we sent tutors and provided social services to distressed communities, were we helping those communities or merely attempting to make up for the fact that the schools and government's social service institutions were deficient?

When we partnered with government institutions, were we working against the interests of local communities and activists? Should we be partnering directly with the communities and local activists rather than with the institutions that were failing them?

With increasing awareness of white racism, combined with increasing discomfort of some blacks and Latinos of having white activists coming into their communities, should we be focusing our efforts on programs that engaged in outreach and education in white communities, including the Columbia community?

When we offered social service programs at Columbia, were we ignoring the fact that Columbia as a slumlord and employer was contributing, like other institutions in society, to the problems in distressed communities? Were we providing Columbia with a way to claim that it was serving the local community when, in fact, it was part of the problem?

Professor Preston Wilcox of Columbia's School of Social Work was an important mentor and guide for us in this process of reflecting on and redefining our mission. He was a political activist and community organizer, deeply involved in Harlem's efforts to develop its own resources and gain control over the institutions in its neighborhoods, a skilled, creative, passionate, and inspiring leader. For example, he developed programs to teach counseling skills to the people in Harlem who served as the informal, nonprofessional therapists: to bartenders, hairdressers, and barbers. He also worked to help whites develop more empathy and respect for black communities, writing a series of brief articles explaining some of the aspects of African American culture that resulted in stereotyping, fear, and prejudice. One of these memos that I remember vividly was a discussion of the phrase "Up against the wall, motherfucker!" Dr. Wilcox explained the origin of this epithet came from the fact that white slaveholders often raped black female slaves. The term "motherfucker" was actually an accurate description of the relationship between slaveholder and the progeny of that rape.

Dr. Wilcox also supported and guided those of us at the Citizenship Council who were struggling with the reevaluation of our mission and helped us develop programs based on our new understanding: developing partnerships with political activists in the communities, increasing research and activism with regard to Columbia's role as an owner of real estate and as an employer, and spurring initiatives for outreach to address racism in white communities. On May 6, 1968, less than a week after the police cleared the five occupied buildings of students, Dr. Wilcox sent the following letter to the Citizenship Council office:

Dear Joel,

Lest you forget, permit me to say to you that what you did demonstrated to C.U. that it is merely an Up South University of Mississippi—that oppresses its consumers, black and white; that it is incapable of change unless it is singled out as the target; that it is organized to program its consumers into compliant participation in the oppression of others; that it is outside of the society to which it claims to address itself. That it has survived is testimony to its self-deception.

Fortunately it has an aroused student body that is capable of turning it around. Keep turning and stay loose!

Sincerely,
Preston Wilcox

There was an intense backlash to this effort to redefine the mission of the Citizenship Council. Not all students supported these changes, nor was the university administration happy with the fact that the Citizenship Council, a respected, school-funded student organization, had become a center for political activism directed against the university and that its offices had been so important to the strikers during the protests. A group of students from the Citizenship Council organized their own protest, issued a declaration that the Citizenship Council was disbanded, and created a new organization that would be focused on community service as it previously had been defined and that would eschew any kind of political activism. As a consequence of this conflict, and also in no small part because of overall changes (economic, political, cultural), which meant that students began to focus more narrowly on their own careers and professional goals, political activism eventually wound down and the era of widespread student volunteering in the community more or less came to an end.

After I graduated, I was burnt out on political activism and pessimistic about my ability to be empowered to achieve meaningful change. SDS had evolved into Weatherman, and even before some friends were killed by an explosion in an apartment where bombs were being built, I was repulsed by the decision to use violence, by those people who had rationalized the idea that for whites to become part of the oppressed class and thereby become legitimate allies, they needed to give up white privilege by doing something that made them outlaws.

As I reflect on that time in my life, I see both the power and strength of our idealism, but also the rigidity and ultimate failure to achieve our goals. We succeeded in stopping construction of the gym, but I don't think we helped the community. Today, in the spot where the gym was to be built, there is mostly unusable land. If we had been more practical, we could have used our protest to increase the amount of space in the facility that could have been available to the community and advocated for significant commitment of resources to provide for staff and programming. The gym could have provided a center in which there would be possibilities for interaction between neighborhood youth and Columbia students.

But even if we didn't succeed with everything we set out to achieve, I and others have learned to temper our idealism with a practical vision, an ability to understand which might be realistic goals and which are not. I hope that I have been able to sustain my commitment to my ideals and vision and work as best I can as an imperfect human being, to achieve those goals to the extent it is possible for me to do so. Today, I am grateful to Columbia. In today's world, with its increasingly narrow understanding of college as a place to kick-start a career, Columbia's continued emphasis on the Core Curriculum and focus on learning for the sake of learning is something that I appreciate every day of my life.

Joel D. Ziff *('69CC), Ed.D., is a psychologist, working for more than thirty-five years as a clinician with individuals, couples, families, and groups. He specializes in the treatment of sexual addiction and is a senior lecturer at Cambridge College. He is author of* Mirrors in Time: The Psycho-Spiritual Journey through the Jewish Year, *as well as numerous articles and chapters in books on psychotherapy, and on Jewish spirituality and psychotherapy. He has three sons and lives in Newton, Massachusetts.*

by Juan Gonzalez

Some moments stamp us forever. They propel our lives onto unexpected paths, awaken emotions we never knew we had, and radically alter how we see the world. Such a moment transpired for many of us at Columbia University in April 1968.

The recollections gathered in this book offer direct testimony from a tiny portion of the thousands who participated on various sides of what became one of the most dramatic and influential university strikes in US history. Fifty years later, the passion and creativity unleashed by that conflict—the mix of rebel ideas and dissident narratives, of naive hopes and bitter disenchantments, of inspired visions for social change, and of personal frustration and regret—remain as vivid as the brilliant spring sun that bathed South Lawn on April 23 of that year.

These marvelous essays made me appreciate how little I understood about the strike that transformed my own life. That's often the way it is with seminal moments. They defy a tidy explanation. The more of their details we learn, the more we discover how little we know. Even for the participants, the passage of time, our selective memory, and just plain ignorance collude to blur our recollection of the "facts." Yes, most of the strikers were white and from families of relative privilege. But so, too, were many of those who opposed the strike. It could not have been any other way at Columbia, or most any other private university, in America in the sixties. Yes, the black students who occupied Hamilton Hall—the

presence of whom meant that for almost an entire week Columbia administrators were reluctant to call in the police—were the pivotal group within
the larger Columbia rebellion. Yes, the inexcusable brutality of the police
in subduing the larger group of mostly white protesters touched off the
broader, campus-wide boycott of classes that followed. And sure, some
strike leaders envisioned their involvement at Columbia as a stepping-
stone to a social revolution at home.

But what young person could be blamed in 1968 for feeling Armageddon
was at hand? After all, Martin Luther King, Jr. had been assassinated that
same month. In the week after King's death, civil disorders erupted in more
than a hundred cities across the country. There were unforgettable pictures
in the press of long lines of white Americans buying guns and ammunition
at stores across the nation. For those of us preparing to graduate—I was
Columbia College, class of 1968—the last thing on our minds was, "What
kind of job will I land?" The bigger question was, "Is the country heading
toward civil war?"

Thus, the student uprisings that year at Columbia and San Francisco
State, in Paris and Mexico City, and on campuses around the globe were
all products of societies in deep crisis. It was that crisis that propelled
so many young people to find common ground, despite our disparate
political views, despite our differences of race, class, and national origin.
For a few short weeks, we put those differences and petty quarrels
aside in a quixotic effort to make a better world and transform a great
university. And once you have experienced the euphoria of creating
a liberated enclave within a repressed society, that feeling of freedom
never leaves you.

Often overlooked in the Columbia narrative, however, is the enormous
impact the strike had beyond white and African American communities.
I, for instance, was born in Puerto Rico, America's last major colony, to
a seamstress and a kitchen worker. Raised in an East Harlem tenement
and the Cypress Hills public housing project in East New York, Brooklyn,
I was the first person in my extended family to attend college. I never
would have landed on the Morningside Heights campus on full scholarship
had it not been for Pauline Buonagura, an amazing journalism teacher at
Franklin K. Lane High School, who instilled in me her endless love affair
with the English language, and Judith Temple, the dogged guidance counselor at Lane who pressed me to apply to Columbia. Once I arrived, only

the steady and gentle support of Professor James Shenton, my adviser, enabled me to navigate the terrifying world of academic arrogance, class entitlement, and white supremacy into which I had been thrust. And I was not the only Columbia striker who didn't quite fit into the black-white dichotomy that was so dominant. There was Samuel Reveron, the son of a legislator in Puerto Rico, who was attending General Studies and who later became a journalist back on the island, and Carmen Chow and Jean Yonemura, Barnard women who went on to play leading roles in one of the most important Chinese-American radical groups of the seventies, I Wor Kuen. There weren't enough Latino and Asian American students at Columbia back then for us to create ethnic student groups as a source of emotional support. Each of us had to find our way through the jumble of class and racial divisions and define ourselves, but once we left Columbia, we immediately returned to our own communities to spread the message of social change.

For me, the friendships I made with Columbia classmates and fellow strikers were instrumental in forging my outlook. There was the brilliant Dave Gilbert, who fearlessly defended Marxist theory in open debates with the most smug of Columbia professors. David spent hours patiently trying to convince me that Vietnam was an unjust imperial war. Even afterward, through his descent into the madness of Weatherman, and through the tragedy of his years in prison, David sought to better the lives of those around him, and he always will have my respect. There was Leon Denmark, who, like me, had been raised in public housing, in York, Pennsylvania, and Nancy Biberman, the middle-class red-diaper baby from suburban Philadelphia with the warmest of smiles and the biggest of hearts. The three of us bonded as volunteers for the Program to Activate Community Talent in Manhattan Valley, one of the Citizenship Council's tutoring projects, with Leon and I rooming together on West 104th Street during senior year. It was this community involvement that got us involved in the neighborhood fight against the gymnasium and brought me to the sundial on April 23. Finally, there was Lewis Cole, the tall, lanky, endearing Students for a Democratic Society leader who taught me more about life and how ordinary people make history than he ever did about Trotsky and Stalin. Lewis remained one of my closest friends for many years afterward. Had he lived, no doubt he would have penned the most passionate essay of all for this collection.

But nostalgia has no value in itself. Like many Columbia strikers, I drew lessons back then that shaped my actions in the years and decades to follow. By 1969, I was part of the Young Lords Party, a group that spurred an entire generation of Puerto Rican and Latino youth into radical politics and social action, and later to the National Congress for Puerto Rican Rights. When I finally settled into a career in daily journalism, the coverage of social and labor movements became my specialty, whether it was general strikes in the Dominican Republic, political troubles in Mexico, Haiti and Central America, or the World Trade Organization protests in Seattle. As a *Daily News* columnist and cohost of the dissident news show *Democracy Now*, my lifelong job was to chronicle injustice, class and racial oppression, and imperial war, exposing the endless corruption of a capitalist society and shining a spotlight on those who seek to change things.

The events during that chaotic spring fifty years ago on Morningside Heights convinced many of us that when enough people stand up, unite around a common cause, and dare to challenge those in power, then another world is indeed possible. This is even truer today. Who could have predicted the vast movements around the world that have emerged over the past few years? From the Fight-for-$15 movement to the immigrant DREAMers (i.e., Development, Relief, and Education for Alien Minors), from the victories around marriage equality to the climate change movement, from the Arab spring to the *indignados* of Spain, from Syriza in Greece to the South Korean masses toppling a corrupt president, from Occupy Wall Street to Black Lives Matter, students and young people have been in the forefront of many major struggles for political and economic change.

Today's right-wing populists, with their law and order agenda, are eerily reminiscent of George Wallace and Richard Nixon fifty years ago. During the Nixon era, however, we on the Left made a terrible mistake: we turned against each other in a mad scramble for political purity (helped along, of course, by the government's secret counterintelligence machinations). We thus left a nascent social movement divided and in tatters. Hopefully, today's rebels have learned from the past and can move forward with the knowledge that those who treasure the unity of a broader social movement over the purity of its individual groups can achieve wonders.

Juan Gonzalez *('68CC) retired from the* Daily News *in 2016 after thirty years as a columnist. He cohosts the radio/TV news show* Democracy Now, *is a professor of journalism at Rutgers University and author of* Harvest of Empire: A History of Latinos in America; News for All the People: The Epic Story of Race and the American Media; *and* Reclaiming Gotham: Bill de Blasio and the Fight to End America's Tale of Two Cities.

INDEX